First World War

and Army of Occupation

War Diary

France, Belgium and Germany

46 DIVISION
138 Infantry Brigade
Leicestershire Regiment
1/4th Battalion
1 February 1915 - 30 June 1919

WO95/2690/1

The Naval & Military Press Ltd
www.nmarchive.com
Published in association with The National Archives

Published by

The Naval & Military Press Ltd

Unit 10 Ridgewood Industrial Park,

Uckfield, East Sussex,

TN22 5QE England

Tel: +44 (0) 1825 749494

www.naval-military-press.com

www.nmarchive.com

This diary has been reprinted in facsimile from the original. Any imperfections are inevitably reproduced and the quality may fall short of modern type and cartographic standards.

Contents

Document type	Place/Title	Date From	Date To
Heading	WO95/2690/1		
Heading	46th Division 138th Infy Bde 4th Bn Leicester Regt Feb 1915-Jun 1919		
Heading	46 1/5 Leicester Regt Feb Vol XI		
Heading	46 1/5 Leicester Regt Vol 14		
Heading	46 1/4 Leices Lirshire Regt Vol XIII		
War Diary	B 10 Hops Stort Farm	01/02/1915	18/02/1915
War Diary	B. Stortford	18/02/1915	26/02/1915
War Diary	Bishop's Stortford	27/02/1915	27/02/1915
War Diary	Southampton	27/02/1915	28/02/1915
War Diary	Fosse 10 by Petit Sains	26/03/1915	20/05/1915
Heading	138th Inf. Bde. 46th Div. Battn. Disembarked Havre From England 3/5. 3.15. 4th Battn. The Leicestershire Regiment. March 1915 June 19		
War Diary	Southampton	01/03/1915	02/03/1915
War Diary	Le Havre	03/03/1915	03/03/1915
War Diary	Southampton	03/03/1915	03/03/1915
War Diary	No 6. Rest Camps Le Havre	04/03/1915	04/03/1915
War Diary	Southampton	04/03/1915	04/03/1915
War Diary	Le Havre	05/03/1915	06/03/1915
War Diary	Cassel	06/03/1915	07/03/1915
War Diary	Zuytpeene	07/03/1915	09/03/1915
War Diary	Strazeele	09/03/1915	11/03/1915
War Diary	Sailly	11/03/1915	14/03/1915
War Diary	Bac St Maur	14/03/1915	16/03/1915
War Diary	Le Chien Blanc	16/03/1915	22/03/1915
War Diary	Steenwerck	22/03/1915	22/03/1915
War Diary	Le Chien Blanc	22/03/1915	23/03/1915
War Diary	Steen Werck	23/03/1915	23/03/1915
War Diary	Le Chien Blanc	23/03/1915	26/03/1915
War Diary	Ref. $ 36.N.W. 1/20,000 Lattargette Armentieres	26/03/1915	27/03/1915
War Diary	Lattargette (Armentieres)	28/03/1915	31/03/1915
Miscellaneous	List of Appendices with War Diary 1/4 Leicestershire Rgt	01/09/1915	01/09/1915
Miscellaneous	Appendices A.1 To A.9		
Operation(al) Order(s)	Operation Order No. 1 By Lieut. Colonel W. A. Harrison T.D. Cmdg. 1/4th Leicestershire Regiment	26/02/1915	26/02/1915
Operation(al) Order(s)	Operation Order No. 2 By Lieut. Colonel W. A. Harrison T.D. Cmdg. 1/4th Leicestershire Regiment	05/03/1915	05/03/1915
Operation(al) Order(s)	Operation Order No. 3 By Lieut. Colonel W.A. Harrison T.D. Cmdg. 1/4th Leicestershire Regiment	08/03/1915	08/03/1915
Miscellaneous	O.C. Coy	11/03/1915	11/03/1915
Operation(al) Order(s)	Operation Order No. 4 by Lieut. Colonel W.A. Harrison T.D. Cmdg. 1/4th Leicestershire Regiment.	09/03/1915	09/03/1915
Miscellaneous	Battalion Order by Lieut. Colonel W.A.Harrion T.D. Cmdg. 1/4th Leicestershire Rgt.	12/03/1915	12/03/1915
Operation(al) Order(s)	Operation Order No. 5 by Lieut. Colonel W. A. Harrison T.D. Cmdg. 1/4th Leicestershire Regiment	15/03/1915	15/03/1915
Miscellaneous	A Form Messages And Signals		

Operation(al) Order(s)	Operation Order No. 6 by Major L.V. Wykes Commanding 1/4th Battalion Leicestershire Regiment	25/03/1915	25/03/1915
Operation(al) Order(s)	Operation Order No. 7 By Major L.V Wykes Commanding 1/4th Leicestershire Regiment	30/03/1915	30/03/1915
Miscellaneous	Appendices B.1 To B.14		
Miscellaneous	Headquarters, 1/1 Lincs & Leic Bde T.F.	15/02/1915	15/02/1915
Miscellaneous	Proposed Order Of Departure Of North Midland Division.	25/02/1915	25/02/1915
Miscellaneous	O.C. 4 Leics	06/03/1915	06/03/1915
Miscellaneous	1/4th Leice Regt.	08/03/1915	08/03/1915
Miscellaneous	Headquarters, Lincoln & Leicester Brigade.	10/03/1915	10/03/1915
Miscellaneous	C Form (Duplicate). Messages And Signals	11/03/1915	11/03/1915
Miscellaneous	O.C., Regt.	11/03/1915	11/03/1915
Miscellaneous	Messages And Signals	12/03/1915	12/03/1915
Miscellaneous	Duplicate Headquarters Linc. & Leics. Bde.	13/03/1915	13/03/1915
Miscellaneous		14/03/1915	14/03/1915
Miscellaneous		23/03/1914	23/03/1914
Operation(al) Order(s)	Operation Order No. 5 by Brigadier General W.R. Clifford Commanding 1/1st Lincs. & Leics. Infty. Bde. T.F.	25/03/1915	25/03/1915
Miscellaneous	Operation Order by Major-General W.F.M. Wilson, C.R. Commanding 4th Division.	30/03/1915	30/03/1915
Miscellaneous	O.C. 4th Leicester	30/03/1915	30/03/1915
Miscellaneous	Appendices C.1 To C.7		
Diagram etc	1/4 Leic Rgt Billetry Area		
Diagram etc	Rough Map		
Diagram etc	1st 4 Leci Regt Billels		
Diagram etc	1/4 Leicestershire		
Diagram etc			
Miscellaneous	Appendix D.1		
War Diary	Brigade Area Orders By Brigade General W.R. Clifford Commanding 1/1st Linc. Leic. Brigade Appendix "D"	22/03/1915	22/03/1915
Miscellaneous	Operation Order by Brig. Gen W.R. Clifford Commanding Lincs. & Leics. Bde. T.F	22/03/1915	22/03/1915
Miscellaneous	Ref. 1/100,000 Hezebouck General Idea		
Diagram etc			
Operation(al) Order(s)	Operation Order No. 1 By Major L.V. Wykes Commanding 1/4th Leicestershire Regiment.	23/03/1915	23/03/1915
Diagram etc			
Miscellaneous	1/4th Battalion Leicestershire Regiment.	25/03/1915	25/03/1915
Miscellaneous	Appendix D.2		
Miscellaneous	Officer Commanding, 4th Leicester	25/03/1915	25/03/1915
Miscellaneous	Instructions for Working Parties on 3rd line	26/03/1915	26/03/1915
Miscellaneous	Training Programme For Battalion North Midland Division.		
Miscellaneous	Battalion Orders by Major L.V. Wykes Commanding 1/4th Leicestershire Regiment.	26/03/1915	26/03/1915
Heading	War Diary 1/4 Liec Rgt		
Miscellaneous	Battalion Order By Major L. V. Wykes Commanding 1/4th Battalion Leicestershire Rgt.	27/03/1915	27/03/1915
Miscellaneous	Battalion Order by Major L.V. Wykes Commanding 1/4th Leicestershire Regiment.	28/03/1915	28/03/1915
Miscellaneous	War Diary App E		
Miscellaneous	War Diary App E	02/03/1915	02/03/1915
Miscellaneous	War Diary App F.	00/03/1915	00/03/1915

Type	Description	Start	End
Heading	138th Inf. Bde. 46th Div. 4th Battn. The Leicestershire Regiment April 1915 Attached. Appendices.		
War Diary	Le Chien Blanc	01/04/1915	01/04/1915
War Diary	Steenwerck	01/04/1915	01/04/1915
War Diary	Forenoon	02/04/1915	02/04/1915
War Diary	Dranoutre	02/04/1915	05/04/1915
War Diary	Trenches	05/04/1915	09/04/1915
War Diary	Dranoutre	09/04/1915	12/04/1915
War Diary	Trenches	12/04/1915	17/04/1915
War Diary	Dranoutre	17/04/1915	20/04/1915
War Diary	Trench Area	20/04/1915	24/04/1915
War Diary	Dranoutre	25/04/1915	28/04/1915
War Diary	Trenches	28/04/1915	30/04/1915
Miscellaneous	Appendices		
Miscellaneous	A Form Messages And Signals.		
Operation(al) Order(s)	Operation Order No. 3 By Brigade General A. W. Clifford Commanding Lincoln And Leicester Infty Bde. T.F.	02/04/1915	02/04/1915
Miscellaneous	A Days In Li En Ches		
Miscellaneous		02/04/1915	02/04/1915
Operation(al) Order(s)	Operation Orders No. 6 By Major L. V. Wykes Commanding 1/4th Bn. Leicestershire Rgt.	02/04/1915	02/04/1915
Miscellaneous	C Form (Duplicate). Messages And Signals.	03/04/1915	03/04/1915
Operation(al) Order(s)	Operation Order No. 6 By Brigade General W.R. Clifford Commanding 1/1st Lincoln & Leicester Infantry Brigade T.F.	04/04/1915	04/04/1915
Miscellaneous	Appendix A.List of Trenches And Garrisons.		
Operation(al) Order(s)	Operation Order No 9 By Major T. T. Gresson, D.S.O. Commanding 1/4th Battalion Leicestershire Rgt.	04/04/1915	04/04/1915
Operation(al) Order(s)	Operation Order No. 7 By Brig.Gen.W.R. Clifford Commanding 1/1 Lincs & Leic Bde. T.F.	07/04/1915	07/04/1915
Miscellaneous	Appendix A		
Miscellaneous			
Operation(al) Order(s)	Operation Order Number 8 By Brigade General W.R. Clifford Commanding 1/1st Lincoln & Leicester Inf. Bde. T.F.	12/04/1915	12/04/1915
Operation(al) Order(s)	Operation Order Number 9 By Brigade General W.R. Clifford Commanding 1/1st Lincoln & Leicester Inf. Bde. T.F.	15/04/1915	15/04/1915
Operation(al) Order(s)	Operation Order Number 11 By Brigadier General W.R. Clifford Commanding 1/1 Lincs. & Leics. Inf. Bde. T.F.	19/04/1915	19/04/1915
Operation(al) Order(s)	Operation Order No. 10 By Major T.T. Gresson D.S.O. Commanding 1/4th Battalion Leicestershire Rgt.	20/04/1915	20/04/1915
Operation(al) Order(s)	Operation Order Number 12 By Brigade General W.R. Clifford Commanding 1/1 Lincs. & Leics. Infty. Bde. T.F.	24/04/1915	24/04/1915
Operation(al) Order(s)	Operation Order Number 13 By Brigade General W.R. Clifford Commanding 1/1 Lincs. & Leics. Infty. Bde. T.F.	27/04/1915	27/04/1915
Diagram etc			
Diagram etc	With Original Copy War Diary		
Heading	138th Inf. Bde. 46th Div. 4th Battn. The Leicestershire Regiment. May 1915		
War Diary	Trenches A & B Coys In Fire Trenches C & D In The Newport D.O.S.	01/05/1915	01/05/1915

War Diary	Trenches	01/05/1915	03/05/1915
War Diary	Dranoutre	04/05/1915	06/05/1915
War Diary	Trenches	07/05/1915	11/05/1915
War Diary	Dranoutre	11/05/1915	11/05/1915
War Diary	Billets	12/05/1915	15/05/1915
War Diary	Trenches	16/05/1915	18/05/1915
War Diary	Dranoutre	19/05/1915	23/05/1915
War Diary	Trenches	23/05/1915	26/05/1915
War Diary	Bivouac	27/05/1915	27/05/1915
War Diary	Dranoutre	27/05/1915	31/05/1915
Miscellaneous	Appendices.		
Miscellaneous	Headquarters, Lincoln & Leicester Brigade.	11/05/1915	11/05/1915
Operation(al) Order(s)	Operation Orders Number 14 By Brigadier General W.R. Clifford Commanding 1/1 Linc & Leic. Infty. Bde. T.F.	01/05/1915	01/05/1915
Operation(al) Order(s)	Operation Order Number 15 By Brigadier General W.R. Clifford Commanding 1/1 Linc. & Infty. Bde. T.F.	05/05/1915	05/05/1915
Operation(al) Order(s)	Operation Order No 19 By Brig Gen W.R. Clifford Commanding 1/1 Lincs. & Leic Bde. T.P.	10/05/1915	10/05/1915
Miscellaneous	After Order Headquarters,	10/05/1915	10/05/1915
Operation(al) Order(s)	Operation Order Number 20. By Brigadier General W.R. Clifford Commanding 1/1 Linc. & Inf. Bde. T.F.	10/05/1915	10/05/1915
Operation(al) Order(s)	Operation Order Number 21. By Brigadier General W.R. Clifford. Commanding 1/1 Linc & Leic Infantry Bde. T.F.	14/05/1915	14/05/1915
Operation(al) Order(s)	Operation Order No. 23 By Brigade General W.R. Clifford Commanding 128th Infantry Brigade.	18/05/1915	18/05/1915
Operation(al) Order(s)	Operation Order No. 25. By Brigade Gen W.R.Clifford Commanding 138th Infantry Bde.	22/05/1915	22/05/1915
Operation(al) Order(s)	Operation Order No. 27 By Brigadier General W.R. Clifford Commanding 138th Infantry Brigade	26/05/1915	26/05/1915
Operation(al) Order(s)	Operation Order No. 28 By Brigadier Gen W.R. Clifford Commanding 138th Infantry Brigade	30/05/1915	30/05/1915
Heading	138th Inf. Bde. 46th Div. 4th Battn. The Leicestershire Regiment. June 1915		
War Diary	Trenches	01/06/1915	02/06/1915
War Diary	(Bivouac) Dranoutre	03/06/1915	06/06/1915
War Diary	Trenches	07/06/1915	09/06/1915
War Diary	(Bivouacs) Dranoutre	10/06/1915	14/06/1915
War Diary	Trenches	14/06/1915	18/06/1915
War Diary	(Bivouacs) Dranoutre	19/06/1915	22/06/1915
War Diary	(Bivouacs) Dranoutre	23/06/1915	29/06/1915
War Diary	Trenches Sanctuary Wood	30/06/1915	30/06/1915
War Diary	Trenches.	30/06/1915	30/06/1915
Heading	138th Inf. Bde. 4Th Battn. The Leicestershire Regiment. July 1915		
Heading	War Diary For Month Of July.1/4th Leicestershire Regt.		
War Diary	Trenches Sanctuary Wood	01/07/1915	02/07/1915
War Diary	Trenches	02/07/1915	06/07/1915
War Diary	Ooderdon	06/07/1915	13/07/1915
War Diary	Trenches Dup Outs I.20.D. Sheet 28	14/07/1915	14/07/1915
War Diary	Trenches	15/07/1915	16/07/1915
War Diary	Trenches Railway Dugouts	17/07/1915	18/07/1915
War Diary	Trenches Lillebeke Lake Dugouts	18/07/1915	20/07/1915
War Diary	Trenches	21/07/1915	26/07/1915

War Diary	Zillebeke Lake Dug. Outs	26/07/1915	31/07/1915
Miscellaneous	Appendices		
Operation(al) Order(s)	Operation Order No 2 By Major J.A. Potter, Cmdg. 1/4th. Leicestershire Regiment	13/07/1915	13/07/1915
Miscellaneous	138th. Inf. Bde. Right Sector.	23/07/1915	23/07/1915
Miscellaneous	Report On Work In Crater In Front Of Trench In 1. 30. C. 7.8. July 24/25/15	24/07/1915	24/07/1915
Miscellaneous	Headquarters 138th Infantry Brigade	27/07/1915	27/07/1915
Diagram etc	Plan		
Miscellaneous	The Brigadier General Commanding 138th. Inf. Bde.	28/07/1915	28/07/1915
Heading	138th Inf. Bde. 46th Div. 4th Battn. The Leicestershire Regiment. August 1915		
Heading	August 1915 1/4 Leicestershire Regt		
War Diary	Zillebeke Lake D.O	01/08/1915	01/08/1915
War Diary	Trenches	02/08/1915	11/08/1915
War Diary	Huts	11/08/1915	22/08/1915
War Diary	Trenches	21/08/1915	22/08/1915
War Diary	Dug-Outs	23/08/1915	28/08/1915
War Diary	Trenches	29/08/1915	31/08/1915
Miscellaneous			
War Diary	138th Inf. Bde. 46th Div. 4th Battn. The Leicestershire Regiment September 1915		
War Diary	Trenches	01/09/1915	03/09/1915
War Diary	Huts	04/09/1915	08/09/1915
War Diary	Trenches	08/09/1915	14/09/1915
War Diary	Bde Reserve	15/09/1915	20/09/1915
War Diary	Trenches	21/09/1915	26/09/1915
War Diary	Huts	26/09/1915	30/09/1915
Heading	138th Inf. Bde. 46th Div. 4th Battn. The Leicestershire Regiment October (1/26.10.15) 1915		
War Diary	Huts Dickebusch	01/10/1915	01/10/1915
War Diary	Windmill Transport Fm W Of Ouder Dom (1500)	02/10/1915	02/10/1915
War Diary	Farms Fivonacs No. p.1	02/10/1915	02/10/1915
War Diary	Gonnehem	03/10/1915	06/10/1915
War Diary	Hesdigneul	07/10/1915	12/10/1915
War Diary	Trenches	13/10/1915	24/10/1915
Heading	138th Inf. Bde. 46th Div. 4th Battn. The Leicestershire Regiment. November 1915		
War Diary	Verquin	21/10/1915	06/11/1915
War Diary	Robecq	07/11/1915	30/11/1915
Heading	138th Inf. Bde. 46th Div. 4th Battn. The Leicestershire Regiment December 1915		
War Diary		01/12/1915	19/12/1915
War Diary		18/12/1915	18/12/1915
War Diary	Le Tannay	19/12/1915	30/12/1915
Heading	1/4 Leicester Regt Jan Vol XI		
War Diary	Le Tannay	01/01/1916	27/01/1916
War Diary	Pont Remy	30/01/1916	30/01/1916
War Diary	Buigny L'Abbe	30/01/1916	30/01/1916
War Diary	N.B.	14/01/1916	14/01/1916
War Diary	Buigny L'Abbe	01/02/1916	11/02/1916
War Diary	Puchevillers	12/02/1916	19/02/1916
War Diary	Fienvillers	20/02/1916	23/02/1916
War Diary	Montrelet	24/02/1916	27/02/1916
War Diary	Gezaincourt	29/02/1916	01/03/1916
War Diary	Doullens	02/03/1916	06/03/1916

War Diary	Sericourt	07/03/1916	09/03/1916
War Diary	Guoy-En-Ternois	10/03/1916	31/03/1916
War Diary	Camblain L'Abbe	02/04/1916	12/04/1916
War Diary	Talus Des Zouaves	12/04/1916	22/04/1916
War Diary	Maizieres	23/04/1916	03/05/1916
War Diary	Savy	04/05/1916	09/05/1916
War Diary	Le Souich	10/05/1916	19/05/1916
War Diary	Humbercamp	20/05/1916	09/06/1916
War Diary	Foncquevillers	12/06/1916	21/06/1916
War Diary	Warlincourt	24/06/1916	24/06/1916
War Diary	Foncquevillers	25/06/1916	30/06/1916
War Diary	St Amand	30/06/1916	30/06/1916
War Diary	Gomme Court Wood Map 57 D.1/40,000	01/07/1916	02/07/1916
War Diary	Maps Foncquevillers 1/10,000 51c Se Monchy 1/10,000 3 & 4	02/07/1916	11/07/1916
War Diary	Saulty	12/07/1916	13/07/1916
War Diary	Bienvillers	14/07/1916	24/07/1916
War Diary	Pommier	25/07/1916	31/07/1916
War Diary	Monchy Trenches	01/08/1916	04/08/1916
War Diary	Bienvillers	04/08/1916	15/08/1916
War Diary	Pommier	16/07/1916	31/07/1916
War Diary	B.E.F. Bienvillers Av-Bois	01/09/1916	02/09/1916
War Diary	Pommier	08/09/1916	08/09/1916
War Diary	Lacauchie	10/09/1916	20/09/1916
War Diary	Bienvillers	21/09/1916	26/09/1916
War Diary	Bienvillers & Monchy	26/09/1916	30/09/1916
War Diary	Trenches Monchy Sector	01/10/1916	02/10/1916
War Diary	La Cauchie	03/10/1916	07/10/1916
War Diary	La Cauchie	06/10/1916	14/10/1916
War Diary	Bienvillers-Au-Bois	14/10/1916	18/10/1916
War Diary	Bienvillers	20/10/1916	25/10/1916
War Diary	Pommier	26/10/1916	27/10/1916
War Diary	Halloy	28/10/1916	31/10/1916
War Diary	Bouquemaison	01/11/1916	01/11/1916
War Diary	Nueux	02/11/1916	02/11/1916
War Diary	Oneux	03/11/1916	03/11/1916
War Diary	Drucat	04/11/1916	07/11/1916
War Diary	Domvast	08/11/1916	12/11/1916
War Diary	Drucat	13/11/1916	21/11/1916
War Diary	Domquevr	22/11/1916	22/11/1916
War Diary	Bonnieres	23/11/1916	24/11/1916
War Diary	Mondicourt	25/11/1916	05/12/1916
War Diary	Bienvillers	06/12/1916	06/12/1916
War Diary	Honnescamps Area	10/12/1916	11/12/1916
War Diary	Bienvillers	13/12/1916	14/12/1916
War Diary	Honnescamps Area	17/12/1916	17/12/1916
War Diary	Souastre	21/12/1916	25/12/1916
War Diary	Honnescamps Area	29/12/1916	29/12/1916
War Diary	Bienvillers	30/12/1916	31/12/1916
War Diary	Bienvillers	01/01/1917	04/01/1917
War Diary	Souastre	06/01/1917	09/01/1917
War Diary	Hannescamps	10/01/1917	12/01/1917
War Diary	Bienvillers	14/01/1917	18/01/1917
War Diary	Hannescamps	22/01/1917	22/01/1917
War Diary	Souastre	23/01/1917	31/01/1917
War Diary	Bienvillers	01/02/1917	02/02/1917

War Diary	Trenches	04/02/1917	07/02/1917
War Diary	Souastre	08/02/1917	10/02/1917
War Diary	Trenches	11/02/1917	13/02/1917
War Diary	Bienvillers	14/02/1917	19/02/1917
War Diary	Trenches	20/02/1917	23/02/1917
War Diary	Souastre	24/02/1917	27/02/1917
War Diary	Trenches	27/02/1917	28/02/1917
War Diary	Gommecourt	28/02/1917	28/02/1917
War Diary	Fonquevillers	01/03/1917	01/03/1917
War Diary	Souastre	02/03/1917	18/03/1917
War Diary	Essarts	19/03/1917	19/03/1917
War Diary	Ayette	20/03/1917	21/03/1917
War Diary	St. Amand	22/03/1917	22/03/1917
War Diary	Berteaucourt	23/03/1917	23/03/1917
War Diary	Raincheval	24/03/1917	31/03/1917
War Diary	Flechin	01/04/1917	03/04/1917
War Diary	Evny St Julien	04/04/1917	09/04/1917
War Diary	Flechin	10/03/1917	16/03/1917
War Diary	Vendin Lez Bethune	17/03/1917	23/03/1917
War Diary	Bully Grenay	24/03/1917	30/03/1917
War Diary	Front Line Trenches	01/05/1917	01/05/1917
War Diary	St Pierre Sector W Of Lens	02/03/1917	06/03/1917
War Diary	Noeux Les Mines	07/05/1917	11/05/1917
War Diary	Lievin	12/05/1917	30/06/1917
War Diary	Cite de Riaumont W of Lens	01/07/1917	09/07/1917
War Diary	Manchy Brelton	10/07/1917	21/07/1917
War Diary	Vaudricourt	22/07/1917	23/07/1917
War Diary	Noeux Les Mines	24/07/1917	27/07/1917
War Diary	Hulluch	28/07/1917	31/07/1917
War Diary	In The Field	01/08/1917	02/08/1917
War Diary	Hight	02/08/1917	31/10/1917
War Diary	In The Field	01/11/1917	30/11/1917
War Diary	Moeux-Les Mines	01/12/1917	07/12/1917
War Diary	Annequin	08/12/1917	08/12/1917
War Diary	Cambrin Right Sub Section	09/12/1917	13/12/1917
War Diary	Beuvry	17/12/1917	26/12/1917
War Diary	Annequin	27/12/1917	07/01/1918
War Diary	Beuvry	02/01/1918	17/01/1918
War Diary	Annequin	18/01/1918	19/01/1918
War Diary	Bethune	20/01/1918	20/01/1918
War Diary	Mt. Bernenchon	21/01/1918	31/01/1918
Miscellaneous	Strength Of Unit For Month Of January, 1918. As Per A.F.B.813		
War Diary	Mont Bernenchon	01/02/1918	01/02/1918
War Diary	Busnes	02/02/1918	08/02/1918
War Diary	Westrehem	09/02/1918	09/02/1918
War Diary	Tactical Scheme	09/02/1918	09/02/1918
War Diary	Coyecque	10/02/1918	01/03/1918
War Diary	Flechin	02/03/1918	02/03/1918
War Diary	Manqueville	03/03/1918	03/03/1918
War Diary	Noeux-Les-Mines	04/03/1918	04/03/1918
War Diary	Cambrin Trench Sector	05/03/1918	16/03/1918
War Diary	Beuvry	17/03/1918	27/03/1918
War Diary	Les Brebis	28/03/1918	31/03/1918
Heading	138th Brigade. 46th Division 1/4th Battalion Leicestershire Regiment April 1918		

War Diary	Trenches	01/04/1918	07/04/1918
War Diary	Bde Support Hill 70	08/04/1918	12/04/1918
War Diary	Sains En Gohelle	13/04/1918	13/04/1918
War Diary	Hersim	14/04/1918	15/04/1918
War Diary	Froissart Camp	16/04/1918	16/04/1918
War Diary	Hersin	17/04/1918	24/04/1918
War Diary	Dvion	25/04/1918	25/04/1918
War Diary	Fouquieres	26/04/1918	28/04/1918
War Diary	Trenches	29/04/1918	06/05/1918
War Diary	Vaudricourt	07/05/1918	10/05/1918
War Diary	Trenches	11/05/1918	18/05/1918
War Diary	Vaudricourt	19/05/1918	22/05/1918
War Diary	Trenches	23/05/1918	30/05/1918
War Diary	Vaudricourt	31/05/1918	03/06/1918
War Diary	Trenches	04/06/1918	11/06/1918
War Diary	Voudricourt	12/06/1918	15/06/1918
War Diary	Trenches	16/06/1918	23/06/1918
War Diary	Vaudricourt	24/06/1918	27/06/1918
War Diary	Trenches	28/06/1918	05/07/1918
War Diary	Vaudricourt	06/07/1918	09/07/1918
War Diary	Trenches	10/07/1918	21/07/1918
War Diary	Vaudricourt	22/07/1918	27/07/1918
War Diary	Trenches	28/07/1918	31/07/1918
Operation(al) Order(s)	1/4th Bn. Leicestershire Regiment Operation Order No. 83 1st July 1918	01/07/1918	01/07/1918
Operation(al) Order(s)	1/4th Leicestershire Regiment Operation Orders No 84	04/07/1918	04/07/1918
Operation(al) Order(s)	1/4th Bn. Leicestershire Regiment Operation Orders No. 84 4th July 1918	04/07/1918	04/07/1918
Operation(al) Order(s)	1/4th Bn Leicestershire Regiment Operation Order No. 84 4th July 1918	04/07/1918	04/07/1918
Operation(al) Order(s)	1/4th Bn Leicestershire Regiment. Operation Order No. 85 9th July 1918	09/07/1918	09/07/1918
Operation(al) Order(s)	1/4th Battn Leicestershire Regt Operation Order No. 86 12 July 1918	12/07/1918	12/07/1918
Operation(al) Order(s)		21/07/1918	21/07/1918
Operation(al) Order(s)	1/4th Bn. Leicestershire Regiment Operation Order No. 88	20/07/1918	20/07/1918
Miscellaneous	1/4th Leicestershire Regiment 21st July 1918	21/07/1918	21/07/1918
Miscellaneous		21/07/1918	21/07/1918
Operation(al) Order(s)	1/4th Leicestershire Regt	21/07/1918	21/07/1918
Operation(al) Order(s)	1/4th Bn Leicestershire Regiment. Operation Order No. 89 27th July 1918	27/07/1918	27/07/1918
Operation(al) Order(s)	1/4th Bn Leicestershire Regiment Operation Order No. 90	30/07/1918	30/07/1918
War Diary	Trenches	01/08/1918	08/08/1918
War Diary	Vaudricourt	09/08/1918	14/08/1918
War Diary	Trenches	15/08/1918	31/08/1918
Operation(al) Order(s)	1/4th Bn. Leicestershire Regiment Operation Order No. 91	03/08/1918	03/08/1918
Operation(al) Order(s)		08/08/1918	08/08/1918
Operation(al) Order(s)	After Order To Operation Order No. 92		
Operation(al) Order(s)	Additions And Corrections Operation Order No. 92	08/08/1918	08/08/1918
Operation(al) Order(s)	1/4th Bn. Leicestershire Regiment Operation Order No. 93	14/08/1918	14/08/1918
Operation(al) Order(s)	1/4th Bn. Leicestershire Regiment Operation Order No. 94	18/08/1918	18/08/1918

Operation(al) Order(s)	1/4th Bn. Leicestershire Reg Operation Order No. 95	23/08/1918	23/08/1918
Map	Note Change Of Colour		
Operation(al) Order(s)	1/4th Battn Leicestershire Regt. Operation Order No. 96	25/08/1918	25/08/1918
War Diary		01/09/1918	30/09/1918
Operation(al) Order(s)	1/4th Leicestershire Regiment Operation Order No. 105	28/09/1918	28/09/1918
Miscellaneous	1/4th Leicestershire Regiment Administrative Instructions	28/09/1918	28/09/1918
Miscellaneous	Operation Carried Out By 1/4th Leicestershire Regt On Sept 29th 1918	29/09/1918	29/09/1918
Operation(al) Order(s)	Operation Order No. 106	29/09/1918	29/09/1918
Miscellaneous			
Operation(al) Order(s)	1/4th Bn. Leicestershire Regiment Operation Order No. 107	30/09/1918	30/09/1918
War Diary		01/10/1918	31/10/1918
Operation(al) Order(s)	1/4th Bn. Leicestershire Regiment Operation Order No. 114	30/10/1918	30/10/1918
War Diary	Busigny	01/11/1918	02/11/1918
War Diary	Molain	03/11/1918	03/11/1918
War Diary	In The Line	04/11/1918	04/11/1918
War Diary	La Groise	05/11/1918	05/11/1918
War Diary	Cartignies	06/11/1918	10/11/1918
War Diary	Sains Du Nord	11/11/1918	12/11/1918
War Diary	Avesnelles	13/11/1918	13/11/1918
War Diary	Bousies	14/11/1918	30/11/1918
Miscellaneous	Report On Operations E. Of The Canal De La Sambre, From 1st To 11th November 1918	11/11/1918	11/11/1918
War Diary	Bousies	01/12/1918	24/02/1919
War Diary	Solesmes	25/02/1919	10/03/1919
War Diary	St Hilaire	10/03/1919	06/04/1919
War Diary	Inchy	09/04/1919	01/05/1919
War Diary	Beaumont	31/05/1919	31/05/1919
War Diary	Inchy	01/06/1919	25/06/1919
War Diary	Caudry	25/06/1919	30/06/1919

46TH DIVISION
138TH INFY BDE.

4TH BN LEICESTER REGT

~~MAR~~ FEB 1915-JUN 1919

46

1/5 Leicester Regt

Feb

Vol XI

46

apl 16

1/4 Leicester Regt

Vol 14

1 46

1/4 Leicestershire Regt.

Vol XIII

1/4 Leic Rgt WAR DIARY 1/2 [illegible] Bde

or

INTELLIGENCE SUMMARY. 1/1st N.M.D

(Erase heading not required.)

Army Form C. 2118.

Instructions regarding War Diaries and Intelligence Summaries are contained in F. S. Regs., Part II. and the Staff Manual respectively. Title pages will be prepared in manuscript.

Hour, Date, Place	Summary of Events and Information	Remarks and references to Appendices
Feb 1915 BISHOPS STORTFORD		
1st Feb. – 5th	50% of officers & men + M.G. Section at LUTON for musketry. Returned 5th inst.	
	Details at Hd Qrs – including 1st Re-inforcements continued elementary training 4-coy system including Bde Operations – Drill Attack & Defence in Gt HALLINGBURY PARK [illegible]	
12th Feb. 3pm	Lecture by G.O.C. on his recent visit to the "Front" [illegible]	
	of [illegible]	
15th	Distinct indication of move [illegible]	[illegible] attached [illegible]
17th – 18	[illegible] for bayonet fighting [illegible]	
3pm 18th	G.O.C. [illegible]	

(9 29 6) W 3332—1107 100,000 10/13 H W V Forms/C. 2118/10.

Instructions regarding War Diaries and Intelligence Summaries are contained in F.S. Regs., Part II. and the Staff Manual respectively. Title pages will be prepared in manuscript.

1/4 Leic Rgt **WAR DIARY** 1/1st L & L Bde

or

~~INTELLIGENCE~~ **SUMMARY.** 1/1st N. M. D.

(*Erase heading not required.*)

Army Form C. 2118.

Feb 15.

Hour, Date, Place	Summary of Events and Information	Remarks and references to Appendices
B. STORTFORD.	Bde Parade at Gt HALLINGBURY PARK - practice	
18th Feb.	for inspection to-morrow	
19th " 11 am.	Inspection of 1/1st N.M.D. by H.M. The KING.	
	Marched past in 8's.	
22nd	Brig. Gen. A. W. TAYLOR relinquished command	
	& " " J. W. CLIFFORD assumed "	
	of 1/1st L & L Bde.	
(6.25 pm. 23.2.15)	Written orders to entrain 27.2.15 - no hour mentioned.	LL. S.D 263.
26th (Midnt)	Remainder of month - as shewn - devoted to	portion retained. B.
	completing to establishment from 2/4th Leic Rgt	
	50 men joined (25th) after short special	
24/2/15	musketry course. Censor Stamp - No 2466 - rec'd	
8 am 26.2.15	Orders giving time of trains issued (8 am 26.2)	LL. S.D 263/2
	received 11.15	

Instructions regarding War Diaries and Intelligence Summaries are contained in F. S. Regs., Part II. and the Staff Manual respectively. Title pages will be prepared in manuscript.

1/4. Leic. Rgt. WAR DIARY ~~or~~ INTELLIGENCE ~~SUMMARY~~. 1/1st Linc & Leic Bde 1/1st N. Mid. Divn

(Erase heading not required.)

Army Form C. 2118.

Feb'y 1915 Hour, Date, Place	Summary of Events and Information	Remarks and references to Appendices
Saturday 6 a.m. 27.2.15. BISHOPS STORTFORD.	1st Trainload - Lt. Col. W.A. HARRISON. T.O + 16 officers & 483 other ranks paraded at CAUSEWAY. Wet & cold. Gt difficulty in obtaining numbers.	X14. Train No.
8 a.m.	2nd Trainload - Major L.V. WYKES - 9 12 officers & 517 other ranks paraded same place. Gt difficulty in obtaining numbers	Copy of orders is attached as. (X17. Train No.)
8.30 a.m.	1st party left B.S. - 50 mins after scheduled time	
11 - a.m.	2nd — 80 mins —	
1-30 p.m — SOUTHAMPTON.	1st Train arrived. 7 officers + 183 + 72 horses to REST CAMP	30 mins late according
4-20 p.m. — —	2nd — — 1. 0 — + 42 to R.C.	100 — } schedule
5-40 p.m. — —	Remainder of Bn to R.C. Transport on S.S. City of DUNKIRK.	
7- p.m — —	Reached R.C. & alloted billets in Camp, Schools & Warehouses	No details kept
10.25 p.m —	Orders re. embarkation recd, but not intelligible. No information obtainable from Camp Office although [illegible] from [illegible] til next day - but orders issued in case of move.	
2 p.m. 28-2-15. —	7 officers & 224 + 5 cycles embark on S.S. C. of D. Berth 32.	
3 p.m.	" — + 290 + 2. — S.S. QUEEN EMPRESS B. A1	
	Also Lt HASLAM + 30 1st HEXTON + 30 2nd ... ditto	
	No start made - very windy & cold. Confined to boat - all ranks.	

(9 29 6) W 3332—1107 100,000 10/13 H W V Forms/C. 2118/10.

Instructions regarding War Diaries and Intelligence Summaries are contained in F. S. Regs., Part II. and the Staff Manual respectively. Title pages will be prepared in manuscript.

WAR DIARY
or
INTELLIGENCE SUMMARY.
(Erase heading not required.)

Army Form C. 2118.

Place	Date	Hour	Summary of Events and Information	Remarks and references to Appendices
FOSSE 10. by Petit Sains	26th		Day spent in rest, cleaning, baths and interior economy	
	27th	9.15am	Church Parade 9.15am in Church Army Hut.	
	28th		Battalion commenced training at MARQUEFFLES FARM. in view of coming operations.	
	29th	30th 31st	Spent in special training under Brigade arrangements.	
			The undermentioned NCOs and men were recommended for Bravery in the field on dates shown.	
	May 15th		No 200550 Sergt WORTHA, 200300. Sergt TREADWELL W. 200188 Pte KIRK C.A. 201346 Pte WHYLEY W.H formed a rescue party to try and extricate five men who had been buried by a heavy enemy trench mortar. They succeeded in rescuing three of the men in face of a very heavy enemy machine and gun fire. Their conduct was magnificent.	
	May 20th		No 200846 Pte Johnson A.W + No 200424 Pte Pratt J.W These two men by their pluck + initiative drove off a party of 20 - 30 Germans who came with the intention of raiding their post which was a very isolated one. The courage and presence of mind of these two men undoubtedly saved their post from a serious incursion. They are deserving of the highest praise	

J. Eric Petley Lieut Colonel
Comdg 4th Leicestershire Regt.

138th Inf.Bde.
46th Div.

Battn. disembarked
Havre from England
3/5.3.15.

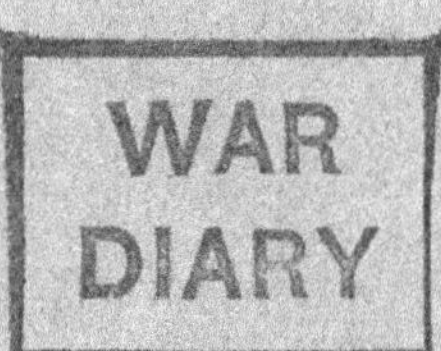

4th BATTN. THE LEICESTERSHIRE REGIMENT.

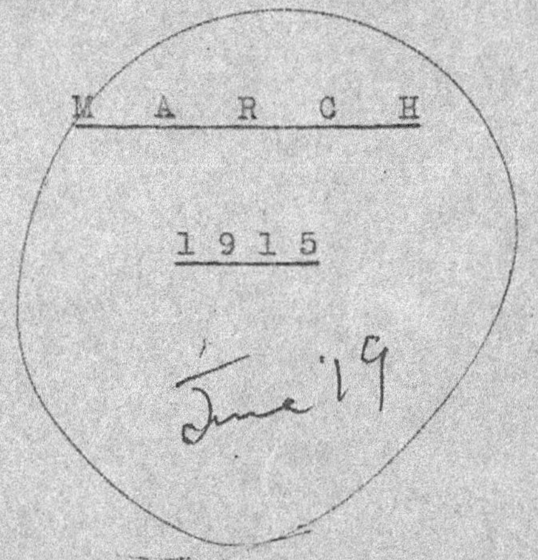

Attached:

1. Appendices A.1 to A.9.
2. Appendices B.1 to B.14.
3. Appendices C.1 to C.7.
4. Appendix D.1.
5. Appendix D.2.
6. Appendix E.
7. Appendix F.

Army Form C. 2118.

(2)

Instructions regarding War Diaries and Intelligence Summaries are contained in F. S. Regs., Part II. and the Staff Manual respectively. Title pages will be prepared in manuscript.

1/4. Leic. Rgt. **WAR DIARY** *or* **INTELLIGENCE SUMMARY.** 1/1st Linc + Leic. Bde 1/1st N. Mid. Divn

(Erase heading not required.)

Hour, Date, Place	Summary of Events and Information	Remarks and references to Appendices
March 1915 ~~Monday~~		
10. am. SOUTHAMPTON. 1.3.15.	"Queen Empress" party ordered to disembark & proceed to Rest Camp. Marched in to R.C. at 12-40 p.m. High wind.	
	"City of Dunkirk" party remained on board ship.	
	Remainder of Bn under Major L.V. WYKES in Rest Camp. RSdB	Pinks ... for ...
3 pm 2.3.15	"Queen Empress" party re-embarked. → [Major L.V. WYKES, 11 officers & 473 other ranks] GOLDEN EAGLE	
4 p.m.	" GOLDEN EAGLE"	
6-45 p.m. "Q.E."	Sailed – Escort of 1 Torpedo Boat Destroyer. Calm Sea.	
8-45 p.m. "G.E."		
	Remainder of Bn in SOUTHAMPTON ~~on~~ ~~board~~ C. of D. RSdB	
3. am. 3.3.15 Le HAVRE	"Queen Empress" reached harbour bar.	
8.15 am *Q.E.	Disembarked & marched to Rest Camp – 4 miles – arr. 10.30 am	* Lt. F.S. Farn 2 Lt. G.E. RUSSELL } No 5 & 6 Platoons & 111 other ranks
9. am. G.E.		
	Above parties under canvas No 6. INF. Rest Camp.	11.30 am Left "Q.E." party at Dock & entrained for unknown destination.
5.00 pm.	M. René Pillot reported for duty as interpreter. Stated had previous experience with 4. ZOUAVES. RSdB	
6.30 pm. SOUTHAMPTON	"City of DUNKIRK" left Berth 32. RSdB	

(9 29 6) W 3332—1107 100,000 10/13 H W V Forms/C. 2118/10.

Instructions regarding War Diaries and Intelligence Summaries are contained in F. S. Regs., Part II. and the Staff Manual respectively. Title pages will be prepared in manuscript.

1/4. Leic. Rgt

WAR DIARY or INTELLIGENCE SUMMARY.

(*Erase heading not required.*)

1/1st Line & Leic. Bde
1/1st N. Mid. Divn

Army Form C. 2118.

(3)

Hour, Date, Place	Summary of Events and Information	Remarks and references to Appendices
March 1915		
4.3.15. No. 6. Rest Camp Le HAVRE	Scotch mist – v. wetting – some exercise only possible. Officers – cipher instruction. Gt deal of time spent censoring correspondence – not enough F. Post Cards available.	
6.30pm. SOUTHAMPTON.	"City of Dunkirk" sailed. RSDB	
5.3.15. 4.30 am. Le HAVRE	"C. of D." off HAVRE. Landed and remained in town.	
2.25 pm.	Bn in No. 6. Camp – received orders to be at POINT A. GARE des MARCHANDISES at 10.30 pm this day	Copy of Bn Orders – Operation (No 2) attached. A.
9 pm	Bn, less fatigue party of 1 + 30 (already quitted camp – 8.15 pm), marched out of camp.	
9.55 pm	Arrived at Point No 4. – joined by "C. of D." party – waiting there.	
10.10 pm.	Commenced entraining. 38 men to wagon. RSDB.	
6.3.15 1-45 Am.	~~[illegible]~~ Entrainment complete.	28 officers – 885 O.R. ranks 72 horses – 9 bicycles & complete transport excepting M.G. & wagon & S.A.A. wagon for same not yet issued.
10.45 pm. (ST. OMER)	Train journey uneventful – no record considered of value. Arrived CASSEL. Journey fatiguing to all. Apparently kept quite secret – destination a surprise. Destination notified – [illegible] attached) B. 3.	

(9 29 6) W 3332—1107 100,000 10/13 H W V Forms/C. 2118/10.

Instructions regarding War Diaries and Intelligence Summaries are contained in F. S. Regs., Part II. and the Staff Manual respectively. Title pages will be prepared in manuscript.

WAR DIARY
or
INTELLIGENCE SUMMARY.
(Erase heading not required.)

1/4 Leic. Rgt — 1/1st Linc & Leic Bde — 1/1st N. Mid. Divn

Army Form C. 2118.

(4)

Hour, Date, Place	Summary of Events and Information	Remarks and references to Appendices
March 1915		
6.3.15. CASSEL	"A" & "B" (less 5 & 6 platoons) billeted in barn near Rly Stn.	
	"C" billeted in Brewery near Stn.	No plan made as Billets ex-tempore for one night only.
	"D" — in & round Café immediately N. of Stn.	
	Spoke to R.M.O. on Stn telephone – could not get thro' to Bde Hdqrs.	
	No's 5 and 6 Platoons billeted in ZUYTPEENE. Recd	
am 10.5 7.3.15. CASSEL	Bn marched to ZUYTPEENE & billeted as shewn in attached rough plan.	[illegible] C.1.
12 noon — ZUYTPEENE	All men billeted – but horses not stabled as much split up. Great deal of correspondence delivered to unit on arrival. A Staff of 2 or 3 clerks apparently still required. Recd	
8.3.15. ZUYTPEENE	Coys route marching – drilling etc in forenoon.	
12.30. pm	Eng. aeroplane compelled to alight near "D" Coy's billet owing to high wind. Report made to 1/1st L&L Bde. & message from "Pilot" to his O.C. at ST OMER forwarded to Bde.	[illegible] message undated

(9 29 6) W 3332—1107 100,000 10/13 H W V Forms/C. 2118/10.

Army Form C. 2118.

(5)

Instructions regarding War Diaries and Intelligence Summaries are contained in F.S. Regs., Part II. and the Staff Manual respectively. Title pages will be prepared in manuscript.

1/4. Leic. Rgt. WAR DIARY 1/1st Linc & Leic Bde
or
INTELLIGENCE SUMMARY. 1/1st N. Mid Divn

(~~Erase heading not required.~~)

Hour, Date, Place	Summary of Events and Information	Remarks and references to Appendices
March 1915 ZUYTPEENE		
8.3.15.	Lt WHITTINGHAM – Interpreter & 2 N.C.O's per Coy (+ 5 cyclists)	
11. am (hour of parade)	to STRAZEELE for billeting. Start greatly delayed –	reason 2 until parties were late
6.30pm.	Telegram by hand (attached) re. move on 9th received.	Original re. attached B 4.
7 pm	Verbal Orders to Os C. Coys – M.G.O., T.O., M.O., QrMr	C.O. 'D' did not receive
9 pm	Typed Op. Orders	copy. 'D' Coy orderly
10.5 pm	Bde Op. Orders received.	failed to find him – also
10.30pm.	Further production of Bn Op. Orders – owing to alterations & additions required on receipt of Bde Orders. RSCC	[illegible] B 3 & 4 Orders referred to are attached
9. a.m. 9.3.15. ZUYTPEENE	Bn paraded outside H.Q. en route for STRAZEELE – less Mac. Gun & all wheeled & pack transport which marched under MAJOR E. SLEIGHT + 1/5 Linc. Rgt – & less 10 sick men unable to march and 6 men to clean billets. Route of Bde as per attached Bde Orders. Bde marched past GEN. SMITH-DORRIEN at CAESTRE. Reached	Distance – approx 9 miles. March casualties
2-40pm. 9.3.15. STRAZEELE	at 2-40 pm. All men billeted by 4-20 pm. Transport in by 5-30 pm. Rough plan of billets attached.	Rough billeting plan C 2 attached. Also rough plan of Divl Bde area. C 2(A)
9-30pm	1/1st L & L. Bde Conference – Bde H.Q. C.Os & Adj's	

(9 29 6) W 3332—1107 100,000 10/13 H W V Forms/C. 2118/10.

1/4. Leic. Rgt

WAR DIARY
or
INTELLIGENCE SUMMARY.
(Erase heading not required.)

1/1. Linc & Leic Bde
1/1st N. Mid Divn

Army Form C. 2118.

Instructions regarding War Diaries and Intelligence Summaries are contained in F.S. Regs., Part II. and the Staff Manual respectively. Title pages will be prepared in manuscript.

Hour, Date, Place (March 1918)	Summary of Events and Information	Remarks and references to Appendices
9-30 p.m. 9.3.15. STRAZEELE	Bde Commander outlined future plans of operations. 1/1st N. Mid Divn to be in Army General Reserve – directly under Commander of Forces British. Advance likely to commence at any moment. Bns to be ready to move at one hours notice probably "fighting order" – no packs. Heavy firing thro' to night – search light rays and flare reflections quite visible in easterly direction. RWB	
10.3.15		
3.55 p.m.	Instructions in case of Divl Advance recd from 1/1st L & L Bde.	Attached.
4 p.m.	Bn parade on Bn Alarm Post in Fighting Order practice parade.	
	3 British Biplanes over during parade moving N. to E.	
	No sound of firing to be heard at night. Direction of wind? RWB	
10.15 AM 11.3.15	Copy of N.M.D. a/1396 recd.	Original attached.
10.47 AM 11.3.15	Order from 1/1st L & L Bde to be ready to move at [illegible] recd over telephone	– Copy recd attached. B.6.
11-40 AM	Copy of message from 1/1st N.M.D. to 1/1st L & L Bde forwarded to 1/4 Leic Rgt.	Attached – B.7.
10.50	Copies of N.M.D. a/1096 sent to Coys & each Coy [illegible] order to get ready to move at once further orders follow. Sent to each Coy.	Original copy recd attached B.5.

Instructions regarding War Diaries and Intelligence Summaries are contained in F. S. Regs., Part II. and the Staff Manual respectively. Title pages will be prepared in manuscript.

1/4 Leic. Rgt

WAR DIARY
or
INTELLIGENCE SUMMARY.

(Erase heading not required.)

1/1st Linc. & Leic. Bde
1/1st N. Mid. Div.

Army Form C. 2118.

(7)

Hour, Date, Place	Summary of Events and Information	Remarks and references to Appendices
March 1915		
11.50 A.M.	Order to Coys to move to S. P. via attached	A 5
10.50 A.M. 11/3/15 STRAZEELE.	This N.M.D. A/1096 acted on as regards Brigading transport – this apparently wrong – N.M.D. A/1096 applying to move by bus.	Order not sufficiently clear for "nearest intelligence"?
	(Bde Route as per attached "order to move") Distance about 11½ miles	
	Impossible to comply with order in time. Bn intact at S. P.	Sick left in STRAZEELE
1.15 P.M.	at 1.15 P.M. Billeting parties only allotted area about 6.30 pm	in N.B. 3 ... 9
7.30 P.M. SAILLY	Bn reached Bg Area – Transport 10 to 75 mins later. [Sample attached C3]	Many sore feet owing to ...
10. P.M.	– Billeted, horses stabled or picketed & vehicles parked.	... – boots not flexible in
	Men very crowded – but v. few in open. Rough plan attached	soles. March Discipline good
Midnight 11/12	Some sniping E.N.W of Bn H.Q. apparently quite close.	B4 Area Plan C 2
12.30 A.m. 12/3/15	B.M. 27 from 1/1st L.L. Bde recd – re ready to move [Rcvd]	
	At one hours notice after 6 a.m. Not recd by an officer (Adjt)	Bde Hq. about 1 m. S. of SAILLY.
	until 12.45 A.m. Lost way 2 hrs finding Bde H.Q.	
1. A.m	Copy Orders re: B.M 27 to A.B. & D Coys. Were warned personally	~~Copy attached~~
	O.C. "C" Coy warned about 5 a.m. "C" Coy at Bn H.Q.	B7(a)
	No move. ... ... required ... STRA... [6.55 p.m.]	Copy of G 50? N.M.D. to Bde Recd 3.? Bn – attached.
6.55 p.m	Bde Area & After Order No 39. re being prepared to move at 6 a.m.	Bn recd copy ...
7.45 p.m	Bn Orders issued to all concerned – re move	Copy attached. B 5a
8.45 p.m	Sniping? or nervous sentry firing near Bn H.Q. Canadians?	

Instructions regarding War Diaries and Intelligence Summaries are contained in F. S. Regs., Part II. and the Staff Manual respectively. Title pages will be prepared in manuscript.

1/1st Linc. Rgt — **WAR DIARY** *or* **INTELLIGENCE SUMMARY.** *(Erase heading not required.)* — 1/1st Linc. & Leic. Bde — 1st N. Mid. Divn.

Army Form C. 2118. (8)

Hour, Date, Place	Summary of Events and Information	Remarks and references to Appendices
March 1915		
6. a.m. 13. 3. 15. SAILLY	Reported to Bde that Bn ready to move & awaiting orders.	
	Heavy artillery firing most of morning. No shells from enemy in neighbourhood of Bn.	
	Gt number of "unable to march" men - sore feet - new boots [illegible] 18	
9.15 a.m.	SL. 278 from Bde - Divn to be "ready to move at 2 hrs notice"	
	Apparently heavy fighting most of the day	
	No move - ready to move tomorrow at 2 hrs notice after	
9.25 P.M.	6 a.m. 14.3.15. Change of billets ordered by N. M. Divn.	[illegible] 51 B. 8.
	Some "sniping" near Hd Qrs during evening Recd	
6 a.m. 14.3.15.	Again ready to move - except that [illegible] "[illegible]" orders [illegible]	
12.30 p.m. BAC ST MAUR	Move to BAC ST MAUR at 12.45 pm [illegible]	
7.40 pm	Billeted [illegible] No [illegible] damage to billets	Plan attached C. 4.
	Information from Bde Major - 1/1st L & L Bde* move at 11 a.m. 15/3 to an [illegible] TRIN. BAYARDS. Special attention to be paid to [illegible]	Much ammunition [illegible] to be found in billets.
	Heavy firing thro' evening	× Notes taken - attached B 9.

(9 29 6) W 3332—1107 100,000 10/13 H W V Forms/C. 2118/10.

Army Form C. 2118. (9.)

Instructions regarding War Diaries and Intelligence Summaries are contained in F.S. Regs., Part II. and the Staff Manual respectively. Title pages will be prepared in manuscript.

1/4 Leic. Rgt WAR DIARY ~~or INTELLIGENCE~~ SUMMARY. 1/1st Linc & Leic Bde 1/1st N. Mid Divn

(*Erase heading not required.*)

Hour, Date, Place	Summary of Events and Information	Remarks and references to Appendices
March 1915		
10.55 P.M. 14/3/15. BAC ST. MAUR	B.M. 24. received from 1/1st L & L Bde & orders issued to coys. – [illegible] called on. [illegible] heavy fighting.	B.M. 24 Copy attached. B.10.
12.35 a.m. 15/3/15	Bde Operation Orders – Copy No. 3 recd & not shown to Adjutant as orders already issued to cover main details of move.	~~Attached~~
7. a.m	Billeting Party under 2/Lt R.C. Harvey at Bn HQ	
9. a.m	Bn Operation Orders [illegible] issued to Coys. (No. 5	Copy not attached 2.6 [illegible]
9.45 a.m	SL 38 rec'd re. standing by in billets at present	
11.35 a.m	B.M. 42 recd. Copy of same sent to all concerned.	Copy of BM 42 attached B.11.
4-30 p.m	Cash for Coys 12.570 fr drawn 1st [illegible]. Billeting Party under 2 Lt R.C. Harvey returned.	
7.13 p.m	B.M. 30 altering hour of start recd – Coys etc notified	
7-30 p.m.	B.M. 30 repeated [illegible] acknowledgment received.	

Instructions regarding War Diaries and Intelligence Summaries are contained in F.S. Regs., Part II. and the Staff Manual respectively. Title pages will be prepared in manuscript.

1/4 Leic. Regt

WAR DIARY
or
~~INTELLIGENCE SUMMARY.~~

(Erase heading not required.)

1/1st Linc & Leic Bde

1/1st N. Mid Div

Army Form C. 2118.

Hour, Date, Place	Summary of Events and Information	Remarks and references to Appendices
March 1915.		
7.45 P.M. BAC ST MAUR 15th	Coys [illegible] — [illegible] arranged for [illegible]	A.7 attached
16.3.15 10.20 AM / BAC ST MAUR	Our [illegible] on Div H.Q. relieved by G.O.C.'s orders before 9 am. Bn passed Bn S.P. as per orders. Marched to new billeting area — vide	about 5 miles [illegible] plan attached C.5.
	Scattered billets — but good otherwise. Tel wires laid out to all coys &	Qrs Stores
	but not satisfactory — reason not traced at [illegible].	
1.30 pm LE CHIEN BLANC	[illegible] Bn billeted [illegible].	
	In touch with Bde by cyclist only — arrangements made to connect with Bde Sig Section (No 2 M.T. [illegible] Sig Coy) at pt ¾ m S. of [illegible] at 9 am 17.3.15.	Bde at [illegible] BARRED
	~~[illegible]~~	
	Bn wires found [illegible] C & B lines. Wire not v. suitable for [illegible] work apparently [illegible] as yet [illegible] — [illegible]	
	R[illegible]	

(9 29 6) W 3332—1107 100,000 10/13 H W V Forms/C. 2118/10

Army Form C. 2118.

(11)

Instructions regarding War Diaries and Intelligence Summaries are contained in F.S. Regs., Part II. and the Staff Manual respectively. Title pages will be prepared in manuscript.

WAR DIARY
or
INTELLIGENCE SUMMARY.
(Erase heading not required.)

1/4. Leic. Regt 1/1st Linc & Leic Bde 1/1st N.M. Div

Hour, Date, Place	Summary of Events and Information	Remarks and references to Appendices
March 1915.		
7.30 A.M. 17th LE CHIEN BLANC	4 G.S. Wagons to Bac St Maur to fetch surplus stores etc.	
Forenoon —	Training & interior economy	
Afternoon —	Inoculation (157 other ranks) by 2nd N.M. F. Amb.	
4.40 pm	B.M. 41 recd "Bde will probably move tomorrow"	Copy not kept
6.5 pm —	Notified Bde – A.L. 29 – that 157 men inoculated etc. – copy	
	Considerable theft? or loss of Iron Rations in "C" Coy	
12.15 am. 18th —	Bde Op. Order No 4. re move recd. Not communicated by officer receiving to Adjt – [illegible]. [illegible] was 6.? am. telephoned to Bde [illegible] to go to Bde H.Q. at 8.30 am. This order misunderstood & [illegible] late to Bde. Message on telephone not repeated – evidently – as officer thought he understood. Fault in [illegible] office (Adjt) [illegible]. Coy [illegible] at [illegible]	Bde H.Q. moved to STEENWERCK
1.30 pm	[illegible] New Area – necessitating change of "A"–"D" portion of "C" Coy – Qr Mr Stores – M.O. – Transport. Changes completed [illegible] – but ½ D Coy in [illegible] Billets. [illegible] "C" & "B" only [illegible] for "A" & "B.D" [illegible] "B"	Plan attached. C.C.

(9 29 6) W 3332—1107 100,000 10/13 H W V Forms/C. 2118/10.

Instructions regarding War Diaries and Intelligence Summaries are contained in F. S. Regs., Part II. and the Staff Manual respectively. Title pages will be prepared in manuscript.

1/4 [illegible] Rgt

WAR DIARY
or
INTELLIGENCE SUMMARY.
(Erase heading not required.)

1/1st [illegible] 1/1st [illegible]

Army Form C. 2118.

Hour, Date, Place	Summary of Events and Information	Remarks and references to Appendices
March 1915		
19th LE CHEF [illegible] BLANC.	Snow during night - cold & bright - Sun soon thawed most of snow. Training in coy [illegible] area. Much diarrhoea amongst troops - origin not at present traceable. Arrangement for instruction in bombing at [illegible] - [illegible] per coy. These [illegible] at [illegible] moments notice - [illegible] not found & officers returned. [illegible] not traced. All hairy coats handed in [illegible] to [illegible] refilling [illegible] Maps of MONS, BRUSSELS, NAMUR, GHENT, [illegible], ANTWERP called in by Bde. Reason not stated. O's C Coys now realizing the weakness of T. F. N. C. O.'s. [illegible] will prove costly. It takes years [illegible] soldiering to make N. C. O. and [illegible] officers - & [illegible] have [illegible] the coming [illegible] [illegible] are [illegible] [illegible] Officers and N. C. O's evidently not well acquainted with N. M. D. War Standing Orders - nor appreciation of fact that promptness in rendering returns - states etc (reasonably accurately) much more important than absolute accuracy - which is impossible & causes such less trouble & delay. Telephone very gt time-saver. Great [illegible] display [illegible] of Bn H.Q	Cash 12370 francs obtained from F^d Cashier - [illegible] - by [illegible] [illegible] not advisable to send [illegible] officers. But the cash not wanted by Coys - O's C deeming [illegible] & better without more. Applications for reduction to ranks or lower grade necessary under A. O. 183 (2)

General summary of Events - no times of importance. Also observations [illegible] [illegible] to date.

RSWB

1/4. Leic Rgt — 1/1st Line Leic Bde — 1/1st N. Mid. Div.

WAR DIARY
or
INTELLIGENCE SUMMARY.
(Erase heading not required.)

Army Form C. 2118. (13)

Instructions regarding War Diaries and Intelligence Summaries are contained in F.S. Regs., Part II. and the Staff Manual respectively. Title pages will be prepared in manuscript.

Hour, Date, Place	Summary of Events and Information	Remarks and references to Appendices
March 1915.		
20th LE CHIEN BLANC	Still more diarrhoea & still not traced. V. bright - warm - frosty night.	Tinned food.
9.30 A.M.	Cpl. KIRK (No. 1517) to ST OMER (14 days M.G. Course). Replaced at MERRIS	
	Lt. Col. W. A. HARRISON - sick in billet - cold - throat.	
	Work - 3hrs in forenoon and 2hrs in afternoon - [illegible]	
	[illegible] exercises - [illegible] Office work, Bn. H.Q. [illegible]	
	& private type [illegible]	
	Difficulty experienced in understanding & completing [illegible] Returns.	
	Still not so clear that "veriest fool can understand"	
2.35 pm	Brit. Bi-Plane due South from Bn. H.Q. heavily shelled, but not apparently touched. Distance away doubtful - but flashes just visible with average glasses. Airship - or captive balloon of airship shape - quite 12 miles S.W. from Bn. H.Q. No other air craft in its neighbourhood. Notified brigade - but made error in thinking it was moving - why not attacked?	As seen thro' glasses. Type not discernable, thought to be enemy. [illegible]
10-45 pm	Heavy gunning - apparently due E - but 2 or 3 guns only. V. little musketry - & only in same direction. Many "fireworks" E & S.	

[illegible initials]

(9 29 6) W 3332—1107 100,000 10/13 H W V Forms/C. 2118/10.

Instructions regarding War Diaries and Intelligence Summaries are contained in F. S. Regs., Part II. and the Staff Manual respectively. Title pages will be prepared in manuscript.

1/4. Leic. Rgt **WAR DIARY** 1/1st Linc & Leic Bde, 1/1st N. Mid. Divn

~~or~~

~~**INTELLIGENCE SUMMARY.**~~

(Erase heading not required.)

Army Form C. 2118. (14)

Hour, Date, Place	Summary of Events and Information	Remarks and references to Appendices
March 1915.		
21st Le CHIEN BLANC	Cold - but beautifully fine. Aeroplanes active - considerably shelled, but no result. Ch parades in Coy areas. Afternoon games & sports - v. popular & men v. cheery & keen.	
12. Noon.	Visit from Captain PRICE DAVIES (V.C. D.S.O.) G.S.O. 1st N.M.D. - getting in touch with units. Sign board directing to Bde H.Q. not conspicuous enough. Various commissions coming in - men unwilling to accept or anxious to stay abroad with unit & not to return home. No apparent escape.	
2. p.m.	Instruction from Captain STONE [illegible] Rgt in [illegible]	1 man [illegible]
Late afternoon.	Captain G. CORAH (5th Bn O.C. Cy C) [illegible] to O.C. Coys - gave some useful hints: trench fighting & sanitation & re various types of Germans to be met, Prussians, Bavarians, Saxons. Don't trust (1), (2) fairly so (3) all against fighting. This confirms rumours.	
9.55 p.m.	Bn Commanders & Adjts ordered to meet Bde Commander at Farm 300x N.E. of M in Le VERRIER. Acknowledged.	[illegible] Ref 1/100,000 HAZEBROUCK map E.F.7.

[illegible signature]

1/4 Leic Regt — **WAR DIARY** *or* **INTELLIGENCE SUMMARY.** — 1/1st Linc & Leic Bde, 1/1st N. Mid. Div

(~~Erase heading not required.~~)

Army Form C. 2118. (15)

Instructions regarding War Diaries and Intelligence Summaries are contained in F. S. Regs., Part II. and the Staff Manual respectively. Title pages will be prepared in manuscript.

Hour, Date, Place	Summary of Events and Information	Remarks and references to Appendices
March 1915.		
22nd Le CHIEN BLANC	Cold & fine – Training 8 – to 11.30am with intervals – Coy areas	
9. am —	Heavy "gunning"	
9.45am —	Bomb & Shovel instruction – Captain STANILAND.	
About 10.30 am	Aeroplane (enemy) brought down slightly E of S from Bn HQ	
3. pm. STEENWERCK	Major L.V. WYKES & Adjt "rendezvous'd" at Fm 300x N.E. of M. of Le KIRLEM. Saw trenches made by Reg Troops? running in line due S of STEENWERCK. 1/5th Linc Regt practising trench box – defence & counter attacks in co-operation with R.A. Not very instructive – not apparently understood by all ranks & isolated efforts made to counter attack.	
4 pm	Instructions from [illegible] Idea & Bde Operation Orders re. our work for 23rd.	
6 pm — Le CHIEN BLANC	Bn Operation Orders prepared – these took nearly 2 hours to complete. This apparent [illegible] length of time due to endeavour to include every necessary detail.	
9 pm.	O's C. Coys assembled at Bn HQ. to hear Bn Op. Orders read & to receive instructions.	
	R.S.D.B.	

(9 29 6) W 3332—1107 100,000 10/13 H W V Forms/C. 2118/10.

Instructions regarding War Diaries and Intelligence Summaries are contained in F. S. Regs., Part II. and the Staff Manual respectively. Title pages will be prepared in manuscript.

1/4 Leic. Rgt

WAR DIARY
or
INTELLIGENCE SUMMARY.
(*Erase heading not required.*)

1/1st Linc. & Leic. Bde
1/1st N. Midl. Div.

Army Form C. 2118.

(16)

Hour, Date, Place March – 1915.	Summary of Events and Information	Remarks and references to Appendices
6.20 a.m. 23rd Le CHIEN BLANC	Bn Op. Orders issued by cyclist orderlies to all concerned + Bde & R.A.	Copy attached also remarks on same as result of criticism of G.O.C. & Brig Gen. D.1
8.45 a.m. "	Bn passed Le GRAND BEAUMART for farm 300x N.E. of M. in le KIRKEM.	
9.15 a.m. " STEENWERCK	Major L.V. WYKES & Adjt met Major CHALLENOR – 3rd STAFFS Battery at Fm indicated in attached sketch. R.A. telephone wire to Battery from Fm not on through. Our line to trenches working well	
10. a.m.	Battery wire still not laid. Reason – not discovered – probably "layer" lost his way. Bombardment presumed to be in progress.	
~~10.20 a.m.~~ 10.19 a.m.	Brig Gen. 1/1st L.L. Bde ordered postponement until 10.35 a.m. – but message could not be got thro' to the Rt flank and D, A & ½ 'B' Coys charged. Charge not absolutely simultaneous & would not have been successful. Query – would the fact that Arty not in touch with Bn H.Q. & R.A. Observing Officer have made any difference? R.A. had definite orders about hours of opening fire – increasing range – objective etc. But would gunners have ever got correct range – without touch with forward observer.	Very instructive morning remarks etc on attached papers marked D.1
11.15 a.m.	Charge repeated – G.O.C. present. No serious criticism. Assault successful at most points – stubborn resistance "presumed" in centre. Eventually successful.	
1.30 p.m.	Bn returned to billets.	

(9 29 6) W 3332—1107 100,000 10/13 H W V Forms/C. 2118/10.

Instructions regarding War Diaries and Intelligence Summaries are contained in F.S. Regs., Part II. and the Staff Manual respectively. Title pages will be prepared in manuscript.

1/4 Leic Rgt **WAR DIARY** *or* **INTELLIGENCE SUMMARY.** 1/1st Linc & Leic Bde, 1/1st N. Mid. Divn

(Erase heading not required.)

Army Form C. 2118. (17)

Hour, Date, Place	Summary of Events and Information	Remarks and references to Appendices
March – 1915		
10.30 am 23rd LE CHIEN BLANC	Lt. Col. W. A. HARRISON T.D. admitted to hospital No 5 HAZEBROUCK – suffering from throat & "ague". Command of Bn devolved upon Major L.V. WYKES.	
	Bde Area Orders – stating probable move to trenches on Friday next 26th inst.	
9.30 pm	L.B.C. 167 from Bde – re training programme. This message took 2 hrs to reach Bn HQ according to A.F. C 398. Statement that ~~the~~ programme not recd till 6.40 pm incorrect, as receipt timed 3.12 pm held by us. This ~~as~~ error not understood – just shows how easily mistakes arise.	L.B.C. 167 B12 b & reply (E.F. 12) B12 a attached

R.S.D.B.

Instructions regarding War Diaries and Intelligence Summaries are contained in F. S. Regs., Part II. and the Staff Manual respectively. Title pages will be prepared in manuscript.

1/4 [illegible] Rgt

WAR DIARY
or
INTELLIGENCE SUMMARY.
(Erase heading not required.)

1/1st [illegible] Bde
1/1st N. [illegible] Div

Army Form C. 2118.

18

Hour, Date, Place	Summary of Events and Information	Remarks and references to Appendices
March 1915		
24th LE CHIEN BLANC 9 a.m. to 12 noon	Route march – route (ref. 1/100,000 HAZEBROUCK) S.P. 300x W.S.W. of Bn H.Q. (not shown on map) on LE VERRIER – SAILLY road – X roads 300x N.N.W. of SAILLY – CROIX du BAC – STEENWERCK – INN about ½ m. [illegible] of STEENWERCK – then S. [illegible] Coys falling out as they passed by H.Qrs. Distance about [illegible] miles for all coys. Roads for most part [illegible] [illegible] still [illegible] (Report that PRZEMYSL captured by RUSSIANS confirmed & GERMAN & AUSTRIAN subjects said to have been advised to quit ITALY) Sandbags and [illegible] tools [illegible] [illegible] coming	Casualties [illegible] principally to [illegible]
9.8 p.m.	Bde [illegible] Orders [illegible] [illegible] [illegible] to be attached to [illegible] for instruction. Bn [illegible] Orders [illegible] [illegible] [illegible] [illegible] and [illegible] called for [illegible] [illegible] [illegible] [illegible] [illegible] [illegible] [illegible] [illegible] to make out [illegible] [illegible] [illegible] [illegible] [illegible] [illegible] [illegible] [illegible] [illegible] [illegible]	
ARMENTIERES	[illegible] [illegible] KINGSWAY [illegible] ARMENTIERES [illegible] [illegible] night	

(9 29 6) W 3332—1107 100,000 10/13 H W V Forms/C. 2118/10

Instructions regarding War Diaries and Intelligence Summaries are contained in F.S. Regs., Part II. and the Staff Manual respectively. Title pages will be prepared in manuscript.

WAR DIARY
or
INTELLIGENCE SUMMARY.
(Erase heading not required.)

1/4 Leic Rgt 1/1st Linc & Leic Bde 1/1st N. Mid Div

Army Form C. 2118. 19

Hour, Date, Place	Summary of Events and Information	Remarks and references to Appendices
March 1915.		
25th LE CHIEN BLANC	Heavy rain in early a.m. Rain at intervals during day. Training at the H.Q. - 8.30 to 11.30 am. Training Operations - Defence Scheme in Trenches [illegible] cancelled owing to wet	Scheme & instructions issued attached D1.
3.30 pm	Instructions re move from Bde. to LE BIZET - 2 [illegible] 1¼ m N. of ARMENTIERES.	
4.17 pm.	Bde Op. Orders No.5 recd. & a vast quantity of other correspondence which necessitated working until early morning. [illegible] [illegible] informed [illegible] [illegible] sick leave [illegible]	Copy No 4 recd attached B/3.
8.30 pm	1/3 Op. Orders No 6 issued to all concerned. Bn Orders - [illegible] [illegible] [illegible] & [illegible] [illegible] issued & [illegible] reported [illegible] receipt of same RSDT	Copy No. 1 attached B/8.

(9 29 6) W 3332—1107 100,000 10/13 H W V Forms/C. 2118/10

Instructions regarding War Diaries and Intelligence Summaries are contained in F. S. Regs., Part II. and the Staff Manual respectively. Title pages will be prepared in manuscript.

1/4 Leic Rgt — **WAR DIARY** *or* **INTELLIGENCE SUMMARY.** (*Erase heading not required.*) — 1st Linc & Leic Bde, 1st N. Mid Div

Army Form C. 2118.

20

Hour, Date, Place	Summary of Events and Information	Remarks and references to Appendices
March 1915		
26th LE CHIEN BLANC	2/Lt K DALGLIESH, his servant, the storeman & 2 sick left in billets (central) under Capt C. 2/N.M. F.A. DALGLIESH i/c of Bde Area Sick	
2.20pm	Major WYKES & Adjt met Brig Commander at Bde S.P. Bde Cdr spoke of importance of all ranks getting instruction during attachment. Importance of cleanliness.	
2.45pm	Bttn [illegible] [illegible] [illegible] for Gen PULTENEY Comdg 3rd Corps, who watched Bde [illegible] [illegible] on S. end of STEENWERCK. Bde [illegible] [illegible] [illegible] [illegible] S. end of S'WERCK [illegible] [illegible] [illegible] [illegible] [illegible] (from platoons [illegible]) & [illegible] [illegible] [illegible] [illegible] (3.5 [illegible]) [illegible] [illegible] [illegible]. Good deal of [illegible] on [illegible]. M.G. [illegible] [illegible] of 7/Essex [illegible] [illegible] of PABOT	Ab [illegible]. No casualty left on road. Distance about [illegible] from Bde S.P.
ARMENTIERES	Reached ARMENTIERES. Billeted as per plan by 6pm	Plan attached C7

Instructions regarding War Diaries and Intelligence Summaries are contained in F.S. Regs., Part II. and the Staff Manual respectively. Title pages will be prepared in manuscript.

1/4 Leic. Rgt **WAR DIARY** 1/1st Lincs & Leics Bde

or

INTELLIGENCE SUMMARY. 1/1st N. Mid Divn

(*Erase heading not required.*)

Army Form C. 2118. (21)

Hour, Date, Place	Summary of Events and Information	Remarks and references to Appendices
March 1915 Ref. S 36. N.W. 1/20,000		
26th LATTARGETTE ARMENTIÈRES.	C.O. & Adj reported at Bde H.Q. 12th Infy Bde. Only Adj Staff Captain in – met Brig. Gen ANNERLEY when returning to Bn H.Q. Found usual daily billets. Men fairly well off. Recd instructions governing attachment. & Bde Major visited billets (H.Q.) Recd	Weather fine – cold. Copies attached & copy of Bn Orders. &c.
27th — 10 am.	To 12th Bde H.Q. C.O., 2nd in C., Adj & M.G.O. for instructions re. attachment of [illegible] to [illegible] [illegible] etc. Afterwards saw exhibition of hand grenade throwing. Coys worked as per instructions. Carried [illegible] with 1/LEICESTERSHIRE. Adj to 16 Inf Bde H.Q. for demonstration of catapult, [illegible] bombs & bomb throwing generally. No troops here having made an attack, no information re: procedure procurable. A & C to trenches (KINGS OWN & MONMOUTHS)	Weather fine – cold

1/4. Leic. Rgt. — WAR DIARY or ~~INTELLIGENCE SUMMARY~~. — 1/1st Line Leic Bde — 1/1st N. M. Div

Army Form C. 2118.

Instructions regarding War Diaries and Intelligence Summaries are contained in F.S. Regs., Part II. and the Staff Manual respectively. Title pages will be prepared in manuscript.

(*Erase heading not required.*)

Hour, Date, Place	Summary of Events and Information	Remarks and references to Appendices
March 1915.		
28th LAMMERGETTE (ARMENTIÈRES.)	Fine bright & cold. Work as per programme & [illegible] Order. Major WYKES (the CO) [illegible] Major [illegible] Adj. reported [illegible] Div. H.Q. [illegible] of [illegible] trenches. [illegible] [illegible] communication trenches [illegible] & interested in the life. Evening – Major Potter [illegible] section of [illegible] trenches [illegible] [illegible]	[illegible]
	[illegible]	[illegible]
1 A.M. 29th	[illegible] careless, which [illegible] Major [illegible]	

Instructions regarding War Diaries and Intelligence Summaries are contained in F.S. Regs., Part II. and the Staff Manual respectively. Title pages will be prepared in manuscript.

WAR DIARY
or
INTELLIGENCE SUMMARY.
(Erase heading not required.)

Army Form C. 2118.

Hour, Date, Place	Summary of Events and Information	Remarks and references to Appendices
[illegible]	[illegible]	[illegible]

(9 29 6) W 3332—1107 100,000 10/13 H W V Forms/C. 2118/10.

Army Form C. 2118.

Instructions regarding War Diaries and Intelligence Summaries are contained in F. S. Regs., Part II. and the Staff Manual respectively. Title pages will be prepared in manuscript.

1/4 [illegible] Rgt

WAR DIARY
or
INTELLIGENCE SUMMARY.

(*Erase heading not required.*)

Hour, Date, Place	Summary of Events and Information	Remarks and references to Appendices
March 1915		
30th KATTARGETTE (ARMENTIERES)	Fine & cold – slight mist. Work as per programme [illegible] Orders Co., 2nd in C & Adj visited K.S.O.W.R. [illegible] portion of [illegible] section of trenches [illegible]	Copy of [illegible] orders attached (D2 file)
	[illegible] Two further casualties of 29th inst reported. Slight wounds.	
2-45 pm	Oper Orders by G.O.C. 4th Div. received & acknowledged from 12th Inf Bde [illegible]	Copy No 7 [illegible] B14
5-45 pm	No further Op Orders being rec'd. Bn Op Orders No 7 issued to all concerned.	
7.30 pm	Copy No 6 of Oper Orders by G.O.C. 4th Div received from 1/1st LINC & LEIC Bde. Not acknowledged as copy of Bn Oper Orders already sent to [illegible] Bde & receipt [illegible]	Copy No 1 attached D9
31st 9.5 am	Bn marched off – 7 men unable to march. O of [illegible] of Bde [illegible] as 1/4 LINC Rgt late at Bde S.P. [illegible] Regt [illegible] followed 1/5 Linc Rgt. Marched past [illegible]	Distance about 8 miles
12.10 pm [illegible]	Billeted in original [illegible]	2 men fell out [illegible] bad feet & [illegible] cause
	Vast number of reports called for – re boots, [illegible]	

(9 29 6) W 3332—1107 100,000 10/13 H W V Forms/C. 2118/10.

45

Feb [illegible] List of Appendices to War Diary
1/4 Leicestershire Rgt.

Appendix.

A. Batt.n Operation Orders & important messages etc issued. only 1 copy.

B. Brigade ([illegible]) ditto only 1 copy

C. Rough plans of Billeting Areas occupied by Batt.n only 1 copy

D.1 Orders, instructions etc issued in connection with training away from firing line. only 1 copy

D2 Orders, instructions etc. — as above training attachment in trenches only 1 copy

E. Nominal Roll of Officers of Batt.n who embarked for foreign service.

48

Feb & March 1915. List of Appendices continued
1/4 Leicestershire Rgt.

Appendix.

F. Average daily number of N.C.O.s & men away from Batt.n in hospital. in duplicate.

March 1915.

R.S. Dyer Bennet
Captain & Adj
1/4 Leic Rgt.

1

A P P E N D I C E S A.1 to A.9.

Copy No 1. . 2.1

OPERATION ORDERS No 1.
by
LIEUT. COLONEL W. A. HARRISON T.D.
Cmdg. 1/4th LEICESTERSHIRE REGIMENT.

Benskin's Brewery,
BISHOP'S STORTFORD.

26th February, 1915.

1 The Battalion will entrain for Port of Embarkation tomorrow, 27th instant as under :-

FIRST TRAIN. (No X14)

HEADQUARTERS (less 2nd in Command, Qmr. Sgt., Transport Sgt., 2 S.A.A.Carts, 1 Water Cart, 1 Tool Wagon, 2 Spare Horses, 2nd in Command's Batman and Horse, 2 Cook's Carts and 3"Train" Transport Wagons (1, Officers'Kits, 1, Blanket. "A" & "B" Coys., and 1, Supply wagon.)
and "A" & "B" Coys. will parade at HOCKERILL BRIDGE at 6 a.m.
Order of March - "A" Coy etc.
Entraining Officer.- Lieut. G. J. Harvey.
Train departs 7-40 a.m. (BISHOP'S STORTFORD G.E.Rly. Stn.)
Train No

SECOND TRAIN (No.X17)

REMAINDER OF HEADQUARTERS, Machine Gun Section, "C" and "D" Coys. will parade as above at 8 a.m.
Order of March "C" Coy. etc.
Entraining Officer-Lieut. T. Whittingham
Train departs 9-40 a.m. (BISHOP'S STORTFORD G.E.Rly. Stn)

PARTIES

(1) Entraining , (2) Unloading & Hold Parties.
Details have been issued to O's.C. "A" & "C" Coys. respectively to supply the above parties
(1) At BISHOP'S STORTFORD
(2) Port of Embarkation.

TRANSPORT Details have been issued to the Transport Officer dealing with the method of entraining horses, wagons, etc.
Also to 2 Lt. L. FORSELL - a/T.O. 2nd train.

Every N.C.O. and man on the strength of the Battalion will parade with his Company or Detachment and march to the Station where the final roll will be called. Only those men who are warned by an Officer to remain behind will not entrain.

DETAILS (Lt.A.Silver) Men ordered to remain will be handed over to the Officer i/c Details.- Lieut. A. Silver - who will march to the station with the first entraining party and remain there until the departure of the second train.

R.S. Dyer-Bennet.

Capt. & Adjutant.
1/4th Leicestershire Regiment.

Copy No 1 War Diary
" 2 1/1st Linc. & Leic. Bde
" 3 Major L V.Wykes
" 4 O.C. "A" Coy
" 5 O.C. "B" Coy
" 6 O.C. "C" Coy
" 7 O.C. "D" Coy

Copy No 8 Transport Officer
" 9 Mac.Gun Officer
" 10 Medical Officer
" 11 Quartermaster
" 12 O. i/c Details.
" 13. Lt. G. J. Harvey
" 14 Lt. T. Whittingham
" 15. 2/Lt. L. Forsell a/T.O. RE..

Issued by orderly at 8 p.m.

Copy No 1 a.2

OPERATION ORDER NO 2
by
LIEUT. COLONEL W.A.HARRISON T.D.
Cmdg. 1/4th LEICESTERSHIRE REGIMENT.

No 6 Rest Camp
le HAVRE

5th March 1915

1 MOVE — The Battalion will move to place of entrainment, GARE des MARCHANDISES, Point No. 4 as under.

Lt. T. WHITTINGHAM — 8-30 p.m. Fall in on Bn. Alarm Post. O. of M. Det. of "A" Coy. "B" "C" & "D" Coys.
Entraining officer.- Lt. T. WHITTINGHAM.

2 RATION PARTY. Lt. H. C. BRICE and 30 N.C.O.'s and men will parade on Bn. Alarm Post at 8 p.m. This party will report to OFFICER i/c DETAIL ISSUE STORES, GARE des MARCHANDISES.
Lt. H.C. BRICE

3 FATIGUE PARTIES. Fatigue parties are detailed as under.-

WAGON LOADING PARTIES.- 2/Lt.F.M.WAITE and No 10 Platoon
2/Lt. K.DALGLIESH and No. 9 Platoon
To assist Transport Section if required.

WAGON SANDING PARTY.- 2/Lt.J.F.Johnson and 20 N.C.O's and men of No.14 Platoon. for sanding Horse wagons.

HORSE ENTRAINING PARTY 2/Lt.R.C.HARVEY and 30 N.C.O's and men to assist in the entraining of horses if required.

RATION PARTY. A second ration party of 40 N.C.O's and men of No 15 platoon under 2/Lt.M.B.DOUGLAS, to stand by in case it is required.

The above fatigue parties are required at the place of entrainment.

4 ~~[illegible]~~. PICQUET

PICKET. 2/Lt. H. F. PAPPRILL and No 16 Platoon will picket all approaches to and exits from place of entrainment.
2/Lt.H.F. PAPPRILL.

5 INSTRUCTIONS. O's.C.Coys. will ensure that all water bottles are full. No drinking water being available atthe entraining station or on the train.
O's.C. Coys.
Every man must be told the station and point of entrainment (Point No.4) before leaving camp.
The entrance to Point No.4 is at 70 COURS de la REPUBLIQUE.

TIME. On FRENCH RAILWAYS the hours of the day are numbered from 0 HEURES (which is mid-night) to 24 HEURES (also mid-night) Thus.- 10 p.m. is 22 HEURES.

SMOKING. Men detailed to travel in wagons containing horses must NOT SMOKE.

R.S. Dyer-Bennet

(sd) R. S. DYER-BENNET Capt. & Adjt.
1/4th Leicestershire Regiment.

Issued verbally to ~~[illegible]~~. Representatives of Companies at 4-30 p.m.
Copies issued as under.

Copy No.	1	War Diary. Filed. ~~[illegible]~~.
"	2	1/1st Linc. & Leic. Inf. Bde.
"	3	Major L. V. WYKES. by Orderly
"	4	O.C. "A" Coy.
"	5	O.C. "B" Coy.
"	6	O.C. "C" Coy.
"	7	O.C. "D" Coy.
"	8	O.C.Detachment. from S.S.DUNKIRK (Capt. B.F.Newill)

OPERATION ORDERS NO 3
by
LIEUT. COLONEL W.A.HARRISON T.D.
CMDG. 1/4TH LEICESTERSHIRE REGIMENT.

Copy No 1. a.3.

"SPANNEUT"
ZUYTPEENE.
8th March 1915.

x Reference 1/100,00 Sheet 5A

1. MOVE. The Bn. will proceed to STRAZEELE tomorrow 9th inst by march route. Pass Bn. Head Quarters at 9-5 a.m. in rear of the 1/4th Linc. Rgt. O. of M. "B" Coy. etc.

1st Line Transport.
The 1st Line Transport(less M.G.Section) will march in rear of the 1/4th Linc. Rgt. 1st Line Transport.
Starting point Level Crossing 1 mile W. of BAVINCHOVE at 11-30 a.m.

R S Dyer Bennet
(sd) R.S.DYER-BENNET Capt. & Adj
1/4th Leicestershire Regiment.

Issued verbally to O's C. Coys. T.O.and M.G.Officer at 7 p.m.

Copy No 1 War Diary
" 2 O.C. "A" Coy
" 3 " "B" "
" 4 " "C" "
" 5 " "D" "
" 6 T.O.
" 7 M.G.O.

Issued by orderly at 9 p.m.

a5.

Each
O.C. [illegible]" Coy.

Coys will move independantly
Starting point
1/4. S. of Z in STRAZEELE
(Ref 5A. 1/100,000)
at once.

O. of M. A. Coy.
STRAZEELE
11.50 am.
11.3.15.

R.S. Dyer Bennet
Capt & Adjt.
1/4 Linc Regt.

OPERATION ORDERS NO 4 Copy No 1.
by
LIEUT. COLONEL W.A.HARRISON T.D.
CMDG. 1/4TH LEICESTERSHIRE REGIMENT.

a.4.

(These orders cancell those issued at 9 p.m. 8/3/'15)

Spanneut,
ZUYTPEENE.
9th March 1915.

Reference 1/100,000. Sheet 5A

1 MOVE. The Bn. will proceed to STRAZEELE to-day by march route. Pass Bn. Head Quarters at 9-5 a.m. in rear of the 1/4th Linc. Rgt. O. of M. "B", "C", "D" & "A" Coys. Reports to Head of Column.

2 1ST LINE TRANSPORT.
The 1st Line Transport will march in rear of the 1/4th Linc. Rgt 1st Line Transport.
Starting Point Level Crossing 1 mile W of BAVINCHOVE at 11-30 a.m.
1st Line Transport will come under orders of Major E. SLEIGHT, 5/Linc. Rgt.

3 SICK. Men unable to march will report to No 2548 L/Cpl.H.W.Hinde Med. Officer's Orderly at ZUYTPEENE Rly. Bridge at 10-10 a.m.

R.S. Dyer-Bennet

(sd) R. S. DYER-BENNET Capt. & Adjt.
1/4th Leicestershire Regiment.

Copy No 1 War Diary
" 2 O.C. "A" Coy Issued at 6 a.m. by orderly
" 3 "B"
" 4 "C"
" 5 "D"
" 6 T.O.
" 7 M.G.O.
" 8 M.O.

BATTALION ORDERS by

LIEUT. COLONEL W.A.HARRISON T.D., CMDG. 1/4TH LEICESTERSHIRE RGT

SAILLY.
12/3/'15.

1 DUTIES.- Capt. of the day Capt. H.Haylock Next Capt. B.F.Newill
Sub. of the day 2/Lt.J.F.Johnson Next 2/Lt.F.M.Wate.

2 INLYING PICQUET.- Inlying Picquet "B" Coy. The Inlying Picquet will always stand to arms ready for an emergency one hour before dawn and a report rendered in writing by the O.C.Coy. to the Bn.Hd.Qrs that everything is in order or otherwise as soon as possible after the inlying picquet has "stood to".

3 MOVE.- The Bn. will prepare to move by 5-45 a.m. tomorrow 13th inst. Blanket wagons and Baggage wagons will be loaded and ready to move by 5-30 a.m.

Breakfast.- 4-45 a.m. An Officer from each Coy. will report personally to the Adjutant by 5 a.m. that the breakfasts were ready at the hour ordered.

The G.O.C. wishes each man to have a full meal for breakfast tomorrow.

IRON RATIONS and WATER BOTTLES.- O's.C.Coys. will at once make sure that Iron Rations are intact and Water Bottles filled with boiled or filtered water. They will report personally to Bn. Hd.Qrs. by 5-45 a.m. tomorrow 13th inst. at latest that everything is correct.

SICK. The Md. Officer will see the sick and men whom O's.C.Coys. consider unfit to do a long march tonight commencing with "A" Coy at 8-30 p.m. These men should parade at Coy.Hd.Qrs. and be marched ~~ex~~ their by their Platoon Sgts. or Section Commander. The O.C.Coy. and Platoon Commanders must be notified immediately after the inspection the Rgtl. Nos. and names of those N.C.O's and men who will be unable to march.

OPERATION ORDERS No 45 by
LIEUT. COLONEL W.A.HARRISON T.D., Cmdg. 1/4TH LEICESTERSHIRE RGT. A6.

BAC SAINT MAUR.
15/3/'16.

Ref.- 1/100,000 Sheet No 5a

1 MOVE.- The Bn. will move to a new area. The Bn. will pass road junction 500 yards W. of B. in BAC ST.MAUR 11-20 a.m. O.of M. Hd.Qrs., "C". "D","A","B",1st ~~and 2nd~~ Line Transport and"Train". The Bn. will march in rear of the 5th Lincolnshire Rgt.

2 REPORTS.- Reports to Head of Column

(sd) R. S. DYER-BENNET Capt. & Adj.
1/4th Leicestershire Regiment.

Issued at 9 a.m. by Cyclist Orderly.

Copy No 1 War Diary
do 2 Linc. & Leic. Inf. Bde.
do 3 "A" Coy
do 4 "B" "
do 5 "C" "
do 6 "D" "
do 7 Transport Officer
do 8 Quartermaster.

Instructions re Billeting party and party for cleaning up as detailed in Bn.Orders dated 14/3/'16.

"A" Form. Army Form C. 2121.

MESSAGES AND SIGNALS.

No. of Message 27

Prefix Code m.	Words	Charge	This message is on a/c of:	Recd. at 7 m.
Office of Origin and Service Instructions.	Sent		Service.	Date
	At m.			From
	To			By
	By		(Signature of "Franking Officer.")	

TO O's C "D", "C", "A" & "B" Coys
Transport Officer, Quartermaster
M.G.O. & Medical Officer

Sender's Number	Day of Month	In reply to Number	AAA
—	Fifteenth	—	

Orders for to-morrows move are as for to day vide Operation Order No 5 of 15.3.'15 AAA except that the hours of parade & starting will be one hour earlier viz for PASS road junction etc at 11/20 A.M. read 10/A.M. The rear party should not be necessary for cleaning up but if it is found to be please notify me by 9-30 A.M. at latest whom you are leaving.

From Adjutant 1/4 LEIC RGT.
Place BAC ST MAUR.
Time 7-45 P.M.

The above may be forwarded as now corrected.

Censor.

(Z) R S Dyer-Bennet Capt.

Signature of Addressor or person authorised to telegraph in his name

* This line should be erased if not required.

158 S. B. Ltd. Wt. W5673/619—50,000. 10/14. Forms C2121/10.

Copy No 1.

A.8.

OPERATION ORDERS No.6 by MAJOR L.V.WYKES
COMMANDING 1/4TH BATTALION LEICESTERSHIRE REGIMENT.

----

le CHIEN BLANC. STEENWERCK.
25th March, 1915.

Ref. 1/40,000 B.36 BELGIUM & FRANCE.

1 INFORMATION. The 1/1ST LINC. & LEIC. BDE. (less 1/5TH LEIC. RGT) with 1/8 BN. NOTTS & DERBY RGT, 60 DIVL. MOUNTED TROOPS (YORKS HUSSARS) 2ND N. MID. FIELD-AMBULANCE and No.2 Coy. DIVISIONAL TRAIN, will proceed for attachment and be billeted on 26th inst.

The Bn. will be attached to the 12TH INFANTRY BDE. and be billeted at LE BIZET.

2 INSTRUCTIONS. The Bn. will march in rear of 1/5TH LINCOLNSHIRE RGT.

STARTING POINT. The Bn. will pass Road Junction at T of le Gd. BEAUMART, proceeding S.E. at 2-30 p.m. tomorrow 26th inst.

Order of March, HEAD QUARTERS, "D", "A", "B", "C" Coys, MACHINE GUNS, 1ST LINE TRANSPORT, and TRAIN.

"C" Coy. "C" Coy. will join the Bn. at the Starting Point, debouching from road running N.E. through I of le ROSIGNOL.

3 ROUTE. STEENWERCK.- le VEAU.- to road junction near T of RABOT.- thence S.E. to NIEPPE.

4 BILLETING PARTY.

The Bn. Billeting party consisting of 2 N.C.O's.

(2/LT.R.C.HARVEY) for Hd.Qrs. and 2 N.C.O's. per Coy as detailed will report to 2/Lt.R.C.HARVEY at road junction immediately E.S.E. of 2nd. E in la RECQUE at 10-30 a.m.

This party will embus at 1/1ST LINC. & LEIC. BDE. Head Qrs. at 11 a.m. The Bn. interpreter will ~~xxxx~~ accompany this party.

5 RATIONS & FORAGE The unconsumedportion of the day's rations will be carried in the mess tin.

The remainder of the day's forage will be carried on the horse in the nosebag.

The 2 supply Wagons will, after issuing on arrival tomorrow, join the 4TH DIVL. TRAIN for attachment.

6 REPORTS.- Reports to the Head of Column.

R.S.Dyer-Bennet

(sd) R. S. DYER-BENNET Capt. & Adjutant,
1/4TH LEICESTERSHIRE REGIMENT.

Issued by Orderly at 8-30 p.m.

+Copy No 1 War Diary
2 1/1ST LINC. & LEIC. INF. BDE.
3 O.C. "A" Coy.
4 "B"
5 "C"
6 "D"
7 Transport Officer
8 M.Gun Officer
9 Med. Officer
10 Quartermaster
11 Billeting Officer
12 Bn. Interpreter.

OPERATION ORDERS NO 7 by MAJOR L.V.WYKES
COMMANDING 1/4TH LEICESTERSHIRE REGIMENT.

Copy No 1.

30/8/'15

A.9

Ref. sheet 5a HAZEBROUCK 1/100,000 & Sheet 36 1/40,000

1 INFORMATION.- The 1/1ST LINC. & LEIC. INF. BDE. (less 1/5TH LEIC. RGT) with 1/8TH BN. NOTTS & DERBY RGT. and 2ND NORTH MIDLAND FIELD AMBULANCE will march to Brigade Area tomorrow, whence Units will move to their own billeting areas. The Battalion will occupy its ~~own~~ original area.

2 INSTRUCTIONS.-The Bn. will march in rear of the 1/5TH LINCOLNSHIRE RGT.
STARTING POINT.- The Battalion will cross R.LYS at point immediately S. of Cotton Factory on le BIZET road. at 9-5 a.m. (Cotton Factory is ½ mile S. of le BIZET)

R. Should be canal

ORDER OF MARCH.- Hd.Qs., "C", "D", "B", "A", M.Gs., 1st L.T. and "Train".

3 ROUTE.- ARMENTIERES - NIEPPE - T of RABOT - STEENWERCK STATION - Cross Roads le Gd.BEAUMART., whence Coys will move to their billets independently.

4 REPORTS.- To Head of the Column.

(sd) R.S.DYER-BENNET Capt. & Adjt.
1/4th Leicestershire Regiment.

Issued by Orderly at 5-45 p.m.

R.S. Dyer Bennet Capt & Adjt
1/4 Leic Rgt

x Copy No 1 War Diary
2 1/1st Linc. & Leic. Inf. Bde
3 12th Inf. Bde
4 O.C. "A" Coy.
5 "B"
6 "C"
7 "D"
8 Transport Officer
9 M.G.Officer
10 Med. Officer
11 Quartermaster.

A P P E N D I C E S B.1 to B.14.

B.1.

Confidential

~~SECRET~~.

N.M.D. P29.
LL ~~SD~~ C7
......

Headquaretrs,
1/1 Lincs & Leic Bde T.F.
....

In view of the early departure of the Division for the Continent. Units are to be prepared to move at short notice and all preparations are to be made accordingly.

sd/ F.H.DANSEY Capt.,
D.A.A. & Q.M.G. 1/1 N.M.D. T.F.

B.STORTFORD,
15/2/15.

2.

O.C., 4/Leics. Regt.
......

For your information and compliance please.

As the Division probably moves in 8 days all furlough ,vaccination or other , is cancelled , and no further vaccination should take place.

4TH B. LEICESTERSHIRE REGT.
No..............
15 FEB. 1915
5.45pm

[signature] Maj.,
Bde Maj. 1/1 Lincs & Leic Bde T.F.

B.STORTFORD,
15/2/15.

B.2.

(Copy)

PROPOSED ORDER OF DEPARTURE OF NORTH MIDLAND DIVISION.

First day Thursday, 25th. February 1915.

Units.	Entraining Stations.
Notts. & Derby Infantry Brigade.	Braintree
No.2 Section Div. Sig. Company	:
1/2nd. North Midland Brigade R.F.A.	Bishop's Stortford
1/2nd. North Midland Field Ambulance	:

Second Day Friday 26th. February 1915.

Divisional Headquarters	Bishop's Stortford
Headquarters Divisional R.A.	:
Headquarters Divisional R.E.	:
2/1st. Field Company R.E.	:
Squadron Yorkshire Hussars	Harlow
North Midland Division Cyclist Company	Bishop's Stortford
1/4th. North Midland How. Brigade R.F.A.	:
1/4th. Bn. Lincolnshire Regiment	:
1/5th. Bn. Leicestershire Regiment	Harlow
1/North Midland (Stafford) Hy. Battery R.G.A.	Bishop's Stortford
1/1st. North Midland Field Ambulance	Braintree
1/2nd. North Midland Field Coy. R.E.	:
Headquarters & No.1 Section North Midland Divisional Signal Company.	Bishop's Stortford

Third Day, Saturday, 27th. February 1915.

Headquarters 1/1st. Lincs. & Leics. Inf. Bde.	Bishop's Stortford
No.4 Section Divisional Signal Company	:
1/5th. Bn. Lincolnshire Regiment	:
+ 1/4th. Bn. Leicestershire Regiment – (7.40 & 9.40 am.) – x	:
1/North Midland Div. Ammn. Column	Luton
1/3rd. North Midland Brigade R.F.A.	Bishop's Stortford

Fourth Day, Sunday 28th. February 1915.

1/1st. Staffordshire Infantry Brigade	Saffron Walden & Audley End.
No.3 Section Divisional Signal Company	Ditto
1/1st. North Midland Brigade R.F.A.	Bishop's Stortford
1/3rd. North Midland Field Ambulance	Elsenham
Headquarters & Headquarter Company Div'l Train	Bishop's Stortford

B. 3.

To/ O.C. 4th Leics.
Detrain Cassel

Billets are allotted
to you at ZUYTPEENE.
1¼ miles N.W. of Cassel Station

Lt. Brigade Hd. Qrs. are at
The Château ¼ mile N. of
WEMAERS.

G. Thorell
Staff Capt.
1/1 North Mid Divn.

6.3.15
St. Omer.

Recd [illegible] 6.3.15

B.4.

1/4th Leicester Regt.

TELEGRAM BY HAND.

10th
RWN.

Tomorrow's move.

Reference 1/100,000 Sheet 5A.

Starting point tomorrow:- QUAESTRAETE 1 mile East of CASSEL at 11 a,m,

Order of March:-
1/8th Notts and Derby Regt.
1/4 ~~1/5th~~ Lincs Regt.
1/4th Leics Regt.
1/5 ~~1/4th~~ Lincs Regt.

~~Starting point for~~
Battalions will move to the starting point independently by road and will not pass South of the Town of CASSEL .

On arrival at STRAZEELE the 1/8th Notts and Derby Regt will proceed to MERRIS and join its Brigade there.

The 2nd Company Divisional Train and the whole of the Transport including 1st Line of the Lincoln and Leicester Brigade and 1st Field Ambulance will march to STRAZEELE by BAVINCHOVE , QUEUE de BAVINCHOVE , LES OISEAUX - LE BREARDE- Road running E. from cross roads ½ mile South of LE BREARDE .

Starting point Level crossing 1 mile W of BAVINCHOVE at 11-30 a.m. and following in rear of the Staffordshire Brigade.

R. L. Abercrombie Maj.,
Bde Maj. 1/1 Lincs & Leic Bde T.F.

Chateau Reumaux ,
WEMAERS CAPPEL.
8/3/15.

2 motor buses will be sent you at 7.15 am tomorrow for surplus Kits

Rec'd 8.3.15 RWB

Headquarters,

Lincoln & Leicester Brigade.

Immediately troops receive orders to be ready packed awaiting orders to move, the sheep skin coats, gum boots and other baggage in excess of field kits will be stored under Battalion arrangements, and left in charge of a small party, who should be chosen from men inefficient from any cause.

The 1st Line Transport will follow the Brigade under charge of the Brigade Transport Officer, destination will be given him at the same time as the order to move.

The blanket wagons will accompany the 1st Line Transport.

The remainder of Transport will receive orders to follow with baggage and a day's supply.

sd/ EDWARD ALLEN, Lieut-Colonel,

A.A. & Q.M.G. 1/1st North Midland Division, T.F.

10/3/15.

To:-

O.C.

1/4th Bn. Leics. Regt.

Forwarded for your information.

Major,

Bde. Major, Linc. & Leics. Infy. Bde. T.F.

STRAZEELE,

10/3/15.

"C" Form (Duplicate). Army Form C. 2123.

MESSAGES AND SIGNALS. No. of Message

KHAM

Charges to Pay. £ s. d. B. 6.

Office Stamp. LEH 11-3-15

Service Instructions.

Handed in at [illegible] Office [illegible] m. Received 10.45 a m.

TO O C 4th LEIC

Sender's Number	Day of Month	In reply to Number	AAA
SC 17	11th		

Be prepared to move at 11.0 am

Recd 10.47 a.m. 11.3.15

[illegible]

FROM L AND L BDE

PLACE & TIME 10.40 am

(24932). M.R.Co.,Ltd. Wt.W9668/1673. 50,000 Pads—1/15. Forms/C.2123.

Following on message "Be ready to move at 11 am." rec^d 10-47 am

B.7.

O.C.,
Regt.

....

The following is a copy of a telephone message received from N.M.D. for your information and necessary action.

" The Division will march to SAILLY today AAA Order of march Lincoln and Leicester Brigade No 2 Company Divisional Train 2nd Field Ambulance (Less Motor Ambulances) AAA Starting point Road junction ¼ mile South of Z in STRAZEELE at 12-5 p.m. AAA Route MERRIS - BLEU - Road Angle South of D in DOULIEU 2nd A of TROU BAYARD AAA Ref Map 5 a. 1/100 000."

Order of March :-

4th Leicestershire Regt.

5th Leicestershire Regt.

4th Lincs Regt.

5th Lincs Regt.

Full Marching Order , no blankets on the Man.

L Anderson

Maj.,

Bde Maj. 1/1 Lincs & Leic Bde t,F,

STRAZEELE ,
11/3/15.

Billeting parties will march in front of the column on each road and will receive instructions as soon as Billeting areas have been allotted to the Division AAA Time of starting NOW ALTERED TO 11-45 a.m.

Rec^d 11-40 am 11.3.15.

R.S.W. Bennet Capt Adjt

Army Form C. 2121.

MESSAGES AND SIGNALS. No. of Message

Prefix	Code	m.	Words	Charge	This message is on a/c of:	Recd. at 4-40 p.m.
Office of Origin and Service Instructions.			Sent		B 7 (A)	Date 12/3/15
			At m.		Service.	From N. M. D.
			To			
			By		(Signature of "Franking Officer.")	By

TO Headquarters
Lincoln & Leicester Brigade

Sender's Number	Day of Month	In reply to Number	
* G. 507	Twelfth	B. M. 44	AAA

Seventh Division have broken through German line between MOULIN DE PIETRE and PIETRE taking several hundred prisoners and are pushing on towards RUE DENEER AAA The North Midland Division will be prepared to move southeast from 6 a.m. to-morrow

N. M. D.

Officer Commanding
4th Bn. Leicestershire Rgt.

For your information

Recd 6-55 pm 12/3/15

From
Place
Time

The above may be forwarded as now corrected. (Z) R. L. Adlercron

Censor. Signature of Addressor or person authorised to telegraph in his name

*This line should be erased if not required.

5682 M. & Co. Ltd. Wt. W929/549—100,000. 6/14. Forms C2121/10.

B.8.

DUPLICATE.

Headquarters

Linc. & Leics. Bdes

The road South and parallel to the Bailly Surla Lys ARMENTIERS Road (Rue due Quesney and Rue Pasaille N.E. of the SALLY STATION Road has ~~bagun~~ been allotted to the Canadian Division for billeting purposes AAA Please cause the Battalion now there to vacate this area early tomorrow morning and move into BAC ST MAUR.

D.A.A. & Q.M.G. North Midland Division.

To:- O.C.

1/4th Bn. Leics. Regt.

Forwarded for your information and necessary action.

9-25 km
13-3-15
WH

sd/ J.E.Viccars, Capt,
Staff Capt, Linc. & Leic. Bde T.F.

B.9.

~~Lin [illegible]~~

Bde will march
~~Starts~~ at 11 a.m. from
Cross Rds ½ mile N.W. of SAILLY Church
marching to CROIX BAYARD.

Billeting Parties at H.Q. at 7 a.m.

No sick men to be left in Billets any men who are sick to go to Hospital

Billets to be left clean, Officer + party to be left behind to clean up

C.O. to be responsible

Division comes in at 12 noon

List of men in Hospital by 3 p.m.

14/3/15 7.40 pm

Service Instructions.

Charges to Pay. £ s. d.

B. 10.

Office Stamp.

LEA 14 3 15

Received 10.42 m

AAA

... marching of ... ready ... short if ... aaa ... sleep ... put ...

Brigade

Service Instructions.

Charges to Pay. £ s. d.

B. 11.

Office Stamp.

LEA 15 3 15

Handed in at Lincoln Brigade Office 11.25 a.m. Received 11.36 a.m.

TO all Battalions

Sender's Number	Day of Month	In reply to Number	AAA
B 17 42	15th		

The Brigade will move to new Billeting area ~~[illegible]~~ tomorrow aaa operation order no 3 will hold good for tomorrow aaa Training and interior economy will proceed aaa Wagons may be unloaded

FROM PLACE & TIME Lincoln Brigade Sailly 11.20 a.m.

(24932). M.R.Co.,Ltd. Wt.W9568/1672. 50,000 Pads—1/15. Forms/C.2123.

Charges to Pay. £ s. d.

B. 10

Office Stamp. LEA 14 3 15

Service Instructions.

Handed in at Lins & Leic Bde Office 10 4 p.m. Received 10 43 p.m.

TO All Battalions

Sender's Number	Day of Month	In reply to Number	AAA
BM 29	14th		

The General Officer Commanding directs that all units of this Brigade should be ready to turn out at short notice during the night if necessity should arise aaa The men are to sleep with their arms and accoutrement ready to put on at shortest notice

10.05 pm

FROM PLACE & TIME 1/1 Lins & Leic Brigade Sailly 10.15 pm

(24932). M.R.Co.,Ltd. Wt.W9668/1672. 50,000 Pads—1/15. Forms/C.2123.

Charges to Pay. £ s. d.

B. 11.

Office Stamp. LEA 15 3 15

Service Instructions.

Handed in at Linc & Leic Brigade Office 11 25 a.m. Received 11 35 a.m.

TO All Battalions

Sender's Number	Day of Month	In reply to Number	AAA
BM 42	15th		

The Brigade will move to new Billeting area tomorrow aaa operation order no 3 will hold good for tomorrow aaa Training and interior economy will proceed aaa Wagons may be unloaded

FROM PLACE & TIME L and L Brigade Sailly 11.20 a.m.

(24932). M.R.Co.,Ltd. Wt.W9668/1672. 50,000 Pads—1/15. Forms/C.2123.

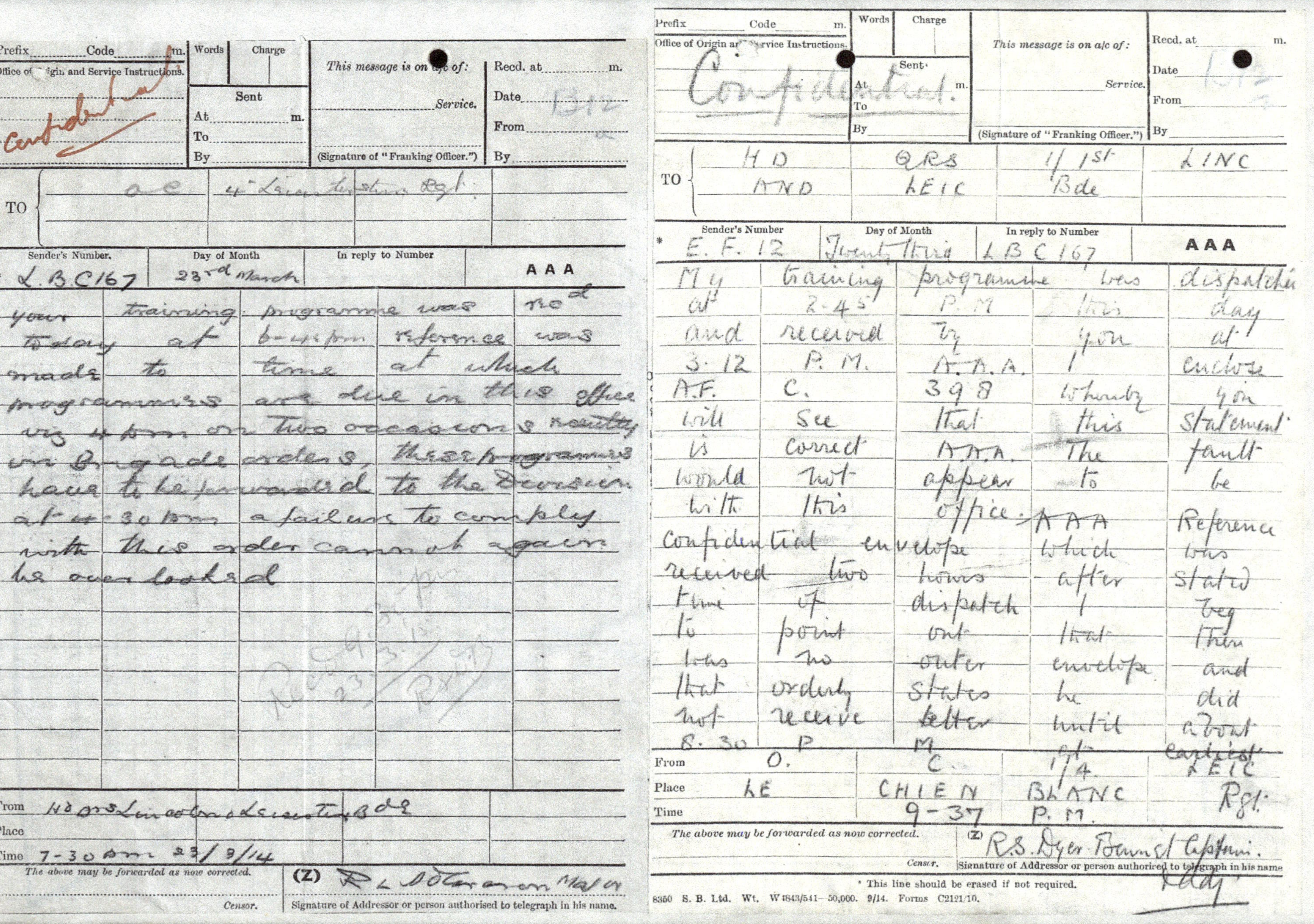

Prefix ..... Code ..... m. | Words | Charge | This message is on a/c of: ..... Service. | Recd. at ..... m. | Date B12 | From | By

Office of Origin and Service Instructions.
Confidential

Sent At ..... m. To By

(Signature of "Franking Officer.")

TO O.C. 4th Leicestershire Regt.

Sender's Number.	Day of Month	In reply to Number	AAA
L.B.C.167	23rd March		

your training programme was recd today at 6-45pm reference was made to time at which programmes are due in this office viz 4pm on two occasions recently in Brigade orders, these programmes have to be forwarded to the Division at 4-30pm a failure to comply with this order cannot again be overlooked

From HdQrs Lincoln & Leicester Bde
Place
Time 7-30am 23/3/14

The above may be forwarded as now corrected.
(Z) R L Adlercron Major

Censor. Signature of Addressor or person authorised to telegraph in his name.

Prefix ..... Code ..... m. | Words | Charge | This message is on a/c of: ..... Service. | Recd. at ..... m. | Date B12 | From | By

Office of Origin and Service Instructions.
Confidential.

Sent At ..... m. To By

(Signature of "Franking Officer.")

TO HD QRS 1/1st LINC AND LEIC Bde

Sender's Number	Day of Month	In reply to Number	AAA
E.F.12	Twenty three	LBC167	

My training programme was dispatched at 2.45 P.M this day and received by you at 3.12 P.M. A.A.A. I enclose A.F. C. 398 whereby you will see that this statement is correct A.A.A. The fault would not appear to be with this office. AAA Reference confidential envelope which was received two hours after stated time of dispatch I beg to point out that then was no outer envelope and that orderly states he did not receive letter until about 8.30 P.M.

From O.C. 1/4 LEIC Rgt.
Place LE CHIEN BLANC
Time 9-37 P.M.

The above may be forwarded as now corrected.
(Z) R.S. Dyer Bennet Captain.

Censor. Signature of Addressor or person authorised to telegraph in his name.

* This line should be erased if not required.

8350 S. B. Ltd. Wt. W1843/541—50,000. 9/14. Forms C2121/10.

Rec^d 4·17 p.m.

(B13)

Copy. No. 4

OPERATION ORDER NO. 5

by

BRIGADIER GENERAL W.R. CLIFFORD

COMMANDING 1/1st Lincs. & Leics. Infty. Bde. T.F.

Reference Map. Belguim & France (B Series) Sheet No. 36 Scale 1/40,000.

1.

STEENWERCK
25/3/15.

1. The Lincoln & Leicester Infantry Brigade (less 1/5th Bn. Leics. Regt) 1/8th Bn. Notts & Derby Regt, 60 Divl. Mounted Troops, 2nd North Midland Field Ambulance and No. 2 Coy, Divisional Train will proceed for attachment and be billeted on the 26th instant as under :-

Unit.	Attached to	Billets.
H.Q. Linc & Leic Infty. Bde. No. 4 Sect. Signal Co.	11th Infty Bde.	Near 11th Bde. Hdqrs West of PLOEGSTEERT
8th Notts & Dorby Regt.	10th -do-	ROMARIN
4th Lincs. Regt.	11th -do-	PLOEGSTEERT Brewery
4th Leics. Regt.	12th -do-	LA BIZET
5th Lincs. Regt.	11th -do-	OOSTHOVE Fm.
60 Yorks Hussars	H.Q. 4th Divn.	NIEPPE
2nd Field Amb'ce (horsed portion)	10th Field Amb'ce.	Near ROMARIN.
No. 2 Coy, Divisional Train	4th Div. Train.	STEENWERCK.

2. Starting point. Cross Roads 1,000 yds South South West of STEENWERCK CHURCH at 2-30 p.m. in the following order of march, Bde. Signal Section, Brigade Headquarters, 4th Lincs. Regt 5th Lincs. Regt, 4th Leics. Regt, 8th Bn. Notts & Derby Regt, 2nd North Midland Field Ambulance, No. 2 Company, Divisional Train, The Divisional Mounted Troops will proceed direct arriving at Cross Roads at T of RABOT in B 3a at 4 p.m.

3. ROUTE. STEENWERCK-LEVEAU to Cross Roads of T of RABOT. On arrival these Units will be met by guides from 4th Division. The YORKSHIRE HUSSARS and 4th LEICESTERSHIRE Regiment will, on arrival at the Cross Roads, turn South East and proceed down the NIEPPE Road.

4. TRANSPORT. All Transport Vehicles will accompany their Batalions.

5. REPORTS. Reports to Head of Column.

sd/ R.L.ADLERCRON, Major,
Brigade Major, Linc. & Leics. Bde. T.F.

Issued by Cyclist Orderly
at to :-

Copy No. 1. 1/8th Bn. Notts & Dorby Regt.
2. 4th Bn. Lincs. Regt.
3. 5th Bn. Lincs. Regt.
4. 4th Bn. Leics. Regt. ✓
5. 2nd North Midland Field Ambulance.
6. No. 2 Company, Divisional Train.
7. Divisional Mounted Troops.
8. North Midland Division.
9. War Diary.

Copy No. 7

Map.
HAZEBROUCK Sheet
1/100,000

Operation Orders by Major-General H.F.M. Wilson, C.B.
Commanding 4th Division.

30th March, 1915.

1. The Lincoln and Leicester Inf. Brig., Signal Section and Field Ambulance attached to the 4th Division from the North Midland Division, will march to the North Midland Area tomorrow.

2. One lorry per battalion will be at the following points at 7-45 a.m. :-

8th Bn. Notts & Derby Regt.	X. of RABOT
4th Bn. Lincoln Regt	Crossroads at PONT DE NIEPPE.
5th Bn. Lincoln Regt.	
4th Bn. Leicester Regt.	Road junction ¼ mile South of LE BIZET.

Battalions will load their rubber boots on these lorries at 7-45 a.m., and the lorries will assemble at the X. of RABOT at 8-30 a.m.

3. Troops will march as under to the Starting Point :-

Unit.	Route to Starting Pt.	Starting Point.	Reach Starting Point.
Bde.H.Q. & Sig.Sec.	ROMARIN-RABOT	X.of RABOT	10 a.m.
8th Bn.Notts & Derby Regt.	- do -	"	10-[illegible] a.m.
4th Bn. Lincoln R.	PLOEGSTEERT -ROMARIN.	"	10-15 a.m.
5th Bn. Lincoln R.	PONT DE NIEPPE -NIEPPE	"	10-25 a.m.
4th Bn.Leicester R.	ARMENTIERES -NIEPPE	"	10-35 a.m.
2nd Fd. Ambulance		"	10-45 a.m.

4. Transport will follow immediately in rear of its units.

5. The Brigade will march via X of RABOT and STEENWERCK Station & village, whence units will move to their billeting areas.

6. The Supply section of the Train (less Yorkshire Hussars portion) will march tonight to refill at N.Midland Div. refilling point tomorrow.

[illegible]
Colonel.,
General Staff.

Issued at 12 noon.

Copy No. 1 N.Mid. Div.
" 2 3rd Corps
" 3 10th Brig.
" 4,5,6. 11th Brig.
" 7 12th Brig.
" 8 A.D.M.S.
" 9 Train
" 10 & 11 Filed.

O.C.

4th Leicesters

Passed to you for information and necessary action.

2.20 pm

30/3/1915

[illegible] Captain

Bde Major 12th Infantry B'de

Recd 2.45 pm

30.3.15

R.E.B.

3

A P P E N D I C E S C.1 to C.7.

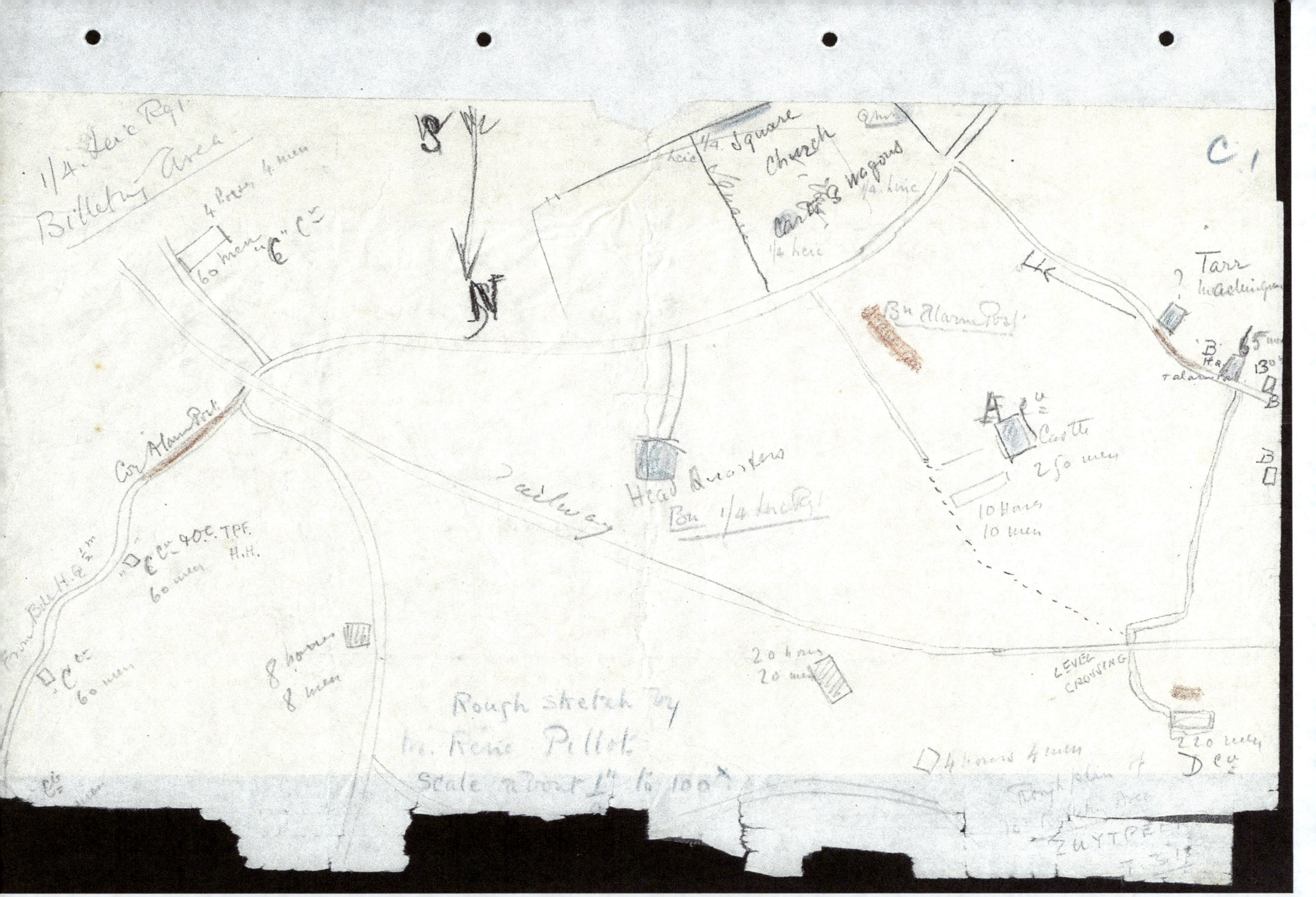
C 1
Billeting Area
Church
Carts & Wagons
Bn Alarm Post
Head Quarters
Railway
Castle
250 men
10 Hors
10 men
Tarr
LEVEL CROSSING
220 men
20 men
8 horses
8 men
60 men
Rough sketch by
Scale

Rough Map
From CASSEL & St Sylvestre
To ECKE
Supply Columns
CAESTRE
D.A.C.
Heavy Battery
FLETRE
1st Bde RFA
3rd Bde RFA
METEREN
2nd Bde RFA
TO BAILLEUL
From HAZEBROUCK
BORRE
Staffs Bde
Div Troops
Pradelles
R.E. Field Co
STRAZEELLE
L.D. Bde
MERRIS
Outtersteene
To Vieux Berquin and Estaires

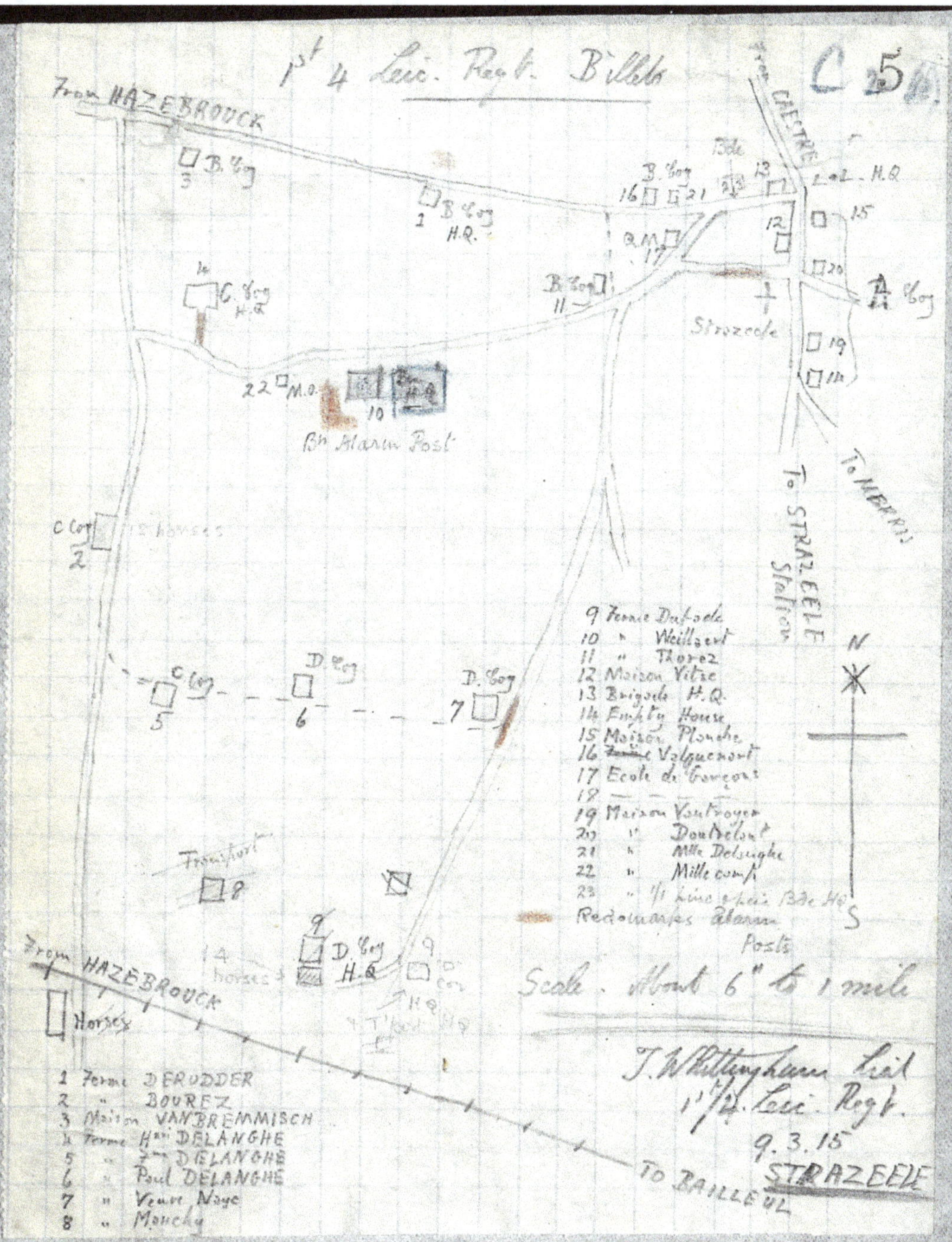

1st 4 Leic. Regt. Billets

C 5

From HAZEBROUCK

From CAESTRE

3 B. Coy

1 B. Coy H.Q.

16 B. Coy

21

Bde

13

Lo2 - H.Q

15

12

Q.M. 17

B. Coy 11

20

A Coy

4 C. Coy H.Q.

Strazeele

19

14

22 M.O.

10

Bn Alarm Post

To STRAZEELE Station

To MERRIS

C Coy 2

C Coy 5

D. Coy 6

D. Coy 7

9 Ferme Dufoele
10 " Weillaert
11 " Thorez
12 Maison Vitse
13 Brigade H.Q.
14 Empty House
15 Maison Planche
16 Ferme Valguenort
17 Ecole de Garçons
18 —
19 Maison Vantroyen
20 " Doutrelont
21 " Mlle Delsighe
22 " Mille comp.
23 " 1/1 Line open Bde HQ

Redmarks Alarm Posts

N

S

Transport 8

9 D. Coy H.Q.

14 horses

9 D Coy H.Q.

From HAZEBROUCK

Horses

Scale. About 6" to 1 mile

1 Ferme DERUDDER
2 " BOUREZ
3 Maison VANBREMMISCH
4 Ferme Hri DELANGHE
5 " Jm DELANGHE
6 " Paul DELANGHE
7 " Veuve Naye
8 " Mouchy

T. Whittingham Lieut
1/4 Leic. Regt.
9.3.15
STRAZEELE

TO BAILLEUL

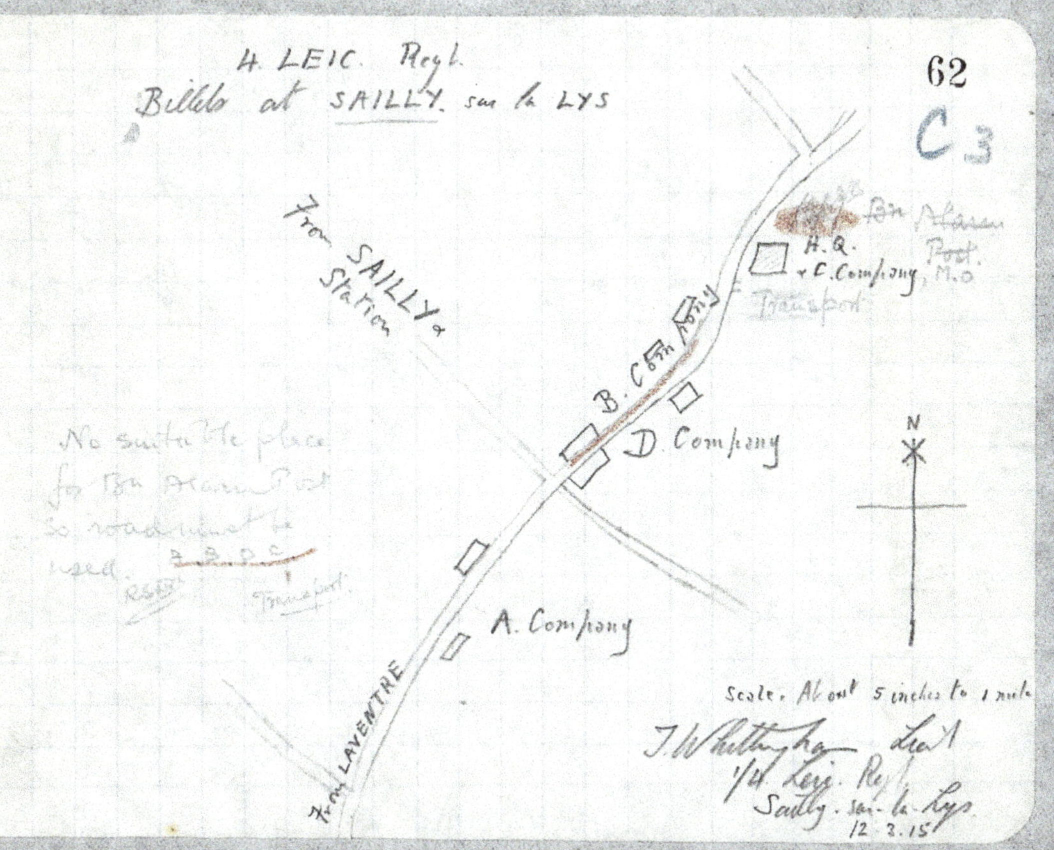

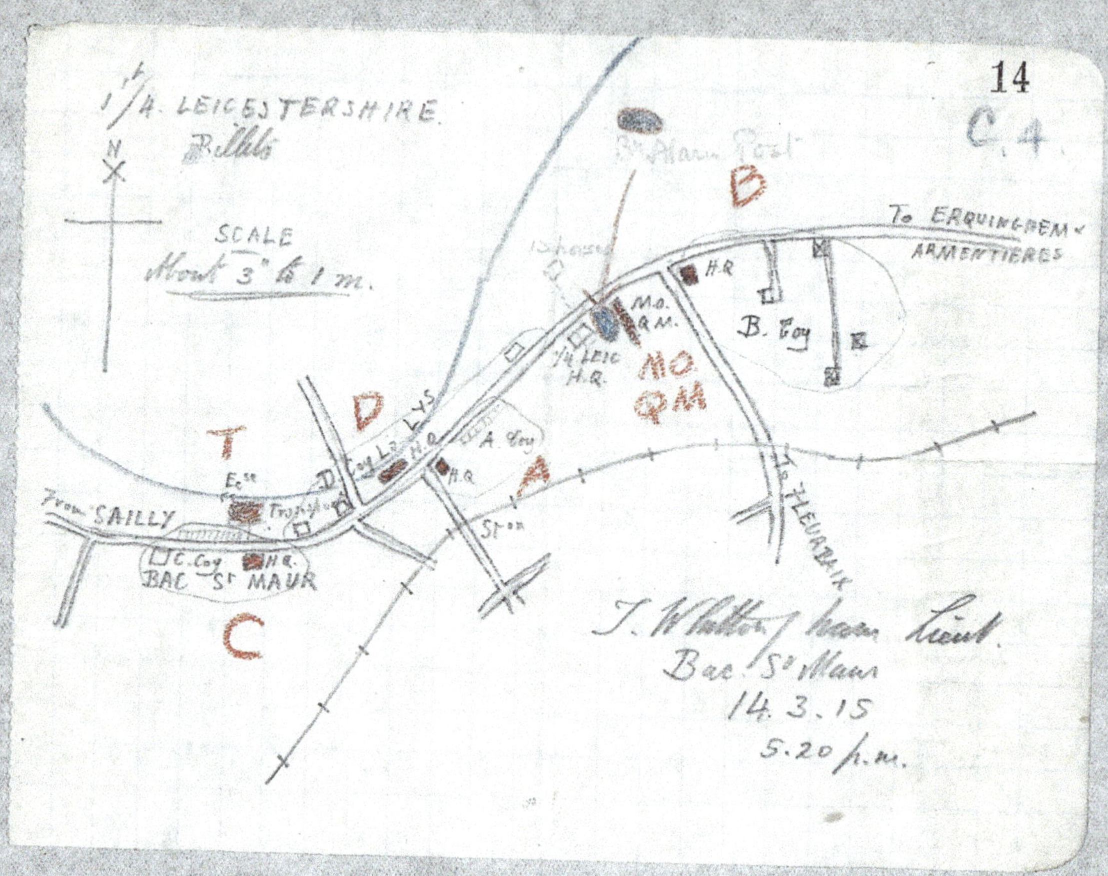
14
C.4
1/4 LEICESTERSHIRE
Billets
N
SCALE
About 3" to 1 m.
B
To ERQUINGHEM ARMENTIERES
H.Q
M.O.
Q.M.
B. Coy
1/4 LEIC
H.Q.
MO
QM
D
T
A. Coy
A
From SAILLY
C. Coy
H.Q.
BAC ST MAUR
C
To FLEURBAIX
Stn
J. Whitton / ham Lieut.
Bac St Maur
14.3.15
5.20 p.m.

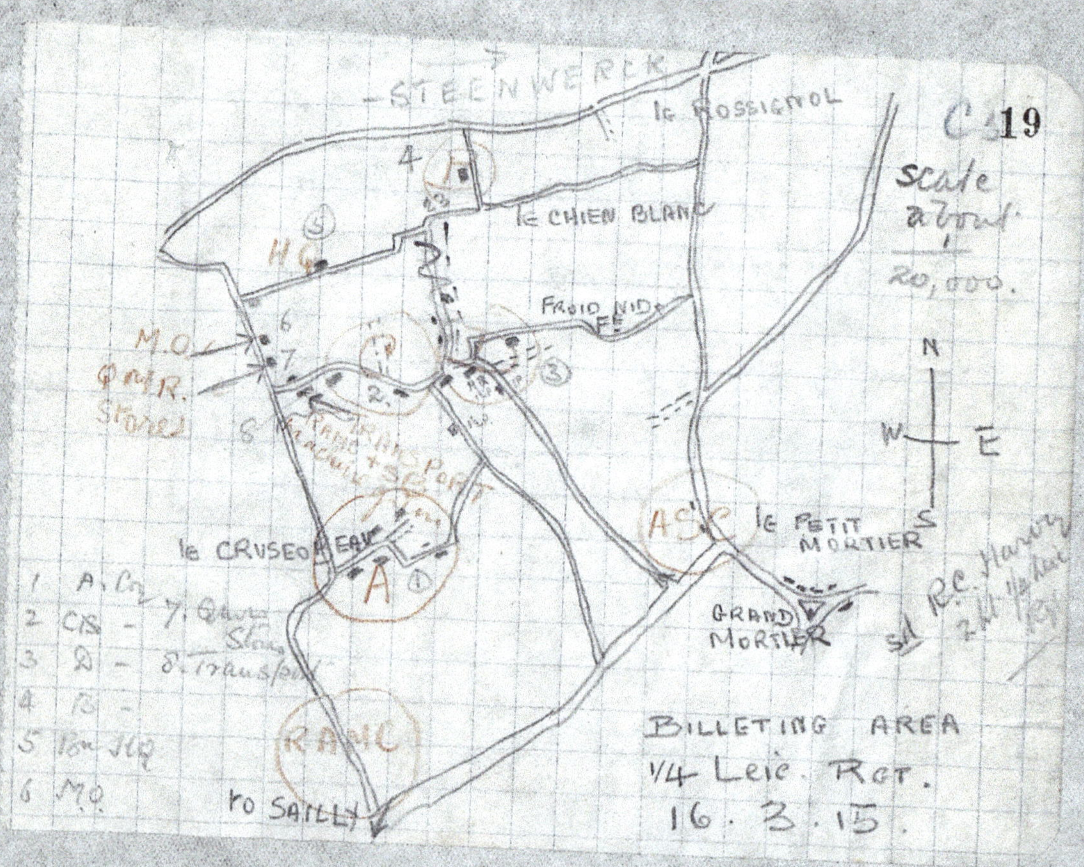
19
STEENWERCK
le ROSSIGNOL
le CHIEN BLANC
HQ
FROID NID
scale
about
1/20,000
N
W
E
S
M.O
QMR.
Stores
TRANSPORT
le CRUSEO EAU
A
ASC
le PETIT MORTIER
GRAND MORTIER
1 A. Coy
2 C. Coy - 7. Q.M. Stores
3 D - 8. Transport
4 B -
5 Bn HQ
6 M.O.
RAMC
to SAILLY
BILLETING AREA
1/4 Leic. Rgt.
16.3.15.

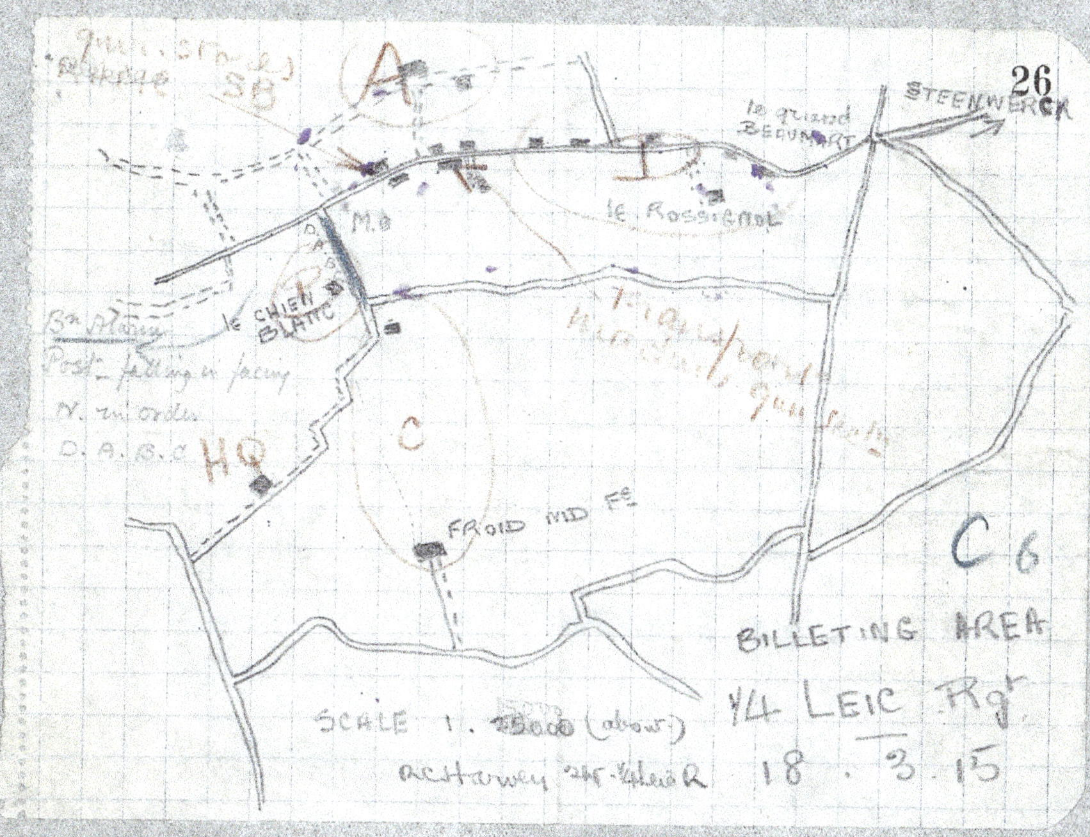
26
A
SB
STEENWERCK
le grand BEAUMART
le ROSSIGNOL
M.O
le CHIEN BLANC
HQ
C
FROID MD Fe.
D. A. B. C
C 6
BILLETING AREA
1/4 LEIC Rgt
18 . 3 . 15
SCALE 1. 15000 (about)

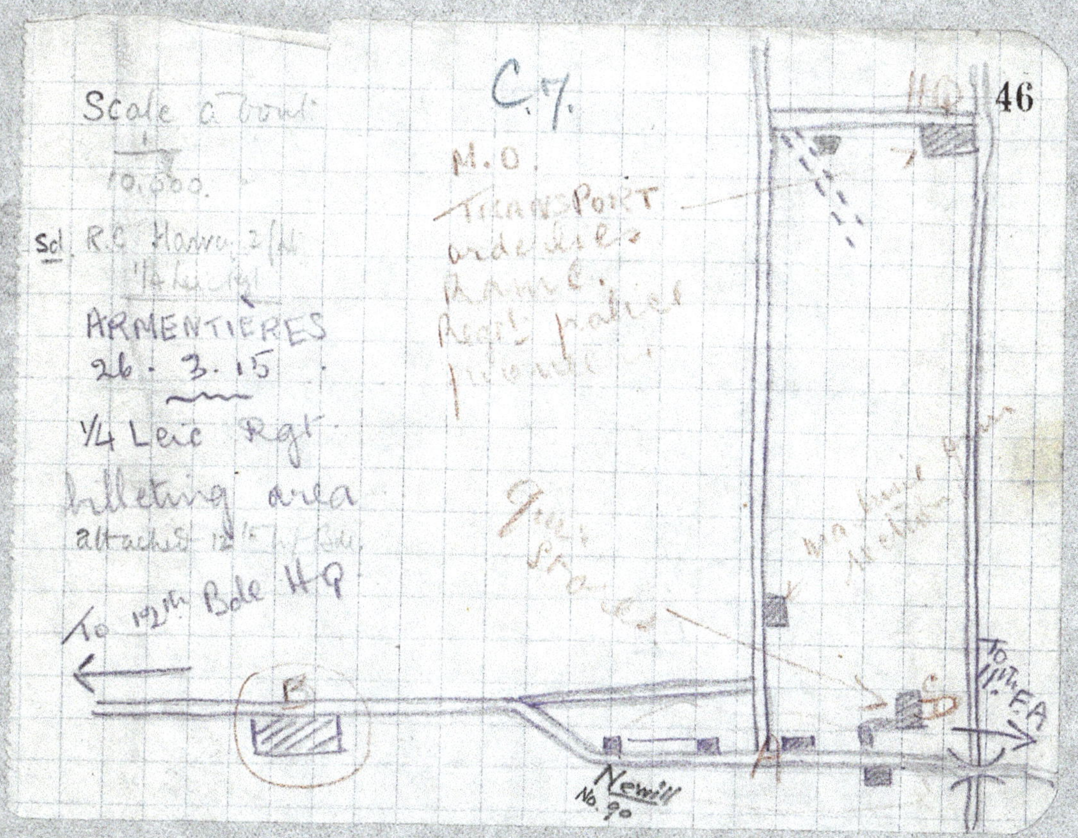
46
C.7.
Scale about
1/10,000.
ARMENTIERES
26 . 3 . 15
1/4 Leic Rgt
billeting area
To 12th Bde HQ
M.O
TRANSPORT
HQ
B
A
D
To 11th F.A
Newill
No. 90

4

A P P E N D I X D.1.

Instruction Appendix "D" 1

BRIGADE AREA ORDERS
by
BRIGADIER GENERAL W.R. CLIFFORD
COMMANDING 1/1st Linc. & Leic. Brigade. T.F.

22nd March, 1915.

86. BATTALION ON DUTY to-morrow :- 1/4th Bn. Leics. Regt.
FIELD OFFICER of the day to-morrow :- Major L.V.WYKES.

87. TRAINING. Reference 1/100,000. HAZEBROUCK. Trench assault operation, Defence operation ~~and~~ in co-operation with Artillery will be carried out by Battalions on dates as follows :-

	Attack 10 a.m	Defence 2 p.m
Tuesday	4/Leics.	5/Lincs.
Wednesday	4/Lincs.	5/Leics.
Thursday	5/Lincs.	4/Leics. Cancelled - wet.

Battalion Commanders will meet the Artillery Commanders ¾ of an hour before the above mentioned time and rendezvous as previousl indicated on the ground viz :- FOR ATTACK Farm immediately S.W. of the 3 of .35 - 1200 yards South of STEENWERCK CHURCH at 9-15 a.m. ~~for Attack and~~

FOR DEFENCE —— Farm immediately South of Road angle 300 yards N.E. of the M in LE KIRLEM ½ mile South of STEENWERCK CHURCH at 1-15 p.m.

Note.

The Battalions carrying out the assault must ensure they have two lines of cable linking trenches with Battalion Headquarters.

sd/ H.L.ANDERSON, Major,

Bde. Major, Linc. & Leic. Bde. T.F.

COPY NO

OPERATION ORDER BY BRIG. GEN. W.R. CLIFFORD
Commanding Lincs. & Leics. Bde. T. F.
****

MOULIN MESSEAN
22/3/15.

Reference 1/100,000 HAZEBROUCK.

INTENTION. 1. The Brigade supported by artillery will attack the Farm which is 300 yards N.E. of the M in LE KIRLEM.

2.(a) The 4th Leicestershire Regt. will carry out the assault on the enemy's trenches on a frontage extending 200 yards N. and 200 yards S. of the abovementioned farm at 10-20 a.m. supported by the fire of No. Battery R.F.A. which will open fire at 10-0 a.m. on this section of the trenches in co-operation with 5 Leicester & 4 Lincs Regts and all Machine Guns on either flank till 10-20 a.m. when all fire will be concentrated on the farm and the infantry assault by the 4 Leicester Regt. will commence.

(b) The front line of trenches now occupied will be held firmly throughout the attack.
The place of the 4 Leicester Regt. will be filled by 5th Lincolnshire Regt. (in Reserve).

DRESSING STATION.
3. Dressing Station at Farmhouse 800 yards South of Headquarters, Windmill.

S.A.A.RESERVE.
4. The Brigade Ammunition Reserve and Tool Carts will be situated at BRIGADE HEADQUARTERS.

REPORTS.
5. Reports to Windmill 500 yards North East of Point 35.

sd/ R.L.ADLERCRON, Maj.,
Bde Maj. L. & L. Bde. T.F.

Issued by Cyclist Orderly at 5 a.m.
to:-
Copy No. 1. War Diary
2. 4/Lincs. Regt.
3. 5/Lincs. Regt.
4. 4/Leics. Regt.
5. 5/Leics. Regt.
6. O.C., R.F.A.
7. O.C., 2nd N.M.F.A.

"D"

1

Ref. 1/100,000.
HAZEBROUCK.

GENERAL IDEA.

A Western Force (Blue) is occupying trenches about 200 yards West of the Beck which runs South from Steenwerck immediately West of Contour 35.

An Eastern Force (Red) is entrenched along the right bank of this beck.

SPECIAL IDEA - RED (Attack).

A Battalion and a Battery R.F.A. (Red Force) have been ordered to attack and capture a section of the Blue trenches 200 yards North and South of the farm, 300 yards North East of the M in LE KIRLEM and farm immediately beyond at 10-a.m. on the instant.

NOTES

1. The O.C. Battalion (Red Force) will meet the O.C. R.F.A. Battery (daily) at 9-15 a.m. at Farm - East edge of Contour 35 - 1200 yards SOUTH of STEENWERCK Church.
2. Object of exercise :- (1) Organization of Trench Duties (2) Co-operation with Artillery (3) Counter attacks (resisting).
3. Points requiring special attention :-
   (1) Syncronising watches with Artillery.
   (2) Communication (a) with Battalions on either Flank (b) with Royal Field Artillery (c) With Brigade Headquarters.
   (3) Machine Gun Fire Co-operation
   (4) Supply of Ammunition.
   (5) Organization of the further attack from trenches.
   (6) The attack of a building beyond the line of trenches.
   (7) Consolidation of position and trenches when captured.
   (8) Platoon Bombing Parties.
   (9) Co-operation with Battalion on either Flank.

Ref. 1/100,000. HAZEBROUCK.

GENERAL IDEA. Cancelled - bad weather

A Western Force (Blue) is occupying trenches about 200 yards West of the Beck which runs South from STEENWERCK immediately West of Contour 35.

An Eastern Force (Red) is entrenched along the right bank of this Beck.

SPECIAL IDEA - (BLUE. Defence).

A Battalion and a Battery R.F.A. are holding a section of trenches North and South of the Farm 300 N.E. of the M in LE KIRLEM It is reported that an attack by the enemy is contemplated at 2 p.m. on the instant.

NOTES.

1. The O.C. Battalion (Blue Force) will meet the O. C. Battery R.F.A. (daily) at 1-15 p.m. at Cross Roads 300 yards N of M in LE KIRLEM.
2. Object of exercise :- Organization of trench duties, co-operation with Artillery, Counter attacks.
3. Points requiring special attention :-
   (1) Syncronising watches with R.F.A.
   (2) Organizing fire, trench and support trench parties.
   (3) Bomb throwers and position of bombs.
   (4) Organization of Machine Gun Fire.
   (5) Communication.
   (6) Supply of Ammunition.

Enlargement to 1:10,000 of A 22.b.d / A 23.a.c of Sheet 36

This plan found to be in-accurate

"D"

Objective Farm

D HQ

A HQ

B HQ

C HQ

Bn HQ

Scale

300 200 100 0 100 200 300 400 500 600 700 yards.

23.3.15.

R. S. Dyer Bennet
Captain & Adjt
1/4 Lincoln Regt

95

Copy No 1 "D" 1

Training Only.

OPERATION ORDER No. 1 by MAJOR L.V.WYKES Commanding 1/4TH LEICESTERSHIRE REGIMENT.

---

le FERME des TIGRES.
23/3/'15.

Reference 1/100,000 HAZEBROUCK, and attached sketch.

1/ INTENTION.- 1. The Bn. will assault the enemy's trenches on a frontage extending 200 yards N. and 200 yards S. of the farm which is 300 yards N.E. of the M in LE KIRLEM. The Artillery, No + Bty. R.F.A. will open fire at 10 a.m. on this section of the trenches and the Bn. will assault at 10-20 a.m. at which moment the Artillery will increase range 200 yards and will concentrate their fire on the above mentioned farm.

+ 3rd S/a/ 1/3

2/ INSTRUCTIONS. 2. The assault will be carried out as under.

FIRST LINE. The first line will consist of the odd numbered platoons of each Company and immediately after the assault will be reorganised with a view to meeting any counter-attack. They will be led by the second in command of Companies.

SECOND LINE The second line, which will follow the first line at 20 paces distance will consist of the Bomb and Sand Bag parties. -The Bomb parties must be prepared to bombard the supporting trenches and also any portion of the firing not immediately taken by the assault. The Sand Bag parties will consist of 12 men per Company., carrying one Sand Bag each will be on the flanks of the Bomb parties. The Sand Bags will be used when necessary to block communication trenches running towards the enemy and to form traverses to isolate such portions of the fire trench as are not immediately taken by the assault.

THIRD LINE The third line, consisting of the even numbered platoons which will follow at 20 paces distance from the second line will carry two spades per section and will form working parties for the purpose of reversing the parapet, repairing trenches and doing any other work that may be found necessary to strengthen the position.

All men except those carrying sand bags and bombs will carry two bandoliers of additional ammunition.

MINES One selected N.C.O. per Coy. will be told off to locate and cut wires to enemy mines.

MACHINE GUNS.- Two Machine Guns will be on each flank of the Bn. and will be pushed forward into the trenches with the third line. They will pay particular attention to the possibility of a counter-attack from the flanks. The M.G. Officer will be with the Machine Gun on the Left Flank. The Officers Commanding Flank Companies will each detail 4 men to act as ammunition carriers for the Machine Guns,- each man to carry two boxes of filled belts.

FIRST AID POST.- A First Aid Post will be established in the trenches from which the assault ismade.

DRESSING STATION.- The Dressing Station will be at Farm House. 800 yards south of Windmill (which is 500 yards N.E. of 5 of Contour 35)

S.A.A.RESERVE.- The ammunition reserve and tool carts will be at Bde.Hd.Qs. at the above mentioned windmill.

RATIONS.- Iron rations will be carried in the haversack.

3/ REPORTS.- Reports to Bn.Hd.Qrs at Farm immediately S.W. of 3 of Contour 35 by telephone from Hd.Qrs. of "A" and "C" Coys. until 10-20 a.m. vide attached sketch. The telephone officer will endeavour to lay lines from "A" and "C" Coys original Hd.Qrs. to the enemy trench by signallers detailed to proceed immediately in rear of third line. (sd) R.S.DYER-BENNET Capt. & Adjt.
1/4th Leicestershire Regiment.

R.S. Dyer Bennet

Issued by orderly at 6-30 a.m.

Copy No		Copy No	
1	War Diary	6	Machine Gun Officer
2	1/1st L. & L. Bde	7	Telephone Officer
3	O.C. No .Bty.R.F.A.	8	O.C. "A" Coy
4	Med. Offr.	9	"B" "
5	Transport Offr.	10	"C" "
		11	"D" "

Omissions - 1). Reference to enemy wire entanglements & special men with wire cutter to finish work not done by art'y
2). Ref. to Bn Ammn Reserve
3) No subdivision of enemy's line into lettered sections

Plan in connection with Defence Scheme (Trench work)

D 1

Cancelled

Enlargement to 1.10,000 of Sheet 36

A. 22. f. d
23. a. c.

Bn HQ.

Scale

25. 3. 15.

R.S. Dyer Bennett
Capt and Adjt
1/4 Leic Regt

10

1/4TH BATTALION LEICESTERSHIRE REGIMENT.

INFORMATION AND INSTRUCTIONS IN CONNECTION WITH TRENCH DEFENCE PRACTISE.
by
MAJOR L. V. WYKES
Cmdg. 1/4th LEICESTERSHIRE REGIMENT.

****

INFORMATION as per General and Special Ideas herewith.
An attack by the enemy is contemplated at 2 p.m.
The Artillery has been instructed to concentrate its fire on the enemy's trenches from 1-30 to 2 p.m. and in the event of a counter attack will then receive instructions to lengthen their range by 100 yards in order to create a screen of fire through which the enemy reinforcements cannot pass.

INSTRUCTIONS.
During the period of the attack the maximum density of fire will be sustained and delivered on the advancing enemy from the fire trench.- as shewn on plan. attached
Machine Guns will endeavour to locate and destroy the enemy's Machine Guns believed to be in the neighbourhood of W. and Z

Should the enemy's attack reach the trenches a counter attack will be made by the troops in the support trenches, who will charge the enemy in two lines, the first line consisting of all men excepting Bomb Throwers and Sandbag Carriers who will form the second line and follow immediately in rear of the first line.

N O T E S

The trenches will be held 200 yards N. and 200 yards S. of centre of farm 300 yards N.E. of the M. in LE KIRLEM, vide attached plan.

The order of the companies will be C, B, A, D.
Each Coy. will have odd numbered platoons in the fire trench and even numbered platoons in the support trench. Grenadier Parties will be in the centre of the Platoons to which they belong.

POINTS REQUIRING SPECIAL ATTENTION. (see notes to General and Special Ideas)

(1) O's.C.Coys will syncronize watches with the O.C. Bn. at the starting point at 1 p.m.
(2) See Notes above.
(3) Position for storage of bombs must be marked out but no actual digging must take place. These would actually be small "dug outs" at the foot of the trench on the side nearest the enemy.
(4) Two machine guns will be on either ~~xxxx~~ flank of the Bn. in the fire trench. The M.G. Officer will be with the guns at the South end of the trenches.
(5) Communication will be by telephone to Bn.Hd.Qrs. at Farm from H.Qs. of "A" and "C" Coys. One orderly per Coy. will be detailed to attend at Bn.Hd.Qs. Messages will be passed laterally by word of mouth and must always state from whom they emanate and ~~from~~ for whom they are intended.
(6) Ammunition will be kept in some convenient position/as near the parapet as possible, at the point from which the firing takes place. Reserve ammunition would be in boxes two to each section and positions for them must be marked out by Platoon Commanders.
(7) Latrines must be indicated by Company Commanders. They should be well in the rear and protected from shell fire as far as possible.

(sd) R.S.DYER-BENNET Capt. & Adjt.
1/4th Leicestershire Regiment.

25/3/'15.

R.S. Dyer-Bennet. Capt & Adj
1/4. Leic Rgt.

A P P E N D I X D.2.

D.2

Subject:- Attachment of a Battalion of the North Midland Divsion to 12th Infantry Brigade.

Officer Commanding,

4th Leicesters

---

1. One Battalion of the North Midland Division will be attached to this Brigade from 26th to 31st March 1915.

Programme of training attached.

2. One officer from this Battalion and one N.C.O. and ten men per Company will be trained in throwing hand grenades. They will parade daily at 9-30.a.m. at Brigade Headquarters whenever their Companies are not in the trenches. On 27th, 28th, 29th and 30th inst. O.C. Lancashire Fusiliers will detail an officer to instruct them and meet them at Bde.H.Q. at 9.30.am. and will provide the dummy hand grenades.

3. For instruction in the trenches Companies of the Territorial Battn of the N.M.Div. will be distributed by single men among the Battalions then in the trenches for the first night and the Companies that go in a second time will be put in by platoons.

Companies of this Territorial Battalion will parade on the evening previous to the day on which they are in the trenches at such hour as Officer Commanding the Battalion to which they will ~~attacked~~ be attached may direct. They will also march to the trenches under his orders.

4. When a Company of the Battn of the N.M.Div. is attached to a Battalion in the trenches the Company Commander will be attached to one of the Company Commanders then in the trenches who will instruct him in details of work in trenches and in relieving and cleaning up after leaving the trenches.

A.McDavis

Captain,

25-3-1915. Brigade Major, 12th Infantry Brigade.

D2

Instructions for working parties on 3rd line.

Officer Commanding,

Battn., North Mid.Div. (4th Leicesters)

Companies for work on 3rd line will meet R.E. Officer at the Cross Roads in square C.14.a (N.E.) as under :-

27th March.	1 Company at 9.a.m.	B Coy
	½ Company at 1-30.p.m.	½ D Coy
	½ Company at 6.p.m.	½ D Coy
28th March.	2 Companies at 9.a.m.	B & D Coys
29th March.	2 Companies at 9.a.m.	A & C Coys
30th March.	1 Company at 9.a.m.	D Coy
	½ Company at 1-30.p.m.	½ B Coy
	½ Company at 6.p.p.	½ B Coy

Each working party is to be completely provided with shovels etc.

C.W. Davies

Captain,

26-3-1915. Brigade Major, 12th Infantry Brigade.

TRAINING PROGRAMME FOR BATTALION NORTH MIDLAND DIVISION.

Coy.	27th March.	28th March	29th March	30th March.
A.	To trenches in the evening.	Trenches King's Own.	3rd Line morning. trenches in the evening.	Trenches. King's Own.
B.	3rd Line.	To trenches in the evening. 3rd line morning.	Trenches. King's Own.	3rd Line.
C.	To trenches in the evening.	Trenches. Monmouths.	3rd line morning. To trenches in the evening.	Trenches. Essex.
D.	3rd line.	3rd Line morning. To trenches in the ~~xx~~evening.	Trenches. Essex.	3rd Line.

Captain,

Brigade Major, 12th Infantry Brigade.

D2

BATTALION ORDERS by MAJOR L.V.WYKES
COMMANDING 1/4TH LEICESTERSHIRE REGIMENT.

26th March, 1915

1 DUTIES.- The Bn. isnext for duty. F.O. Major J.A.POTTER.
Capt. of the day Capt. H. HAYLOCK Next Capt. B.F.NEWILL
Sub. of the day 2/LT.M.B.DOUGLAS Next 2/LT.G.E.RUSSELL
Inlying Picquet "D" Coy Next "A" Coy.
Guard on Bn.Hd.Qs. "B" Coy.. Next "C" Coy.

2 PARADES Sick.- The Medical Officer will visit the sick, commencing at "B" Coy at 7 a.m. then proceeding to "A", "C", & "D" Coys.
Grenade Throwing party, Consisting of Lt.G.J.HARVEY, and 1 N.C.O. and 10 men per Coy. will parade at 13th Inf. Bde. H.Qs. at 9-25 a.m. where they will be met by an officer detailed by the O.C. Lancashire Fusiliers to instruct them.
The 13th Inf. Bde. H.Qs. are at road angle C 13 d (sheet 36 1/40,000)
Other work as per programme.
The transport ~~xxxxxxx~~ Officer will arrange to have all tools at "B" Coys. H.Qs. at 7-45 a.m.

3 PRECAUTIONS.- O's.C.Coys. will ensure that when their Coys are in the open, moving to or from place of instruction, the Platoons are from two to three hundred yards apart.- small bodies being less likely to attract the attention of aircraft.
Particular attention is directed to pamphlets issued to Coys. this day bearing on (1) Crossing to the right bank of the river LYS etc, and (2) Precautions to be taken against observation from the German Lines.

4 ATTACHMENT.-The Officer Commanding wishes all ranks to take full advantage of the attachment, so that when the time comes for the Battalion to take its place as a Unit in the trenches or elsewhere, they will do so with the utmost confidence, thereby maintaining the good name of the Leicestershire Regiment

(sd) R. S. DYER-BENNET, Captain & Adjutant
1/4TH LEICESTERSHIRE REGIMENT.

War Diary
1/4 Ser Rgt
Original

+ Statement
Original

BATTALION ORDERS by MAJOR L.V.WYKES
COMMANDING 1/4TH BATTALION LEICESTERSHIRE RGT.

27th March, 1915.

1 DUTIES.- The Bn. is on duty. F.O. Major J.A.POTTER.
Capt. of the day Capt. B.F.NEWILL Next Capt. T.P.FIELDING-JOHNSON.
Sub. of the day 2/LT.G.E.RUSSELL Next 2/LT.J.F.JOHNSON.
Inlying Picquet "B" Coy. Next "C" Coy.
Guard on Bn.Hd.Qrs. "B" Coy. XXXXXXXXXXXX.

2 PARADES. Sick. The Med. Offr. will inspect the sick as for to-day.
Grenade Throwing Party, Consisting of 2/Lt.M.B.Douglas and 1 N.C.O. and 10 men from "B" and "D" Coys will parade at 12th Inf. Bde. H.Qs. at 9-25 a.m. where they will be met by an officer detailed by the O.C. Lancashire Fusiliers to instruct them. (HQ's road angle - C 13 d (Sheet 36 1/40,000))
The Transport Officer will arrange to have the tools delivered as follows. ½ to "B" Coy's. H.Qs. and ½ to "D" Coy'. H.Qs. by 7-45 a.m.. Other work as per programme.

3 OPERATION ORDERS.- With reference to N.M.D. WSO's Sec. 5, para (1) (a), an acknowledgement in message form is required, it is not sufficient to receipt the envelope.
Similar action is required when the word "acknowledge" is added at the end of a message.

4 MEDICAL.- When an officer is placed on sick list the M.O. i/c is to notify this at once to the O.C. the Unit or Formation to which the sick officer belongs.

5 CHURCH.- O's.C.Coys. will arrange to hold a short Devine Service tomorrow.

6 INTERIOR ECONOMY.- Time not occupied by training should be devoted to interior economy, including bathing.

7 TRENCHES.- The O's.C. "B" and "D" Coys. will report to the O's.C. Kings Own. and Essex Rgt, respectively, at 12 noon tomorrow.

8 GUARD.- The Machine Gun Officer will find the Guard for Bn.Hd.Qs. tomorrow, 28th inst. This guard will mount at 5-30 p.m.

(sd) R.S.DYER-BENNET Capt. & Adjt.
1/4th Leicestershire Regiment.

BATTALION ORDERS by MAJOR L.V.WYKES
COMMANDING 1/4TH LEICESTERSHIRE REGIMENT.

28th March, 1915

1 DUTIES.- Capt. of the day Capt. E.P.FIELDING-JOHNSON Next Capt.A.C.COOPER
Sub. of the day 2/Lt.J.F.JOHNSON Next 2/Lt.F.M.WAITE
Guard on Bn.Hd.Qs. M.G. Sectiob. Next M.G.Section.

2 PARADES.- The sick will be inspected under the same arrangements as for to-day.
Grenade Throwing party.- Consisting of Lt.T.Whittingham and 1 N.C.O. and 10 men from "A" and "C" Coys will parade at 12th Inf. Bde. H.Qs. at 9-25 a.m. where they will be met by an officer detailed by the O.C.Lancashire Fusiliers to instruct them. 12th Bde. H.Qs. are at road angle C 13 d ref sheet 36 1/40,000.
The Transport Officer will arrange to have the tools delivered as follows, ½ to "A" Coy. and ½ to "C" Coy by 7-45 a.m.
Extra tools can be drawn from 12th Bde. Hd.Qs.
Other work as per programme.

3 DISCIPLINE.- Attention is drawn to pamphlet on "Discipline" which has been issued to Coys. this day.

(sd) R.S.DYER-BENNET Capt. & Adjt.
1/4th Battalion Leicestershire Regiment.

BATTALION ORDERS by MAJOR L.V.WYKES.
COMMANDING 1/4TH LEICESTERSHIRE REGIMENT.

D.2

29th March, 1915.

1 DUTIES.- Capt. of the day Capt. A.C.COOPER Next Capt. R.A.FAIRE
Sub. of the day 2/LT.F.M.WAITE. Next 2/Lt.R.C.HARVEY
Guard on Bn.Hd.Qrs. M.G.Section Next "B" Coy.

2 PARADES.- The sick will be inspected under the same arrangements as for to-day.
Grenade Throwing party.- Consisting of 2Lt. G.E.F.RUSSELL and 1 N.C.O. and 10 men from "B" and "D" Coys will parade at 12th Inf. Bde. Hd.Qs at 9-25 a.m. where they will be met by an officer detailed by the O.C. Lancashire Fusiliers to instruct them. 12th Bde. H.Qs. are at road angle C 13 d (ref sheet 36 1/40,000)
The transport Officer will arrange to have the tools delivered ~~as follows ½ to "B" Coy and ½~~ to "D" Coys. H.Qs. by 7-45 a.m.
Extra tools can be drawn from 12th Bde. H.Qs.
Other work as per programme.

3 REPORTS.- Officers Commanding Coys. will render a report to this office as soon as possible after the attachment to the 12th Inf. Bde has been completed, dealing with Instruction Received, Important Points brought to notice and terminating with any suggestions considered of value for future guidance in Trench Warfare.

(sd) R.S.DYER-BENNET Capt. & Adjt.
1/4th Leicestershire Regiment.

To.- O's.C.Coys.,
1/4th Leicestershire Regiment.

The Officer Commanding wishes to remind all ranks that every reasonable precaution should be taken to avoid unnecessary risks.

He would point out that any officer, N.C.O. or man who unnecessarily exposes himself to the danger of death or injury, commits a crime.

It should, moreover, be the aim and object of all ranks to keep themselves fit for the purpose of maintaining the fighting efficiency of the Battalion.

(sd) R.S.DYER-BENNET Capt. & Adjutent.
29/3/'15. 1/4th Leicestershire Regiment.

A P P E N D I X   E.

War Diary.

43

App. E

Nominal Roll
of Officers of 1/4 Leicestershire Regt
who embarked for foreign service on
dates as shown – at SOUTHAMPTON

Rank	Initials	Name		Dates
Lieut. Col.	W.A.	Harrison	T. D.	2. 3. 1915
Major.	L. V.	Wykes		do
"	J. A.	Potter		do
Captain	A. C.	Cooper		do
"	T. P.	Fielding Johnson		do
"	B. F.	Hewitt		4. 3. 1915
"	H.	Haylock		2. 3. 1915
"	L.	Corah		do
"	J.	Milne		do
"	R. A.	Faire		do
Lieutenant.	W. B.	Jarvis	T.O.	4. 3. 1915
"	G. J.	Harvey		do
"	F. N.	Tarr	M.G.O	2. 3. 1915
"	J. G.	Abell	Telephone O.	4. 3. 1915
"	F. S.	Farr	Res. M.G.O	2. 3. 1915
"	T.	Whittingham	Scout O.	do
"	H. C.	Brice		do
"	A. C.	Clarke		4. 3. 1915
"	L.	Forsell	Res. T.O.	do
"	R. C.	Harvey		2. 3. 1915
"	F. M.	Waite		do
"	K.	Dalgliesh		do

War Diary. App: E. 44

	Rank	Name	Date
	2nd. Lieutenant.	J. F. Johnson	2.3.1915
	" "	G. S. F. Russell	do
		M. G. Douglas	do
		H. F. Papprill	do
	" "	W. N. Dunn	4.3.1915
2.3.'15	Captain & Adj.	R. S. Dyer-Bennet (Leic. Rgt)	
	Lieutenant.	G. A. Brogden. RAM. C.(T.)	
	Lieut & Qmr	G. E. Ball	
	Interpreter.	P. Pillot.	of 4/Zouaves.

March 1915.

R. S. Dyer Bennet
Captain & Adj
1/4 Leic. Rgt.

7

A P P E N D I X F.

4a

War Diary App. F

Average daily number of N.C.Os & men away from Batn in hospital

— 18 —

March 1915.

R. S. Dyer-Bennet
Captain & Adjt
1/4. Leic. Regt.

138th Inf.Bde.
46th Div.

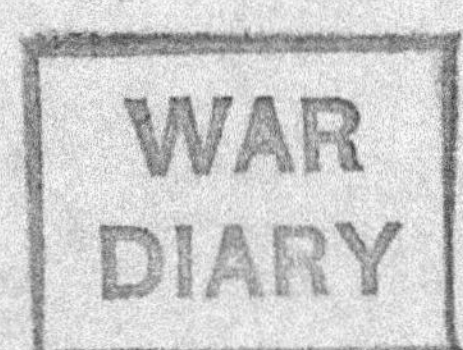

4th BATTN. THE LEICESTERSHIRE REGIMENT.

A P R I L

1 9 1 5

Attached:

Appendices.

Confidential

Original

1/4 [illegible] Regt.

WAR DIARY
or
INTELLIGENCE SUMMARY.
(Erase heading not required.)

Army Form C. 2118.

Instructions regarding War Diaries and Intelligence Summaries are contained in F. S. Regs., Part II. and the Staff Manual respectively. Title pages will be prepared in manuscript.

Hour, Date, Place	Summary of Events and Information	Remarks and references to Appendices
April 1915		
[illegible]	Fine, bright + warm. [illegible]	
	Interior economy in billets [illegible]	
STEENWERCK 12 noon	[illegible]	
	[illegible]	
1 pm	[illegible]	
Good Friday Forenoon	Interior Economy – CO visited all coys.	
6. pm	Coys – [illegible] – 4 Guns [illegible] orders issued re	Revaille B fast [illegible] Attached
9.25 pm	Bde Op: Order No 3 (Copy No 5) recd – Secret	
11.45 pm	Battn Op: [illegible] No 8 typed, [illegible] not issued until Saturday	
12 noon	early morning – [illegible] delay occasioned by No. of copies reqd + trouble in getting same [illegible] enveloped – addressed – [illegible]	
8.15 am	Marched to DRANOUTRE – distance 8 miles.	
	Billets as per plan	Billeting Plan C
Evening DRANOUTRE	Major T. T. GRESSON D.S.O. (York + Lanc Regt) [illegible] C.O. [illegible] – O.C. Coys [illegible]	

C. & O.C. [illegible]

(9 29 6) W 3332—1107 100,000 10/13 H W V Forms/C. 2118/10

1/4 Linc Rgt 1/1st Linc & Leic Bde 1/1st N. M. Divn

Army Form C. 2118.

Instructions regarding War Diaries and Intelligence Summaries are contained in F. S. Regs., Part II. and the Staff Manual respectively. Title pages will be prepared in manuscript.

WAR DIARY
or
INTELLIGENCE SUMMARY.
(Erase heading not required.)

Hour, Date, Place	Summary of Events and Information	Remarks and references to Appendices
April 1915		
3rd DRANOUTRE	Visited trenches of CENTRE SECTOR - 84th Bde - Inf - held by 1st MONMOUTHSHIRE Rgt. Coy officers remained in their trenches	Plan of trenches D attached
4th 4 A.M.	H.Q. officers returned to Billets	
11. A.M.	Bn Parade Service C of E	
12.10 P.M.	LA 4. recd - ordered to trenches right of A/5th	Copy recd - attached B
4.45 P.M.	Bn Op. Order No. 9 issued	Copy No 1 attached
7. P.M.	Bde Op - No 6 (copy No. 3) recd	
8.30 P.M.	Bn marched to relief of 1/MONMOUTHSHIRE Rgt	
10. P.M.	Bn reached new HQ ONE TREE Fm - about 3 miles	
5th 3.50 A.M.	Relief completed - no casualties. V. quiet night. Distribution of Coys as per attached plan & report. Situation normal - very quiet day. Some difficulty with telephone communication - owing to wire betn F2 & E2 broken and mended at dusk	
2.30 P.M.	Fatigue parties for R.E. carrying material for mining etc Work. PICCADILLY & REGENT ST	

(9 29 6) W 3332—1107 100,000 10/13 H W V Forms/C. 2118/10.

Army Form C. 2118. 3.

Instructions regarding War Diaries and Intelligence Summaries are contained in F.S. Regs., Part II. and the Staff Manual respectively. Title pages will be prepared in manuscript.

WAR DIARY
or
~~INTELLIGENCE~~ SUMMARY.
(Erase heading not required.)

[illegible] Regt 1[illegible] [illegible] Bde 4[illegible] [illegible] Div

Hour, Date, Place	Summary of Events and Information	Remarks and references to Appendices
April 1915 5th Trenches	R.E. Lce Cpl guiding fatigue party gave a sorry demonstration of nerves – falling on his face when ever flare went up – wife & 5 children at home etc. A good many men "got lost" during the night & wandered aimlessly [illegible] until daylight. Attribute to lack of experience. Gum boots – 30 prs per Coy were issued for use in trenches. Trench [illegible] [illegible] Regt [illegible] [illegible] not understood & men walking in them. Fatigue & other parties in F.S. [illegible] [illegible] default of other orders – [illegible] a great mistake [illegible] [illegible] [illegible] fatigue. ([illegible] [illegible] [illegible] [illegible] are necessary?) R.S.D.B.	

(9 29 6) W 3332—1107 100,000 10/13 H W V Forms/C. 2118/10

Instructions regarding War Diaries and Intelligence Summaries are contained in F. S. Regs., Part II. and the Staff Manual respectively. Title pages will be prepared in manuscript.

1/4 Leic Rgt 1/1st L & L Bde 1/1st N. M. Div.

WAR DIARY
or
INTELLIGENCE SUMMARY.
(~~Erase heading not required.~~)

Army Form C. 2118. (4)

Hour, Date, Place	Summary of Events and Information	Remarks and references to Appendices
April 1915.		
Trench Area 6th	Quiet, normal day. Without [illegible] of the day	1 man killed
	C & D Coys endeavoured to relieve A & B, but owing	1 " wounded
	to C Coy becoming dismembered & majority losing their	Lieut T. Whittingham hit
(7th 2.30 am)	way, relief of A only partially effected. D effected	by spent bullet in toe
	relief about 2.30 am all dead beat owing to	during relief, not serious
	[illegible] Recent [illegible] Faulty organisation and un-	Unnecessary use of communication
	due safety precautions lead led to block in R. St.	trenches but [illegible] not [illegible] covered unnecessary [illegible] bends
Afternoon	B Coy came out & proceeded via Piccadilly to	
	Newport [illegible] in broad daylight, no casualties	
6th & 7th	Usual fatigue & working parties busy all available	
	time. Working mostly on cleaning, but very little	
	to show for labour.	
	Men rather exhausted evidently [illegible] conditions [illegible]	

(9 29 6) W 3332—1107 100,000 10/13 H W V Forms/C. 2118/10.

Army Form C. 2118.

Instructions regarding War Diaries and Intelligence Summaries are contained in F. S. Regs., Part II. and the Staff Manual respectively. Title pages will be prepared in manuscript.

WAR DIARY *or* INTELLIGENCE SUMMARY. 1/1st [illegible] Bde 1/1st N. M. [illegible]

(*Erase heading not required.*)

Hour, Date, Place	Summary of Events and Information	Remarks and references to Appendices
[illegible] 1915		
[illegible] Trenches noon	[illegible] between [illegible] Shells [illegible] near E1, killing [illegible] [illegible] Our artillery [illegible] shot [illegible] [illegible] drawing [illegible] Quiet day	[illegible]
	E. [illegible]	
8th —	Quiet day – Special work on Regent St under supervision of Major [illegible]	
	Enemy sniper reported to have been seen by listening post [illegible] E1 right – he dropped [illegible] and was not [illegible] or seen again.	
6.15 pm	4 heavy enemy shells dropped near [illegible] [illegible] No damage done.	

(9 29 6) W 3332—1107 100,000 10/13 H W V Forms/C. 2118/10

Army Form C. 2118.

Instructions regarding War Diaries and Intelligence Summaries are contained in F.S. Regs., Part II. and the Staff Manual respectively. Title pages will be prepared in manuscript.

WAR DIARY
or
INTELLIGENCE SUMMARY.
(Erase heading not required.)

Hour, Date, Place	Summary of Events and Information	Remarks and references to Appendices

(9 29 6) W 3332—1107 100,000 10/13 H W V Forms/C. 2118/10.

Army Form C. 2118. (7)

Instructions regarding War Diaries and Intelligence Summaries are contained in F. S. Regs., Part II. and the Staff Manual respectively. Title pages will be prepared in manuscript.

WAR DIARY
or
INTELLIGENCE SUMMARY.
(~~Erase heading not required.~~)

Hour, Date, Place	Summary of Events and Information	Remarks and references to Appendices
[illegible] 1 [illegible]	"A" & "B" bathing - Bde arrangements - C & D Coy baths	1 man shot himself
3 P.M. 11th	[illegible] Service in [illegible] field [illegible] held	in foot - C. of I. produced
	by Bde Chaplain P. ASHBY	evidence tending to prove "accidental" of careless.
10 a.m. - 1 p.m. 12th	CO inspected Company billets. Not a good show	
	after 3 days to clean up.	
	V. large no. of rifles damaged owing to firing with	
	muzzles stopped with mud of Regent St. & Piccadilly	
	Shows necessity of muzzle covers as well as	
	breech covers already in general use.	
7.15 pm	Bn marched off to trenches arriving 8.35 pm at	
	ONE TREE Fm	
9.15 pm Trenches	Relief commenced	
11.40 pm	" completed	No casualties
11.15 pm	" Zeppelin passed over left Sector going N. E.	Our guns fired but no apparent result.

(9 29 6) W 3332—1107 100,000 10/13 H W V Forms/C. 2118/10.

1/4 Leic. Rgt. [illegible] 1/1st [illegible] Bde 1/1st N.M. Div

Instructions regarding War Diaries and Intelligence Summaries are contained in F. S. Regs., Part II. and the Staff Manual respectively. Title pages will be prepared in manuscript.

WAR DIARY
or
INTELLIGENCE SUMMARY.
(*Erase heading not required.*)

Army Form C. 2118.

Hour, Date, Place	Summary of Events and Information	Remarks and references to Appendices
April 1915		
1.15 A.M. 13th Trenches	Heavy fire bursts in neighbourhood of 15 - right sector. Adj went to all trenches except SP2a. V. little work done - except on parapets. E2 working [illegible] seemed to effect our men badly [illegible] from E2 not far out.	
3.15 pm	Quiet day - until Germans commenced shelling Frenchmans farm [illegible] & [illegible] killing 1 officer & [illegible] (8? - 1/4 Linc Rgt. After which continuous stream of men seen [illegible] from Packhorse Fm after carrying wounded) [illegible] - "[illegible]" 30 officers 100 men from Newport Dug Outs [illegible] worked in Regent St.	

1/4 Linc Rgt — 1/1st Linc & Leic Bde — 46th N. M. Div

Army Form C. 2118.

Instructions regarding War Diaries and Intelligence Summaries are contained in F. S. Regs., Part II. and the Staff Manual respectively. Title pages will be prepared in manuscript.

WAR DIARY
or
INTELLIGENCE SUMMARY.
(~~Erase heading not required.~~)

Hour, Date, Place	Summary of Events and Information	Remarks and references to Appendices
April 1915 Trenches. 13th	Shelling of Frenchmans or R.A. redoubt [illegible] efforts of Bn HQ which practically completed a very fair dug out immediately West of ONE TREE Fm. This at a pinch would hold 40 m. Communication arranged for	
8-30pm.	Lt G S HARVEY seriously wounded in [illegible] by rifle bullet in back of head — ricochet off tree on left flank or sandbag on parapet (N [illegible]) or thro' sand bag. Took about 3½ hrs. to get him to Dressing Stn — delay due to his being kept some time in trench as he was very sick when moved and communication trenches narrow and very difficult for stretcher bearers.	1 officer wounded (2 men slightly wounded) before he was brought. S' bearers from trenches & N.D.O's meet at R. [illegible] Fm

Every available N.C.O. & man from C & D Coys employed — fatigues & working parties.

(9 29 6) W 3332—1107 100,000 10/13 H W V Forms/C. 2118/10.

1/4 Leic R[illegible] 1/1st [illegible] Bde 1/1st N.M. Div

Army Form C. 2118.

(10)

Instructions regarding War Diaries and Intelligence Summaries are contained in F. S. Regs., Part II. and the Staff Manual respectively. Title pages will be prepared in manuscript.

WAR DIARY
or
INTELLIGENCE SUMMARY.
(Erase heading not required.)

Hour, Date, Place	Summary of Events and Information	Remarks and references to Appendices
April 1915		
14th Trenches	CO & 2nd in C round 'A' Coy in v. early morning. A wet night.	
2.30am	Fatigue party of 40 under 2Lt DALGLIESH reported for work with RE – but 40 men went off under w[illegible] to another party of RE by mistake. A case of incompetent N.CO – not looking after his men whilst his officer away getting orders.	No casualties.
	100 men working in Regent St morning & afternoon for 6 hrs in all	
	All [illegible] at Bn HQ moved into special dug out.	
	Usual evening fatigues & ration parties. Ten sentups in [illegible] this ready made – very satisfactory arrangement when [illegible] finished	
6.45 P.m.	Germans shelled Mt KEMMEL – no apparent result.	
	2nd in C round trenches – also Bde Major and RE Officers.	
15th Trenches	Very fine – bright & warm.	2 men killed (1 in E1, 1 in F2)
	No German shelling – tho' expected	4 RE wounded working [illegible]
8 p.m.	RE wiring party covered by ½ coy [illegible] Rgt – laying French wire from E1 left (left end) to [illegible] of E2. Start delayed owing to report that Germans held RED COTTAGE – but not confirmed and wire finally laid.	1 wounded E2 or F2

(9 29 6) W 3332—1107 100,000 10/13 H W V Forms/C. 2118/10

Instructions regarding War Diaries and Intelligence Summaries are contained in F. S. Regs., Part II. and the Staff Manual respectively. Title pages will be prepared in manuscript.

WAR DIARY
or
INTELLIGENCE SUMMARY.
(*Erase heading not required.*)

1/4 [illegible] Rgt 1/1st [illegible] Bde 1/1st [illegible]

Army Form C. 2118.

(11)

Hour, Date, Place	Summary of Events and Information	Remarks and references to Appendices
April 1915		
15th Trenches 10.45 pm	Adj rec^d long message from Bde Major on telephone re anticipated attack by Germans on YPRES [illegible] use of asphyxiating gases expected. Men to use "damped" handkerchiefs to counteract. Very still night however.	
16th Trenches	V. quiet all day. Fine & warm. Sharp [illegible] in N.E. direction shortly after daybreak. C.O. out with guide, guide wounded	1 [illegible] 2 [illegible] 1 — in Piccadilly
8.30 pm	1/5 [illegible] Rgt arrived to relieve. Very dark and	
9. pm	Relief commenced	
17th Trenches	Relief completed [illegible] but not reported until a late [illegible] owing to [illegible] relieving officer to report [illegible]. Men [illegible] exhausted than after first tour in trenches.	

(9 29 6) W 3332--1107 100,000 10/13 H W V Forms/C. 2118/10.

Instructions regarding War Diaries and Intelligence Summaries are contained in F.S. Regs., Part II. and the Staff Manual respectively. Title pages will be prepared in manuscript.

WAR DIARY
or
INTELLIGENCE SUMMARY.
(Erase heading not required.)

Army Form C. 2118.

Hour, Date, Place	Summary of Events and Information	Remarks and references to Appendices
April 1918		
17th [illegible]	[illegible]	
7pm	Very heavy gunning from direction of [illegible] [illegible]	
18th 10 am	[illegible]	
5 pm	[illegible]	
19th	[illegible]	

Instructions regarding War Diaries and Intelligence Summaries are contained in F. S. Regs., Part II. and the Staff Manual respectively. Title pages will be prepared in manuscript.

1/4 Leic Rgt **WAR DIARY** *or* **INTELLIGENCE SUMMARY.** 1/1st L. & L. Bde 1/1st N. M. Div

(*Erase heading not required.*)

Army Form C. 2118.

13

Place	Date	Hour	Summary of Events and Information	Remarks and references to Appendices
DRANOUTRE	April 1916	7.30 p.m.	Bn moved to Trench Area. Bn Op. Orders attached. {M. René PILLOT (interpreter) left for ST OMER succeeded by Belgian –	
	20th	8.45	Arrived ONE TREE Fm.	
Trench Area		9.15.	Relief commenced	
		11.0	" completed	O.R. 1 man wounded but returned to duty (slightly) after being wounded. Hit by [illegible] New post [illegible]
			Adj made complete tour of trenches and S.Ps. returning 4.30 a.m. following day. Enemy inactive except in neighbourhood of SPANBROEKMOLEN – near which a trench mortar was busy – but not aimed our way. Good work had been done in trenches since our last visit – by R.E. & 1/5 Linc. Rgt – also on Regent St.	
	21st	2 a.m.	Several civilians – apparently labourers – beyond boundary limit – not found after first seen – tho' searched for by party of Sherwoods & ourselves – 300x N. of SP27.	Ref. B.
		7.25		
		noon 12	Enemy shelling WULVERGHEM – very mildly.	
		p.m. 3.40 to 3.45	Art. Test of E1 Right & F2 – fairly speedy reply to call for fire	
			Usual working parties – Regent St in day time.	

1/4 Leic Rgt — WAR DIARY or INTELLIGENCE SUMMARY. — 1/1st L. I. Bde. — 1/1st N. M. Div.

Army Form C. 2118.

Instructions regarding War Diaries and Intelligence Summaries are contained in F. S. Regs., Part II. and the Staff Manual respectively. Title pages will be prepared in manuscript.

(Erase heading not required.)

Place	Date April 1915	Hour	Summary of Events and Information	Remarks and references to Appendices
Trench Area	21st	3.55 pm	Enemy apparently located our Regent St working party – with result that 7 to 10 shells were dropped near SP4 Fm – no casualties. Some impact some air bursts. 3 fuzes found 50. 52 & 53 (numbered) – & lettered K.K – & sent to R.A.	Casualties: 1 other rank killed. O.R. wounded working on Dug Out E.6 12.50 pm rifle bullets
			H.Q. retired to dug outs (2) in rear – very glad of 5th Line Rgts handiwork in building 2nd. German, wearing dark cap with yellow band, seen opposite E1 R. Remainder of day normal.	
		Evening	An R.A. officer 3rd Staffs Battery – went up to trench F2 for night & day.	
			R.S.M.B.	
	22nd	3.30 am	Heavy rifle firing N. & S. of our sector.	
		4.30	Communication from SP27 to fire trenches interrupted – found to be due to shell fire, when repairing party went out at dusk. We were able to get thro' to trenches via R.R. line.	1 wounded O.R.
		Between 4 pm to 5-45 pm	Enemy apparently tried to find our guns W. of Bn H.Q. with 5.9" shells – C.O. & M.O. out, but remainder of H.Q. retired to Dug Outs in rear. No damage done. About 15 rounds fired. Captive balloon (Ger) located E.S.E from E6. (attached – 3rd Staffs Bty)	
		9 pm	Col Bruce & Major Challenor went round E2 & F2 with C.O. Col Bruce brought report that French & Canadians given way slightly – N. of YPRES✗. Attack thought to be likely. Complaints of sore eyes in fire trenches. Nothing materialised. R.S.M.B.	✗ due to use of gasses

Instructions regarding War Diaries and Intelligence Summaries are contained in F. S. Regs., Part II. and the Staff Manual respectively. Title pages will be prepared in manuscript.

1/4 Leic Regt. 1/1st L. & L. ... 1st N. M. Div.

WAR DIARY
or
INTELLIGENCE SUMMARY.
(Erase heading not required.)

Army Form C. 2118.

15

Place	Date April 1915.	Hour	Summary of Events and Information	Remarks and references to Appendices
Trench Area	23rd		Normal day.	Casualty O.R.
			No enemy shelling – Bn HQ. retired to Dug Out for ½ hr.	1 killed E1 R
			R.S.D.B.	1 wounded E1 L
	24th	.	Quiet night & day – except for v. heavy cannonade N & N.E. – YPRES. ? Locally, our guns seemed to shoot well.	
			Lt. Col. W.A. HARRISON – returned from hospital – quite unexpectedly – did not resume command.	3. O.R. wounded
		8.20 p.m.	1/5 Leic. Rgt. arrived at ONE TREE Fm to relieve us.	1 – guide, going up with relief
		8.50.	Relief commenced & expeditiously carried out. Reflection of gt blaze in sky N.E. YPRES?	just N. of FRENCHMANS Fm
		10.30	" completed.	2 – in trench E
		11.55.	Bn HQ. – the last to leave except working party – reached billets – quickest performance to date	3.
			R.S.D.B.	
DRANOUTRE	25th		Bathing & usual billet routine.	
		3pm	Bn Ch. Parade, 1/5 Leic. Rgt. Band.	
			Heavy distant artillery.	
			R.S.D.B.	
	26th		"A" Coy moved into DETTINGEN Huts. Still hear heavy firing.	O.R.
		Commencing onwards	Working party (B Coy) E4 & E6 – wiring – after instruction in forenoon from R.E.	2 wounded (Same billet)
		5.30 pm	C.O. lectured & catechised Officers & N.C.Os of 'A' & 'C' & afterwards inspected transport at INKERMAN Fr. R.S.D.B.	

Instructions regarding War Diaries and Intelligence Summaries are contained in F. S. Regs., Part II. and the Staff Manual respectively. Title pages will be prepared in manuscript.

WAR DIARY
or
INTELLIGENCE SUMMARY.
(*Erase heading not required.*)

1/4. Leic Rgt 1/1st Linc & Leic Bde 1/1st N. M. Divn

Army Form C. 2118.

16

Place	Date April 1915	Hour	Summary of Events and Information	Remarks and references to Appendices
DRANOUTRE	27th	10am	C.O. inspected "A" "C" & "D" Coys at huts & billets. Turnout "A" & "D" good – "C" still v. poor. "B" excused until following day owing to all-night work in trench area.	
			Heavy gunning all day to N. & N.E.	
			Cold day. Sort of sea mist in evening.	
		5.30 pm	C.O. lectured & catechised Officers & N.C.Os of "B" & "D" near "B's" billet. These "shows" are gt success. N.C.Os very keen & feel interest being taken in them – improves their morale.	
		7pm	Heavy gunning to N & N.E. [illegible]	
			— ^ —	
			Orders	
		8am	Bde Op. O. No 13. Copy No 5 received –	
"	28th	11am	C.O. inspected "B" Coy – turn out & kits good – except boots, which were somewhat poor. Present issue of boots to men seems of inferior quality. This is the opinion of officers who are boot experts. Men evidently don't use dubbin but ordinarily extravagantly.	Warm, bright day – some wind
		12 noon	C.O. went thro' N.C.Os roll re promotion with O's C Coys – who could not recommend a large number of N.C.Os – senior ones mostly "older hands" but not very bright & so considered less fit than younger to officers	
		Afternoon		
		7.40 pm	Bn. moved to trench area	Very bright moonlight night
		8.45	– arrived ONE TREE Fm.	
		9.20	– commenced relief	

1577 Wt. W10791/1773 500,000 1/15 D. D. & L. A.D.S.S./Forms/C. 2118.

1/1 Leic. Regt — 1/1st Linc & Leic Bde — 1/1st N.M. Div

Army Form C. 2118. 17

WAR DIARY
or
INTELLIGENCE SUMMARY.
(*Erase heading not required.*)

Instructions regarding War Diaries and Intelligence Summaries are contained in F. S. Regs., Part II. and the Staff Manual respectively. Title pages will be prepared in manuscript.

Place	Date April 1915.	Hour	Summary of Events and Information	Remarks and references to Appendices
Trenches	28th	p.m. 11.5	Bn completed relief of 1/5 Linc Rgt. very light night. Experimental rifle-rests inserted in E1 L & E2	
			RSDB.	
–	29th	a.m. 7.30	CO met Bde Major up at E1 & with other officers made special reconnaissance with a view to locating enemy sap believed to be in neighbourhood of right of E1 Left. No result. 2Lts RUSSELL & DOUGLAS out on similar enterprise – negative information.	S. Bearers now meet wounded near New Dug Outs.
		8 am	Adj: tried to locate work above ground with glasses from FRENCHMANS Fm but none visible – tho: it looked as if there was commencement of sap from a jutting out portion of enemy trench opp R of E1. right. Very excellent view obtained from F's Fm of whole of our line & opposing trenches. The line of trees against Piccadilly where it passes F's Fm appears far safer than way thro Fm judging from reports and inspection of these [illegible]	Casualties 1 killed, 5 wounded OR (1 killed & 2 wounded in Piccadilly – 1 guide to S. P. 2 a & 2 running E1 of E1 Left [illegible])
		11 am	Enemy commenced morning shelling NEUVE EGLISE – COOKER Fm & short of it also 100x to 150x N. of SP2 a. No damage done	
		4 pm	Visit from Div Sanitary Experts – in connection with corpses, carcasses – disposal of	

1577 Wt. W10791/1773 500,000 1/15 D. D. & L. A.D.S.S./Forms/C. 2118.

Instructions regarding War Diaries and Intelligence Summaries are contained in F. S. Regs., Part II. and the Staff Manual respectively. Title pages will be prepared in manuscript.

1/4 Leic Rgt. 1/1st L & L Bde 1/1st N. M. Divn

WAR DIARY
or
INTELLIGENCE SUMMARY.
(Erase heading not required.)

Army Form C. 2118. 18.

Place	Date April 1915	Hour	Summary of Events and Information	Remarks and references to Appendices
Trenches	29th	Evening	Adj. to E2, G3, right & left - also listening posts & nothing of note seen - The men obviously feeling much more at home & firing with confidence. Trenches look very different to 3 weeks ago.	
		9pm	Report rec'd at Bn HQ that signalling visible from ~~[illegible]~~ in German lines. Signallers could not read signals - probability is that light was in G. captive balloon - RSDB	
	30th		V. warm & bright day	Casualties O.R.
		10.30 am	G.O.C. visited Bn HQ	
		11 am	Enemy shelled 2nd & 3rd Staffs Batteries - damaging officers hut	1 killed, N. entrance of left 9.20 am
		Afternoon	Our guns put 22 shots into enemy trenches opp E2 damaging parapets very little, but apparently successfully touching up trenches	2 wounded in Piccadilly slightly, 1 of S [illegible] [illegible] same spot 3.5 & 3.15 am
		11 pm	CO. visited trenches.	2 wounded immediately W. of Newport D.O. [illegible]

Casualties when falling in for fatigue same bullet apparently 8.20 pm
1 wounded 50x N.E. of Newport D.O. ration party - 9.30 pm

R S Dyer-Bennet
Capt & Adj
1/4 Leic Rgt.

1577 Wt. W10791/1773 500,000 1/15 D. D. & L. A.D.S.S./Forms/C. 2118.

Killed. No 3334. Pte S. BLOUNT
"B" Coy

Wounded. No. 2629. Pte C. SABIN
"C" Coy.

" 1657. " C. A. GENT.) "D" Coy
" 2708 " L. HOPKINSON)

A P P E N D I C E S .

SECRET.

OP[...]

BRIGADI[...] C[...]
Linco[...]

Reference Maps:-
FRANCE Shee[...]
BELGIUM She[...]
HAZEBROUCK [...]

"A" Form. Army Form C. 2121.

MESSAGES AND SIGNALS.

No. of Message

Prefix Code m. | Words | Charge

Office of Origin and Service Instructions.

Secret

This message is on a/c of:

Service.

Sent At m. To By

(Signature of "Franking Officer.")

Recd. at m. Date From By

TO H^d Quarters 4th Leic R.

Sender's Number	Day of Month	In reply to Number	AAA
LBM. LA4	4th		

Reference	Operation	order	No	5
para	7	your	Battalion	will
take	over	trenches	to-night	the
4/5	inst	instead	of	5/6
~~inst~~	April	as	therein	stated

Recd 12.10 pm
Recd by
Capt ...

From L + L Bde
Place
Time 11-45.

The above may be forwarded as now corrected (Z)

Censor. Signature of Addressor or person authorised to telegraph in his name

*This line should be erased if not required.

3652 M. & Co. Ltd. Wt. W929/549-100,000. 6/14. Forms C2121/10.

[signature] for Brigade Major.

1. The North Mid[...]
now held by t[...]
Headquarters [...]
Divisional [...]
Staffs Inf[...]
Lincs & Le[...]
Notts & De[...]

2. Hdqrs.L & L Bde. L.& L.Bde(less 1/4th Lincs & 1/5th Lincs) The [...] The [...] and [...] ORD[...] Regt[...] 2nd [...] STAR[...] PONT[...]

the [...] (She[...] TIME[...] 12-1[...] ROUT[...] in [...] 5a.[...] DRA[...]

3. 1/4th Lincs Regt. 1/5th Lincs Regt. (Lt Col JESSOP Commanding) The [...] J.W[...] mar[...] ORD[...] STA[...] TIM[...] ROU[...]

4. BILLETING PARTIES.

1/4th Leics Regt) 1/5th Leics Regt) Billeting parties from the 1/4th Leicestershire Regt and the 1/5th Leicestershire Regt. will report to the Staff Captain at the present Brigade Headquarters at 8 a.m. April 3rd /15.

1/4th Lincs Regt) 1/5th Lincs Regt) Billeting parties from the 1/4th Lincs Regt and the 1/5th Lincs Regt will report to the Staff Capt at Brigade Headquart[...] DRANOUTRE at 11 a.m. April 6th /15.

5. TRANSPORT. Transport Vehicles including Train wagons will march in rear of the Unit to which they belong.

6. AMBULANCE. One Motor Ambulance from the 2nd N.M.Field Ambulance will follow in rear of the transport of the 2nd Infantry Batt. on each day.

SECRET.

OPERATION ORDER NO 5
by
BRIGADIER GENERAL A. W. CLIFFORD COMMANDING
Lincoln and Leicester Infty Bde.T.F.

Reference Maps:-
FRANCE Sheet 36 LILLE.)Scale 1/40000
BELGIUM Sheet 28 YPRES)
HAZEBROUCK Sheet 5a.Scale 1/100000.

Copy No. 5

Bde Headquarters,
2/4/15.

....

1. The North Midland Division will take over the line of trenches now held by the 5th Division When this has been completed Headquarters will be established as follows:-
Divisional Headquarters.... ST.JANS CAPPELLE (now 5th Divl.Hdqrs)
Staffs Infty Bde ...WESTHOF FARM (T.19 a.) (now 83rd Bde Hdqrs)
Lincs & Leic Bde...DRANOUTRE (M.36) (now 84th Bde Hdqrs)
Notts & Derby Bde..KEMMEL CHATEAU (N 21) (now 14th Bde Hdqrs)

2.
Hdqrs.L & L Bde.
L.& L.Bde(less 1/4th Lincs & 1/5th Lincs)

The LINCOLN AND LEICESTER INFANTRY Brigade (less 1/4th Lincs and 1/5th Lincs Regts) One Motor Ambulance will march as follo
ORDER OF MARCH. Brigade Headquarters 1/4th Leicestershire Regt. 1/5th Leicestershire Regt. and 1 Motor Ambulance from 2nd North Midland Field Ambulance.
STARTING POINT. Road junction immediately S.W. of l in le PONT DE PIERRE - Sheet 36 LILLE A.10 a.c.
The 1/5th Leicestershire Regt. will join the column at the level crossing at S of CALAIS in CHIN DE FER DE CALAIS (Sheet 28 YPRES S.27 a.) .
TIME. The Head of the Column will pass the starting point at 12-15 p.m. April 3rd.
ROUTE. LE PONT DE PIERRE - Level crossing at S. of CALAIS in CHIN DE FER DE CALAIS - BAILLEUL - Lunatic Asylum (Sheet 5a.HAZEBROUCK) - HAEGEDOORNE - HILLE - CHAPle (S.5 b.) - DRANOUTRE.

3.
1/4th Lincs Regt.
1/5th Lincs Regt.
(Lt Col JESSOP Commanding)

The 1/4th Lincs Regt and the 1/5th Lincs Regt. under Lt.Col. J.W.JESSOP will leave their present billets on April 6th and march to DRANOUTRE as follows:-
ORDER OF MARCH. 1/5th Lincs Regt - 1/4th Lincs Regt.
STARTING POINT. As in para 2.
TIME. 12-15 p.m. April 6th 1915.
ROUTE . As in para 2.

4. BILLETING PARTIES.
1/4th Leics Regt)
1/5th Leics Regt)
Billeting parties from the 1/4th Leicestershire Regt and the 1/5th Leicestershire Regt. will report to the Staff Captain at the present Brigade Headquarters at 8 a.m. April 3rd /15.
1/4th Lincs Regt)
1/5th Lincs Regt)
Billeting parties from the 1/4th Lincs Regt and the 1/5th Lincs Regt will report to the Staff Capt at Brigade Headquart DRANOUTRE at 11 a.m. April 6th /15.

5. TRANSPORT. Transport Vehicles including Train wagons will march in rear of the Unit to which they belong .

6. AMBULANCE. One Motor Ambulance from the 2nd N.M.Field Ambulance will follow in rear of the transport of the 2nd Infantry Batt. on each day.

4 days in trenches.

on return probably some readjust[ment]
of billets.

Probably ~~[illegible]~~ 2 extra
bandoliers.

Once on his post the Sentr[y]
will not leave his post —

will be shot.

If he ~~falls~~ wishes to fall o[ut]
must be relieved.

13

7. TAKING OVER TRENCHES. The 5th Leicestershire Regt. will take over trenches from the 84th Infantry Brigade on the night of 4/5 April and the 4th Leicestershire Regt on the night of 5/6 April . Commanding Officers Adjutants and O.C. Companies and 2nd in Command of Companies of the 1/4th Leics Regt and 1/5th Leics Regt. will be prepared to go into the trenches immediately on arrival at destination . The above Officers of the 5th Leicestershire Regt. will leave the trenches the same night : the above Officers of the 4th Leicestershire Regt. will remain in the Trenches for 24 hours . The same Officers of the 4th and 5th Lincs Regt. will similarly be prepared to proceed immedaitely to the trenches on arrival on 6th April if so ordered. Further orders as to taking over will be issued later. Battalion Commrs. are reminded that the trenches can only be entered at night.

4th Leics Regt.
5th Leics Regt.

4th Lincs Regt.
5th Lincs Regt.

8. COMMAND. The G.O.C. 5th Division will command the line until all Infantry reliefs have been completed throughout the Division.

9. ALTERATION TO ORDERS. These orders are subject to alteration being dependent on the moves of other Divisions.

10. PARTIES. Drag Rope parties should be detailed by Battalions to be in readiness to assist wagons on DRANOUTRE Hill.

11. REPORTS. During the march on April the 3rd Reports to Head of Column. During the march on April the 6th. Reports to Head of 4th Lincs Regt.

sd/ R.L.ADLERCRON Maj.,
Bde Maj. 1/1 Lincs & Leic Bde T.F.

ISSUED by Cyclist Orderly
at 7-30 p.m. to

Copy No 1. Brigade Maj.for Brig Gen Commanding
2. Staff Capt.
3. 4/Lincs Regt.
4. 5/Lincs Regt.
5. 4/Leics Regt.
6. 5/Leics Regt.
7. 2nd N.M.F.A.(for information)
8. N.M.D.
9. 84th Infantry Brigade.
10. War Diary.

Secret.

Copy No *1*.

OPERATION ORDERS No 6
by
MAJOR L. V. WYKES
COMMANDING 1/4TH BN. LEICESTERSHIRE RGT.

Battn. H.Q.,
2nd April 1915

Reference Maps FRANCE sheet 36 1/40,000
BELGIUM 28 1/40,000

1 INFORMATION.- The 1/1st LINC. & LEIC. INF. BDE. will take over the trenches now held by the 84th BDE. with Bde. H.Q. at DRANOUTRE (sheet 28 M 36)

2 INSTRUCTIONS.-The Battn will pass 1 of le Gd. Beaumart proceeding N to 1 of le Pont de Pierre (sheet 36) (Bde. Starting Point) at 11-55 a.m. to-morrow 3/4/'15 and march in rear of Bde. H.Q.
O. of M. Battn. H.Q., "A", "D", "B", "C" Coys., Mac. Guns, 1st Line Transport and "Train".

<u>ROUTE</u>- le Pont de Pierre - level crossing at <u>S</u> of CALAI<u>S</u> in Chem de fer de CALAI<u>S</u> (sheet 28) - BAILLEUL - Lunatic Asylum - HAEGEDOORNE - HILLE - CHAPle (S. 5 b) - DRANOUTRE.

3 BILLETING PARTY.- (2/LT. R. C. HARVEY) The Battn. Billeting party will assemble at road junction 100 yards W of "D" Coys. H.Q. at 7-15 a.m. under 2/LT.R.C.HARVEY and march to Bde.H.Q., reporting to Bde. Staff Captain at 8 a.m.

4 AMBULANCE One Motor Ambulance will follow in rear of the Bde.

5 TAKING OVER TRENCHES. The C.O., Adj., O's C.Coys. and 2nd in C. of Coys. will be prepared to go into the trenches immediately on arrival at destination and will remain in the trenches for 24 hours.
The Battn. will take over the trenches allotted to it on the night of the 5/6th April.
Further orders as to taking over will be issued later.
The trenches can only be entered at night.

6 DRAGROPE PARTIES The O.C. "C" Coy. will detail parties to assist the Transport and "Train" on DRANOUTRE hill by means of drag ropes provided by the Transport Officer.

7 REPORTS Reports to Head of Battn.

Issued by Cyclist Orderly at *11.55* p.m.

R S Dyer Bennet,
Captain & Adj,
1/4 Leic Rgt

Copy No 1 War Diary
2 "
3 Adj. for C.O.
4 1/1st Linc. & Leic. Inf. Bde
5 O.C. "A" Coy
6 "B"
7 "C"
8 "D"
9 Billeting Officer
10 Transport Officer
11 Machine Gun Officer
12 Medical Officer
13 Quartermaster.

War Diary

"C" Form (Duplicate). Army Form C. 2123 A.

MESSAGES AND SIGNALS. No. of Message..................

Service Instructions.	Charges to Pay £ s. d.	Office Stamp. LEA 3/4/15

Handed in at the L & L Office, at 8 30 a m. Received here at 8 36 a m.

TO O C 4th Leic

Sender's Number	Day of Month	In reply to Number	AAA
L 151/23	3rd		

Following	telegram	from	Second
Corps	begins	aaa	MAJOR
T	GRESSON	D.S.O	of
Yorks	and	Lancs	Regt
appointed	to	temporary	
Command	of	4th	Leics
Regt	aaa	Move	ordered
aaa	Message	ends	

FROM L & L Brigade
PLACE
TIME 8 18 am

SALE & POLDEN, LTD. PRINTERS, ALDERSHOT.
(60,017). Wt. 7981—448. 40,000 Pads. 4/15. W.

Secret *Copy No 3*

OPERATION ORDER No. 6
by
BRIGADIER GENERAL W.R.CLIFFORD
Commanding 1/1st Lincoln & Leicester Infantry Brigade T.F.

Headquarters,
4th April, 1915.

Ref. 1/10,000 KEMMEL WYTSC HAETE.

1. The enemy are reported to be improving their work by the addition of a salient opposite 15 and unverified reports have been received as to mining opposite E 1 Officers Commanding Units in taking over from their opposite numbers should make a special point of obtaining the latest information of the enemy.

2. The Lincoln & Leicester Brigade will occupy the Trench line from Trench 14 on the ~~sector~~ *flank* to the point where trench F. 2 intersects the road from STORE FARM to SPANBROEK MOLLEN. The line will be divided into two sectors. Right sector from 14 inclusive 14s, 15, 15s, E.4, SP1, with following accommodation in rear :- COOKER FARM, Dig outs N. 35, POND FARM with Battalion Headquarters at FRENCH MANS FARM.
Left Sector E.1, E.3, E.2, E.6, F.2 to road (marked by sandbag butrlss) inside breastwork), SP2a, SP2b. accommodation in rear NEWPORT DUG OUTS, PACKHORSE FARM, Battalion Headquarters ONE TREE FARM.

3. The Right Sector will be held by 5th Leicestershire Regiment under Lt. Colonel, JONES T.D. and will take *over* from the 1st Welsh Regiment on the night of the 5th April. The O.C. Welsh Regiment will remain in command of the sector until the relief is completed
The Left Sector will be held by the 4th Leicestershire Regiment under Major T.T.Gresson D.S.O. will take over from the 1st Monmouth Regiment (with Suffolk detachment in F.2 Suffolk M.G. detachment in SP2b and Welsh Garrison in E.1) The O.C. 1st Monmouthshire Regiment will remain in command of this sector until the relief is completed.

4. TIME OF RELIEFS. The 5th Leicester Regt. is due at PACK HORSE FARM at 11-30 p.m. and will be met there by two Guides 1st Welsh Regt. for each of the following trenches viz:- 14, 14s 15 15s and SP1 Battalion Headquarters COOK FARM, POND FARM, and 35 N dug outs. Reliefs will start from PACK HORSE FARM at 12 midnight.
The 4th Leics. Regt. is due at ONE TREE FARM at 10 p.m. and will be met there by 2 guides 1st Monmouth Regt. for each of the following trenches E.1, E.2, E.3, E.6, F.2 SP2a SP2b NEWPORT DUG OUTS.
Note. To arrive at destination by the time mentioned.
Battalions will pass through DANOUTRE 1½ hrs. before the time they are due to arrive.

5. DISTRIBUTION. Each Battalion will have 2 Companies in Fire trenches and support points and two Companies in Battalion Reserve APPx A shows present garrison of trenches and support points, and should be generally adheared to.

6. MACHINE GUNS. Right Sector one in 14 and one in 15.
Left Sector E3 and F2.

7. TRANSPORT. Machine Gun Wagon, Tool Cart, Maltese Cart to follow Battalions to PACK HORSE FARM and ONE TREE FARM but no tools to go up with the trench Companies. The remainder of the Transport is left in Transport Stables. Transport from ONE TREE FARM will not return until PACKHORSE FARM is clear.

13

8. DETAILS. The following details will remain in billets, Quarters Master, Quarter Master Sergeant, Sergeant Shoemaker, Armourer Sergeant, Company Quarter Master Sergeants, 1 Cook per Company Sgt. Tailor, 1 Groom per 2 horses. Transport details, Sergeant Drummer and 2 men Orderly Room Clerk.

9. Men. Each man will carry
   (a) Water bottle full (they must last 24 hours)
   (b) 1 Extra Bandolier
   (c) Some fuel in pack.
   (d) 1 pair Gum Boots if available
   (e) 2 Sandbags one filled with coke or charcoal.

10. WORK TO BE DONE. Commanding Officers will ascertain from the Officers Commanding the Battalion they releave the details of all work at present in progress and will continue the same. Particular attention is directed to any maintenance work required.

11. REPORTS Reports will be sent to arrive at this Office at 7-30 a.m. and 7-30 p.m. detailing the situation. Exceptional circumstances will be reported immediately. A daily report as per Pro Forma A herewith showing work done during preceeding 24 hours will be sent to arrive at this Office by 7 p.m.. A daily report as per proforma B will be rendered daily by the O.C. to arrive at this Office at 7-30 a.m. The Log Book at present kept by Battalions will be kept up.

12. TRENCH STORES Battalions will send a list of stores taken over in each trench to Brigade Headquarters and keep a duplicate copy themselves. This procedure will be followed with future relief.

13. COMMUNICATION WITH ENEMY. Any communication with the enemy is absolutely forbidden. Officers must firmly repress any attempts on the part of the enemy to fraternise with us. Any overtures made by them with this intention must be absolutely ignored.

14. BRIGADE HEADQUARTERS. In the event of an attack Brigade Headquarters will be moved to Dug Out in sand pit 100 yards East of LINDENHOEK Cross Roads on South Side of road to SPY FARM. One Orderly per Battalion will be sent to this point on the event of an attack.

sd/ R.L.ADLERCRON, Major,
Bde. Major, 1/1st Linc. & Leic. Inf. Bde. T.F.

Issued by Cyclist
Orderly at ? p.m. to :-

Copy No. 1. Bde. Major per Brig. Genl,
2. Staff Captain,
3. 4th Leics. Regt.
4. 5th Leics. Regt.
5. 84th Infantry Brigade.
6. War Diary.

Rec 7. p.m.

13

APPENDIX A.

LIST OF TRENCHES AND GARRISONS.

Trench.	Rifles.	Machine Gun	T'phone	Remarks.
14	30	1	T	Formerly called 14 b Good Breastwork approached by good communication trench.
14s	40	-		Support trench.
15	140	1	T	Good Breastwork with communication trench with it. Connection with 14 b desirable. Existing old trench muddy connects with E3 but this part not yet occupied or fully sandbagged.
15s	50	-	-	Good dug outs.
X E1	50	-	T	This trench is in two parts E1 right & E1 left, separated by 30x-40x old trench now being worked at. E1 right has 30 rifles E1 left has 20, each should have an Officer. Exposed position and liable to enfilade fire and sudden assault, but very important, has communication trench right up from SP1. Men should only be in this trench 24 hours and then relieved. Ground all round is insanitary.
X E3	35	1	-	Good dry trench with improved rifle pits, firing across gaps between E1 & E2 & E and 15.
E4	40	-	-	Line of dug outs along edge of wood, indifferent and liable to shelling. Fire trench just in front.
SP1	50	1	T	Good redoubt, has two days supplies, allround fire but is shelled. Garrison must hold out at all cost and not be used for other purposes quite comfortable.
X E2	40	1	T	Very good breastwork. To Right Front is Red Cottage which is occupied by us every night by 6 men who run there hard as Officer going with them & returning after posting men.
X E5	60	-	-	Good breastwork covers gap between E1 & E2 is now extended to North but Northern part is not fully sandbagged yet and is not yet occupied and should be.

(Though held by 84th Brigade F.4 F.5 and 100 of F3 are taken over by Notts & Derbys Brigade).

Trench.	Rifles.	Machine Gun	T'phone	Remarks.
F6	60	-	-	Will hold quite 100 good support trench with fire parapet. Parapet requires sandbagging.

13

Trench.	Rifles.	Machine Gun.	T'phone.	Remarks.
SP2a	25∅	1	T.	New small work with good field of fire; drainage wants attention Garrison must remain hidden.
SP2b	50	1	T.	Redoubt recently improved has six dug outs and a T shaped trench at head for machine gun to be put there when required. Well wired all round; wires should not be put further forward or will be visible.
SP3	50	1	T.	Similar to SP2b.

OPERATION ORDERS NO 9 Copy No 1

by

MAJOR T. T. GRESSON, D. S. O.

COMMANDING 1/4TH BATTALION LEICESTERSHIRE RGT.

Bn. Headquarters.
4/4/'15

Ref. BELGIUM sheet 28, 1/40,000
and plan of trenches which may be seen in the O.R.
copies of which will be issued.

1 INFORMATION.- The Bn. will take over the centre sector of the trenches allotted to the 1/1st N. M. DIV. on the night of 4/5th April, 1915, relieving 1ST MONMOUTHSHIRE REGIMENT.

2 INSTRUCTIONS.- Starting point.- 600 yards E. of DRANOUTRE CHURCH Approximately under N--of DRANOUTRE.

TIME.- 8-30 p.m.

ORDER OF MARCH.- Hd.Qs. "A", "B", "C", "D", Coys., M.G's. and Transport as detailed.

DRESS.- F.S.M.O., wearing Great Coats.

AMMUNITION.- Every N.C.O. and man will carry two extra bandoliers, making in all 220 rounds per man.

TRENCHES.- Trenches will be taken over as under.

"A" Coy. E1. R one officer and 30 men - L one officer and 20 men
E3. One officer and 35 men (plus one M.G. & 8 men)
E6. One officer and 50 men. (with rations for 3 days - 2 days of these will be sent up later)
Any surplus men from "A" Company in SP2a and SP2b.

"B" " E2. Two Officers and 40 men (plus one M.G. and 8 men)
F2. Two officers and 100 men
Surplus in SP2b.

"C" " Completes SP2a & SP2b if not already containing one officer and 25 and one officer and 50 respectively with remainder in NEWPORT DUG OUTS.

"D" " In "NEWPORT DUG OUTS".

GUARDS.- Permanent Guards will be found at Bn. H.Q., at each end of NEWPORT "DUG OUTS", and also at SP2a and SP2b.

LISTENING POST.- The O.C. "B" Coy will detail a party of one officer and 6 men as Listening Post at RED COTTAGE, E.S.E. of E2. This party will rush in at dusk and out just before dawn.

TAKING OVER TRENCHES.- On arrival at ONE TREE FARM (Bn.H.Qs), "A" Coy led by guide of 1/ST MONMOUTHSHIRE RGT will proceed by COOKER FARM to its trenches.
"B" Coy. will move by REGENT STREET, leaving NEWPORT "DUG OUTS" on its right (East)., going in at F6.
When the front has been reported clear, the remainder of "C" Coy. and "D" Coy. will move straight into NEWPORT. "DUG OUTS"

3 REPORTS.- O's.C.Coys. will report to Bn.H.Q. by telephone when they have taken over and in future at 4 a.m. daily stating "Situation Norman" or otherwise.
Occurances of importance must be reported at once.

4 RATIONS.- Except where otherwise ordered, ~~and~~ one day's rations will be carried on the man.

(sd) R. S. DYER-BENNET Capt. & Adjt.
1/4TH LEICESTERSHIRE REGIMENT.

Issued by Cyclist Orderly at 4-45 p.m.

Copy No 1 War Diary
2 "
3 Adjt. (for C.O.)
4 1/1ST LINC. & LEIC. INF. BDE.
5 O.C. "A" Coy
6 "B"
7 "C"
8 "D"
9 Transport Officer
10 Machine Gun Officer
11 Medical Officer
12 Quartermaster.

Copy No 5 13

SECRET.

OPERATION ORDER NO 7 BY BRIG.GEN.W.R.
CLIFFORD COMMANDING 1/1 Lincs & Leic Bde T.F.

Headquarters,
7/4/15.

Reference 1/10000 KEMMEL WYTSC HAETE.

1. Trench Battalions will be relieved on night 8th/9th and 9th/10th
   (a) 4th Lincs Regt. releiving 5th Leicester Regt. in right sector on night 9th/10th .
   (b) 5th Lincs Regt. releiving 4th Leicester Regt on night 8th/9th on left sector.

   The allotment of trenches and accomodation in rear to be taken over is shewn in Appendix A attached .

2. (a) The 5th Lincs Regt will pass through DRANOUTRE Square at 6-45 p on 8th inst. and march via LINDENHOEK Guard and Packhorse Farm to arrive at ONETREE at 8-15 p.m.
   (b) The 1/4 Bn. Leics. Regiment will arrange for two guides for each trench and farm to be taken over to be at ONE TREE FARM 8-15 p.m. whence the relief will start at 8-45 p.m. The 4th LEICS TRANSPORT OFFICER will arrange for two guides to meet the 5th LINCOLN REGIMENT at DRANOUTRE and guide it to ONE TREE FARM.

3. (a) The 4th LINCOLN REGIMENT will pass through DRANOUTRE SQUARE at 6-45 p.m. on 9th instant and will march via LINDENHOEK Guard to PACKHORSE FARM to arrive there by 8 p.m.
   (b) The 5th Leicester Regiment will arrange for two guides for each trench and farm to be taken over to be at PACKHORSE FARM at 8 p.m. whence the relief will start at 8-30 p.m. The Transport Officer 5th Leicester Regiment will provide two guides to meet the 4th LINCOLN REGIMENT at DRANOUTRE and guide it to PACKHORSE FARM.

4. TRANSPORT to accompany Battalions is shown on Appendix "B" attached.

5. EMPTY TRANSPORT to bring in 4th and 5th Leicester Regiment will leave DRANOUTRE SQUARE at 6-30 p.m. and will not start to come back till 9-30 p.m.

6. AFTER RELIEF 4th and 5th LEICESTER REGIMENTS will return to billets in DRANOUTRE AREA.

7. APPENDIX "B", Copy of Operation Order number 6 is attached. The attention of relieving Battalions is directed to paras. 1, 5,7,10,13 and 14.

8. MAXIM GUNS. The attention of Officers Commanding 4th and 5th LEICESTER REGIMENTS is directed to paragraph 9 Routine Order No. 1 6 men will be left with each Gun. The 4th LINCOLN REGIMENT will hand over one machine gun with its detachment and limber to the Machine Gun Officer of the 5th LINCOLN REGIMENT before noon on the 8th instant.

   The 5th LINCOLN REGIMENT will post the three machine guns as follows :- E2 one, SP2a one, SP2b one - ex 4th Lincoln Regiment.

   The 4th LINCOLN REGIMENT will post their remaining machine gun in SP1. Machine Guns will then be as follows in the trenches.

RIGHT SECTOR

Trench.	No.	Found from.
14	1	5/LEICS
15	1	5/LEICS
SP1	1	4/LINCS

LEFT SECTOR.

Trench.	No.	Found from.
Sq1' × E3	1	4/LEICS.
E2	1	5/LINCS.
C/d × F2	1	4/LEICS.
SP2a	1	5/LINCS.
SP2b	1	4/LINCS.

9. REPORTS as to completion of relief will be telegraphed to BRIGADE HEADQUARTERS by the relieving Battalion.

10. AMMUNITION. Battalions relieved will bring back with them all their unexpended ammunition including the extra bandolier taken with them to the trenches.

Maxim gun detachments will take with them to the trenches 10,000 per gun.

sd/ RL. AYLMERCRON, Major,

Brigade Major, 1/1st Linc. & Leics. Bde. T.F.

Issued by Orderly
at p.m. to :-

Copy No. 1 Brigade Major for Brigadier
2 Staff Captain
3 4/LINCS REGIMENT
4 5/LINCS REGIMENT
5 4/LEICS REGIMENT
6 5/LEICS REGIMENT
7 WAR DIARY.

13

APPENDIX A.

TABLE SHEWING TRENCHES AND DISTRIBUTION OF RIFLES.

RIGHT SECTOR.

BATTALION HEADQUARTERS
FRENCHMANS FARM.

Trench.	Rifles.	Machine Gun.
14	40	1
14s	30	
15	140	1
15s	50	
E4	40	
SP1	50	1
	350	3

LEFT SECTOR.

BATTALION HEADQUARTERS
ONE TREE FARM

Trench	Rifles	Machine Gun.
E1 right	30	
E1 left	20	
E3	35	1
E2	40	1
E6	50	
F2	70	1
SP2a	25	1
SP2b	50	1
	325	5

Accommodation in rear for Battalion Reserves.

COOKER FARM	1 Company	PACKHORSE FARM	1 Company
POND FARM	1 Company	NEWPORT DUG OUTS	1½ Companies.
DUG OUTS N35	100 men		

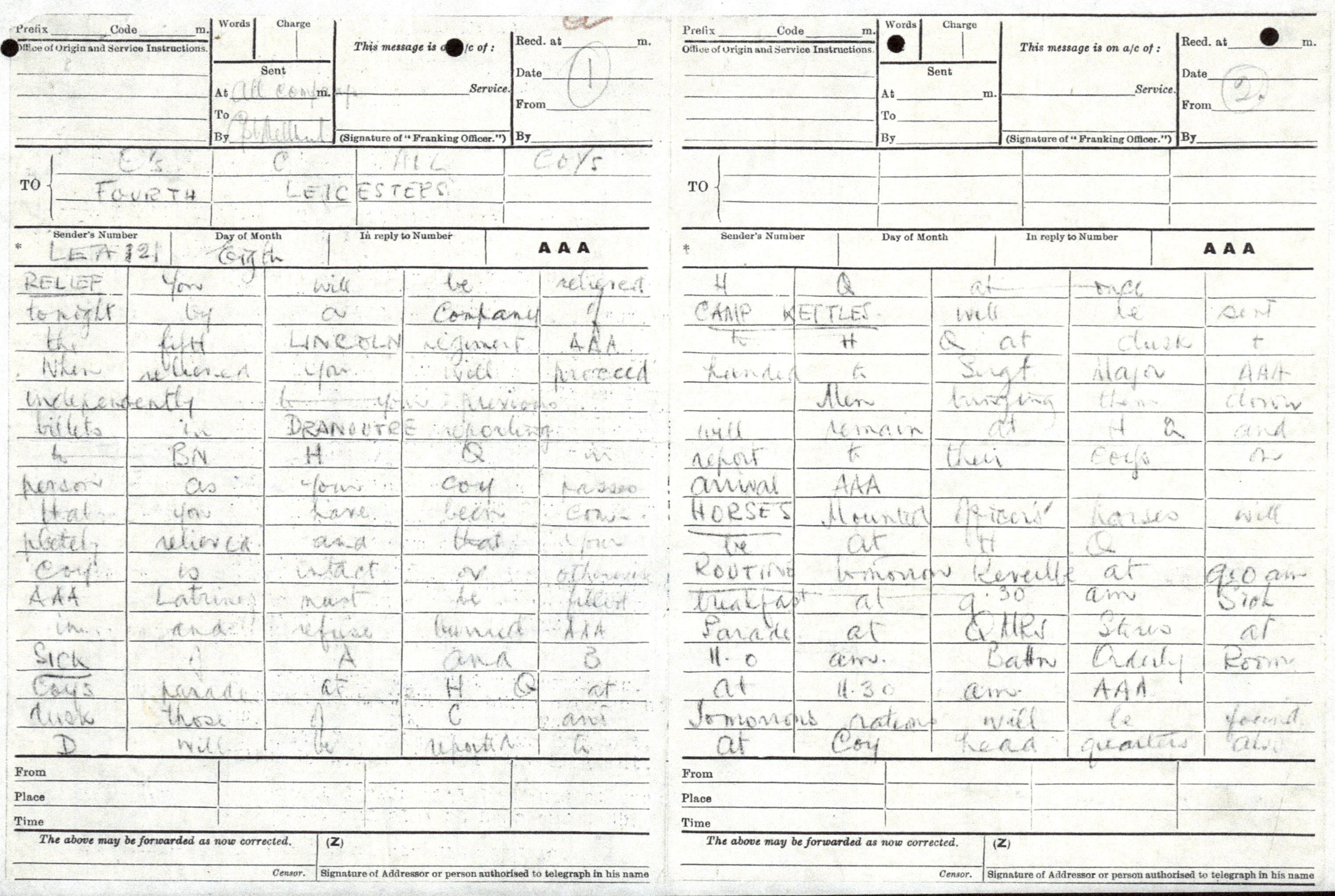

Prefix Code m. Words Charge
Office of Origin and Service Instructions.
Sent At All coys m. To By
This message is on a/c of: Service.
(Signature of "Franking Officer.")
Recd. at m. Date (1) From By

TO C's C All Coys
FOURTH LEICESTERS

Sender's Number LEA 121 | Day of Month 29th | In reply to Number | AAA

RELIEF You will be relieved tonight by A Company of the fifth LINCOLN regiment AAA When relieved you will proceed independently to your previous billets in DRANOUTRE reporting to BN H Q in person as soon as you have been completely relieved and that your Coy is intact or otherwise AAA Latrines must be filled in and refuse buried AAA Sick of A and B Coys parade at H Q at dusk those of C and D will be reported to

From
Place
Time
The above may be forwarded as now corrected. (Z)
Censor. Signature of Addressor or person authorised to telegraph in his name

Prefix Code m. Words Charge
Office of Origin and Service Instructions.
Sent At m. To By
This message is on a/c of: Service.
(Signature of "Franking Officer.")
Recd. at m. Date (2) From By

TO

Sender's Number | Day of Month | In reply to Number | AAA

H Q at once CAMP KETTLES will be sent to H Q at dusk to be handed to Sergt Major AAA Men bringing them down will remain at H Q and report to their Coys on arrival AAA HORSES Mounted Officers' horses will be at H Q ROUTINE tomorrow Reveille at 8.0 am Breakfast at 9.30 am Sick Parade at QMRS Stores at 11.0 am Battn Orderly Room at 11.30 am AAA Tomorrows rations will be found at Coy head quarters also

From
Place
Time
The above may be forwarded as now corrected. (Z)
Censor. Signature of Addressor or person authorised to telegraph in his name

Prefix ______ Code ______ m. | Words | Charge | This message is on a/c of: | Recd. at ______ m.

Office of Origin and Service Instructions.

Sent At ______ m. To ______ By ______ | Service. (Signature of "Franking Officer.") | Date ______ From ______ (3) By ______

TO

Sender's Number | Day of Month | In reply to Number | AAA

Blankets	AAA			
INDENTS	for	equipment	clothing	and
nccessaries	required	will	be	telephoned
to	H Q	by	E.O.	p.m.
tonight	AAA			
PARADE	STATES	covering	all	men
on	company	parade	list.	will
be	at	Bn	H Q	by
1 pm	tomorrow			
A	final	situation	and	work
report	will	be	sent	in
by	10.30	pm.	tonight	at
latest	AAA			
MACHINE	GUNS	The	machine	guns
and	one	NCO	and	four
men	per	gun	will	remain
in	the	trenches		

From ______ Place ______ Time ______

The above may be forwarded as now corrected. (Z)

Censor. Signature of Addressor or person authorised to telegraph in his name

---

Prefix ______ Code ______ m. | Words | Charge | This message is on a/c of: | Recd. at ______ m.

Office of Origin and Service Instructions.

Sent At ______ m. To ______ By ______ | Service. (Signature of "Franking Officer.") | Date ______ From ______ (4) By ______

TO

Sender's Number | Day of Month | In reply to Number | AAA

SUPPORTING	POINTS:	You	will	issue
the	necessary	orders	to	your
supporting	points.	The	officers	i/c
which	will	report	to	Bn
Hqrs	on	passing		

From ADJ 1/4 LEICESTERS

Place

Time 3.48 pm

The above may be forwarded as now corrected. (Z) [illegible]

Censor. Signature of Addressor or person authorised to telegraph in his name

SECRET. Copy No. 5

OPERATION ORDER Number 8

-by-

BRIGADIER GENERAL W. R. CLIFFORD

Commanding 1/1st Lincoln & Leicester Inf.Bde.T.F.

Headquarters,
12th April, 1915.

1. Trench Battalions will be relieved on nights of 12/13 and 13/14 instant.
   (a) The 4th LEICESTER REGIMENT will relieve the ~~5th~~ 5th LINCOLN REGIMENT on night of the 12/13th inst.
   (b) 5th LEICESTER REGIMENT will relieve the 4th LINCOLN REGIMENT on night 13/14 instant.

2. The Relieving Battalions will arrive (a) at ONETREE FARM and (b) at PACKHORSE FARM at 8-30 p.m. each night, where they will be met by guides from Battalions to be relieved. Reliefs will commence at 9 p.m.

3. TRANSPORT. Transport of the Relieving Battalion will follow in rear of the Battalion. Transport of the Battalion to be relieved will follow in rear of the relieving Battalion.Transport On night 13/14 4th LEICESTER Transport will be passed PACKHORSE FARM by 8 p.m.

4. BILLETS. The 5th LINCOLN REGIMENT and 4th LINCOLN REGIMENT will return to billets in the DRANOUTRE AREA when relieved.

5. REPORTS. Relieving Battalions will report by telegraph when the relief is completed.

R L Adlercron,
Major,

Brigade Major, 1/1 Linc. & Leic. Inf. Bde T.F.

Issued by Cyclist Orderly at to:-

Copy No. 1 Brigade Major for Brigadier
2 Staff Captain.
3. 4th Lincoln Regiment.
4. 5th Lincoln Regiment.
×5. 4th Leicester Regiment.
6. 5th Leicester Regiment.
7. War Diary.

13

S E C R E T.

Copy no. 5

OPERATION ORDER Number 9

-by-

BRIGADIER GENERAL W. R. CLIFFORD

Commanding 1/1st Lincoln & Leicester Inf.Bde.T.F.

Headquarters,
15th April,1915.

1. Trench Battalions will be relieved on nights of 16/17 and 17/18 instant.
   (a) The 5th LINCOLN REGIMENT will relieve the 4th LEICESTER REGIMENT on night of the 16/17 instant.
   (b) The 4th Lincoln Regiment will relieve the 5th LEICESTER REGIMENT on night 17/18 instant.

2. The Relieving Battalions will arrive (a) at ONE TREE FARM and (b) at PACKHORSE FARM at 8-30 p.m. each night, where they will be met by guides from Battalions to be relieved. Reliefs will commence at 9 p.m.

3. TRANSPORT. The arrangements for transport will be those detailed in Trench Routine Order No. 5 para. 1. On night of the 16/17 instant the 5th Leicester Transport will follow in rear of the 5th Lincoln Transport. On night of the 17/18 5th Lincoln Transport will follow in rear of the 4th Lincoln Transport. The 4th Lincoln Transport making way to allow the 5th Lincoln Transport to pass at PACKHORSE FARM.

4. MACHINE GUNS. Attention is directed to Trench Routine Orders No. 8 of 15/4/15.

5. BILLETS. The 4th Leicester Regiment and 5th Leicester Regiment will return to Billets in the DRANOUTRE AREA when relieved.

6. REPORTS. Relieving Battalions will report by telegraph when the relief is completed.

[illegible signature] Major,
Brigade Major, 1/1st Linc. & Leics. Inf. Bde. T.F.

Issued by Cyclist
Orderly at .m. to :-

Copy No. 1 Brigade Major for Brigadier
2. Staff Captain
3. 4th Lincoln Regiment
4. 5th Lincoln Regiment
5. 4th Leicester Regiment
6. 5th Leicester Regiment
7. WAR DIARY.

SECRET.   Copy No. 5

OPERATION ORDER Number 11

-:by:-

BRIGADIER GENERAL W. R. CLIFFORD

Commanding 1/1 Lincs. & Leics. Inf. Bde. T. F.

Headquarters
19th April, 1915.

1. Trench Battalions will be relieved on nights of 20/21 and 22/23 instant.

(a) The 4th LEICESTER REGIMENT will relieve the 5th LINCOLN REGIMENT on night of the 20/21 instant.

(b) The 5th LEICESTER REGIMENT will relieve the 4th LINCOLN REGIMENT on night of the 22/23 instant.

2. The Relieving Battalions will arrive (a) at ONE TREE FARM and (b) at PACKHORSE FARM at 8-45 p.m. each night, where they will be met by guides from Battalions to be relieved. Reliefs will commence at 9-15 p.m.

3. TRANSPORT. The arrangements for Transport will be those detailed in Trench Routine Order No. 9 Part II paragraph 3. On nightn of the 20/21 instant the 4th Lincoln Transport will follow in rear of the 4th Leicester Regiment. On night of 22/23rd instant the 4th Leicester Transport will move after the 4th Lincoln Transport but in front of the 5th Leicester Regiment passing PACKHORSE at 8-15 p.m.

4. BILLETS. The 5th Lincoln and 4th Lincoln Regiments will return to Billets in the DRANOUTRE AREA when relieved.

5. REPORTS. Relieving Battalions will report by telegraph when the relief is completed.

R. L. Adlercron Major,
Brigade Major, 1/1 Linc. & Leic. Inf. Bde. T.F.

Issued by Cyclist
Orderly at 11.30 p.m. to :-

Copy No. 1. Brigade Major for Brigadier.
2. Staff Captain,
3. 4th Lincoln Regt.
4. 5th Lincoln Regt.
5. 4th Leicester Regiment.
6. 5th Leicester Regiment.
7. WAR DIARY.

Copy No 1. a

OPERATION ORDERS No 10
by
MAJOR T. T. GRESSON D. S. O.
COMMANDING 1/4TH BATTALION LEICESTERSHIRE RGT.

Bn. Headquarters,
30/4/'15

Ref. BELGIUM, sheet 28, 1/40,000
and plan of trenches.

1 INFORMATION.- The Battalion will relieve the 1/5th Bn. Lincolnshire Regiment this night.

2 INSTRUCTIONS.-
STARTING POINT.- 600 yards S. of DRANOUTRE CHURCH.
TIME.- 7-30 p.m.
ORDER OF MARCH.- Guides, H.Q., "C", "D", "A", "B" Coys. Transport.
DRESS.- F.S.M.O. wearing Great Coats.
AMMUNITION.- 170 rounds per man
DETAILS.- M.Gunners, Signallers for trenches and Dug outs, and Police will parade with their Coys.
TRENCHES will be taken over as under.

"D" Coy. E1. R one officer and 30 men L- one officer and 20 men
E3 One officer and 35 men
E6 One officer and 50 men.
Any surplus men from "D" Coy. in Sp2a and Sp2b.

"C" " E8. Two officers and 40 men
F2. Two officers and 100 men
Surplus in Sp2b.

"B" " Completes Sp2a and Sp2b if not already containing one officer and 25 and one officer and 50 respectively, with remainder in NEWPORT DUG OUTS.

"A" " In NEWPORT DUG OUTS.

The above are the minimum garrisons.
MACHINE GUNS Will be taken over as under.
E3, E8, F2 Sp2a.
by 1/4th Bn. Leicestershire Regiment, 6 men per gun.
SP2b, by 1/4th Lincolnshire Regiment.

GUARDS.- permanent Guards will be found at each end of NEWPORT DUG OUTS, and also at Sp2a and Sp2b.

REPORTS.- As per trench standing Orders.

sd/ R.S.DYER-BENNET Capt. & Adjt.
1/4th Bn. Leicestershire Regiment.

Issued by Cyclist orderly at 12 noon.

Copy No 1 War Diary
2 do
3 Adjutant, for C.O.
4 1/1st Linc. & Leic. Inf. Bde.
5 O. C. "A" Coy.
6 "B" "
7 "C" "
8 "D" "
9 Transport Officer
10 Machine Gun Officer
11 Medical Officer
12 Quartermaster.

S E C R E T. Copy No. 5

1 B.

OPERATION ORDER Number 12
by
BRIGADIER GENERAL W. R. CLIFFORD
Commanding 1/1 Lincs. & Leics. Infty. Bde. T.F.

Headquarters
24th April, 1915.

1. Trench Battalions will be relieved on nights of 24/25th and 26/27th instant.

   (a) The 5th LINCOLN REGIMENT will relieve the 4th LEICESTER REGIMENT on night 24/25th.

   (b) The 4th LINCOLN REGIMENT will relieve the 5th LEICESTER REGIMENT on night 26/27th.

2. The Relieving Battalions will arrive (a) at ONE TREE FARM and (b) at PACKHORSE FARM at 8-45 p.m. each night where they will be met by guides from Battalions to be relieved. Reliefs will commence at 9-15 p.m.

3. TRANSPORT. The arrangements for Transport will be those detailed in Trench Routine Order No. 9 Part II paragraph 3.

4. The 4th LEICESTER REGIMENT and 5th LEICESTER REGIMENT will return to Billets in the Dranoutre Area when relieved.

5. REPORTS. Relieving Battalions will report by telegraph when the relief is completed.

R. L. Peterson Major,

Brigade Major, 1/1 Linc. & Leic. Inf.Bde.
T.F.

Issued by Cyclist
Orderly at 11 a.m. to:-
Copy No. 1. Brigade Major for Brigadier.
2. Staff Captain.
3. 4th Lincoln Regiment.
4. 5th Lincoln Regiment.
5. 4th Leicester Regiment.
6. 5th Leicester Regiment.
7. WAR DIARY.

10 la

Recd
8 pm
24.4.15.

S E C R E T.

Copy No. 5

OPERATION ORDER Number 13
by
BRIGADIER GENERAL W. R. CLIFFORD
Commanding 1/1 Lincs. & Leics. Infty. Bde. T.F.

Headquarters,
27th April, 1915.

1. Trench Battalions will be relieved on nights of 28/29, and 30 Apl/1 May.

   (a) The 4th LEICESTER REGIMENT will relieve the 5th LINCOLN REGIMENT on night28/29th instant.

   (b) The 5th LEICESTER REGIMENT will relieve the 4th LINCOLN REGIMENT on night 30 Apl/1st May.

2. The Relieving Battalions will arrive (a) at ONE TREE FARM and (b) at PACKHORSE FARM at 9-0. p.m. each night where they will be met by guides from Battalions to be relieved. Reliefs will commence at 9-30 p.m.

3. TRANSPORT. The arrangements for Transport will be those detailed in Trench Routine Order No. 9 Part II paragraph 3.

4. The 4th LINCOLN REGIMENT and 5th LINCOLN REGIMENT will return to Billets in the DRANOUTRE AREA when relieved.

5. REPORTS. Relieving Battalions will report by telegraph when the relief is completed.

sd/ R. L. ADLERCRON, Major,

Brigade Major, 1/1 Linc. & Leic. Inf. Bde.
T.F.

Issued by Cyclist
Orderly at 9 p.m. to:-

Copy No. 1. Brigade Major for Brigadier.
2. Staff Captain.
3. 4th Lincoln Regiment.
4. 5th Lincoln Regiment.
5. 4th Leicester Regiment.
6. 5th Leicester Regiment.
7. WAR DIARY.

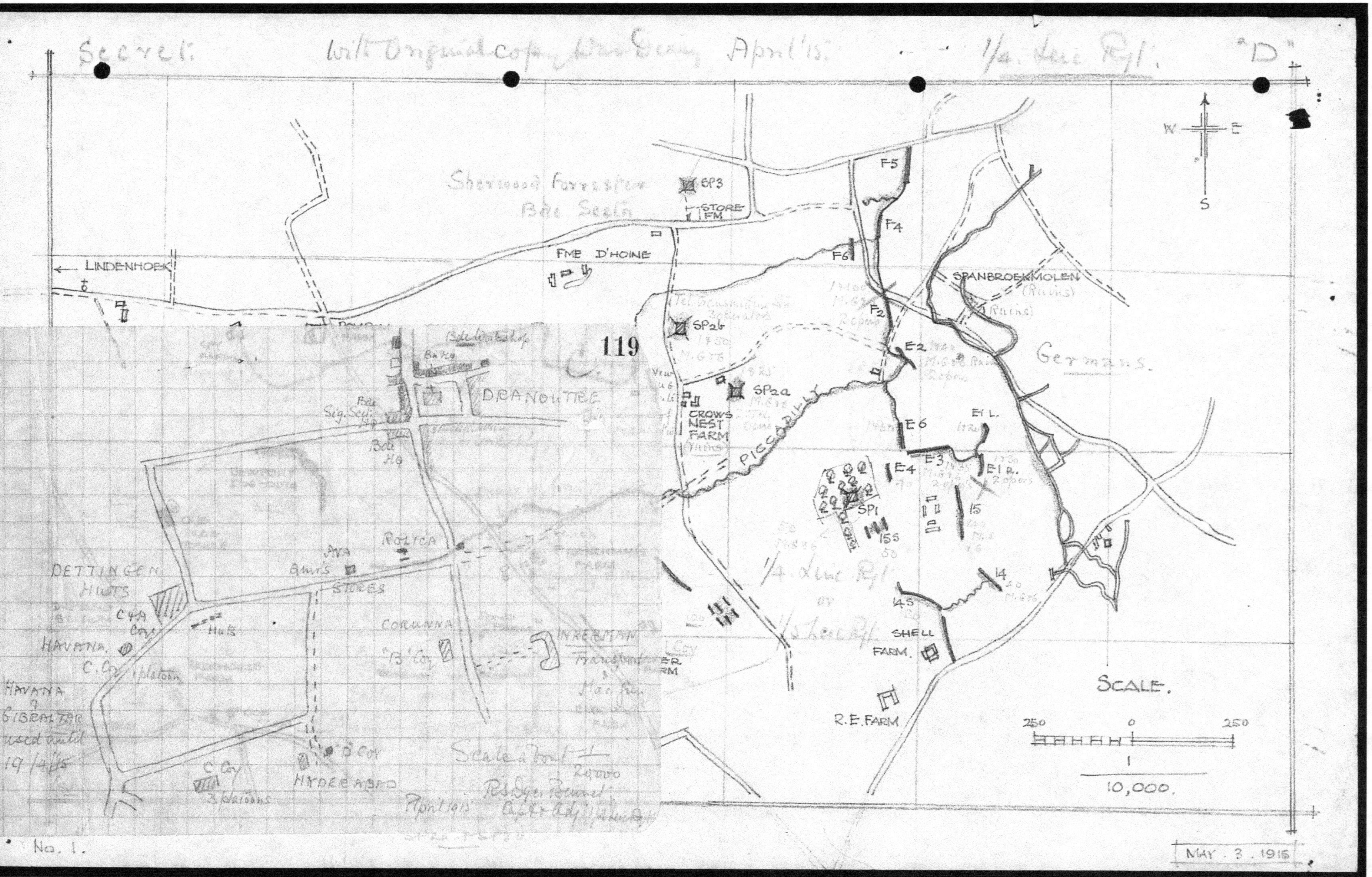

Secret.
"D"
W
E
S
LINDENHOEK
Sherwood Forresters
FME D'HOINE
SP3
STORE FM
F5
F4
F6
F2
E2
E6
E3
E4
E1 L.
E1 R.
SPANBROEKMOLEN
(Ruins)
Germans.
SP2b
SP2a
CROWS NEST FARM
PICCADILLY
SP1
15
14
155
145
1/4. Line Ryl.
SHELL FARM.
R. E. FARM
SCALE.
250
0
250
1
10,000.
119
DRANOUTRE
Bde Sig. Sect. HQ
Bde HQ
DETTINGEN HUTS
HAVANA
C. Coy
Huts
STORES
CORUNNA
'B' Coy
INKERMAN
FARM
'D' Coy
HYDERABAD
C Coy
3 platoons
HAVANA & GIBRALTAR used until 19/4/15
April 1915
No. 1.
MAY . 3 . 1915

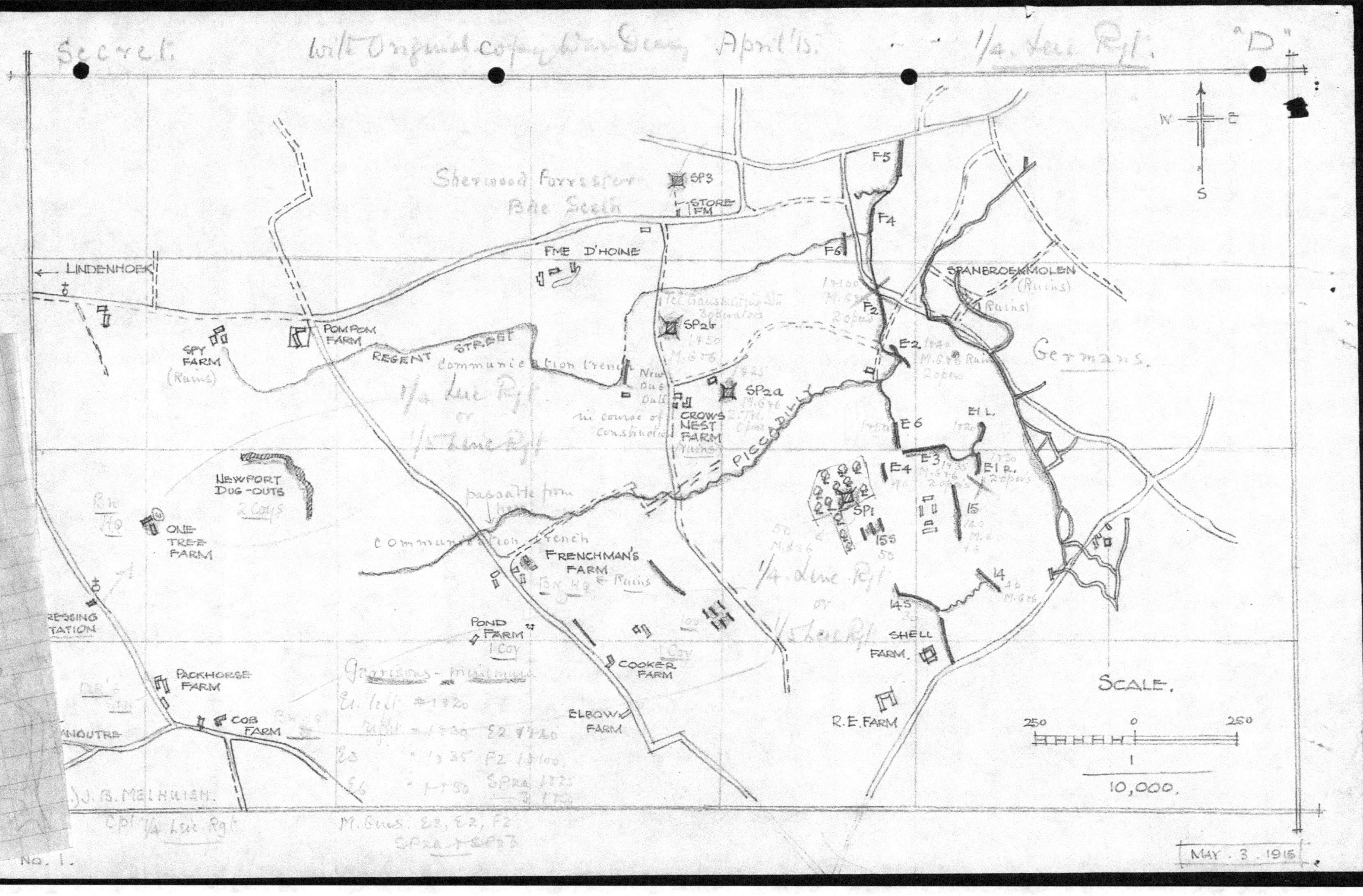

Secret.
1/4. Leic Rgt.
"D"
W
E
S
Sherwood Forrester
LINDENHOEK
SP3
STORE FM
FME D'HOINE
F5
F4
F6
F2
E2
SPANBROEKMOLEN
(Ruins)
Germans.
SP2b
SP2a
POM POM FARM
SPY FARM
(Ruins)
REGENT STREET
Communication trench
1/4 Leic Rgt
or
1/5 Leic Rgt
in course of construction
CROWS NEST FARM
PICCADILLY
E6
E1 L.
E4
E3
E1 R.
SP1
15
155
NEWPORT DUG-OUTS
2 Coys
Bn HQ
ONE-TREE-FARM
Communication trench
FRENCHMAN'S FARM
Bn HQ
Ruins
14
14S
SHELL FARM.
DRESSING STATION
POND FARM
1 Coy
COOKER FARM
1 Coy
PACKHORSE FARM
COB FARM
ELBOW FARM
R.E. FARM
SCALE.
250
0
250
1
10,000.
Garrisons
J. B. MELHUISH.
Cpl 1/4 Leic Rgt
M. Guns. E3, E2, F2
SP2a + SP2b
No. 1.
MAY . 3 . 1915

138th Inf.Bde.
46th Div.

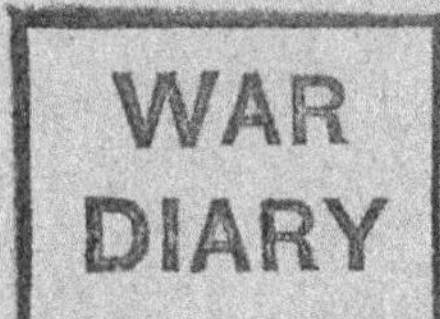

4th BATTN. THE LEICESTERSHIRE REGIMENT.

M A Y

1 9 1 5

Attached:

Appendices.

Confidential

1/4 Leicestershire Regt. 1/4 Leic Rgt. May '15 1/1st Lincs & Leic Bde 1/1st N. M. Divn

Instructions regarding War Diaries and Intelligence Summaries are contained in F. S. Regs., Part II. and the Staff Manual respectively. Title pages will be prepared in manuscript.

WAR DIARY
or
INTELLIGENCE SUMMARY.
(*Erase heading not required.*)

Army Form C. 2118.

1.

Place	Date May 1915	Hour	Summary of Events and Information	Remarks and references to Appendices
Trenches	1st		Light rain early a.m.	
A & B Coys in fire trenches C & D in the Newport [illegible]			Quiet night 30th Ap/1st May, but large number of bullets going v. high over Dug Outs – one man (4/5 Leic Rgt.) hit near Packhorse Fm. Reason – Germans had parties out mending parapet where broken [illegible] their sentries fired high(?) – this has been noticed before.	Casualties. 1 N.C.O. killed 2nd [illegible] F2 [illegible] 2 wounded E1 [illegible] standing on platform Same bullet
		4 a.m.	C.O. returned from visit to trenches 4 a.m. Adj out.	
		Over	Aeroplanes v. busy over Ger. lines	
			Fine & warm day – very quiet on both sides.	1 wounded in E1 night
		6 p.m.	Star Shell dropped from aeroplane – observed from fire trenches reported by 2 Lt. Clarke from SP2 [illegible]. This was followed by v. heavy shelling by enemy. No damage done. Our guns replied & apparently shut enemy up. Ger. Shells – High explosive & Shrapnel – all 200x W. of F2 – F4 & Northwards.	
			Ger. parapets damaged & working parties afforded good targets at night.	
			4.7" shells somewhat erratic – 1 short [illegible] SP2a – did not burst.	
	Evening		Captain Faire out with E1 listening post saw 2 or 3 Germans working with planks & about 12 came [illegible] or covering. Faire & his 4 men with [illegible] & lead. Ger. came to within 9 or 10x. Germans disappeared eventually [illegible] so. It seems that enemy must be sapping towards E1 or perhaps E15. Faire should have shot them	

1577 Wt. W10791/1773 500,000 1/15 D. D. & L. A.D.S.S./Forms/C. 2118.

1/4 Leic. Rgt [illegible] Bde. 1/1st N.M. Div.

Army Form C. 2118.

2.

Instructions regarding War Diaries and Intelligence Summaries are contained in F. S. Regs., Part II. and the Staff Manual respectively. Title pages will be prepared in manuscript.

WAR DIARY
or
INTELLIGENCE SUMMARY.

(Erase heading not required.)

Place	Date May 1915	Hour	Summary of Events and Information	Remarks and references to Appendices
Trenches	1st	Early am	Fain's reason being he wanted to leave them with feeling of security. Has lost opportunity of securing prisoner or even dead German?	
		6 pm	Small flag seen on Ger. parapet opp. S. end E1 left - fired at & withdrawn to be replaced by blue & white flag & man apparently in civilian cap & jacket. About same place - lamp on metal rod noticed. This was removed on being fired at.	
			2 for Rifle Grenades used during day - were apparently successful in 50% of cases. [illegible initials]	
	2nd	3.15 am	2 Lt K DALGLIESH wounded severely in left arm & also somewhat in left leg going out to ordering E1 & Left listening post withdraw. Brought down to E3 & fitted in by M.O. probably saving his life by prompt & skilled attention. Dalgliesh considered he had been careless in running out, but bullet was probably a chance shot. A quiet day.	Casualties 1 Officer wounded E1 [illegible] 2 O.R. wounded
		6.30 pm	Secret communication that relief to be 3 hrs later than arranged and orders issued	

Army Form C. 2118. 3

3.

1/4 Linc Rgt — 1/1st L & L Bde — 1/1st N.M. Div

Instructions regarding War Diaries and Intelligence Summaries are contained in F. S. Regs., Part II. and the Staff Manual respectively. Title pages will be prepared in manuscript.

WAR DIARY
or
INTELLIGENCE SUMMARY.
(*Erase heading not required.*)

Place	Date May 1915.	Hour	Summary of Events and Information	Remarks and references to Appendices
Trenches	2nd	6.30 pm	to observe & report on bullets coming over at Bn H.Q., Newport Dug Outs, Piccadilly & end of (E) Regent St. Very few except from neighbourhood of last bend in Regent St where large no. came over. No apparent attempt being made to fire on special points in rear of fire trenches.	
			The Bde Orderly who brought the Secret Orders re. relief came up to Bn H.Q. in full daylight with Orderly for 1/5 Linc Rgt. Spotted?	Casualties. 1 O.R. severely wounded in Vigo St 100 N of Piccadilly died on way to Dressing Stn.
			Working party 'C' Coy to complete VIGO St (comm trench betn Regent St & Piccadilly) & ... party under ...	
	2/3	11.30 pm 11.45	1/5 Linc. Rgt arrived to relieve. Relief commenced	
"	3rd	1-50 am	Relief completed. N.B. Captain L. Cowan ... for this Bn being sick in billets. R.S.B.	1 O.R. slightly wounded during relief 400 W of F2 - hand
DRANOUTRE			Fine & warm day	
		5.30 pm	C.O. questioned all officers on Routine & other ... R.S.B.	1 O.R. wounded severely in ... & body.
	4th	12.30 pm	Vast competition for Temporary Commissions in Reg Army & that C.O. unable to take any steps without impairing efficiency of Bn.	... 2 ... 13 ...
		5.30 pm	C.O. examined N.C.Os on T.R.C. (A & B Coys) - gt improvement shewn	

1577 Wt. W10791/1773 500,000 1/15 D. D. & L. A.D.S.S./Forms/C. 2118.

1/4 Leic. Rgt. **WAR DIARY** or ~~INTELLIGENCE SUMMARY.~~ 1/1st L & L Bde 1/1st N. M. Div

(Erase heading not required.)

Army Form C. 2118. 4

Instructions regarding War Diaries and Intelligence Summaries are contained in F. S. Regs., Part II. and the Staff Manual respectively. Title pages will be prepared in manuscript.

Place	Date May 1915	Hour	Summary of Events and Information	Remarks and references to Appendices
DRANOUTRE	4th	Even'g	'C' Coy working on VIGO St - communication trench betn Piccadilly & Regent St.	Casualties 1 OR wounded 200 W. of W. end Regent St.
			'D' " — — New Dug Outs in valley rear of ground betn SP2a & SP2b under RE supervision.	
			Above parties worked from 9 pm. till about 2 am. 5th	
			RSDB	
"	5th	pm. 4.45	Bomb & grenade lecture & demonstration by 2. Lt. Russell & Lt A.A. Ellwood at CORUNNA Fm	
		5.45	C.O. examined N.C.O's of 'C' & 'D' on T.R.O. same place.	
			Bde O.O. No 15. Copy No 5 recd. 2 Lt R.C. Harvey granted 48 hrs leave to go to BOULOGNE to see brother & people RSDB	Copy No 5 attached
"	6th	am 10.30	C.O. inspected 'C' Coy - gt improvement in turn out & general efficiency	
		2.30 pm	C.O. saw Os C. Coys re. gasses used by Germans	
		4.50	L.A. 25 re. postponement of time of relief - i.e. alteration in Bde O.O. 15 - received	LA 25 attached
		6.45	Orders to stand fast until further orders issued to all concerned	Copies issued of orders attached
		9.0	" re. starting time issued to all concerned	
		10.	Transport passed thro' DRANOUTRE	

1577 Wt. W10791/1773 500,000 1/15 D. D. & L. A.D.S.S./Forms/C. 2118.

Instructions regarding War Diaries and Intelligence Summaries are contained in F. S. Regs., Part II. and the Staff Manual respectively. Title pages will be prepared in manuscript.

WAR DIARY
or
INTELLIGENCE SUMMARY.

(*Erase heading not required.*)

1/4th Leic. Regt. 1/1st L. & L. Bde. 1/1st N. M. Divn.

Army Form C. 2118. 5

Place	Date May 1915.	Hour	Summary of Events and Information	Remarks and references to Appendices
DRANOUTRE	6th	pm. 10.15	Bn started for trenches. Lt. F. S. Parr sick in billets.	
		11.30	— arrived ONE TREE Fm. 187 German pattern respirators issued.	
		12. mn	Relief commenced. "C" in E1 R & L, E3, E6 & S P20 (21 men & 2/Lt Clarke from "D"). "D" in E2, E2 and [illegible] men of B in S P23 [illegible] including [illegible]	
Trenches	7th	am. 2.10	Relief completed. Very quiet night - fairly bright - early morning mist.	
			Adjutant visited all trenches & supporting points. Nothing unusual occurred.	
		11.30.	2Lt R. C. HARVEY returned to DRANOUTRE from 48 hrs leave.	
			CO. & MO. visited trenches returning 3.30 pm.	
			Platoon worked from 9 [illegible] [illegible] paying special attention to drains.	
		pm. 2.15	Our artillery shelling [illegible] & enemy shelling E15.	
		8.45	Received 4 KNAPSACK SPRAYS for use on [illegible] screens for use by [illegible] when enemy using gasses. Screens [illegible] muslin on frame [illegible] stretched across. Hyposulphite of soda [illegible] for spraying. All men now in possession of respirators of various kinds. Salt & [illegible] in the trenches as emetics. Arrangements made to connect telephone [illegible] wires on high part of parapets so to ensure [illegible] of communication [illegible]. Now experiencing difficulty in finding enough men for R.E. work & ration [illegible] parties. Draft badly needed - also officers. [illegible]	[illegible] Bonfire wood sent [illegible] R.E. [illegible] signals [illegible] [illegible] [illegible] using gasses

1577 Wt. W10791/1773 500,000 1/15 D. D. & L. A.D.S.S./Forms/C. 2118.

1/4 [illegible] Rgt 1/1st [illegible] Bde 1/1st N.M. Divn

Army Form C. 2118.

6.

Instructions regarding War Diaries and Intelligence Summaries are contained in F. S. Regs., Part II. and the Staff Manual respectively. Title pages will be prepared in manuscript.

WAR DIARY
or
INTELLIGENCE SUMMARY.
(Erase heading not required.)

Place	Date May 1915	Hour	Summary of Events and Information	Remarks and references to Appendices
Trenches	8th	am 4.15	Last working party returned – Shows were kept at it	1 O.R. wounded
			Orders rec'd to wire in front of E2 & F2.	
			Quiet day – started permanent look-out men at Bn H.Q. with A.B. 153 for notes of observers.	
			These O.B.'s go to pt 20x N. of Fm during day & into roof by night.	
			Mistake made by R.E. about staples for wiring – put on [illegible] wagon with tools for Regent St Dug Outs. Wiring : not done.	
			Adj visited all trenches & SPs & listening posts (E1 R. rt post, E1 L. left post) all normal.	
			R.S.O.R.	
–	9th		Just after midnight 8/9 5 grenades – possibly hand – arrived just short of E1 L. A similar reply quietened them.	
			Peaceful day	
		5pm	Our guns fired over E1 R, but seemed to pitch well over. caught supports?	
		4-0 to 4.30	Just previous to this, Brit aeroplane brought down Ger. Plane – which nosed down into Ger lines	
		6.45 to 7.15	V. heavy art. fire on both sides	
		7.10	E2 mine exploded rather livening matters up. 15x to 20x Ger parapet blown up according to report	
			About this time E1 R & L bombarded MESSINES – 2500x bearing of 124°	
			for ¼ hr "rapid". This brought on heavy German	

1577 Wt. W10791/1773 500,000 1/15 D. D. & L. A.D.S.S./Forms/C. 2118.

1/4 Leic. Rgt **WAR DIARY** *or* **INTELLIGENCE SUMMARY.** 1/1st L & L. Bde 1/1st N. M. Div.

(Erase heading not required.)

Army Form C. 2118.

Instructions regarding War Diaries and Intelligence Summaries are contained in F. S. Regs., Part II. and the Staff Manual respectively. Title pages will be prepared in manuscript.

Place	Date May 1915	Hour	Summary of Events and Information	Remarks and references to Appendices
Trenches	9th	Betn 7 & 7.45 pm	rifle fire and some shelling. Major T. T. Greeson slightly wounded when in E1 L & one Shrapnel in E6 burst just absolutely right unfortunately - 10 casualties. 30 hand & 20 rifle grenades used. Most of former fell short - but latter got home or v. near E1 R. certainly had Germans under this fire.	1 off 1 O.R. killed & 8 wounded in E6. 3 wounded in E1 L. C.O. not returned as casualty
			120x Fence & barbed wire put up from 21 (S. end) of E2 running N. by B Coy party in 1¾ hrs actual work. No casualties.	
			Adj visited all trenches	
	10th		(50 men employed) Very busy working on Vego St all day until finished except flooring (RE work)	
		pm 3.40	A few Ger. shells near Bn HQ. - retired to Dug Outs - nothing doing.	
			Change taking place in line - 1/4 Linc Rgt moving into Notts & Derby Sector - all battns in Bde in up near trenches.	
		pm 11.30	5 or 6 Germans (5th Bavarian Inf) bombed E1 left - causing garrison, somewhat weakened by listening posts, who saw nothing, to quit, all in authority having been killed or wounded. Full report by C.O. attached. Marked X.	1 Off killed [illegible] 1 O.R. " 8 " wounded E1 L
			1/5 Linc Rgt arrived to relieve.	
	11th	am 12.30	Situation normal again.	1 O.R. killed 1 " wounded E1 R
		2.10	Relief completed. Bn drifted home - disgusted on a/c of no proper show.	

1577 Wt. W10791/1773 500,000 1/15 D. D. & L. A.D.S.S./Forms/C. 2118.

1/4 Leic Rgt. **WAR DIARY** 1/1st Linc & Leic Bde

or

INTELLIGENCE SUMMARY.

1/1st N. Mid. Div.

(Erase heading not required.)

Army Form C. 2118.

8

Instructions regarding War Diaries and Intelligence Summaries are contained in F. S. Regs., Part II. and the Staff Manual respectively. Title pages will be prepared in manuscript.

Place	Date	Hour	Summary of Events and Information	Remarks and references to Appendices
DRANOUTRE	May 1915 11th		C.O. investigated E1 L affair immediately on return. Identity disc 645 → N. R. (...) ... (... Company) TRANSP... Effects of dead German in E1 L. handed in to Bde – Mauser rifle & pistol, good deal of ammunition – watch shows fast but keeping good time. German time is 1 hr ahead of us. Captain HAYLOCK's funeral at ONE TREE Fm	R.E.D.B.
Billets	12th		Interior Economy – R.E. instruction for Officers & N.C.Os. 1/1 L & L Bde becomes 138th Inf Bde, 1/1 N.M. Divn – 46th Divn. 'A' & 'B' Coys worked on 2nd Line G.H.Q. from 9 pm to 2 am 13th inst.	R.E.D.B. Instructions & ... attached
	13th		C.O. & those concerned to Divl H.Q. to see G.O.C. in ... ... Coy Officers & N.C.Os (full) under R.E. again	R.E.D.B.
	14th		Prepared to move into trenches W of MT KEMMEL – but move cancelled	
		4 pm	Instructions to wire in front of F2 15/16 night recd	
		10.10	Bn moved to TRENCHES. Lt. H.C. BRICE rejoined from Grenade Course. 2nd Lt F.M. WAITE joined 2 ...	Bde
	(approx)	11.15	– arrived ONE TREE Fm	
		11.45	– commenced relief. 'A' Coy ... E1 R, L, E3 & E2. 'B' Coy E6, E2 & F2. 'D' ... SP2A & remainder in Reserve ... 'C' Coy in ...	
2/Lt M.B. DOUGLAS his servant & 2 men Bn to ST OMER for Mac. Gun Course Evening	15th	2 am	Relief completed – Adj. accompanied relief – visited listening posts ... had been somewhat altered. New work ... Sap ... New Sap 20, New trench E4 ... We are now Rt Sector of 138th Bde (46th Divn) 4/Lincs ... Staffs Bde (137th Bde) on our rt (S) & on our left (N) Notts & Derby Bde (139th Bde). About 150x French wire laid – operations curtailed. CAPTAIN A.C. COOPER – badly wounded & men brought in – most of them somewhat ... – see over. Quiet day	R.E.D.B. 2 OR killed (12 noon 16.5.15)

1577 Wt. W10791/1773 500,000 1/15 D. D. & L. A.D.S.S./Forms/C. 2118.

Instructions regarding War Diaries and Intelligence Summaries are contained in F. S. Regs., Part II. and the Staff Manual respectively. Title pages will be prepared in manuscript.

WAR DIARY *or* INTELLIGENCE SUMMARY.

(*Erase heading not required.*)

1/4 Leic Rgt 138th Inf Bde 46th Div

Army Form C. 2118.

9

Place	Date	Hour	Summary of Events and Information	Remarks and references to Appendices
	May 1915		CO & Adj round fire trenches	
Trenches	16th	am 12.15	Captain A. C. COOPER out in front of centre of F2 with wiring party & 2nd Lt R.C. HARVEY — badly wounded — probably by ricochet off tree. Smashed left hand and two left through into inside. Brought back over parapet by Cpl. BROWN (No.) & Sapper	Casualties CAPTAIN A.C. COOPER killed
			thence taken to Bn Dressing Stn & carefully tended — but heart weak	
		am 6.30	Captain COOPER died.	
			V. quiet day — fine but cold.	
		pm 8.30	Germans got busy with rifles — but were "downed" at once with a salvo from 2nd [illegible].	
		about midnight	2 Lt. R.C. HARVEY, 1 cpl & 3 men continued wiring front of F2. no troubles	
	17th	am 1.30	Lt H.C BRICE & 3 grenadiers went out from rt (S) of E1R & threw 8 grenades at little "work" of Germans ¼ rt from E1 R. One didn't explode, rest seemed all right.	
			Listening posts thought Germans relieved last night — SAXONS out — BAVARIANS in	
			Wet & "muggy" day after promising start.	
		am 8.30 to 12 noon	V. heavy firing could be heard to S & S.W. British & Fr pushing on.	
			Our line v. quiet all day.	
		pm about 8.30	N. Staffs reported ~~to have~~ seeing civilian in rear (W.) of com. trench betn E4 & 15. [alter state N. Staffs ... of 15 ...]	
			No patrols sent out by us — lack of enterprise. Staffs didn't get him.	
			Received information that Germans are now poisoning the water running from their trenches — not unexpected from THEM.	
			Very dark night — "going" awful.	

1577 Wt. W10791/1773 500,000 1/15 D. D. & L. A.D.S.S./Forms/C. 2118.

RSM [illegible]

Instructions regarding War Diaries and Intelligence Summaries are contained in F. S. Regs., Part II. and the Staff Manual respectively. Title pages will be prepared in manuscript.

1/4. Leic Rgt

WAR DIARY
or
~~INTELLIGENCE SUMMARY.~~

138th Inf Bde
46th Divn

(Erase heading not required.)

Army Form C. 2118.

10.

Place	Date May 1915	Hour	Summary of Events and Information	Remarks and references to Appendices
Trenches	18th		Adj round fire trenches – during night ~~working~~ [illegible] for carrying parties [illegible] late back (not about 4.30am)	1 O.R. killed
			Arrangements made to dump trench stores at E6 & E3 corner – E2 & F2 junc at NEW DUG OUTS – at Bn HQ – all above [illegible] hurried [illegible] forward from trenches.	
			CO round fire trenches 5pm to 7.30pm	
			Very wet & cold day – particularly towards evening.	N.B. [illegible]
			Hardly any artillery fire & battle sounds from S only just audible.	[illegible]
		pm 9.3	Red Very light sent up from E2 & F2 junction in error. Gunners never saw it [illegible]	[illegible] hand [illegible]
			[illegible] Bde. Disaster (to Germans) averted	[illegible] down
		10.30	1/5 Leic Rgt arrived to relieve. [illegible] delay in commencing [illegible] – some [illegible]	Piccadilly [illegible]
		11.30	Relief commenced – a v. slow job, the going being awful & men [illegible] in [illegible] trenches	[illegible]
			[illegible] outside, with result that	ONE TREE Fm
	19th		Relief completed	
DRANOUTRE		am 4	Bn got back to billets	
		12 noon	[illegible] inspected by A.D.M.S. [illegible]	[illegible]
	20th	3	Germans 85 exploded mine under [illegible] of [illegible] not greatly damaged.	
		8.40	Orders to move [illegible] to [illegible] Adj visited [illegible]	
		4.55	C [illegible] 100 [illegible] extension westward of [illegible] D helped carry [illegible]	
		8/1012	D [illegible] 150 [illegible] 9pm	

1577 Wt. W10791/1773 500,000 1/15 D. D. & L. A.D.S.S./Forms/C. 2118.

1/4 Leic Rgt 138th

WAR DIARY
or
INTELLIGENCE SUMMARY.
(Erase heading not required.)

Instructions regarding War Diaries and Intelligence Summaries are contained in F. S. Regs., Part II. and the Staff Manual respectively. Title pages will be prepared in manuscript.

Place	Date May 1915	Hour	Summary of Events and Information
DRANOUTRE	21st		Party of 1 + 30 urgently called for to help [illegible]
			Digging at [illegible] [illegible] [illegible] Fine [illegible]
			Bn moved into bivouac* on slope W of KEMMEL [illegible]
		6 pm	Divine Service close to Bivouac. H.Q. remained in DRANOUTRE
		8.30 pm	Mine opp "12" exploded & 15 to 20 Ger. parapet downed [illegible]
	22nd	10 am	Two C.S.M. of [illegible] Leic Rgt [illegible] (a) Stealing from Comrades [illegible] (b) Deserting his post [illegible] [illegible] charges 18 [illegible]
			Very fine & warm day. [illegible] FORSELL [illegible] CAPELLE [illegible]
			Major R E MARTIN arrived from 5 Leic Rgt to command [illegible]
			[illegible] to York & Lancs Rgt to command [illegible]
		9.15 pm	Bn to trenches. [illegible] all officers having gone up [illegible]
		10.30	— arrived
		10.45	Relief commenced. Capt [illegible] in command [illegible] 'D' Coy in E1, E1a, E3 & E4 'C' — in E6, E2 & P2 [illegible] & Regent St. C.O. 'A' in Newport [illegible]
	23rd	1.15 am	Relief completed. Continuous [illegible] work on [illegible] 2 bodies recovered
			V. fine & warm day
			C.O. made thorough inspection of fire trenches & SP27 — 7 hours inspecting. Enemy shelled Piccadilly & [illegible] most of afternoon — slightly damaged trench in places.

Rough Plan of Bivouac occupied by 1/4 Leics Rgt (T.F.) [illegible]

1577 Wt. W10791/1773 500,000 1/15 D. D. & L. A.D.S.S./Forms/C. 2118.

Instructions regarding War Diaries and Intelligence Summaries are contained in F. S. Regs., Part II. and the Staff Manual respectively. Title pages will be prepared in manuscript.

1/4 Leic Rgt 138th

WAR DIARY
or
INTELLIGENCE SUMMARY.

(Erase heading not required.)

Place	Date May 1915	Hour	Summary of Events and Information	Remarks and references to Appendices
DRANOUTRE	21st		Party of 1 & 30 urgently called for to help [illegible] Rgt [illegible] worked all day under Lt ABELL	
			Digging at present still going on. Fine & warm day	
			Bn moved into bivouac× on slope W of KEMMEL windmill (Transport & specialists to [illegible])	× [illegible] attached
		6 pm	Divine Service close to Bivouac. H.Q. remained in DRANOUTRE	
		8.30 pm	Mine opp 12 exploded & 15 to 20 Ger parapet downed. [illegible]	
			(F.P. No 1) RSB	
	22nd	10 am	Two C.S.M. of ½ Leic Rgt tried (1) Stealing from Comrades [illegible] (2) Deserting his post & causing unnecessary alarm [illegible] Charged [illegible] – [illegible] suspended	
			Very fine & warm day. (Lt FORSELL [illegible] St JAN CAPELLE for a rest – [illegible] down)	
			Major R E MARTIN arrived from 1/5 Leic Rgt to command 1/4 Leic Rgt & Major T. E. GRESSON DSO to return to York & Lancs Rgt to command after rest at St Jan CAPELLE [illegible]	went to U.K. eventually
		9.15 pm	Bn to trenches. Nearly all officers having gone up to take over trenches & stores at 6 pm	
		10.30	– arrived	
		10.45	Relief commenced → Captain [illegible] in command. "D" Coy in E1, R & 2, E3 & E4 "B" Coy SP2 & 7 & Regent St [illegible] "C" – in E6, E2 & F2 "A" in Newport [illegible]	RSB
	23rd	1.15 am	Relief completed. Continuous [illegible] work on E1 [illegible] 2 bodies recovered	
			V. fine & warm day	
			C.O. made thorough inspection of fire trenches & SP27 – 7 hours inspection. Enemy shelled	
			Piccadilly & [illegible] most of afternoon. Slightly damaged trench in places	

Army Form C. 2118.

Instructions regarding War Diaries and Intelligence Summaries are contained in F. S. Regs., Part II. and the Staff Manual respectively. Title pages will be prepared in manuscript.

WAR DIARY
or
INTELLIGENCE SUMMARY.
(*Erase heading not required.*)

1/4 Leic. Rgt 138th Inf Bde 46th Divn

12

Place	Date May 1915	Hour	Summary of Events and Information	Remarks and references to Appendices
Trenches	23rd	–	E.R. garrison cleared out for howitzers to fire periodical shots on [illegible] each day	O.R. 3 wounded [illegible]
			Idea prevalent that enemy after mining E.R.	
			for grenades E.R. – garrison had to cease work & retire temporarily	
			Report rec'd (via F2) that Germans had blown up portion of their own [illegible] by mistake [illegible]	
			thought that they paid for this indiscretion later. This was opp. 12. [illegible] wounded [illegible]	
			General mob'n ordered in ITALY. [illegible] trenches	
			2nd in C round trenches by night. A 2nd in C at Bn HQ or new institution for this Bn. work made easier for C.O. & Adj.	
			R.E.D.B.	
	24th		Whit Monday. No holiday but glorious day for one.	
		a.m. 12.5	Red flare or rocket seen to N. of F2 just after midnight	O.R. 3 wounded (2 merely [illegible] scope wounds)
		3 am	ZEPPELIN reported from S.P. 2 [illegible] going N.W. [illegible] 5 or 6 miles away moving v. fast	
		6 am	TAUBE came over Bn H.Q.	
			Sounds of [illegible] firing [illegible] alarm.	
			ITALY declares war against AUSTRIA.	
		p.m. 12.30	Ant[i] gas bombs in E6 blew up – no one damaged – cause probably heat [illegible] – ammonia gas – very volatile [illegible] have the punctured. No other bombs or grenades went off. [illegible] 2 [illegible] damaged.	
			C.O. & Adj spent 8 hrs in Fire Trenches	
		6.16 p.m. 7.35	Regular little Art'y duel – mostly in Ex. H.Q. neighbourhood. No damage done. [illegible] parapet damaged opp F4.3	

1577 Wt. W10791/1773 500,000 1/15 D. D. & L. A.D.S.S./Forms/C. 2118.

Army Form C. 2118.

13

Instructions regarding War Diaries and Intelligence Summaries are contained in F. S. Regs., Part II. and the Staff Manual respectively. Title pages will be prepared in manuscript.

WAR DIARY
or
INTELLIGENCE SUMMARY.

(Erase heading not required.)

1/4. Leic. Rgt   138th Inf Bde. 46th Divn.

Place	Date May 1915	Hour	Summary of Events and Information	Remarks and references to Appendices
Trenches.	24th		Some damage apparently done opp E2. Result of our howitzers [illegible] [illegible] was [illegible] [illegible] [illegible]. ? [illegible] result of gas used [illegible]?	
		9.30 pm	[illegible] flare [illegible] thought to be German	
		9.40	[illegible]	
			Heavy rifle fire in Evening	
			During [illegible] portion of [illegible] one of our men got hit [illegible] outside Piccadilly mending wire [illegible] [illegible] pulled in by [illegible] [illegible] 2nd Staffs [illegible] one WEAVOR Regt No. 3	[illegible]
	25th	2.20 am	Reported [illegible] [illegible] ZEPPELIN going W. in early hours of morning [illegible] [illegible]	
	14th Inf Bde		Fine [illegible] warm day – very peaceful day	
			CO [illegible] from 9.15 am to [illegible] [illegible]	
		5.15 pm	Germans [illegible] fired [illegible] (N. of Pom-Pom) [illegible] [illegible] [illegible]	1 O.R. Killed
		8.45	Another heavy blaze S. of [illegible] Fm – probably [illegible] Fm [illegible] [illegible] [illegible] spreads rapidly. It appears that some one is busy burning [illegible] [illegible] [illegible] occupied by Germans [illegible] by Shell fire. [illegible] [illegible] [illegible] [illegible] [illegible] [illegible] [illegible] [illegible] Trip round all fire trenches [illegible] [illegible] [illegible] [illegible] [illegible]	[illegible]
	26th	3.30 am	G' plane came over Bn HQ. & Mt Kemmel – [illegible] [illegible] [illegible] [illegible] G' lines. Same manoeuvre performed later in day [illegible]	[illegible]
			V. quiet – holiday. CO round all trenches. [illegible] [illegible] [illegible]	[illegible]

1577 Wt. W10791/1773 500,000 1/15 D. D. & L. A.D.S.S./Forms/C. 2118.

Instructions regarding War Diaries and Intelligence Summaries are contained in F. S. Regs., Part II. and the Staff Manual respectively. Title pages will be prepared in manuscript.

1/4 Leic Rgt — 138th Inf Bde — 46th Divn.

WAR DIARY
or
INTELLIGENCE SUMMARY.
(Erase heading not required.)

Army Form C. 2118.

14

Place	Date May 1915	Hour	Summary of Events and Information	Remarks and references to Appendices
BIVOUAC DRANOUTRE	27th		C.O. inspected bivouacs. Promulgation of (1) 3 months F.P. No 1. for Stealing goods property of comrade & (2) 18 months Impt with H.L. for Deserting his post etc (suspended)	
			Apparently a quiet day. Warmish except in wind, which was v. cold - bright. Place becoming dusty	R.G.M.
	28th		Fine & fairly warm day. 81st Inf Bde under Brig. Gen H.L. CROKER (late Cmdg 1st Leic. Rgt) rested in DRANOUTRE en route for ARMENTIERES from YPRES. C.M. of 2 Ptes - (1) for drunkenness in trenches which should have been also for Not complying with an order etc & using threatening & insubordinate language to an N.C.O. - but these charges ordered to be withdrawn. Court acquitted accused on charge of B. in spite of officer's & 2 Sgts evidence. Result of civilian lawyer's quibbles? (2) Refusing to comply and using obscene language to an N.C.O. & found guilty - 12 months Impt with H.L.	for ARMENTIERES from YPRES.
			Interpreter Comte LIEDERKERKE goes to C.R.E. (who visited bivouacs about noon) & replaced by Belgian merchant service officer - M. . 7/R.B. of K's Army arrived for attachment & instruction	R.G.M.
	29th	10. am	G.O.C. 46th Divn held conference of C.O.s at 138th Inf Bde's H.Q. & afterwards visited bivouacs	
		noon 12.	C.O. inspected all coys - F.S.M.O. "A" & "B" good - C poor - & "D" pretty good except in wood deficiency.	Xmess tins - for which no reason found.
		pm 3.45	M.O. gave lecture to all officers - C.S.Ms & Platoon Sgts - Subject "Haemorrhage". C.O. talked to all officers on matters brought up at G.O.C's conference	
		8pm	French reported to be delivering an attack N. of YPRES. A quiet - bright & warm day.	R.G.M.

1577 Wt. W10791/1773 500,000 1/15 D. D. & L. A.D.S.S./Forms/C. 2118.

1/4. Leic Rgt   **WAR DIARY** *or* **INTELLIGENCE SUMMARY.**   138th Inf Bde. 46th Divn

(Erase heading not required.)

Army Form C. 2118.

15

Instructions regarding War Diaries and Intelligence Summaries are contained in F. S. Regs., Part II. and the Staff Manual respectively. Title pages will be prepared in manuscript.

Place	Hour, Date, Place (May 1915)	Hour	Summary of Events and Information	Remarks and references to Appendices
DRANOUTRE	30th	10am	Divine Service at foot of hill immediately W. of bivouac	Casualties
			C.R.E. & Bde Gen. Cmdg 138th Inf Bde present	Captain [illegible] [illegible]
		5pm	Officers [illegible] [illegible] [illegible] [illegible] Thrower [illegible]	[illegible] [illegible] [illegible]
		9.30pm	Bn quitted bivouac for trenches	wounded by rifle grenade
		10.30pm	" arrived [illegible]	2/Lt [illegible] rejoined
		11.20pm	Relief commenced late owing to necessity of rearranging	from [illegible] [illegible]
			distribution of officers. Major [illegible] to command [illegible]	[illegible] [illegible] to
				2/Lt J.F. [illegible] [illegible]
			Cold frosty night [illegible]	[illegible]
	31st	1.10am	Relief completed [illegible] [illegible]	
			[illegible] E4	
			(Bn also took over [illegible] for [illegible] [illegible])	Casualties
			"B" [illegible] E2 F2	1 O.R. wounded 4 Leic Rg
			C. SP8 (old [illegible]) SP9 (old [illegible]) [illegible] Regent St [illegible]	1 O.R. — 5/ [illegible]
			D. [illegible] [illegible] [illegible] [illegible]	afterwards died
			[illegible] [illegible] Piccadilly F2	
		9.15pm	C Coy 7/[illegible] came up [illegible] [illegible] [illegible] trenches	2 [illegible] in [illegible]
			as shown	3
			Quiet day except for enemy shelling [illegible] [illegible] F2 about 7.30pm	
			They appear to have [illegible] [illegible] range of [illegible] [illegible]	

A P P E N D I C E S .

CONFIDENTIAL C O P Y

For Original of War Diary p.7. May

Headquarters,
Lincoln & Leicester Brigade.

About 11-40 p.m. on 10th May I was attending the funeral service of the late 2/Lieut. A. C. Clarke at ONE TREE FARM when news was brought to me that E1 left was in possession of the Germans and that the garrison had been exterminated. I at once ordered Capt. A. C. Cooper to take whatever men he could collect of his Company ("B" Coy.) and make a counter attack on E1 left. I gave Capt. Newill ("A" Coy.) orders to proceed at once to the REGENT STREET dugouts and act as a reserve. I asked Lt. Col. Sandall 5th Lincoln Rgt. who had just arrived to carry out the relief of my Regiment to send (2) two Companies to E2. Capt. Dyer-Bennet and I then proceeded to the trenches and on reaching NEWPORT DUGOUTS saw a party of "B" Coy. falling in. There were 3 Sergts. and 71 men. We took these men on with us. I arrived in E3 trench at 12-30 a.m. 11th inst. On hearing the situation and that E1 left had been retaken and that the firing was dying down I sent a message to the Batteries to cease fire. At 12-40 a.m. I sent a message to Lt. Col. Sandall explaining the situation. In acknowledging my message he stated that he had placed one Company in F2 and one Company in E2. A few minutes later I informed the Brigade. Before I left ONE TREE FARM I telephoned to Capt. Fielding-Johnson, O.C. "C" Coy. which held the right of the line, to launch a counter attack from E6. After collecting the bomb throwers he entrusted the command to 2/Lt. Peake who had only reached the trenches on the previous night. On getting into E1 left about 12-23 he found it deserted, except for Capt. Haylock severely wounded and one dead German. Capt. Fielding-Johnson ordered fire to be opened from E3 and E6 on E1 left.

Major

Major Potter's Company fired from F2 and E2 trenches without eliciting any response.

It appears from enquiries I have made that the Germans threw about seven bombs, of which two exploded in the trench. Capt. Haylock ordered the men to open fire, but after the second explosion he was badly wounded. Sgt. Jacques was killed and Cpl. Reading and Lce. Cpl. Goadby wounded. The men then, being without officer or N.C.O's, evidently lost heart and quitted the trench. Three men who were carrying sandbags along the communication trench say they were swept back into E3 by the stream of men flowing from E1 left.

X I can account for the whole of the garrison and no one was taken prisoner. The casualties in E1 left were

Killed 1 Sergt.

Wounded 1 Officer, Capt. Haylock, since dead.

In E1 right the casualties were 1 killed and 1 wounded.

The right post remained out and saw the Germans and took no action.

The left post remained out but about 10-30 p.m. Lce. Cpl. Goadby went and reported to Capt. Haylock. At 11-30 p.m. Pte. Jones hearing the bombing going on and Lce. Cpl. Goadby not having returned went into E1 left and found it empty at 11-35 p.m. He then went to E1 right but does not appear to have reported to anybody.

11th May, 1915.

sd/ T. T. GRESSON, Major,
Cmdg. 1/4th Bn. Leicestershire Regiment.

X This was afterwards found to be incorrect as No. 2444 Pte A ICLIFFE, who was not a member of the Garrison, was never seen after approximately 11.10 p.m. 10th at which time he was resting in E1 L from fatigue.

May 31st 1915.

R S Dyer-Bennet Capt & Adjt
1/4 Leic Regt

SECRET.

Copy No. 5 "B"

OPERATION ORDER Number 14
by
BRIGADIER GENERAL W.R. CLIFFORD
Commanding 1/1 Linc. & Leic. Infty. Bde. T. F.

Headquarters
1st May 1915.

1. Trench Battalions will be relieved on nights of 2nd/3rd and 4th/5th instants.

   (a) The 5th LINCOLN REGIMENT will relieve the 4th LEICESTER REGIMENT on night 2/3rd instant.

   (a) The 4th LINCOLN REGIMENT will relieve the 5th LEICESTER REGIMENT on night 4/5th instant.

2. The Relieving Battalions will arrive (a) at ONE TREE FARM and (b) at PACKHORSE FARM at 9-0 p.m. each night where they will be met by guides from Battalions to be relieved. Reliefs will commence at 9-30 p.m.

3. TRANSPORT. The arrangements for Transport will be those detailed in Trench Routine Order No. 9 Part II paragraph 3.

4. The 4th LEICESTER REGIMENT and 5th LEICESTER REGIMENT will return to Billets in the DRANOUTRE AREA when relieved.

5. REPORTS. Relieving Battalions will report by telegraph when the relief is completed.

sd/ R. L. ADLERCRON, Major,

Brigade Major, 1/1 Linc. & Leic. Inf. Bde. T.F.

Issued by Cyclist Orderly at 6p.m to:-

Copy No. 1. Brigade Major, for Brigadier.
2. Staff Captain,
3. 4th Lincoln Regiment.
4. 5th Lincoln Regiment.
5. 4th Bn. Leicester Regiment.
6. 5th Bn. Leicester Regiment.
7. WAR DIARY.

SECRET. Copy. No. 5

OPERATION ORDER Number 18
by
BRIGADIER GENERAL W.R. CLIFFORD
Commanding 1/1 Lincs. & Leic. Infty. Bde. T.F.

Headquarters
5th May, 1915.

1. Trench Battalions will be relieved on nights of 6/7th and 8/9th instants.

(a) The 4th LEICESTER REGIMENT will relieve the 5th LINCOLN REGIMENT on night 6/7th instant.

(b) The 5th LEICESTER REGIMENT will relieve the 4th LINCOLN REGIMENT on night 8/9th instant.

2. The Relieving Battalions will arrive (a) at ONE TREE FARM and (b) at PACKHORSE FARM at 9 p.m. each night where they will be met by guides from Battalions to be relieved. Reliefs will commence at 9-30 p.m.

3. TRANSPORT. The arrangements for Transport will be those detailed in Trench Routine Order No. 9 Part II para. 5.

4. The 5th LINCOLN REGIMENT and 4th LINCOLN REGIMENT will return to Billets in the DRANOUTRE AREA when relieved.

5. REPORTS& Relieving Battalions will report by telegraph when the relief is completed.

E L Adderson Major,
Bde. Major, 1/1 Linc. & Leic. Infty. Bd
T. F.

Issued by Cyclist
Orderly at 9 p.m. to:-

Copy No. 1 Brigade Major, for Brigadier.
2 Staff Captain.
3 4th Lincoln Regiment
4 5th Lincoln Regiment
5 4th Leicester Regiment.
6. 5th Leicester Regiment.
7 War Diary.

O.O.
4th Leicesters

SECRET.

COPY NO. 5

OPERATION ORDER NO 19
by
BRIG.GEN. F.R.CLIFFORD Commanding 1/1 Lincs. & Leic Bde T.F.

....

1. The North Midland Division has received orders temporarily to extend its present front Northwards as far as trenches L 4 and L 6 inclusive so as to free other troops for offensive action elsewhere . The operations will extend over the nights of 9th/10th 10th/11th and 11th/12th May.

2. On the night of the 10/11 May the Lincoln and Leicester Infantry Brigade will take over from the Notts and Derby Infantry Brigade the trenches held by the right Battalion of the Notts and Derby Brigade, G2 inclusive . The Lincoln and Leicester Brigade will then have three Battalions in the trenches .

3. On the night of the 11/12 May the Staffordshire Infantry Brigade will take over from the Lincoln and Leicester Infantry Brigade as far as trench 15 inclusive and S 1.

4. Artillery will continue to cover their present area.

5. On night of 10/11 May the 4/Lincoln Regt. will relieve the 5th Notts & Derby Regt. in the trenches from left of 4/Leicester Regt in F.2 to G. 2 inclusive.

6. On night of 11/12 May the 5th Leicester Regt will be relieved by the Staffordshire Infantry Brigade and will return to billets in DRANOUTRE when relieved . Details and times of this relief will be communicated later. The 5th LINCOLN Regt. will on night of 11/12 May take over F4 & E dug out from 5th LEICS Regt. Battalions concerned (5 LIN. & 5 LEI) will make arrangements for transfer of E & dug out themselves.

7. The 4th Lincolnshire Regt will arrive at LINDENHOEK Cross Roads (N 27 c 98) at 8-45 p.m. where it will be met by guides from 5th Notts and Derby Regt.

8. Battalion Commanding Officer, Company Commanders, Machine Gun Officer and Bomb Officer will arrange to meet their opposite numbers in 5th Notts and Derby Regt this afternoon . The 4th Lincs. Regt will make their own arrangements with the 5th Notts and Derby Regt to effect this.

9. Trench Stores will be left in trenches except hand and rifle grenades which will accompany units . A receipt will be obtained for any trench stores handed over & a copy of such receipt & of any receipt given to an outgoing Battalion will be forwarded to this Office.

10. The 4th Lincs Regt. will receive from Notts and Derby RegtInfty. Bde. tonight two machine guns lent to the Notts and Derby Brigade by this Brigade last night under the following arrangements :-

(a) The 2 Machine Guns in "G1" and "G2" will be withdrawn at 8 p.m. and the and the two machine guns which were handed over to the Notts and Derby Brigade last night will be handed back to the M.G. Officer of the 4th Lincoln Regt at that hour at the left of "G2" trench .A party to receive them will be detailed by the O.C. 4th Lincs Regt.

(b) The Machine guns at present in F 4 and F 5 will be withdrawn at 8 p.m. Their emplacements will be taken over at that hour by the 4th Lincoln Regt . These guns must be withdrawn at this hour punctually as they are required elsewhere tonight .

(c) The Machine Gun in S P 3 will be withdrawn when the garrison is relieved by the 4th Lincolnshire Regt.

11. Transport will march in rear of the 4th Lincoln Regt tonight.

12. WORK TO BE DONE. Commanding Officer will ascertain from O.C. 5th Notts and Derby Regt. the work at present in progress and arrange to continue the same until further orders are issued. Particular attention is directed to continuation of any necessary maintainance work.

13. O.C. Brigade Signal Section will arrange to meet O.C. Notts and Derby Brigade Signal Section this afternoon and arrange for taking over the signal communication in this area and coupling up same to Lincs & Leic Bde Headquarters . He will report to this Office when new communications have been established. He will also arrange for communication with Headquarters 14th ~~[illegible]~~ R.H.A. Brigade ~~[illegible]~~

14. DISTRIBUTION of TROOPS. Pending further orders distribution of troops in trenches taken over from Notts and Derby Brigade will be the sam as the present distribution of 5th Notts and Derby Regt. as follows:-

S.P.3 One Platoon and 1 Machine Gun.
F.4. Three Platoons and 1 Machine Gun.
F.5. Three Platoons and 1 Machine Gun.
F.6. One Platoon.
G.1.)
G.2.) One Company. (One Machine Gun in G.1. (One Machine Gun in G.3.
G.3.)
One Company in reserve at LINDENHOEK Cross Roads.

15. O.C. 5th Notts and Derby Regt. will be in Command of this Sector until Relief is completed.

16. O.C. 4th Lincolnshire Regt. will report to this Office when he takes over.

Issued by Orderly at 1 p.m.
to :-

Copy No1 Brigade Major for Brigadier.
2. Notts and Derby Brigade.
3. 4/Lincs Regt.
4. 5/Lincs Regt.
5. 4/Leicester Regt.
6. 5/Leicester Regt.
7. Brigade Signal Section.

sd/ H.L. ADLERCRON Maj.,
Bde Maj Lincs & Leic Bde T.F.
Headquarters.
10/5/15 .

(4)

SECRET.

AFTER ORDER .

Headquarters,
10/5/15.

To OPERATION ORDER No 19 by Brig.Gen. W.R. Clifford Commanding Lincs & Leic Bde dated this day

ADD:-

1. One Officer and One N.C.O. per Company from the 6th NORTH STAFFORDSHIRE Regt will be at R.E. Farm at 5 p.m. to take over Trench Stores , they will be met at R.E. Farm by by 2nd in Command of Companies ,5th Leicestershire Regt.who will hand over trench stores for which they will obtain a receipt in duplicate.

2. The 6th NORTH STAFFORDSHIRE REGT will relieve the 5th LEICESTERSHIRE Regt. on night 11/12th May (in right sector excluding E 4) . Relief commencing from R.E. Farm at at 8 p.m. The 5th Leicestershire Regt. will arrange for an adequate supply of guides for all trenches and support point being at R.E. Farm at 7-30 p.m. . They will be in charge of a responsible N.C.O. who will report their arrival to O.C. 6th North Staffprdshire Regt. at R.E.Farm.

3. O.C. 5th Leicestershire Regt will command Right sector until relief is completed .

4. O.C. 5th Lincolnshire Regt will arrange with O.C. 5th Leic. Regt to relieve 5th Leicestershire Regt. in trench E 4 before 7-30 p.m. Immediately this relief is completed E.4 will become part of Sector commanded by O.C. 5th Lincs Regt.

5. From 8 p.m. 11th May. Trenches E 4 to F 2 with support trenches and support points will be known as the"right sector" Trenches F 4 to G 2 as the "left Sector"

sd/ R.L.ADLERCRON , Maj.,
Bde Maj. Lincs & Leic Bde T.F.

ISSUED at 11-30 p.m.by Messenger

Copy No 1 Bde Maj for Brigade Commander
2 4/Lincs. Regt.
3 5/Lincs Regt.
4 4/Leics Regt.
5 5/Leics Regt.
6 Staffordshire Infty Bde.
7 Bde Signal Officer.
8. War Diary.

S E C R E T. Copy No. 4.

OPERATION ORDER Number 20.
by
BRIGADIER GENERAL W. R. CLIFFORD
Commanding 1/1 Linc. & Leic. Inf. Bde. T. F.

Headquarters
10th May, 1915.

1. The 4th Leicester Regiment will be relieved on night of 10/11 by the 5th Lincoln Regiment.

2. The Relieving Battalion will arrive at ONE TREE FARM at 11-30 p.m. where they will be met by guides from 4th Leicester Regiment. Relief will commence at midnight.

3. TRANSPORT. The arrangements for transport will be those detailed in Trench Routine Order No. 9 Part II para. 5. The 4th Leicester Transport will leave DRANOUTRE at 9-30 p.m.

4. The 4th Leicester Regiment will return to Billets in the DRANOUTRE AREA when relieved.

5. REPORTS. Relieving Battalion will report by telegraph when the relief is completed.

[signature] Major,
Bde. Major, Linc. & Leic. Inf. Bde. T. F.

Issued by Cyclist
Orderly at 8 p.m. to :-

Copy No. 1. Brigade Major for Brigadier.
2. Staff Captain.
3. 5th Lincoln Regiment.
4. 4th Leicester Regiment.
5. WAR DIARY.

Rec'd ... 10.5 ...

SECRET. Copy No. 5.

OPERATION ORDER Number 21.
by
BRIGADIER GENERAL W.R.CLIFFORD.
Commanding 1/1 Linc & Leic Infantry Bde T.F.

Headquarters,
14th May 1915.

1. The 5th Lincoln Regiment will be relieved on night of 14/15 by the 4th Leicester Regiment.

2. The relieving Battalion will arrive at ONE TREE FARM at 11-30 p.m. They will be met by guides from ~~4th Leicester~~ 5th Lincoln Regiment. Relief will commence at midnight.

3. TRANSPORT. The arrangements for transport will be those detailed in ~~Trench~~ Standing Order No 9, Part 11, para 3. The 5th Lincolns Transport will leave DRANOUTRE at 9-30 p.m.

4. The 5th Lincoln Regiment will return to Billets in the DRANOUTRE AREA when relieved.

5. REPORTS. Relieving Battalion will report by telegraph when the relief is completed.

R. L. [illegible] Major,

Bde. Major, Linc & Leic Inf Bde T.F.

Issued by Cyclist
Orderly at 3 p.m. to :-

Copy No 1. Brigade Major for Brigadier.
2. Staff Captain.
3. 5th Lincoln Regiment.
4. 4th Leicester Regiment.
5. War Diary.

Recd [illegible] 14.5.15

SECRET. Copy No. 4.

OPERATION ORDER No. 23.
by
BRIGADIER GENERAL W.R.CLIFFORD
Commanding 138th Infantry Brigade.

Headquarters,
18th May, 1915.

1. The 4th LEICESTER REGIMENT will be relieved on night of 18/19 instant by the 5th LINCOLN REGIMENT.

2. The relieving Battalion will arrive at ONE TREE FARM at 10-30 p.m. They will be met by guides from 4th LEICESTER Regiment. Relief will commence at 11 p.m.

3. TRANSPORT. The arrangements for Transport will be those detailed in STANDING ORDERS, Part XI, paras. 2 and 3. The 4th LEICESTER TRANSPORT will leave DRANOUTRE at 8-45 p.m.

4. The 4th LEICESTER REGIMENT will return to Billets in the DRANOUTRE AREA when relieved.

5. REPORTS. The Relieving Battalion will report by telegraph when the relief is completed.

[signature] Major,
Brigade Major, 138th Infantry Brigade.

Issued by Cyclist Orderly
at 3-30 p.m. to :-

Copy No. 1. Brigade Major for Brigadier.
2. Staff Captain.
3. 5th LINCOLN REGIMENT.
4. 4th LEICESTER REGIMENT.
5. War Diary.

Recd A.5 p.m.
18-5-15

Secret. Copy No. 4

Operation Order No 25.
by
Brigadier Gen W.R.Clifford
Commanding 138th Infantry Bde.
......

Hdqrs.,
22/5/15.

1. The 5th Lincoln Regt will be releieved on night of 22/23 inst by the 4/Leicester Regt.

2. The releaving Battalion will arrive at One Tree Farm at 10-30 p.m. They will be met by guides from the 5th Lincs Regt. Relief will commence at 11 p.m.

3. Transport. The arrangements for transport will be those detailed in Standing Orders Part II paras 2 and 3 The 5th Lincoln Transport will ~~arrive~~ leave Dranoutre at 8-45 p.m.

4. The 5th Lincoln Regt will return to billets in the Dranoutre Area when relaaved.

5. Reports . The relieving battalion will report by telegraph, when the relief is completed.

sd/ R.L.ADLERCRON Maj.,
Bde Maj 138th Infantry Bde

Issued by Cyclist Orderly
at 11 a.m. to
Copy No 1.Bde Maj. for Brigadier.
2.Staff Capt.
3.5th Lincs Regt.
4.4th Leics Regt.
5. War Diary.

SECRET. Copy No. 4

Operation Order No. 27
by
Brigadier General W.R. Clifford
Commanding 138th Infantry Brigade

Headquarters,
26th May, 1915.

1. The 4th LEICESTER REGIMENT will be relieved on night of 26/27th instant by the 5th LINCOLN REGIMENT.

2. The Relieving Battalion will arrive at ONE TREE FARM at 10-30 p.m. They will be met by guides from the 4th LEICESTER REGIMENT. Relief will commence at 11 p.m.

3. The 4th LEICESTER REGIMENT will return to Bivouacs in the DRANOUTRE AREA when relieved.

4. Reports. The Relieving Battalion will report by telegraph when the relief is completed.

sd/ R.L.ADLERCRON, Major,
Bde. Major, 138th Inf. Bde.

Issued by Cyclist Orderly
at 12 noon to :-
Copy No. 1. Brigade Major for Brigadier
2. Staff Captain.
3. 5th LINCOLN Regiment.
4. 4th LEICESTER Regiment.
5. War Diary.

Recd 2pm
26.5.15

S E C R E T .   Copy No. 4

O P E R A T I O N   O R D E R   NO 28
------ by --------
BRIGADIER GEN. W.R.CLIFFORD
Commanding 138th Infantry Brigade .

Headquarters,
30th May 1915.
....

1. The 5th LINCOLNSHIRE Regt will be releived on night of 30/31 st by the 4th LEICESTERSHIRE Regt.

2. The relieving Battalion will arrive at ONE TREE FARM at 10-30 p.m. They will be met by guides from the 5th LINCOLNSHIRE REGT . RELIEF will COMMENCE at 11 p.m.

3. The ATTACHMENT COMPANY of the 7th Battalion RIFLE -BRIGADE will remain in the places allotted to them by the 5th LINCOLNSHIRE Regt. until the 4th LEICESTERSHIRE Regt. have completely taken over:their positions may then be changed by the O.C.,4th LEICESTERSHIRE Regt. if he so desires.

4. The 5th LINCOLNSHIRE Regt will return to bivouacs in the DRANOUTRE Area when relieved .

5. REPORTS. The Relieving Battalion will report by telegraph when therelief is completed .

sd/ R.L.ADLERCRON Maj.,
Bde Maj 138th Infantry Bde.

ISSUED by CYCLIST ORDERLY at
11 a.m. to:-

Copy No 1.Brigade Major for Brigade Commander.
2.Staff Captain
3.5th Lincolnshire Regt.
4.4th Leicestershire Regt.
5.7th Battalion Rifle Brigade.
6.War Diary.

138th Inf.Bde.
46th Div.

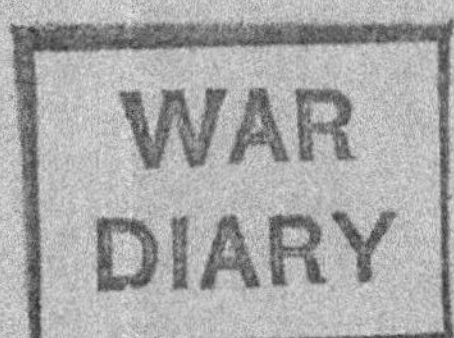

4th BATTN. THE LEICESTERSHIRE REGIMENT.

J U N E

1 9 1 5

Army Form C. 2118.

Instructions regarding War Diaries and Intelligence Summaries are contained in F.S. Regs., Part II. and the Staff Manual respectively. Title pages will be prepared in manuscript.

1/4. Leic. Rgt

WAR DIARY or INTELLIGENCE SUMMARY.

138th Inf Bde
40th Div

(*Erase heading not required.*)

Place	Hour, Date, Place (June 1915)	Hour	Summary of Events and Information	Remarks and references to Appendices
Trenches.	1st June		Fine [illegible] cool day – very quiet except for enemy shelling S. end of F2 again in evening	[illegible] hill
	2nd	am 1.15	Just after report [illegible] from Bde that Zeppelin [illegible] the noise of some sort of aircraft was plainly heard over [illegible] as far as could be judged Packhorse Fm. – moving N.W.	
			A quiet warm day	
			CO [illegible] visited all fire trenches	
		4.30pm	3 red rockets fired experimentally from [illegible] hardly visible (except one knew they were going up) [illegible]	
			These do not appear to be any [illegible] day	
		9.3 pm	3 similar rockets fired [illegible] [illegible] successful [illegible] plainly visible.	
		11 pm	On relief [illegible] Bde [illegible] Section [illegible] HQ. The Chalet [illegible]	[illegible] of R. Bde returned [illegible] Dranoutre.
	3rd	1.30	Relief [illegible]	

Instructions regarding War Diaries and Intelligence Summaries are contained in F. S. Regs., Part II. and the Staff Manual respectively. Title pages will be prepared in manuscript.

1/4. Leic Rgt ~~WAR DIARY~~ or **INTELLIGENCE SUMMARY.** 138th Inf Bde 46th Divn

(*Erase heading not required.*)

2

June 1915.

Place	Hour, Date, Place	Summary of Events and Information	Remarks and references to Appendices
(Bivouac) DRANOUTRE	3rd	This unusual procedure – viz 3 days only in [illegible] [illegible] by readjustment of line 138th Inf Bde taking over increased frontage.	
		Quiet [illegible] day.	
	3.30pm	[illegible] of [illegible] – 1 year [illegible] of refusing to comply & using obscene language to a N.C.O. [illegible] not suspended.	
	4 pm	Adj [illegible] 2 C. [illegible] 7/R Bde at [illegible] [illegible]	
	Evening	[illegible] of [illegible] of artillery fire [illegible] [illegible] use of gas shells.	RS&T
		[illegible] [illegible] relief [illegible] 3 days [illegible]	
4th	8am	Lt. Col. [illegible] killed – (Cmdg 1/4 Leic: Regt) [illegible] [illegible] [illegible] wounded (– of Leic Rgt) [illegible] [illegible] killed [illegible] [illegible] [illegible] [illegible] this took place in KEMMEL	

(9 29 6) W 3332—1107 100,000 10/13 H W V Forms/C. 2118/10.

Instructions regarding War Diaries and Intelligence Summaries are contained in F. S. Regs., Part II. and the Staff Manual respectively. Title pages will be prepared in manuscript.

1/4 Linc Rgt ~~WAR DIARY~~ or 138th Inf

INTELLIGENCE SUMMARY.

(*Erase heading not required.*)

46th Div

3

June 1915

Place	Hour, Date, Place	Summary of Events and Information	Remarks and references to Appendices
(Bivouac) DRANOUTRE	5th 9.30 am	G.O.C. 46th Div inspected 'A' & 'D' Coys - rapid fire. No dummies. The idea was to see [illegible] from physical & [illegible] [illegible] been [illegible] [illegible] to maintain continuous high rate of fire [illegible] 2 minutes or so [illegible] 'sketchy' firing over parapets have not been conducive to keeping [illegible] up to the mark as regards [illegible].	
	About noon	Three or four shells came [illegible] over [illegible] [illegible] [illegible] [illegible]	
	3pm	Funeral of Lt. Col. JESSOP 4th Linc Rgt - 10 officers & 20 other ranks attended - impression [illegible] [illegible] [illegible] [illegible] [illegible] [illegible] [illegible] [illegible] [illegible] with.	
		Heavy Art. Fire to S. and to N.	
	6th 10. am	Divine Service - immediately W. of bivouac - Bde [illegible] attended	
	12.30pm	O.C. [illegible] 5th Ox & Bucks L.I. came to bivouac re attachment of their [illegible]	
	(9.30pm	Ox & Bucks L.I. 'A' Coy having joined Coys to which attached for	Casualty
	7th 9.15pm	2 Lt. F. M. WAITE wounded when standing at S. end of [illegible] [illegible] [illegible] (one eye) facing [illegible]. He died following day	2Lt. F. M. WAITE killed

(9 29 6) W 3332—1107 100,000 10/13 H W V Forms/C. 2118/10.

Instructions regarding War Diaries and Intelligence Summaries are contained in F.S. Regs., Part II. and the Staff Manual respectively. Title pages will be prepared in manuscript.

1/4 Leicester Regt. 138 Inf Bde 46th Div. 4

~~WAR DIARY~~ or INTELLIGENCE SUMMARY.

(Erase heading not required.)

June 1915

Place	Hour, Date, Place	Hour	Summary of Events and Information	Remarks and references to Appendices
Trenches	7th	2 am	2/Lieut E M WHITE died [illegible] R.S. [illegible] LINDENHOEK DRESSING St.	
			2nd in C. visited F trenches - v. quiet night.	
			Misty morning [illegible] wind.	
		2 pm	CO 2nd in C. Adj. and Signalling Officers of 5th [illegible] and Bucks Bn arrived at Chalet for tour of inspection.	
		5 pm	Germans shelled junction E2 - F2. No damage.	
		6-45 pm	Grenades fired from E2.	
		7-15 pm	" " " F2.	
		7-30 pm	Support Trenches in rear of F2 & F4 shelled, resulting in damage to Pall Mall.	
			About same time Trench Mortar was fired from East end of E3. Damage to enemy parapet reported.	
	8th		Very hot sultry day. All quiet	

(9 29 6) W 3332—1107 100,000 10/13 H W V Forms/C. 2118/10.

Instructions regarding War Diaries and Intelligence Summaries are contained in F. S. Regs., Part II. and the Staff Manual respectively. Title pages will be prepared in manuscript.

1/4 Leic. Regt. ~~INTELLIGENCE~~ ~~or~~ SUMMARY. 138th Inf Bde 46th Division

(Erase heading not required.)

Place	~~Hour~~, Date, ~~Place~~	hour	Summary of Events and Information	Remarks and references to Appendices
Trenches	June 8th	2 pm	Bde Gen. came to H.Q. about 2 p.m.	
		5 pm	C.O. visited Trenches. Returned 11 p.m.	
		11-30 pm	Adj. & Adj. Bdr Books Lt visited Trenches. The Adjutant wounded by bullet wound in ~~the~~ calf of leg. During the afternoon of this day a German newspaper (Bamburger Tagblatt) was found near E1L, apparently blown there by a Grenade rifle. Sent (with translation of certain parts by Major Potter) to Bde. H.Q.	
	9th	10 am	Bde Gen. visited Trenches	
		" "	Lt. F.W. Farr reported at H.Q. for duty as temporary adj.	Casualty. Lieut. H.C. Barce was seriously wounded by the premature explosion of a converted rifle grenade. About 4 pm.
		5 pm	C.O. visited Trenches. Returned 11-30 p.m. Wind - mild N. <u>Note</u>. Hostile Aeroplane was observed about 7-a.m. flying from a Northerly direction.	

(9 29 6) W 3332—1107 100,000 10/13 H W V Forms/C. 2118/10.

Instructions regarding War Diaries and Intelligence Summaries are contained in F. S. Regs., Part II. and the Staff Manual respectively. Title pages will be prepared in manuscript.

or INTELLIGENCE SUMMARY.

1/4 Leic Regt. (~~Erase heading not required.~~) 138th Inf Bde 46th Division

Place	June 1915 ~~Hour,~~ Date, ~~Place~~ hour	Summary of Events and Information	Remarks and references to Appendices
(Bivouac) Dranoutre	10th	Battalion returned from the Trenches and was finally settled in bivouacs by 4-30 am. Rouse 11-am.	
	12 noon	Telegram received that Lieut. H.C. Brice died at 11.25 a.m. at No 3 Casualty Clearing Hospital Bailleul.	
		Weather fine - but sultry.	
"	12th	Fine - very hot. Rouse 7-30 a.m. Battalion found Guards for Lindenhoek - Brigade H.Q. - and 2nd Bde R.F.A.	
	8am.	A Coy paraded for digging fatigue. Work commenced at 10 a.m. Work completed - North end of Regent St - levelled and drained. Regent St Extension - Drained - 16 grids laid and staked and 38 grids laid temporarily in bad places. A Coy was brought up to fatigue strength	

Instructions regarding War Diaries and Intelligence Summaries are contained in F. S. Regs., Part II. and the Staff Manual respectively. Title pages will be prepared in manuscript.

or

~~WAR DIARY~~ INTELLIGENCE ~~SUMMARY~~. 1/4 Leic Regt 138th Inf Bde 46th Division

(~~Erase heading not required.~~)

Place	~~Hour~~, Date, ~~Place~~ Hour	Summary of Events and Information	Remarks and references to Appendices
(Brouxes) Dranoutre	June 12	of 180 by addition of a draft from B Coy. Pall Mall extension also levelled and drained. Company ceased work at 2 pm	
"	12 noon	C Coy supplemented by D Coy paraded to relieve A Coy digging fatigue. Digging commenced 2 pm. Work done – continuation of mornings work. Work stopped 6 pm.	
"	10 a.m.	Funeral of Lieut. H C Bruce. The following officers attended – Capt J.E. Viccars – Major J.A. Potter – Capt. B F. Newill – Capt L Corah – Lieut W.B. Jarvis – Lieut. F.N. Tarr – Lieut F.S. Parr. Also 40 N.C.O.s and men from Grenade Section. Service taken by Rev. Upten.	

(9 29 6) W 3332—1107 100,000 10/13 H W V Forms/C. 2118/10.

Instructions regarding War Diaries and Intelligence Summaries are contained in F. S. Regs., Part II. and the Staff Manual respectively. Title pages will be prepared in manuscript.

~~WAR DIARY or INTELLIGENCE~~ SUMMARY.

1/4 Leic. Regt. (~~Erase heading not required.~~) 138th Inf Bde 46th Division

Place	Hour, Date, ~~Place~~	Summary of Events and Information	Remarks and references to Appendices
(Bivouacs) Dranoutre	June 12th		
	4-30 pm	Concert party gave performance in field in rear of 2nd N.M. Field Ambulance. First official concert. All men of Battn not on duty attended.	
		C.M. of a Pte for using insubordinate language to an N.C.O.	
"	9-30 pm.	C.O. spoke to O's C. Coys on subject of work and reliefs. Suggestions for removal of grass in front of fire trenches and for harassing the enemy.	
		Heavy firing heard in northerly direction between 8 pm and 9-30 p.m.	
"	13th	Fine and warm.	
	10 am	Church Parade. Service taken by Rev. Ashby Brigade Chaplain. The C.R.A. attended the service. Regimental march was played by band of 5th Leics: at end of service for first time	

(9 29 6) W 3332—1107 100,000 10/13 H W V Forms/C. 2118/10.

Instructions regarding War Diaries and Intelligence Summaries are contained in F. S. Regs., Part II. and the Staff Manual respectively. Title pages will be prepared in manuscript.

or ~~INTELLIGENCE~~ SUMMARY.

1/4 Leic. Regt. (Erase heading not required.) 138th Inf Bde 46th Division

Place	~~Hour~~, Date, ~~Place~~ hour	Summary of Events and Information	Remarks and references to Appendices
(Bivouacs) Dranoutre	June 13th	Our aeroplanes seem to have been unusually busy today; several flying over.	
"	" 14th	Fine day.	
"	10 a.m.	C. O. inspected B Coy. Dress - fighting order.	
"	11 a.m.	C. O inspected D Coy. " "	
		Both Companies were good.	
	11-45 a.m.	The C.O. and 2nd in Command of 10th D.L.I. visited the Bivouacs to discuss their coming trench attachment with the C.O.	
	9 pm	The Battn was paraded for the promulgation of the F.G.C.M. held on a Pte [illegible] on the 12th inst.	
Trenches	" 11-35 pm.	Relief of 5th Lincs. Regt completed without mishap.	
		C. Coy of the 10th D.L.I. is attached to us	
		Total Strength in Trenches is:-	
		4th Leicesters - 15 Officers 621 O.R.	
		10th D.L.I - 5 " 160 "	
		5th Leicesters - 24 Machine Gunners.	
		Pigeon Flyer - 1.	

(9 29 6) W 3332—1107 100,000 10/13 H W V Forms/C. 2118/10

Instructions regarding War Diaries and Intelligence Summaries are contained in F. S. Regs., Part II. and the Staff Manual respectively. Title pages will be prepared in manuscript.

~~WAR DIARY~~ or INTELLIGENCE ~~SUMMARY~~. 1/4 Leic Regt 138th Inf Bde 46th Division

(Erase heading not required.)

Place	Hour, Date, Place Time Hour	Summary of Events and Information	Remarks and references to Appendices
Trenches	June 15th	Another ~~[illegible]~~ tour in the Trenches has begun. Capt. A.B. Johnson (5th Leices) is again at H.Q. for the purpose of carrying on his survey of the district	Casualty
	7-45 am	Enemy Aeroplane reported as having passed over F5 from a Northerly direction.	7-20 am 1 O.R. wounded in E1L – Right end. Dangerous Corner there
	9-30 am	Battle practise ordered by Brigade entailing the removal of Battalion H.Q. from the Chalet to Regent St Dug Outs.	
	10 am	Removal completed. Report of same sent to Brigade H.Q. Trench Runners to R.S.? O assembled and certain tests made viz from F2 – 8 mins. " 74 – 12 mins. " E3 – 13 mins	
	1 pm	Brig. General Clifford and staff arrive at dugouts. He is accompanied by 2 representatives of the Press – Most unusual.	
	2-15 pm	Battle ended. Return of H.Q. to Chalet.	

(9 29 6) W 3332—1107 100,000 10/13 H W V Forms/C. 2118/10.

Instructions regarding War Diaries and Intelligence Summaries are contained in F. S. Regs., Part II. and the Staff Manual respectively. Title pages will be prepared in manuscript.

or

~~INTELLIGENCE SUMMARY.~~ 1/4 Leic Regt. 138th Inf Bde. 46th Division

~~(Erase heading not required.)~~

Place	~~Hour~~, Date, ~~Place~~ Time	Summary of Events and Information	Remarks and references to Appendices
Trenches.	June 15th	On return journey met Major General Milne. He made a complimentary reference to the condition of Regent St.	
		The weather is very fine, with mild Northerly Wind.	
	5-15 pm	a 2/3 White and 1/3 Prussian Blue flag was held up for a short time over the German parapet to the right of E1R.	
	9-15 pm	Heavy firing on left - apparently shell fire, Trench Mortar, and rifle fire. There seemed also to be a mine explosion.	
		Heavy rifle fire also from our own trenches.	
		F4 & 5 were shelled a little by Enemy. Our guns (2nd Battery) replied.	
		C.O. at R.S.D.O. during this affair	
	9-45 pm	all quiet again on immediate front. Very spasmodic gun firing on left continues.	
	11-15 pm	C.O. returned from trenches.	

(9 29 6) W 3332—1107 100,000 10/13 H W V Forms/C. 2118/10.

Instructions regarding War Diaries and Intelligence Summaries are contained in F. S. Regs., Part II. and the Staff Manual respectively. Title pages will be prepared in manuscript.

~~WAR DIARY~~ or INTELLIGENCE ~~SUMMARY~~.

(~~Erase heading not required.~~)

1/4 Leic. Regt. 138th Inf Bde 46th Division

Place	~~Hour~~, Date, ~~Place~~ Hour	Summary of Events and Information	Remarks and references to Appendices
Trenches	June 15th 10.45 pm	From F2 it is reported seeing 3 lights (white) dropped from what appeared to be a dark cloud.	
"	" 16th	Weather fine. Wind - Gentle Northerly.	
	9.45 am	Enemy dropped two high explosive shells (Howitzer) into F2 40 yds and 85 yds N. of Tree. The second of these resulted in 9 casualties. They had previously shot over 207 field gun Shrapnell at same target without any damage being done.	Casualties Killed 1 O.R. Wounded 7 O.R. also wounded 1 O.R. of the D.L.I. attached
		Aggressive Squad put in some good work during day, causing 8 loopholes to be closed up and doing much damage to top row sandbags.	
	3 pm	C.O. & second in C. visited Trenches, returned 9.30 pm.	
	10 pm	C Coy 10th D.L.I. relieved by B Coy of same Unit	10 pm C Coy 10 D.L.I. returned [illegible]
		Leave has been cancelled suddenly, at 2 pm today.	

(9 29 6) W 3332—1107 100,000 10/13 H W V Forms/C. 2118/10.

Instructions regarding War Diaries and Intelligence Summaries are contained in F. S. Regs., Part II. and the Staff Manual respectively. Title pages will be prepared in manuscript.

~~INTELLIGENCE~~ SUMMARY.

(Erase heading not required.)

1/4 Leic. Regt. 138th Inf. Bde. 46th Division

Place ~~Hour~~, Date, ~~Place~~ hour	Summary of Events and Information	Remarks and references to Appendices
Trenches. June 18th	Fine day. Wind gentle & Northerly	
	Centenary of Waterloo	
9-30 am	Enemy aeroplane observed flying over our lines in S.E. direction	
2 pm	Visit from two Officers of York & Lancaster Regt. Their division Corps reserve and they had come forward to view the country & lines.	
3 pm	C.O. & Adj visited Trenches; returning 11 p.m.	
11-15 pm	Relief by 5th Leics. completed	
12-30 pm	H.Q. returned to Bivouacs	

(9 29 6) W 3332—1107 100,000 10/13 H W V Forms/C. 2118/10.

Instructions regarding War Diaries and Intelligence Summaries are contained in F.S. Regs., Part II. and the Staff Manual respectively. Title pages will be prepared in manuscript.

~~INTELLIGENCE~~ SUMMARY.

1/4 Leics Regt (*Erase heading not required.*) 138th Inf. Bde. 46th Division

Place ~~Hour,~~ June Date, ~~Place~~ Hour	Summary of Events and Information	Remarks and references to Appendices
(Bivouacs) Dranoutre June 19th	Fine day - Cooler - Wind mild Northerly	
9 am	Rouse	
	Uneventful day	
20th	Very fine - Wind mild Northerly	
11.30 am	The Battn was visited by Sir Charles Fergusson (commanding 2nd Corps), accompanied by the Bde General and Brigade Major. The Corps Commander spoke in terms of appreciation of the work of the 46th Division since they had taken over a portion of the line Trenches. He said that the Division is being temporarily lent to the 2nd Corps and expressed the hope that before long it would again be back under his own command.	

Instructions regarding War Diaries and Intelligence Summaries are contained in F. S. Regs., Part II. and the Staff Manual respectively. Title pages will be prepared in manuscript.

~~WAR DIARY~~ or ~~INTELLIGENCE SUMMARY.~~ (~~Erase heading not required.~~)

1/4 Leic Regt — 138th Inf. Bde — 46th Division

Place / Hour, Date, Place / Hour	Summary of Events and Information	Remarks and references to Appendices
(Bivouacs) Dranoutre June 20th	Major Martin was today informed of his promotion to temp. Colonel, the news being first announced on Batt. parade by Lt. Charles Ferguson	
3 p.m.	Church Parade. Service taken by Rev. Ashby attended by the Bde General and Staff captain	
" 21st	Fine - hot - wind very gentle Northerly	
10-45 am	Battalion paraded packed and loaded ready to move from present station, and was inspected by Bde General Clifford. The Bde General expressed satisfaction at the appearance of the Battalion	
12-45 pm	Battalion returned to Bivouacs	

(9 29 6) W 3332—1107 100,000 10/13 H W V Forms/C. 2118/10

Army Form C. 2118.

Instructions regarding War Diaries and Intelligence Summaries are contained in F. S. Regs., Part II. and the Staff Manual respectively. Title pages will be prepared in manuscript.

or

~~WAR DIARY~~ INTELLIGENCE ~~SUMMARY.~~

(Erase heading not required.)

1/4 Leic. Regt.

138th Inf. Bde
46th Division

Place	Date	Hour	Summary of Events and Information	Remarks and references to Appendices
(Bivouacs) Dranoutre	June 22nd		Fine - Hot - Wind gentle Northerly.	
		2 am	5th Leices. Regt. returned from the Trenches and joined us in Bivouacs, 4th Leic Regt taking the Northern - 5th Leics Southern field. The Brigade is under orders to move from Dranoutre to a new station to-day.	
		8-20 pm	Battn fell in.	
		8-45 pm	Battn marched out of Dranoutre.	
		11-15 pm	Arrived at our new station.	
		12 midnight	Battn was settled down for the night, bivouacing in an open field. The Machine Gun section left in trenches with their guns until relieved by the incoming Brigade	

(9 29 6) W 3332—1107 100,000 10/13 H W V Forms/C. 2118/10.

Instructions regarding War Diaries and Intelligence Summaries are contained in F. S. Regs., Part II. and the Staff Manual respectively. Title pages will be prepared in manuscript.

or

~~INTELLIGENCE~~ SUMMARY.

1/4 Leic Regt (*Erase heading not required.*)

138th Inf Bde
46th Division

Place ~~Hour~~, June Date, ~~Place~~ Hour	Summary of Events and Information	Remarks and references to Appendices
(Bivouacs) Ouderdom June 23rd	Fine – wind SW mild.	
9 am.	Rouse. Washing places and latrines put up	
5-45 pm	Battalion paraded for route march.	
" June 24th 8 am.	Rouse.	
10-30 am	Battalion paraded under company arrangements. Training – muscle excercises – rapid firing – bayonet fighting – physical excercises	
5-45 pm.	Battalion Route march.	
" June 25th 8 am	Rouse. Training as for June 24th. Foot inspection.	At 1-45 am on the 25th inst. the Gun section under Lieut. Douglas rejoined the Battalion

Instructions regarding War Diaries and Intelligence Summaries are contained in F. S. Regs., Part II. and the Staff Manual respectively. Title pages will be prepared in manuscript.

~~WAR DIARY~~ or **INTELLIGENCE ~~SUMMARY~~.** 1/4 Leic Regt. 138th Inf Bde 46th Division

(Erase heading not required.)

Place	June Date, Hour	Summary of Events and Information	Remarks and references to Appendices
(Bivouacs) Ouderdom	June 25th	a heavy thunderstorm in the afternoon accompanied by torrential rain. The bivouacs practically flooded out, but the men remained cheerful.	
"		The C.O. and 2nd in C. visited the trenches the Battn is to take over.	
"		The C.O. left for England on 5 days leave.	
"	" 26th	Fine again	
	8 am	Rouse	
	10-30 am	Companies paraded under Coy arrangements. Training as on two previous days.	
"	" 27th	Cloudy. Heavy showers during day. Wind mild Westerly. Church parade was held in a corner of the Bivouac field. Service taken by Brigade Chaplain – Sermon by Mr Uffen. Routemarch in evening cancelled owing to rain.	

(9 29 6) W 3332—1107 100,000 10/13 H W V Forms/C. 2118/10.

Instructions regarding War Diaries and Intelligence Summaries are contained in F. S. Regs., Part II. and the Staff Manual respectively. Title pages will be prepared in manuscript.

or

~~INTELLIGENCE SUMMARY.~~

(Erase heading not required.)

1/4 Leic Regt 138th Inf Bde 46th Division

Place ~~Hour~~, June Date, ~~Place~~ Hour		Summary of Events and Information	Remarks and references to Appendices
(Bivouacs) Ouderdom.	June 28th	Fine Wind mild S.W.	
		Training Two hours training in morning under Company arrangements, special attention being paid to musketry exercises - rapid loading and firing - physical exercises	
		Draft of 91 men (including 3 Sergts) arrived at Poperinghe at 1-30 pm and were brought to Bivouacs under Lieut. Parr.	
	3 pm	Major Potter, Company Commanders, and Adjt visited support points in Sanctuary Wood and Maple Copse	
"	" 29th	Fine Wind S.W.	
	am 10.30	New Draft paraded at Bde H.Q. for inspection by Major General Stuart-Wortley and the Bde General	

Instructions regarding War Diaries and Intelligence Summaries are contained in F. S. Regs., Part II. and the Staff Manual respectively. Title pages will be prepared in manuscript.

1/4 Leic. Regt.

~~INTELLIGENCE~~ or SUMMARY.

(~~Erase heading not required.~~)

138th Inf Bde.
46th Division

Place	~~Hour~~, Date, ~~Place~~ hour	Summary of Events and Information	Remarks and references to Appendices
(Bivouacs) Ouderdom	June 29		
	7. p.m.	Battn paraded to proceed to relieve 5th Bn Notts & Derby Regt in Sanctuary Wood	
	10 p.m.	Battn was met by Guides at Kruistraat and Conducted by Companies to Sanctuary Wood	
Trenches Sanctuary Wood.	" 30th 1-30 am	Relief of 5th Notts & Derby Regt Completed. Situation remained normal throughout the day; but enemy artillery was ~~very~~ active from 1-45 p.m. onwards.	Casualties Wounded 1. O.R.
		No fires may be lighted in the wood between 3 a.m. and 9-30 p.m.	
		Look outs for Aeroplanes are posted at various points. On aeroplane approaching they blow whistle & all men remain still under nearest tree until it is past.	

(9 29 6) W 3332—1107 100,000 10/13 H W V Forms/C. 2118/10

Instructions regarding War Diaries and Intelligence Summaries are contained in F. S. Regs., Part II. and the Staff Manual respectively. Title pages will be prepared in manuscript.

or

INTELLIGENCE SUMMARY. 138th Inf. Bde. 46th Division

1/4 Leic. Regt. *(Erase heading not required.)*

Place, ~~Hour~~, Date, ~~Place~~ June Hour	Summary of Events and Information	Remarks and references to Appendices
Trenches June 30th 9 p.m.	C Coy relieved one Coy of 4th Lincs. in Strong Points A. B. C. and E.	
	Certified Correct F. L. Barr Lieut A/adjt 1/4th Leicestershire Regt 1st July 1915.	

138th Inf.Bde.
46th Div.

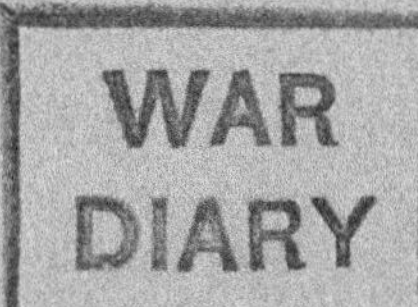

4th BATTN. THE LEICESTERSHIRE REGIMENT.

J U L Y

1 9 1 5

Attached:

Appendices.

"War Diary"

for the month of JULY.

1/4th LEICESTERSHIRE REGT.

Instructions regarding War Diaries and Intelligence Summaries are contained in F. S. Regs., Part II. and the Staff Manual respectively. Title pages will be prepared in manuscript.

~~WAR DIARY~~ ~~or~~ ~~INTELLIGENCE SUMMARY.~~ 1/4 Leic. Regt (~~Erase heading not required.~~) 138th Inf. Bde. 46th Division

Place	Date	Hour	Summary of Events and Information	Remarks and references to Appendices
Trenches Sanctuary Wood.	July 1st	-	Cloudy and cool. Wind mild Westerly	Casualties
		5 pm.	C.O. returned from leave.	1 man killed
		7 pm.	A and B Coys relieved 2 Companies of 5th Leicesters in fire Trenches A taking 5 & 6, B taking 7 & 8.	2 other ranks wounded
			D Coy garrisoned S.P. D and relieved Cheshires in Maple Copse, remainder of D Coy remaining in C2 in Sanctuary Wood.	
			Enemy Artillery very active between 6 & 7 p.m. — a large number of gas shells came over N.W. of Sanctuary Wood. The night was quiet.	
"	2nd		Warm. Wind nil in morning — mild Westerly towards evening	
		12 midday	Enemy sent 4 shrapnell shells into North end of Sanctuary Wood near Bn H.Q. dug out wounding one man. At 4 p.m. another fell by North extremity of Wood wounding another and killing a third.	Casualties wounded:— 2 other ranks
		2 pm	C.O. & 2nd in C visited Maple Copse to select site for Medical	Killed 1 other rank

1577 Wt. W10791/1773 500,000 1/15 D. D. & L. A.D.S.S./Forms/C. 2118.

Instructions regarding War Diaries and Intelligence Summaries are contained in F. S. Regs., Part II. and the Staff Manual respectively. Title pages will be prepared in manuscript.

or

INTELLIGENCE SUMMARY.

1/4 Leic. Regt. (Erase heading not required.) 138th Inf. Bde. 46th Division.

Place	Date	Hour	Summary of Events and Information	Remarks and references to Appendices
	~~July~~ June			
Trenches	2nd		aid post and dugouts.	
		6.30 pm	C.O. and a/adj. visited fire Trenches.	
		1-45 pm	2nd in C. visited fire Trenches.	
"	3rd		Very hot - wind gentle westerly.	Casualties
		pm 12.30	Enemy shelled Sanctuary Wood and Maple Copse for about 20 mins; but did no damage	1 O.R. Killed 3 O.R. Wounded
		6 pm	C.O. visited trenches	
			Trenches 7 & 8 were shelled between 4 & 5 pm. the former being much damaged. Also from 11 AM to 1 pm and 1.30 - 3 pm Night was quiet.	
	4th		Again very hot - wind nil.	Casualties
			C.O. sent to hospital by M.O. with temperature.	2 O.R. Killed
		1 pm	Enemy shelled trenches 7 & 8 again damaging the former, ~~and also S~~	4 O.R. Wounded

1577 Wt. W10791/1773 500,000 1/15 D. D. & L. A.D.S.S./Forms/C. 2118.

Instructions regarding War Diaries and Intelligence Summaries are contained in F. S. Regs., Part II. and the Staff Manual respectively. Title pages will be prepared in manuscript.

~~or~~ INTELLIGENCE SUMMARY.

1/4 Leic. Regt ~~(Erase heading not required.)~~ 138th Inf. Bde. 46th Division

Place	Date	Hour	Summary of Events and Information	Remarks and references to Appendices
Trenches	July 4th		This was continued until 2 p.m., but was ~~[illegible]~~ again began at 5 pm lasting an hour. Sanctuary Wood also shelled during this hour.	
		pm 7.25	Enemy artillery began to shell Sanctuary Wood with Shrapnell in direction of dumps. This was continued for 20 mins and was followed by 15 mins very rapid rifle fire.	
		10 pm	All again quiet.	
		11-47 p.m.	A green light was observed behind enemy's lines.	
"	5th	am 1-30	Enemy again shelled Sanctuary Wood with Howitzers and Shrapnell and continued it until 2-15 am. A similar practice was	
		pm 12.30	carried out by him for the same period commencing about 12.30 Noon, & a few howitzer shells fell in SANCTUARY WOOD about 4 pm.	~~Casualties~~
		6 pm	Major Potter visited trenches with various instructions regarding relief.	2 O.R. killed 4 O.R. Wounded

1577 Wt. W10791/1773 500,000 1/15 D. D. & L. A.D.S.S./Forms/C. 2118.

Instructions regarding War Diaries and Intelligence Summaries are contained in F. S. Regs., Part II. and the Staff Manual respectively. Title pages will be prepared in manuscript.

or

INTELLIGENCE SUMMARY.

(Erase heading not required.)

Place	Date	Hour	Summary of Events and Information	Remarks and references to Appendices
	July			
Trenches	5th	8pm	Howitzer and shrapnel shelling of Sanctuary Wood again repeated and in consequence Battalion Headquarters were removed to MAPLE COPSE.	
		9.30pm	Guides met relieving battn. 6th South Staffords at Bridge 4 YPRES at 9.30 pm. & led them to the trenches arriving	
		11.40pm	here at about 11.40 pm. the delay being caused by a working party blocking the route; insufficient gaps in hedges; bad route through ZILLEBEKE, and a maze of badly laid telephone wires. Subject to this the relief was expeditiously carried out the corresponding companies of each battalion relieving each other, our last party on returning passing headquarters of	
	6th	1.20am	our battalion at 1.20 am without suffering any casualties during this period.	
			One machine gun team failed to arrive & consequently six men of the battn. of necessity extended their tour	

1577 Wt. W10791/1773 500,000 1/15 D. D. & L. A.D.S.S./Forms/C. 2118.

Instructions regarding War Diaries and Intelligence Summaries are contained in F. S. Regs., Part II. and the Staff Manual respectively. Title pages will be prepared in manuscript.

INTELLIGENCE SUMMARY.

(Erase heading not required.)

Place	Date	Hour	Summary of Events and Information	Remarks and references to Appendices
	1915		for a further six hours.	
OODERDOM.	July 6th	5am	Companies, Bombers, Machine Gunners &c. marched home independently arriving in bivouacs at OODERDOM about 4.45 am. – total distance from trenches about 8 miles.	
			Throughout the day companies were at the disposal of their officers commanding for Interior Economy, Rifle inspections, Collection of Respirators &c; one parade only being held.	
			Wind – mild S.W.	
ditto.	7	10.30 am till 12.30 pm	Companies paraded for Physical drill, Muscle exercises, Bayonet fighting & Musketry under Company commanders	
		3 pm	Battalion route march for 1½ hours.	
			Wind gusty S.W.	
ditto.	8th		During previous evening & night of 7th/8th much rain fell & the men having practically nothing but waterproof sheets with which to make bivouacs, found weather	

1577 Wt. W10791/1773 500,000 1/15 D. D. & L. A.D.S.S./Forms/C. 2118.

Instructions regarding War Diaries and Intelligence Summaries are contained in F. S. Regs., Part II. and the Staff Manual respectively. Title pages will be prepared in manuscript.

or

INTELLIGENCE SUMMARY.

(*Erase heading not required.*)

Place	Date	Hour	Summary of Events and Information	Remarks and references to Appendices
	1915			
OUDERDOM	July 8		conditions most uncomfortable. Serge great-coats when once wet through - very difficult to dry.	
		10.30 am till 12.30 pm	Companies at disposal of company commanders for programme of work similar to yesterday, with lecture on lessons from last trench tour.	
		3 pm	Battn route march. Digging shelter trenches.	
		4.15.	Five shrapnel shells fell about 3/4 mile S.S.E of bivouacs, while 3 howitzer shells passed over bivouacs coming from same direction.	
			Wind squally mainly S.	
do.	9		Brigadier intimated to C.O. personally that he desired men to be occupied for six hours when out of trenches after first day.	
		7 am	Running drill in loose order.	
		9.30 am till 12.30 pm	Companies at disposal of their O.Cs. for programme of work similar to two previous days.	

1577 Wt. W10791/1773 500,000 1/15 D. D. & L. A.D.S.S./Forms/C. 2118.

Instructions regarding War Diaries and Intelligence Summaries are contained in F. S. Regs., Part II. and the Staff Manual respectively. Title pages will be prepared in manuscript.

or

INTELLIGENCE SUMMARY.

(Erase heading not required.)

Place	Date	Hour	Summary of Events and Information	Remarks and references to Appendices
	1915			
OUDERDOM	July 9	3 pm	Battalion route march. Rained during afternoon. Wind Gentle SW.	
do.	10	9.30 am till 12.30 pm	Programme of training during morning similar to previous days: Diarrhoea prevalent probably owing to unsweetened lemonade issue. Wind Gentle SSW.	
do.	11	4 am 5 9 am till 3 pm	Reveille Battn. 600 strong paraded for digging fatigue round white chateau in H 22 B. Ref. BELGIUM & FRANCE sheet 28, & complimented by CRE 46th Div. on results of the six hours work. Wind SW Gusty.	
do.	12	9.30 am till 2.30 pm	Programme of work similar to previous days. CO and company commanders visited Headquarters of 1st Bn. Dorset Regt. in railway embankment in I 20 c ref. BELGIUM & FRANCE sheet 28. and the approaches from there to the headquarters of the other battalions of the	

1577 Wt. W10791/1773 500,000 1/15 D. D. & L. A.D.S.S./Forms/C. 2118.

Instructions regarding War Diaries and Intelligence Summaries are contained in F. S. Regs., Part II. and the Staff Manual respectively. Title pages will be prepared in manuscript.

~~WAR DIARY or~~ INTELLIGENCE SUMMARY. 1/4 Leic. Regt. 138th Inf. Bde. 46th Division.

(Erase heading not required.)

Place	Date	Hour	Summary of Events and Information	Remarks and references to Appendices
	1915			
OUDERDOM	July 12	10 am to 6 pm	15th Bde 5th Division whom the 138th Inf Bde are relieving tonight & tomorrow. 270 men of the latter visited baths at POPERINGHE	
			Wind mild W.	
"	13		Warm. Wind - Nil	
		8 pm	Battalion moved off from Bivouacs for trenches to take over dugouts and strong points held by 1st Dorsets in I.20.D Sheet 28 As per Battn Operation Orders No 2 by Major G.A. Potter.	
		11-31 pm	Relief completed.	
Trenches Dug Outs I.20.D. Sheet 28.	" 14		Fine Warm. Wind - breezy north westerly.	
		12 midday	C.O. 2nd in C visited Trenches held by 1/4 Lincs: Regt.	
		5 pm	Enemy shelled neighbourhood of Bde H.Q. ~~one shell hitting the H.Q.~~	
		9-30 pm	Heavy rifle fire with some Artillery fire heard to S.W. lasted for about 20 mins.	
			Very heavy rain in night.	

1577 Wt. W10791/1773 500,000 1/15 D. D. & L. A.D.S.S./Forms/C. 2118.

Instructions regarding War Diaries and Intelligence Summaries are contained in F. S. Regs., Part II. and the Staff Manual respectively. Title pages will be prepared in manuscript.

or

INTELLIGENCE SUMMARY.

1/4 Leic. Regt. (Erase heading not required.) 138th Inf. Bde. 46th Division.

Place	Date	Hour	Summary of Events and Information	Remarks and references to Appendices
Trenches	July 15th		Cool & Cloudy. Wind S.E.	Casualty
		12 midday	A/C.O. visited strong points and trenches held by 1/4 Lincs. Regt.	1. O.R. wounded slight.
		5 pm	Enemy shelled Bde H.Q. hitting it once. No damage done.	
		10 pm	~~C.O.~~ Lt. Col. Martin returned to duty from Sick leave.	
"	16th		Cool & Cloudy. Wind S.E.	
		am 9-45	Enemy shelled ground 500x North of Dugouts apparently searching for Batteries in that neighbourhood. This lasted for about 30 mins.	
		4 pm	Enemy shelled BDE H.Q. making four hits. Continued for about ½ hour.	
			C.O. and 2nd in C. visited trenches.	
			Brigade moved to new H.Q. at Kruisstaat.	

1577 Wt. W10791/1773 500,000 1/15 D. D. & L. A.D.S.S./Forms/C. 2118.

Instructions regarding War Diaries and Intelligence Summaries are contained in F. S. Regs., Part II. and the Staff Manual respectively. Title pages will be prepared in manuscript.

INTELLIGENCE SUMMARY.

1/4 Leic. Regt. (Erase heading not required.) 138th Inf. Bde. 46th Division.

Place	Date	Hour	Summary of Events and Information	Remarks and references to Appendices
Trenches	July			
Railway Dug Outs	17th		Cloudy and cool. Much rain during day and night.	Casualty
			Wind - Strong S.W.	1. O.R.
		2-30 pm.	Court Martial held in H.Q. dugout on a Lce: Corpl: on a charge of neglect.	wounded 10 p.m.
			President of Court. Major Robinson 5th Lincs.	
			Members. - Capt Stanland 4th Lincs. Lt. Shields 5th Leic.	
			Prisoner acquitted.	
		2-45 pm.	C.O. and 2nd in C visited Support point I.28.D and trenches 47 and 48.	
			Very little shelling today — only 3 or 4 fired by enemy about 500x N. of dugouts, apparently searching for guns.	
			Enemy did not fire on late B.de H.Q. today	
"	18th		Fine - Wind breezy North	
		5.40 pm	Lt. F.N. Tarr (Adjt.) was killed by splinter from Crump whilst visiting ZILLEBEKE LAKE DUG-OUTS. 2nd Lieut	Killed Lt. F N TARR

1577 Wt. W10791/1773 500,000 1/15 D. D. & L. A.D.S.S./Forms/C. 2118.

Instructions regarding War Diaries and Intelligence Summaries are contained in F. S. Regs., Part II. and the Staff Manual respectively. Title pages will be prepared in manuscript.

or

~~INTELLIGENCE SUMMARY.~~

1/4 LEIC. REGT. (Erase heading not required.) 138th Infantry Bde. 46th Division.

Place	Date	Hour	Summary of Events and Information	Remarks and references to Appendices
Trenches. Zillebeke Lake dugouts	July 18th.		R C Harvey took over duties of adj.	
		9.30 pm	Batt. relieved 5th Lincs. at ZILLEBEKE LAKE dugouts	
	19th		Situation normal Wind S.E.	WOUNDED. 2 O.R.
	20th	1 am	Batt. relieved 5th Lincs in "Right Sector" at 1 am. Companies were distributed as follows:-	Killed 1 O.R. Wounded 5 O.R.
			42a dug-outs "B" Coy (3 platoons)	
			47 + 47S "A" Coy	
			48 + 48S "C" Coy	
			49 + 49S "D" Coy	
			SPR1 "B" Coy (1 platoon)	
			Headquarters situated 100 yds NW of N end of trench 49 in dead ground from immediate front. M.O. in 42a dug-outs. Battalion dumping ground NW corner of MAPLE COPSE.	
			Trenches were in bad conditions. Little or no barbed wire entanglements. Practically	

1577 Wt. W10791/1773 500,000 1/15 D. D. & L. A.D.S.S./Forms/C. 2118.

Instructions regarding War Diaries and Intelligence Summaries are contained in F. S. Regs., Part II. and the Staff Manual respectively. Title pages will be prepared in manuscript.

INTELLIGENCE SUMMARY.

1/4 LEIC REGT. (Erase heading not required.) 138th Infantry Bde. 46th Division.

Place	Date	Hour	Summary of Events and Information	Remarks and references to Appendices
Trenches	JULY		no system of drainage. In places the parapet was dangerously low. Number of dugouts quite insufficient. Sanitary condition deplorable	
			Enemy fairly quiet. During the evening Trench 48 was trench-mortared; this ceased however, when our artillery replied	
	21st	7 am	Wind gentle SW.	Wounded 1 O.R.
		6 pm	5 officers of 51st Brigade joined the Batt. for 24 hours instruction. RIGHT and LEFT SECTOR Headquarters joined by buried cable.	
			Several times during night Trench 47 was trench-mortared (sausage type)	
	22nd	7 am	Situation quiet. Wind SW. During the night enemy were particularly quiet. During the night they were heard hammering stakes in for wire entanglements in front of trench 49	Killed 1 O.R. Wounded 9 O.R.

Instructions regarding War Diaries and Intelligence Summaries are contained in F. S. Regs., Part II. and the Staff Manual respectively. Title pages will be prepared in manuscript.

~~INTELLIGENCE~~ SUMMARY.

1/4 LEIC. REGT. (Erase heading not required.) 138th Infantry Bde. 46th Division

Place	Date	Hour	Summary of Events and Information	Remarks and references to Appendices
TRENCHES	JULY			
	23	7am	Situation normal. Wind SW.	Killed 1 O.R. Wounded 7 O.R.
		9am	The following officers, who arrived with the transport on the previous night, were thus posted:– Lt. T. Whittingham to "C" coy. Lt. G. J. Nugee " "B" " 2Lt. P. W. Scholes " "A" "	
		6.55pm	First charge exploded under enemy's forward parallel	
		7.1pm	Main charge exploded under enemy's parapet.	
		7.1pm	to 7.15pm. Our artillery fired over trenches 1 and 2.	
		9.35pm	Enemy exploded mine just short of trench 50. (for details see attached report)	
	24	7am	Situation quiet. Wind gentle SW.	Killed 1 O.R. Wounded 16 O.R.
		9.15pm	Crater made by enemy's mine immediately in front of trench 50 was occupied by 4th and 5th Leicesters. A working party began to put crater into state of defense, joining same to N end of trench 49	

1577 Wt. W10791/1773 500,000 1/15 D. D. & L. A.D.S.S./Forms/C. 2118.

Instructions regarding War Diaries and Intelligence Summaries are contained in F. S. Regs., Part II. and the Staff Manual respectively. Title pages will be prepared in manuscript.

~~INTELLIGENCE SUMMARY.~~

1/4 LEIC. REGT. (Erase heading not required.) 138th Infantry Bde 46th Division.

Place	Date	Hour	Summary of Events and Information	Remarks and references to Appendices
TRENCHES.	JULY.		by deepening old trench running parallel to S end of trench 50. (for details see attached.)	
	25	12.10am	Enemy threw time-fuze trench-mortar-bomb into crater. It was followed by two more which fell short.	Wounded 3 OR
		7am	Situation quiet. Wind W.	
		3pm	Enemy shelled N end of 49 trench and immediate vicinity to Headquarters. (whizz-bangs.)	
		9pm	Working party carried on work begun on previous night in crater and forward trench.	
	26	1am	Battalion, completely relieved by 5th LINCS., proceeded to ZILLEBEKE DUG-OUTS, which the 5th LINCS. had just vacated.	
ZILLEBEKE LAKE DUG-OUTS		7am	Situation normal. Wind SW by W. Battalion rested.	
		6pm	C.O. saw company commanders. Battalion dump in field at S end of ZILLEBEKE LAKE DUG-OUTS.	

Instructions regarding War Diaries and Intelligence Summaries are contained in F. S. Regs., Part II. and the Staff Manual respectively. Title pages will be prepared in manuscript.

~~INTELLIGENCE SUMMARY.~~

1/4 LEIC. REGT. (Erase heading not required.) 138th Infantry Bde. 46th Division

Place	Date	Hour	Summary of Events and Information	Remarks and references to Appendices
ZILLEBEKE LAKE D.O.	JULY			
	27	7am	Situation normal. Wind SW.	
		3pm	Fatigue party of 1 officer + 20 men worked at Bde HQ. till 7pm. This fatigue party is provided daily by battalion whilst in Brigade Reserve.	Wounded 1 O.R.
		6pm	Capt. Faire accompanied Bde Major in order to plan out new C.T. ZILLEBEKE - BATTERSEA FARM - SQUARE WOOD.	
		9pm	7 officers + 360 O.R. worked on above trench till 1.30 am.	
	28	7am	Situation normal. Wind SW.	
		9pm	Fatigues as on previous night	
	29	7am	Situation quiet. Wind nil.	F.A. Lt. F. S. PARR
		3pm	C.O saw company commanders. Progress of C.T. discussed	
		6pm	C.O and Capt. Faire met Brigade Major at SQUARE WOOD to further discuss + plan out C.T.	
		9.16pm	Dirty underclothing sent back on transport to divisional laundry.	

1577 Wt. W10791/1773 500,000 1/15 D. D. & L. A.D.S.S./Forms/C. 2118.

Instructions regarding War Diaries and Intelligence Summaries are contained in F. S. Regs., Part II. and the Staff Manual respectively. Title pages will be prepared in manuscript.

~~INTELLIGENCE~~ SUMMARY.

(*Erase heading not required.*)

1/4 LEIC REGT. 138th INFANTRY BDE. 46th DIVISION

Place	Date	Hour	Summary of Events and Information	Remarks and references to Appendices
ZILLEBEKE LAKE D.O.	JULY			
	29		2nd Lieut. M.B. Douglas took over command of M.G. section.	
	30	5.50am	Wind nil. Early this morning Germans attacked sector immediately on our left. At about 3.30 am our artillery opened a heavy fire, objective N of Brigade sector. This continued during greater part of the day.	Wounded. 3 O.R.
		9.30am	Verbal message to hold ourselves in readiness.	
	31	7am	Situation normal. Wind gentle SW.	
		10.30am	Carrying party of 3 officers + 120 O.R. took over 160 gallons of water up to battle headquarters of 41st Infantry Brigade.	Wounded 4 O.R. F.A. 2Lt C.B.P. Peake
		7pm	N end of ZILLEBEKE LAKE DUG-OUTS severely shelled with percussion shrapnel.	6 O.R
		8pm	about this time 8th Sherwood Foresters attacked. Enemy repulsed. Exchange in our favour. Our artillery support excellent. The enemy made not further	

1577 Wt. W10791/1773 500,000 1/15 D. D. & L. A.D.S.S./Forms/C. 2118.

Instructions regarding War Diaries and Intelligence Summaries are contained in F. S. Regs., Part II. and the Staff Manual respectively. Title pages will be prepared in manuscript.

~~INTELLIGENCE SUMMARY.~~

1/4 LEIC. REGT (*Erase heading not required.*) 138th Infantry Bde 46th Division

Place	Date	Hour	Summary of Events and Information	Remarks and references to Appendices
ZILLEBEKE LAKE D.O.	JULY			
	31		attempts to bomb our trenches. Our artillery kept up a heavy fire till 9.15 pm. Enemy's effort to silence our guns was feeble.	
		9.30pm	The situation was again quiet.	
		9.45pm	Transport arrived	
			2Lt. J. E. Barker joined the battalion for duty. Lt. Leeson returned from leave. Coy. Sgt. Major Bromley relieved Batt. Sgt. Major Davenport who returned to Quartermaster's Stores on "LIGHT DUTY".	2Lt. J. E. BARKER joined batt. Batt. Sgt. Major for Light duty.
			25 war-worn O.R returned to Qmr. Stores en route for base.	25 O.R. Sent to Base.
		11.15pm	1st LEICESTERS arrived at NW corner of ZILLEBEKE LAKE in div. reserve for 14th Div. They there received orders to return to billets.	

R.C. Harvey 2Lt. a/adj
1/4th Leicestershire Regiment
1.8.15

A P P E N D I C E S .

RET.

OPERATION ORDERS NO 2.

by

Major J.A.Potter, Cmdg. 1/4th. Leicestershire Regiment.

Ref. FRANCE & BELGIUM Sheet 28, OUDERDOM. 13/7/15.

1.

The Battalion will take over the Railway Embankment Dugouts & Strong Points now held by the 1st. Dorset Regt. in I 20, D. ref. sheet 28, tonight.

2.

The battalion will march at 7-45 p.m. and rendevous at the Railway crossing in I 20 a. LILLE ROAD COURTRAI RY. at 10 p.m.

O. of M.

Headquarters.
Signallers.
1 Platoon "D" Coy. & 1 Sgt. and 9 men.
C. A. B. & the remainder of D Coy.
Grenadiers, Machine Gunners, and Scabies Cases.
1st. Line of Transport.

Parties will be met at the rendevous by guides from the battalion being relieved and will be led independantly to the S.P.'s and dugouts to be occupied by them. O.C. Coys. will render reports to Bn. H.Q. together with copies in duplicate of trench stores taken over, immediately on completion of the relief.

3. Immediately on arrival at dugouts OC.Coys. will detail a party to fill all available water tins from the water cart accompanying the battalion which will be at the dump.

Dump. The dump for all rations and stores for all battalions is BDE. H.Q. I 20 c 8.9 ref. 1/10000.

4. On arrival, one guard of 1 N.C.O. and 3 men will be furnished by each company to prevent men straying away from the embankment and to watch for aeroplanes. The O.C. "A" Coy. will detail a guard of similar strength for Bn. Hqrs.

No fires will be lit between the hours of 3 a.m. and 9 p.m.

SD B.F.NEWILL. Capt.
A.A. 1/4th. Leicestershire Regiment.

No. 1. "A" Coy.
2. "B" "
3. "C" "
4. "D" "
5. M.G.O.
6. G.O.
7. War Dairy.

COPY.

138TH. INF. BDE. RIGHT SECTOR.

REPORT ON EVENTS ON EVENING AND NIGHT JULY 23/24th.

July 23rd. 6-55 p.m. First charge exploded under enemy's forward parallel.

7-1 p.m. Main charge exploded under enemy's parapet.

7-1 to 7-15 p.m. Our artillery fired over 1 and 2 trenches.

Trench Commanders in Right Sector had been warned the previous day and all subordinate commanders had been instructed bythem; nothing was said to the men.

9-35 p.m. Violent explosion apparently in direction of trench 50; considerable amount of debris fell all over and around Battalion Hqrs. I immediately telephoned to trench 49 Capt. Milne had gone to interview the officer in charge of wo rk on OBSERVATORY RIDGE pursuant to Bde. order; 2/Lt. Douglas who was in command, informed me that the explosion seemed to be in trench 50 or a1. I ordered the Bomb Officer to assemble his men at the junction of 49 and 50 and informed the O.C. 5th. Leicesters (Left sector) that I had done so. The machine gun officer reported that his guns were all ready for action within two minutes of the explosion. Some time elapsed before I could get any accurate information as to what had happened. While making inquiries I sent every available man from hqrs. with shovels and all empty sandbags to trench 49 in case the parapet had been destroyed. In the meantime 2/Lt. Douglas had stopped a ration party from trench 48 who were passing through 49 and added them (40 in number) to the garrison. Capt. Milne had heard the explosion while on his way to observatoryridge . He ran back to his trench and having found that the garrison were standing to, he left Lt. Douglas in command and went up trench 50; he found 3 or 4 traverses at the end of that part of the trench which normally occupied empty of men. The garrison were buried in debris. He sent for 10 men with shovels and then posted some 4th. Leicester bombers and other men as garrison. He then superintended the digging out of the men. Capt. Griffiths 5th. Leicesters came from the other end of the trench and asked Capt. Milne to send round the short forward trench to see if the 5th. Leicester listening patrol were still there.

Capt. Milne took a bomber and crawled round the forward trench about 40x up it he found what seemed to be a large crater at the place approx. at which the 5th. Leicester patrol was posted. He returned and reported to Capt. G riffiths and then continued to help in the digging out of buried men and the replacing of sandbags on the parapet. After hearing Capt. Milne's report I told the O. C. 5th Leic. to keep my men who were garrisoning the S end of 50 as long as he considered necessary.

At about 1 a.m. I was infomed by the O. C. 5th Leic. that a party of the enemy were reported to be in the centre crater and that he proposed to have them bombed out.

I ordered my Bomb Officer to confer with the 5th Leic. Officer and co-operate. He did so, and they threw several bombs into the Crater ; afterwards a flare was sent up and they satisfied them-selves that the Crater was empty.

The enemy rifle fire died down about midnight to its normal intensity.

NOTE After the explosion of our second charge, the enemy sent up an irregular succession of red and white flares from opposite 49.

flares opposite 49.

This appeared to be a signal for artillery support.

The casulties in this Batallion were as follows :-

Bruises from falling debris	3.
Bruises and wounds from falling sandbags	2.
Bruises from being buried	1.
Crushed and bullet wounds.	2.

No damage was done to the parapet of Trench 49 though large quantities of falling debris fell into it and the trenches in rear of it.

(sd) R. E. MARTIN.
Lt. Col.
Comdg 1/4th Leic, Rt.

24. 7. 15.

COPY.

Report on work in crater in front of Trench in 1. 30. C. 7.8. July 24/25/15.

---

(1) At 9-35 p.m. on July23rd , in retaliation for two mines exploded by us , the enemy fired a mine in front of Trench 50 in 1.30. C.7.8. A large crater was formed of a width estimated at 40 feet across at the centre at a distance of about 20 to 25 yards from the parapet of the trench. A report of the explosion and of the subsequent action taken that night was forwarded under myG.X. 1938 on the 25th instant.

(2) On the 24th Julyiy was decided to push forward our position by occupying the forward lip of the crater . As soon as it was dark work was started in clearing the forward trench in front of Trench 50 of trees and other obstructions. and by 9-29 p.m. the work was sufficiently far advanced to allow of diggers from the 4th Battn Leicester Rt entering the trench . deepening it and filling sandbags. The work was slow and difficult as it had to be performed kneeling. At the same time a drift was commenced bymen of the 175th Tunnelling Coy R. E. under the parapet of Trench 50 to permit of the crater being entered in daylight without exposure.

~~3EX~~ (3) At 9-50 p.m. an N.C.O. and 8 men of the 1/1 Field Co. 4R. E. and 8 men of the 5th Battn Leics Regt specially selected for proficiency in building a sandbag breastwork entered the crater and began to cut a ledge about 5'6" below the lip of the crater on its inner fact (eastn side) The Bombers of the 4th and 5th Leics Regt formed a screen along the front of the trench and of the crater to protect the working party.

(4) At 10-45 p.m. sandbags began to arrive from the Brigade store and were passed from man to man along the trench and over the parapet and into the crater where other men began to fill them. Sandbags filled in Trench 50 were rolled over the parapet into the Crater . A line of men passed the sandbags as theywere filled up to the ledge of the crater where the builders made a revetment.Under the direction of Col. Martin (O.C. 4th Battn Leics Regt) who had now come up to superintend the work in the crater. two traverses were built on the ledge. the one at the N end and the other at the outer face- about the centre of the outer face of the parapet.

(5) At 11-30 p.m. the second relief of builders consisting of 1 N.C. O. and 8 men of the 1/1 Field Co. R. E. and 8 men of the 4th Bn Leicester Regt arrived in the crater and in order to push on with the work as much as possible before dawn both reliefs were kept at work. Including the men filling and passing sandbags there were thus 35 to 40 men in the crater . At 12-10 p.m. the enemy threw a trench mortor bomb from a catapult which fell in the crater and killed 1 men and wounded 21 others. Major Potter who remained in the crater throughout attended to the wounded and those of the working party not engaged in evacuating the wounded continued their work. Meanwhile Col. Martin left to receive instructions from the Brigadier as to the continuance of the work. At 12-45 a.m. orders were received to suspend the work for half an hour to see if more bombs would be thrown. Two more bombs were thown but fell outside the crater causing no more casulties.

(6) By this time it had become too light to resume work

on the crater, but a few men remained in the forward trench which joins up the old trench with the crater to deepen the shallowest places. By daylight it was possible to crawl into the crater without being seen except from the trees. A bench 4 to 5 ft wide had been dug for 20 yards in the bank of the crater and revetted with a sandbag wall, and the two traverses had been completed. The drift under the parapet of trench 50 had also been driven in a length of 4ft and was in a state to be pushed through into the crater before nightfall. The Bombers were withdrawn at dawn and the sandbags were covered with earth as far as possible.

The work was completed the following evening.

(COPY)

HEADQUARTERS
138th INFANTRY BRIGADE.

Report on work done in connection with Mine Crater in front of Trench 50.

I have the honour to report that pursuant to orders from the Brigade, and after conference on the afternoon of the 24th with Capt. Price Davies, 46th. Division and Major Cowen R.E., I arranged with Major Toller, the following:-

(1) The section of the 1/1st. Field Co. R.E. at present in Armagh Wood, 16 sappers and 2 N.C.O's, should be strengthed an by the addition of 8 men from the 4th. and 8 from the 5th. Leicesters; all to be selected for skill in laying sandbags.

(2) 50 men of the 4th. Leicesters should meet the transport on arrival and carry the sandbags (specially sent up) direct to trench 49.

(3) 50 men 4th. Leicesters should work as sandbag fillers and carriers.

(4) The 4th. Leicesters should clear the forward trench in front of 50 sufficiently to allow the passage of men crawling and of the handing forward of sandbags.

(5) The 5th. Leicesters should bring up to trench 50 the 500 sandbags filled two days ago in readiness for the mine exploded on the 23rd., and should fill as many as possible during the night; these should be passed over the parapet and rolled down in the crater.

(6) A trench or ledge should be cut round the E slope of the crater, at such a level that a 4foot 6 inches wall should have its top about a foot to 18 inches below the crest of the earth run of the crater.

(7) The 4th. and 5th. Leicesters bombers should form a screen along the front of the forward trench and the crater so as to keep off any attempted attack. Work to begin as soon as it was dark and to continue until dawn.

(8) A drift should be made under the parapet of 50, to run out into the crater and allow of its being entered without exposure. This work was begun forthwith by the mining Coy. R.E.

(9) By 9-20p.m. Major Potter had cleared the forward trench of fallen trees and other obstructions. The diggers were then passed into the trench and proceeded to deepen it and fill sandbags. This work was necessarily slow and difficult, having to be done kneeling. By about 9-50 p.m. the first shift (N.C.O. and 8) of sappers had gone forward into the crater and began to cut the ledge. The 5th, Leicesters sandbag men went with them.

(10) At 10-45 p.m. or thereabouts the sandbags from the Brigade store began to arrive. These were passed along from hand to hand by the men in the trench and the foremost were sent down into the crater to fill them. Filled sandbags were thrown over the parapet of 50 and rolled into the crater lines of men being formed to pass them up to the ledge, where the sappers laid them.

(11) The work had proceeded so far under Major Potters direction. At about 10-45 p.m. after satisfying myself that the arragements for the supply of sandbags were working properly, I went forwarded into the crater. I directed the N.C.O. of sappers to build a travess in about the centre of the enemy face of the crater, & remained in the crater myself in order to ensure so far as possible that no time should be lost in any way and to supervise generally.

(12) At 11-30 p.m. the second shift of sappers came on. I consulted with the Sgt. as to the progress of the work and arranged that both shifts should continue at work in order to make full use of the hours of darkness. This involved an addition to the numberof men in the crater who filling and passing sandbags. Finally they were about 35 or 40 men at work.

(13) At about 12-10 a.m. the enemy through a time fuse trench mortar bomb, probably from a catapult, as no noise was heard before the explosion. It burst in the centre of the crater, killing 1 man and wounding 21 others some of them severely. The crater was filled with smoke and there was some confusion.

(14) Helped by MajorPotter I fell in the unwounded men, less those required to help the badly hurt along the trench. Major Potter attended personally to some of the worst cases in the bottom of the crater. I made my way after leaving him in charge, to Hqrs. and explained the position to the Bde. Major , who after consulting the General toled me that the General approved of the work being suspended for half an hour in order to see whether any more bombs would be thrown. Two more were in fact thrown at about 12-15 and 12-20 both exploded near the south edge of the crater but outside it.

(15) After getting the wounded dressed and sent out, Major Potter resumed work with the men who were left. At about 12-45 a.m. he received my order to withdraw the men from the crater. I returned from Hqrs. to the trench and found the remains of the working party coming from the forward trench. I sent for the R.E. Sgt. and after consultation with him decided that it was too light to resume work in the crater. A few men were kept in the forward trench until the light became pronounced, to deepen the shallow places. When they were finally withdrawn this trench was passable by crawling throughout and access could be got to the crater by day, without exposure to view except to any enemy in the trees.

(16) The work accomplished in the crater consisted of the cutting of a trench about 4'6" to 5' wide for a length of about 20 yds. round the outer circumference of the hollow. A sandbagged wall about 3'6" high has been built, the length of the ledge; two traverses have carried up at the northern end at about the centre of the outer face as shown on the sketch.

(17) The drift under the parapet of 50 had been driven to a length of 4' . The R.E. Officer expressed himself of as confident that it would be threw into the crater before this evening.

(18) The comparatively large number of casualties was due, of course, to the crowding of men in the crater. This was inevitable if any effective attempt was to be made to complete the consolidation of the forward edge in one night. A very large number of sandbags had to be filled and handed up a steep slope by lines of men to the ledge near the top. in view of the urgent character of the order which I had received, I did not consider myself at liberty to order a cessation of work without reference to the Brigade.

(19) I would suggest very strongly that when the work is resumed sandbags should be passed through the new drift and not over the parapet. I think it almost certain that the enemy were made aware of the fact that work was going on in the crater through seeing the bags rolled down the front of the parapet during a time when the cloud had cleared and the moon shone out. Without the bags thus supplied the work could not have been carried as far as it was; but as soon as any other method of getting them into the crater is available, it should most certainly be used. The bombers were left in position until dawn and the sandbags were covered with earth so far as possible.

SD. R.E.MARTIN. Lieut. Col.
Cmdg. 1/4th. Leicestershire Regiment.

25/7/15.
5-15 a.m.

4

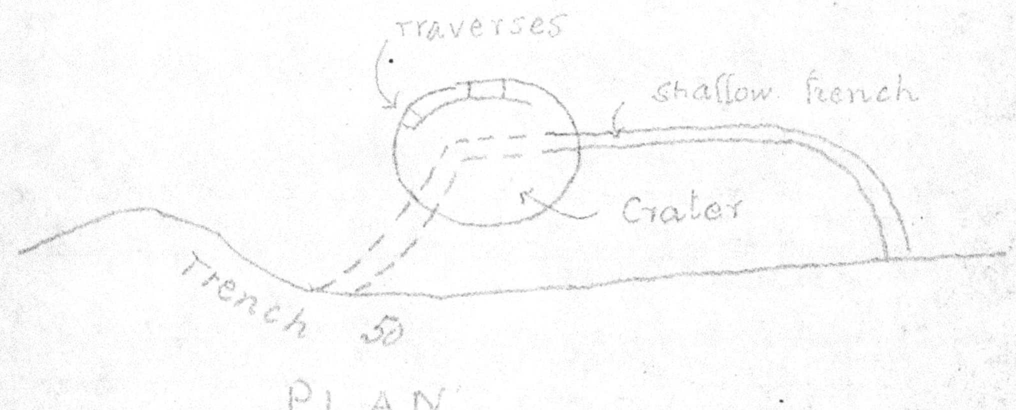

PLAN

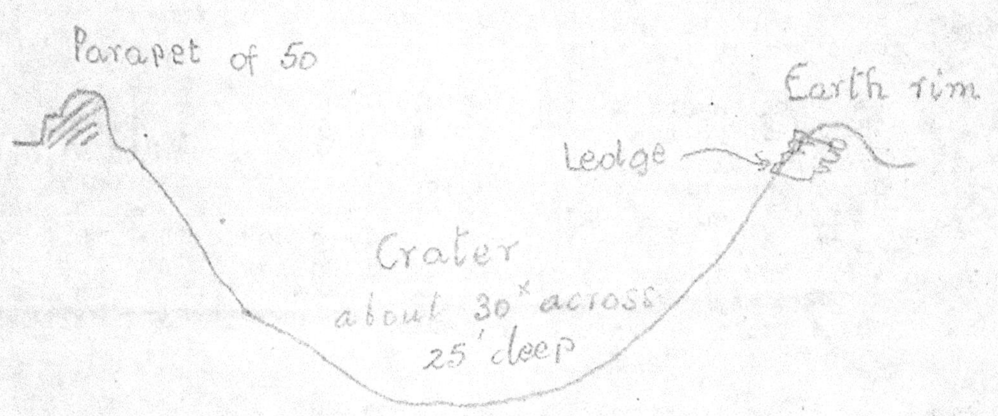

SECTION THROUGH CRATER

The Brigadier General,
Commanding 138th. Inf. Bde.

Sir,

I have the honour to enclose for your information reports from Major Potter and Capt. Milne upon the conduct of men under fire on July ~~24/25~~ 4th., 22nd., and the night of July 24/25th.

(1). Between a dozen and twenty shells fell in the wood where the party referred to in Capt. Milne's report were carrying the stretcher, and I would submit for your notice the behaviour of PTES. LOWE and ALEXANDER under these circumstances.

(2) The shelling in SANCTUARYVWOOD on July 4th. was fairly severe and the three stretcher bearers named of whom PTE LOWE above mentioned was one, had to go about 100 yds across the ground where they were falling in order to reach the wounded man.

(3) The ground in rear of trench 6, over which SGT: BIRD and the three stretcher bearers passed on July 4th. is quite open to the enemy's view and fire, and it was broad daylight at the time.

(4) With regard to the behaviour of PTES. LETTS & WHEELBAND in the crater on the night of July 24/25th., I would point out that these men were assembled with the other unwounded men by Major Potter under the only available cover, which was afforded by the mass of earth on the S.W. rim of the crater. This cover they left of their own accord to assist Major Potter in tending the man who was delirious, and continued working with him while two further trench mortar bombs exploded on the edge of the crater.

(5) I can confirm of my own knowledge what Major Potter says of the difficulty of conveying the wounded along the forward trench. It was at that time both shallower and more obstructed than it is at present and the management of a delirious patient under such circumstances was an operation of no small difficulty and danger.

(6) In my report dated 25th. inst I brought to notice the services rendered by Major Potter inmanaging the working parties in the forward trench and the crater and in carrying on the work after the explosion of the bombs.

I had not then had an opportunity of learning what was done in the matter of the treatment of the wounded, but I should like to be allowed to bring to notice the manner in which Major Potter organized and led this work. He showed the same coolness and resource in the difficulty task of removing a delirious patient, and afterwards the body of a man who was killed, up the side of the crater and along the trench, that he had displayed during the earlier part of the night. His personal example was of the greatest value in steadying the men and setting them to work again.

I am, Sir,

Your obedient servant,

Lieut. Col.

Cmdg. 4th. Leicestershire Regiment.

28/7/15.

138th Inf.Bde.
46th Div.

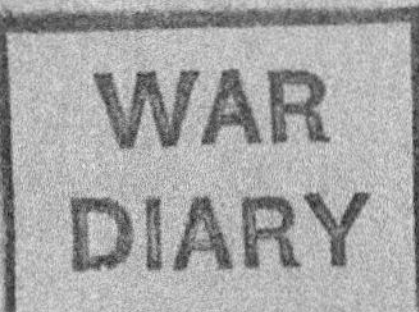

4th BATTN. THE LEICESTERSHIRE REGIMENT.

A U G U S T

1 9 1 5

Instructions regarding War Diaries and Intelligence Summaries are contained in F. S. Regs., Part II. and the Staff Manual respectively. Title pages will be prepared in manuscript.

or

~~INTELLIGENCE SUMMARY.~~

(Erase heading not required.)

Place	Date	Hour	Summary of Events and Information	Remarks and references to Appendices
			August 1915	
			1/4 Leicestershire Regt.	

1577 Wt. W10791/1773 500,000 1/15 D. D. & L. A.D.S.S./Forms/C. 2118.

Instructions regarding War Diaries and Intelligence Summaries are contained in F. S. Regs., Part II. and the Staff Manual respectively. Title pages will be prepared in manuscript.

or
~~INTELLIGENCE SUMMARY.~~
(Erase heading not required.)

1/4 LEIC REGT. 138th Infantry Bde, 46th Division.

Place	Date	Hour	Summary of Events and Information	Remarks and references to Appendices
ZILLEBEKE LAKE D.O	AUGUST			
	1	7am	Situation quiet. Wind nil.	F.A. 3 O.R.
		3pm	Battalion office held	
		4pm	C.O. saw company commanders.	
			The relieving 25 O.R from base joined the battalion for duty this day.	
		9pm	Companies left ZILLEBEKE LAKE DUG-OUTS to take over RIGHT SECTOR from 5th Lincs. Trenches were allotted to companies as follows:-	
			D coy (3 platoons) 42a dug-outs	
			B " 47 and 47S	
			A " 48 Rifle pits and SQUARE WOOD.	
			C " 49 and 49S	
			D " (1 platoon.) SPR1	
			Garrisons of 42a dugouts and 47 proceeded via Railway line and remainder by ZILLEBEKE C.T.	
		11.30pm	Relief completed.	

1577 Wt. W10791/1773 500,000 1/15 D. D. & L. A.D.S.S./Forms/C. 2118.

Instructions regarding War Diaries and Intelligence Summaries are contained in F. S. Regs., Part II. and the Staff Manual respectively. Title pages will be prepared in manuscript.

or

INTELLIGENCE SUMMARY.

1/4 LEIC. REGT. (Erase heading not required.) 138th Infantry Bde. 46th Division.

Place	Date	Hour	Summary of Events and Information	Remarks and references to Appendices
TRENCHES	AUGUST			
	2	7am	Situation quiet. Wind SW	Wounded 1 O.R.
		8.15am	An explosion occurred about 30 yds in front of German parapet opposite R.P.2. Apparently at sap head exploded	F.A. 6 O.R.
		3.30pm	Ground between 42a dugouts and 47s shelled by enemy's howitzers & whizz-bangs.	
	3.	7am	Situation quiet. Wind S by W. Gusty	
		12.30pm	Col. Hewitt 5th York & Lancaster Regt arrived for attachment.	
		2.40pm	O.C. 47 reported suspicion of enemy mining near red cottage.	Wounded 1 O.R.
		5pm	60 pr. Batty fired 30 rounds over 47 trench. Many good hits on German parapet. C.O. visited trenches with Col. Hewitt	F.A. Capt. NEWILL 2 O.R.
		7.15pm	Enemy threw heavy T.M. bombs on trench 50. Our Howitzers & Field Bty replied.	
	4.	3am	ZOUAVE WOOD heavily shelled for over an hour.	Wounded 1 O.R. F.A. 2/Lt. LEESON
		7am	Situation normal. Wind S.W.	

Instructions regarding War Diaries and Intelligence Summaries are contained in F. S. Regs., Part II. and the Staff Manual respectively. Title pages will be prepared in manuscript.

INTELLIGENCE SUMMARY.

(Erase heading not required.)

1/4 Leic Regt. 138th Bde. 46th Division

Place	Date	Hour	Summary of Events and Information	Remarks and references to Appendices
TRENCHES	AUGUST			
	4	3pm	Working party seen in C.T. in rear of crater made on previous day in front of 48 trench.	F.A. 4 O.R.
		5pm	2nd Derby Howitzer Batt.y fired rds at German first line trench opposite 47 and 48.	
		6.30pm	Headquarters "whizz-banged".	
		7.0pm	Enemy threw 3 heavy trench mortar bombs into trench 50. Our howitzers replied by shelling wood opposite S end of trench 49 where trench mortar was thought to be.	
	5	3.30am	Our artillery heavily shelled HOOGE sector for about one hour.	Wounded Lt. McGEE 1 O.R.
		7am	Situation quiet again. Wind S.W. gentle.	
		3.30pm	Germans threw 3 heavy T.M. bombs in trench 50.	F.A. 5 O.R.
		3.30pm	Lt F.J. McGEE wounded in both shoulders by shrapnel from whizz-bang at E end of trench 47S.	
		4.15pm	18pr Battery fired high explosive shell at German	

Instructions regarding War Diaries and Intelligence Summaries are contained in F. S. Regs., Part II. and the Staff Manual respectively. Title pages will be prepared in manuscript.

or

INTELLIGENCE SUMMARY.

(*Erase heading not required.*)

Place	Date	Hour	Summary of Events and Information	Remarks and references to Appendices
TRENCHES	AUGUST			
			parapet opposite trench 48. Enemy's parapet badly damaged.	
		6.54pm	ARMAGH WOOD whizz-banged. Our artillery replied	
			REMARKS:- From the following incidents we are led to believe that enemy opposite this sector have recently been relieved:-	
			(a) During the day a white sheet was hoisted from trench opposite 47. with WARSHAW HAS FALLEN on it	
			(b) Some German shouted from opposite 47 "Vy vas you so quiet?"	
			(c) Flares were sent up from different places and 2 or 3 men were seen to fire together	
	6	7am	Situation quiet. Wind SW	Wounded 1 O.R.
			Little rifle fire during the morning	
		3pm - 5pm	47a and CT to 47S shelled with "Crumps"	

Instructions regarding War Diaries and Intelligence Summaries are contained in F. S. Regs., Part II. and the Staff Manual respectively. Title pages will be prepared in manuscript.

or

~~INTELLIGENCE~~ SUMMARY.

1/4 Leic. Regt. (*Erase heading not required.*) 138th Brigade 46th Division

Place	Date	Hour	Summary of Events and Information	Remarks and references to Appendices
TRENCHES	AUG			
			and whizz-bangs	
		9pm	3 sausages thrown over 48 trench. No damage done.	
	7th.	7am.	Situation quiet. Wind S.W.	
		11 am.	Headquarters "whizz-banged".	F.A. 2 O.R.
		6pm.	48 trench "sausaged". 2Lt. W. N. DUNN wounded by piece of sausage in calf.	WOUNDED. 2Lt. DUNN 2 O.R.
	8th.	7am.	Situation normal. Little rifle fire. Wind SW.	
		10 am.	49 & 50 trenches whizz-banged	
		4pm.	42a & 47s crumped & whizz-banged	
	9th.	7am.	Situation quiet wind. SW.	F.A. 5 O.R.
		9.30 am	49 & 50 trenches "whizz-banged."	
			During the morning our howitzers fired onto German front line trenches opposite 49 & 50 trenches. Enemy retaliated by whizz-banging 49 & crump-ing 42 a dugouts	

1577 Wt. W10791/1773 500,000 1/15 D. D. & L. A.D.S.S./Forms/C. 2118.

Instructions regarding War Diaries and Intelligence Summaries are contained in F. S. Regs., Part II. and the Staff Manual respectively. Title pages will be prepared in manuscript.

~~INTELLIGENCE SUMMARY.~~

(*Erase heading not required.*)

Place	Date	Hour	Summary of Events and Information	Remarks and references to Appendices
TRENCHES.	AUG.			
	10.	7 am	Situation quiet. Wind nil.	F.A.
			During the day 47S + C.T. leading to 42a dugouts were "crumped"	5 o.R.
			The Battalion was relieved by 5th Lincs. Relief completed 11 pm. Coys returned independantly, garrisons of 42a dugouts, 47, 47S + 48 moving via railway, and remainder by Batt H.Q. MAPLE COPSE – ZILLEBEKE. Guides met Companies at Bde H.Q and conducted them to H.23.a.b. where batt. rested	
	11	7 am	Situation normal. Wind W.	
		9 am	Breakfast.	
		11.15 am.	Battalion paraded. and moved off by Companies at 5 minutes interval to huts H 13 d.9.1.	
		6 pm	G.O.C. came to see Battalion	
			The following officers arrived and were posted	

Instructions regarding War Diaries and Intelligence Summaries are contained in F. S. Regs., Part II. and the Staff Manual respectively. Title pages will be prepared in manuscript.

INTELLIGENCE SUMMARY.

(*Erase heading not required.*)

Place	Date	Hour	Summary of Events and Information	Remarks and references to Appendices
HUTS.	AUG			
	11.		to companies thus :–	
			Lt J. G. ABELL to "A" Coy	
			2Lt W. H. B. MOGGRIDGE " "C" "	
			2Lt W. N. RILEY " "D" "	
	12.	7am	Situation normal. Wind nil.	
			Battalion rested. Armt Sgt. inspected rifles.	
		9.30am	2Lt SCHOLES & 32 O.R. paraded under Capt. ELLWOOD for instruction in grenade throwing	
		2pm – 3pm	Bde band played	
		5.30pm – 7pm	" "	
		5.0pm	C.O. visited HQ 6th LEIC Regt. at M 29 d 2.3 (Belgium 28)	
	13	7am	Situation normal. Wind nil. Wet day.	FA.
			Battalion bathed & rested.	4 O.R.
		6pm	C.O. visited transport lines & Qmr stores. Bde band played 6 – 7.30pm.	
	14	7am	Situation normal. Wind W.	1.

Instructions regarding War Diaries and Intelligence Summaries are contained in F. S. Regs., Part II. and the Staff Manual respectively. Title pages will be prepared in manuscript.

~~INTELLIGENCE SUMMARY.~~

1/4 LEIC. REGT (*Erase heading not required.*) 138th Infantry Bde 46th Division

Place	Date	Hour	Summary of Events and Information	Remarks and references to Appendices
HUTS	AUG			
	14		The following digging parties were provided —	
			2 officers 150 O.R. working 8.30 am to 2.30 pm under 1/1 [illegible] Coy R.E.	
			2 officers 150 O.R. working 9 am to 3 pm under 2/1 Field Coy R.E.	
			1 officer & 30 O.R. working from 9 am to 3 pm at Brigade HQ.	
		5.30 pm	Battalion office.	
		6 pm	C.O. & Adj. went to Brigade HQ	
	15	7 am	Situation normal [illegible]	
			Brig-Gen [illegible] Clifford relinquished the command of 138th Infantry Brigade. Brig-Gen G.C. KEMP took over command.	F.A. 2 O.R
		10.15 am	[illegible] church parade.	
		12.1 pm	C.O. went to Divisional HQ.	
		5 pm - 7 pm	Brigade band played.	
		7 pm	Retreat blown	

1577 Wt. W10791/1773 500,000 1/15 D. D. & L. A.D.S.S./Forms/C. 2118.

Instructions regarding War Diaries and Intelligence Summaries are contained in F. S. Regs., Part II. and the Staff Manual respectively. Title pages will be prepared in manuscript.

INTELLIGENCE SUMMARY.

(Erase heading not required.)

Place	Date	Hour	Summary of Events and Information	Remarks and references to Appendices
HUTS.	AUG.			
	16th	7am	Situation normal. Wind	
		9.30am.	C.O. inspected companies with a view to finding out what deficiencies had not yet been replaced.	
		4.0pm.	Battalion paraded in mass formation for inspection by G.O.C. He commented on smart turn-out, and was apparently pleased with state of clothing and equipment.	
		6.30pm.	Battalion left huts en route for trenches.	
		8.0pm.	Battalion passed Bridge 16, proceeding to relieve 5th Lincs in RIGHT SECTOR. Distribution of battalion:	
			42a dug-outs — "C" Coy	
			47s, 47 — "D" Coy	
			48, SQUARE WOOD — "B" Coy	
			49, 49s — "A" Coy	

Instructions regarding War Diaries and Intelligence Summaries are contained in F. S. Regs., Part II. and the Staff Manual respectively. Title pages will be prepared in manuscript.

INTELLIGENCE SUMMARY.

(*Erase heading not required.*)

1/4 LEIC REGT. 138th Infantry BRIGADE. 46th Division.

Place	Date	Hour	Summary of Events and Information	Remarks and references to Appendices
TRENCHES	AUG.		SR1 "C" Coy.	
			Relief completed by 11.45 pm.	
			During period of rest 2Lt. SCHOLES + 32 O.R. had 4 days instruction in "bomb-throwing" under Capt. Elwood. The 138th Brigade sent the battalion a maxim gun on arrival at huts, and 2Lt. DOUGLAS proceeded to instruct daily latest batch of his recruits.	
	17	7am	Situation quiet. Wind N.W.	Killed 1 O.R.
		1.30pm	47S shelled with crumps & shrapnel till 2.30 pm and after from 3.15pm to 4pm. Enemy lengthened range with shrapnel as far as 42a. 49 "whizz-banged" from 3.30pm - 4pm.	F.A. 1 O.R.
		10-pm	Gas slightly smelt throughout sector	
	18	7am	Situation normal. Wind N.W.	
		3.30pm 5.45pm	Lt. DUMBELL 41st Friends Howitzer Batt. wounded (G.S.) neck & right shoulder junction 47 & 48	Wounded Lt. DUMBELL 3 O.R. F.A. 2 O.R.

1577 Wt. W10791/1773 500,000 1/15 D. D. & L. A.D.S.S./Forms/C. 2118.

Instructions regarding War Diaries and Intelligence Summaries are contained in F. S. Regs., Part II. and the Staff Manual respectively. Title pages will be prepared in manuscript.

~~INTELLIGENCE SUMMARY.~~

(*Erase heading not required.*)

1/4 LEIC. REGT. 138th Infantry Bde 46th Division

Place	Date	Hour	Summary of Events and Information	Remarks and references to Appendices
TRENCHES	AUG.			
	19.	7am	Situation normal. Wind NW.	WOUNDED 2 O.R. F.A. 4 O.R.
		11.30am	Lieut. W. G. MARSHALL, 2nd Lincs Batt. shot through head while looking through periscope from junction 47 & 48 at trenches opposite 50. He died shortly afterwards. On the 18th inst. a German aeroplane dropped several copies of the "GAZETTE DES ARDENNES" behind 48 trench. Two copies dated 4th & 18th July were picked up to-day.	
			Brig. Gen. Kemp visited sector during afternoon.	
	20	7am	Situation normal. Wind W.	WOUNDED 1 O.R. F.A. 3 O.R.
		3pm	1st DERBY How. fired 10 rds. over 49 trench at German salient. Observer reports that shells were all over parapet. 2nd DERBY Hows. fired over 47.	
			Trench between 47S & 42a de "cramped" & "whizz-banged".	

1577 Wt. W10791/1773 500,000 1/15 D. D. & L. A.D.S.S./Forms/C. 2118.

Instructions regarding War Diaries and Intelligence Summaries are contained in F. S. Regs., Part II. and the Staff Manual respectively. Title pages will be prepared in manuscript.

~~INTELLIGENCE SUMMARY.~~

1/4th LEIC. REGT. (Erase heading not required.) 138 Brigade 46th Division.

Place	Date	Hour	Summary of Events and Information	Remarks and references to Appendices
TRENCHES	AUG			
	21	7am	Situation quiet. Wind NW.	KILLED. 1 O.R.
		2.30pm.	Small 'crumps' and whizz-bangs dropping short of 42a dug-outs.	F.A 3 O.R.
			Rifle-firing very quiet.	
	22	7am.	Situation quiet. Wind NW.	
			47S shelled. No damage.	F.A 2 O.R.
		5pm to 5.30pm.	E end of 49 + ground behind trench 50 whizz-banged.	
			Battalion was relieved in RIGHT sector by 5 LINCS. RIGHT SECTOR was modified. 49 was given up to LEFT SECTOR battalion with SPR1, and 5 LINCS took over from 41a. 41 + 42 from 137th Bde. Companies returned to dug-outs independently by 42a. 47S. 47 by railway. 48. 49. 49S + SPR1 by observation rd.	

1577 Wt. W10791/1773 500,000 1/15 D. D. & L. A.D.S.S./Forms/C. 2118.

Instructions regarding War Diaries and Intelligence Summaries are contained in F. S. Regs., Part II. and the Staff Manual respectively. Title pages will be prepared in manuscript.

INTELLIGENCE SUMMARY.

(Erase heading not required.)

Place	Date	Hour	Summary of Events and Information	Remarks and references to Appendices
DUG-OUTS	AUG.			
			HQ., HQ staff, A & B coys occupied ZILLEBEKE LAKE DUG-OUTS. C & D coys machine gun & grenade sections bivouacing in H.23 b. The latter had field kitchens with them.	
	23	7am	Situation normal. Wind NW.	WOUNDED 3 O.R.
			Battalion rested.	F.A. 2 O.R.
			During period in Brigade reserve, battalion found daily 155 O.R for work on 2nd line defenses.	
		4.30pm.	Lt. PARR & 2Lt DOUGLAS with M.G. section proceeded to E HUTS (	
			2Lt. SCHOLES & 32 men also proceeded to 'E' HUTS to complete grenade course of training	
	24	7am	Situation normal. Wind N.W.	F.A.
		6pm.	Battalion moved from ZILLEBEKE LAKE DUG-OUTS to W end of RAILWAY DUG-OUTS. Batt. HQ at	4 O.R.
	25	7am	Situation normal. Wind N.W.	

Instructions regarding War Diaries and Intelligence Summaries are contained in F. S. Regs., Part II. and the Staff Manual respectively. Title pages will be prepared in manuscript.

INTELLIGENCE SUMMARY.

1/4 Leic. Regt. (Erase heading not required.) 138th Brigade. 46th Division.

Place	Date	Hour	Summary of Events and Information	Remarks and references to Appendices
DUG-OUTS.	AUG.			
			Weather fine. Day was quiet.	
		8.15pm.	4 percussion shells fell on battalion dump. Effect very local. No damage.	
		8.45pm.	Transport arrived.	
	26	7am.	Situation normal. Wind N.W. Weather fine.	
			Day was quiet, and only marked by aircraft duels.	
	27	7am.	Situation normal. Wind N.W.	WOUNDED 1 O.R.
			Aircraft active. Little artillery fire.	F.A. 2 O.R.
		11.30pm	Some aircraft passed over ZILLEBEKE CHURCH travelling in a N.W. direction.	
	28.	7am.	Situation normal. Wind S.E.	F.A.
			Fatigue parties of 20 men provided to fetch building material from Ypres.	Lt. M.B. DOUGLAS 5 O.R.
		7.15pm	C & D coys, M.G. section left H.23.b. en route for trenches, proceeding by Bridge 16 & TRANSPORT FARM.	
		8pm	A & B coys left RAILWAY DUG-OUTS.	

1577 Wt. W10791/1773 500,000 1/15 D. D. & L. A.D.S.S./Forms/C. 2118.

Instructions regarding War Diaries and Intelligence Summaries are contained in F. S. Regs., Part II. and the Staff Manual respectively. Title pages will be prepared in manuscript.

INTELLIGENCE SUMMARY.

1/4 Leic. Regt. (Erase heading not required.) 138th Brigade. 46th Division.

Place	Date	Hour	Summary of Events and Information	Remarks and references to Appendices
TRENCHES	AUG.			
			Companies relieved 5th Lincs as follows:—	
			A Coy. 42a and SQUAREWOOD DUG-OUTS.	
			B Coy. 41, 41a and 41S.	
			C Coy 47S & 47	
			D Coy 48 and 49S.	
		10.45pm	Relief Completed.	
	29	7am	Situation quiet. Wind W by SW.	F.A. 1.
		7.30pm.	Post card (copy attached) and a sheet of the FRANKFÜRTER ZEITUNG thrown into 47 trench over barrier. No arm was exposed.	
	30.	7am	Situation quiet. Wind WNW.	
		5pm.	Enemy shelled 47S and neighbouring trenches with 'whizz-bangs' in retaliation to our Howitzer fire.	Wounded 2 F.A. 1
		8pm.	Brigadier & Capt. Viccars dined at Batt. HQ.	
		9pm.	2Lts HOBBS and WAGSTAFF Arrived from Qmr stores.	
		10.30pm.	Brigadier & Co. visited barricade from 47 trench.	

1577 Wt. W10791/1773 500,000 1/15 D. D. & L. A.D.S.S./Forms/C. 2118.

Instructions regarding War Diaries and Intelligence Summaries are contained in F. S. Regs., Part II. and the Staff Manual respectively. Title pages will be prepared in manuscript.

or

INTELLIGENCE SUMMARY.

1/4 Leic. Regt. (Erase heading not required.) 138th Infantry Brigade. 46th Division

Place	Date	Hour	Summary of Events and Information	Remarks and references to Appendices
TRENCHES	AUG.			
	31	4 am 7 am.	Situation normal. Wind W by NW.	WOUNDED 2 O.R. Sick 1 O.R.
		8.30 am	to 9 am. 42a, 47s and ARMAGH WOOD whizz-banged.	
		10 am	a note in a flare case tied to a piece of shell thrown into end of 49 TRENCH.	
		7.30 pm.	minenwerfer bomb thrown over A2, followed by 2 more. No damage done. 5th Leicesters report that they had previously heard the minenwerfer being push up behind enemy's trenches on rails.	
			R.C. Harvey 2Lt & Adjt. 1/4th Leicestershire Regt.	

1577 Wt. W10791/1773 500,000 1/15 D. D. & L. A.D.S.S./Forms/C. 2118.

Copy of message Thrown into end of 47 at 10am on Aug. 31st wrapped up in flare case.

Good bye englishmen
Have you frenchmen here?
and of what party of this Country speaks any of yours our language?

a dutchman.

—

we beg to give answer but not by yours Cannons.

Copy of message thrown into 47 TRENCH at 7.30 pm on 29th August 1915. Message written in pencil on a Feld-Postkart, and copy of Frankfurter [illegible] attached.

Ce journal montre notre front en Russie. J'ai une prière. Aussitôt que vous avez reçu cette papier, je tiendrai la main sur le wall. Tirez! Tirez dans mon bras en cette partie ↘ la cause de ma prière je ne puis pas dire. Nos officiers! Je tiendrai un journal à la main. Tirez alors et blessez moi de la main tiendrai sur le wall ce soir et au matin demain quelque fois. Tirez alors!

138th Inf.Bde.
46th Div.

WAR DIARY

4th BATTN. THE LEICESTERSHIRE REGIMENT.

S E P T E M B E R

1 9 1 5

Confidential

Instructions regarding War Diaries and Intelligence Summaries are contained in F. S. Regs., Part II. and the Staff Manual respectively. Title pages will be prepared in manuscript.

WAR DIARY
or
~~INTELLIGENCE SUMMARY.~~
(Erase heading not required.)

1/4th Leicestershire Regt. 138th Brigade 46th Division

Army Form C. 2118.

Place	Date 1915	Hour	Summary of Events and Information	Remarks and references to Appendices
TRENCHES	SEP.			T of F.A. means "Sick"
Where? evidently just NE of 2nd Battalion No 1 Zillebeke	1.	7am.	Situation quiet. Wind W. Day was quiet throughout. Little artillery fire. 49 & 50 trenches were whizz-banged during afternoon. No damage.	Wounded 1 O.R. F.A. 3 O.R.
	2.	7am.	Situation quiet. Wind SW. Little rifle fire.	Wounded 2 O.R. F.A. 5 O.R.
		3.30pm	Enemy shelled CT 47S - 42a.	
		8pm	48 trench sausaged.	
	3.	7am	Situation quiet. Wind NW.	Wounded 2 O.R.
		11am	49S whizz-banged.	
		10.50pm	Batt. completely relieved by 4th Lincs. Weather caused delay in relieving. It had been wet throughout day. Battalion returned to DICKEBUSCHE HUTS companies marching independantly.	F.A. Nil.

Army Form C. 2118.

WAR DIARY
or
~~INTELLIGENCE SUMMARY.~~
(Erase heading not required.)

Instructions regarding War Diaries and Intelligence Summaries are contained in F. S. Regs., Part II. and the Staff Manual respectively. Title pages will be prepared in manuscript.

1/4 LEIC. 138th. Bde: 46th Division.

Place	1915 Date	Hour	Summary of Events and Information	Remarks and references to Appendices
HUTS.	SEP.			
	4.	7am.	Situation quiet. Wind N.W. Weather wet. Interior economy. Inspection by Army Commander cancelled.	F.A. 9 O.R.
	5.	7am.	Situation quiet. Wind N.W. Showery.	F.A. 6 O.R.
		2.30pm.	Battalion inspected by Army Commander Gen. PLUMER. Coys paraded at coy. alarm posts. Dress:– drill order with waterproof sheets.	
	6.	7am.	Situation normal. Batt. bathed & rested. Interior economy.	F.A. 3 O.R.
	7.	7am.	Situation normal. Wind N.W. Weather fine.	F.A.
		11.30am.	Batt. church parade for C. of E. & Wesleyans.	3. O.R.
		1pm.	Capt. R.S. DYER - BENNETT returned from England, and took over duties as Adjutant.	
	8.	7am.	Situation normal. Wind W. During morning C.O. inspected coys independently. Dress F.S.M.O.	F.A. 6 O.R.

R.H. Harvey Lt. & a/adj.

Army Form C. 2118.

WAR DIARY
or
~~INTELLIGENCE SUMMARY.~~
(Erase heading not required.)

Instructions regarding War Diaries and Intelligence Summaries are contained in F. S. Regs., Part II. and the Staff Manual respectively. Title pages will be prepared in manuscript.

1/4 Leic. Rgt 138th Inf Bde 46th Divn

Place	Date	Hour	Summary of Events and Information	Remarks and references to Appendices
Trenches	1915. Septr			
	8th	pm 5.30	Bn moved to trenches in bodies not greater than 2 platoons.	
		10.30	" completed relief of 1/5 Linc: Rgt distributed as follows. 'A' Coy 41 & 41 S 'B' Coy 42 S & 89 wood Do 'C' " 48 & 49 S 'D' " 47 & 47 S	2 O.R. wounded.
			Quiet night. No wind	
			2/Lts JARVIS, ABELL & PARR to be Capts – 2/Lt HARVEY & JOHNSON to be Lieuts. R.L.B.	
	9th		Fine – warm – wind – . Lieut R.C HARVEY took over Bde Intelligence Duties	1 O.R. killed 5 O.R. wounded
Lt. Col. SANDALL temporarily in command of Bde. General on leave			Quiet, except for "crumping" A 2 S. C.O round with Adj:	
			Bottom (W.) end of 49 – the barricade fell in on front of about 5 yds – ground in front very Sodden & work done at night to drain thro' – Germans unaware & didn't fire. Barricade temporarily built up for 24 hrs. R.L.B.	1 O.R. Sick FA
	10th		Fine & warm after cold night. Quiet day	1 O.R. Sick FA
			CO & Adj round trenches	
			49 suffered somewhat from shrapnel (enemy) R.L.B.	
	11th		V. cold night – fine, bright day. Germans put over 6 large "sausages" about 1 pm near left Bn's H.Q. no damage of importance. Our T.M. men fired 3 (50lbs) to range – 1 failure. Germans "crumped" over 50 & near left Bn's H.Q. – little damage. Later crumped C.T. between 42 S & 47 S 41 S & 43 – some damage no casualties. R.L.B.	2 O.R. Sick FA

1577 Wt. W10791/1773 500,000 1/15 D. D. & L. A.D.S.S./Forms/C. 2118.

Army Form C. 2118.

Instructions regarding War Diaries and Intelligence Summaries are contained in F. S. Regs., Part II. and the Staff Manual respectively. Title pages will be prepared in manuscript.

WAR DIARY
or
~~INTELLIGENCE SUMMARY.~~
(Erase heading not required.)

1/4 Leic. Rgt 138th Inf Bde – 46th Div.

Place	Date	Hour	Summary of Events and Information	Remarks and references to Appendices
Trenches	1915 Sept			
	12		Fine - bright day. Situation normal, but heavy "crumping" near Bn HQ. and in neighbourhood of R.P. 3 & 2. The former v. considerably damaged and evening spent in rebuilding parapet and also at a pt near rt (W) end of A9. Very good work done. Germans inactive either through ignorance or laziness - work unhindered. C.O. & adj spent dead of afternoon & all night. Lt Col SANDALL (5 Linc Rgt) a/Bde Gen, Bde Major & Captain WILSON (Div Staff) visited trenches.	1 OR wounded; 3 OR sick FA
Fine	13	6 am to 6.30 am	6" Hows did good work on enemy salient opp A1 - quantities of timber, corrugated iron & sandbags turned up. Germans replied with "crumps" - one landed in Bn HQ. no damage. Enemy again v. busy in afternoon until about 4.30pm. crumping round Bn HQ. very heavily - no damage. "Shrapnel in R.P. 3 & 2 caused some damage & a few casualties - 2 Lt WRIGHT had several slight head wounds. 4.2s crumped somewhat. Bde Major, Major PRICE DAVIES (46 Div Staff) visited trenches. C.O. & Adj to RPs - SQ wood & D.O. in evening & later at the repair work in R.P. 3 etc. Quiet day on the whole - fine, warm, slight S.W. wind. Very little aerial activity.	1 off wounded; 6 OR; 7 OR sick FA; [illegible]
	14		Fine and SW. Quiet day - except for crumping of SQ Wood in aft'noon & again about 7 pm. in salvos. Some damage to D.O. but no casualties. There C.O. & adj round all trenches to inspect.	1 OR wounded; 2 OR sick FA
		pm 9.30	Relieved by 1/5 Linc Rgt. Bn to Bde Res. "B" to DEEPING D.O. "D" to Rly D.O. "A" & "C" to KRUISSTADT. Bn D.O. ditto.	[illegible]

5.

Army Form C. 2118.

WAR DIARY
or
~~INTELLIGENCE SUMMARY.~~
(Erase heading not required.)

Instructions regarding War Diaries and Intelligence Summaries are contained in F. S. Regs., Part II. and the Staff Manual respectively. Title pages will be prepared in manuscript.

1/4 Leic. Rgt 138th Inf Bde. 46th Divn.

Place	Date 1915 Sept.	Hour	Summary of Events and Information	Remarks and references to Appendices
Bde Reserve	15.		No wind. Fine - warm - Quiet. Major McALLISTER HEWLINGS (M.O.) to A.S.C. and Captain J. A. COWAN from 2nd N.M. F.A. in former's place as RMO. Usual working parties under O i/c Works - Captain FAIRE. 1 Officer & 25 O.R. (new draft) arrived Qmr's stores. 2/Lt COX	O.R. 2 wounded 1 sick FA. [initials]
	16		Fine warm quiet day except for reported shelling of RP3 which entailed our sending 20 men to help 1/5 LINC RGT for work in RP3. Usual working parties. Bde Gen KEMP resumed command after leave	2 O.R. sick FA [initials]
	17		Weirerec shelling leave closed for time being. C.O. at 1 day M.G. course WISQUES	
		10 am to 11.30 am	Our artillery v busy shelling Germans	
			Usual working parties am. & pm	
		3 pm to 6 pm	Enemy shrapnelled neighbourhood of Rly D.O. heavily & considerable art activity was displayed by both sides - somewhat intermittent firing but heavy at times. Germans seriously damaged A.T.S (A8 & A7 somewhat) & R P's with heavy shells but only 2 casualties	1 O.R. wounded [initials]

1577 Wt. W10791/1773 500,000 1/15 D. D. & L. A.D.S.S./Forms/C. 2118.

6

Instructions regarding War Diaries and Intelligence Summaries are contained in F. S. Regs., Part II. and the Staff Manual respectively. Title pages will be prepared in manuscript.

WAR DIARY
or
INTELLIGENCE SUMMARY.
(Erase heading not required.)

Army Form C. 2118.

1/4 Linc Rgt 138th Inf Bde 46th Div

Place	Date 1915 Sept	Hour	Summary of Events and Information	Remarks and references to Appendices
Bde Res've				
	18.	10am	Some artillery activity on our part apparently directed HOOGE way. Enemy did not reply in	1 OR W F A
		12 & [illegible]	this direction until about 4 pm and then heavy shrapnel bursts mostly to the E some 300–500	
		2/45 pm	after batteries in our neighbourhood.	
			Approx 170 of our men under Capt NEWINS assisted 1/5 Linc Rgt to dig out 47? – some 10? of which were flat. No casualties and good work done.	[illegible]
	19		Fine – much cooler – little local art action – no German shells in neighbourhood. No evening working parties.	[illegible]
	20	8am	Op. O. 7. copy 5 re relief rec^d. Working parties till 1 pm	
		12 noon	3 large shells landed near Bty D.O. [illegible] in ground. Bty [illegible] moved up [illegible] + [illegible] shelling took place.	4 OR to F A
		5.30 pm	KRUISSTRAAT [illegible] marched to relieve 1/5 Linc Rgt – other coys [illegible] later	1 OR wounded
Trenches		8.53 pm	Relief of 1/5 Linc Rgt completed.	[illegible]
			Quiet night – cold – bright moon – work in open impracticable.	
	21		Quiet day – enemy scored direct hit on m.g. tripod [illegible] + 9 ([illegible] end) [illegible] gun [illegible] damaged.	[illegible]
			Enemy also scored direct hit on m.g. emplacement [illegible] – no damage [illegible]	

Instructions regarding War Diaries and Intelligence Summaries are contained in F. S. Regs., Part II. and the Staff Manual respectively. Title pages will be prepared in manuscript.

WAR DIARY
or
INTELLIGENCE SUMMARY.
(Erase heading not required.)

Army Form C. 2118.

7

1/4 Leic Rgt. 138th Inf Bde 46th Div.

Place	Date 1915 Sept	Hour	Summary of Events and Information	Remarks and references to Appendices
Trenches	21.		CO & Adj visited all trenches to day & A5, BPs 47, 2A & 3 A1 to night. 50% line Rgt worked 3 hrs on repairing 47S. Very light night but Germans quiet. RSW	1 OR wounded 1 — to F.A.
	22		Quiet day – v little enemy shelling, but art from 3rd, 14th, 17th & 46th Divs were busy in	
		4pm–5.3pm	firing on German lines firing in our sector mostly over 47 & 48 – results good apparently. CO & Adj round all fire trenches aftn until 8 pm – again later	
	23	4 am to 4.45	Early morning bombardment by our guns – HOOGE direction apparently. No reply our way. Brigadier & B Major round right sector with CO & Adj during pm. CO & Adj visited HQ 6/S. Staffs Very close day – thunderstorm at night & heavy rain. Very heavy rumbling of Art. heard a long way S. General impression that "something doing" – air full of rumours of push commencing.	discussed demonstration on 25th. 2 OR wounded 1 — to F.A.
	24.	4.20 to 4.55 am	Bombardment by our art & Belgian 75 cm guns recently attached 2nd Line Batt to replace 2 15 pounders – fired over A7 – Shrapnel & H.E. No particular result. More rain – trenches very wet & muddy – necessity for complete gridding of all trenches obviously essential	2 OR wounded 1 — to F.A.

8.

Army Form C. 2118.

Instructions regarding War Diaries and Intelligence Summaries are contained in F. S. Regs., Part II. and the Staff Manual respectively. Title pages will be prepared in manuscript.

WAR DIARY
or
INTELLIGENCE SUMMARY.
(Erase heading not required.)

1/4. Leic. RGT. 138TH Bde – 46th Div

Place	Date 1915 Sept	Hour	Summary of Events and Information	Remarks and references to Appendices
			Major RL ADLERCRON – Bde Major – left Bde to command 6th W. RIDINGS.	
Trenches	24.		Quiet day. CO & Adj round trenches until 8pm. – received orders re. bombardment 25th & attack also re: part to be played by 138th Bde.	OO 8. Opus Para 76
				N. New form of gas expected from Ger's
			Straw for smoke screen in front of A1 carried up & prepared.	1 OR. killed 1 – wounded
	25	1.40 am	Secret instructions re. disposal of trench and other stores in case of advance rec'd.	SC/5/4
			Quiet night – rifle fire normal. Our art' occasionally fired HOOGE Direction	
			Copy of report on country to E of our present position.	
		3.30 am	V. heavy bombardment begins.	
		4.20	Stated time for our Inf 3rd & 14th Div to assault – but impossible to tell if they did as art fire hardly seemed to slacken.	
		4.50	6 B. Staffs report that no straw will be ignited & smoke bomb business postponed till 5.50 am.	
		5.50	Rifle fire (mostly from periscopic rifles) some mac gun fire & bomb throwing from mac lines begin. Fifth LEISTERS lit straw opp 50 – wind wrong way & came back over them & being shrapnelled from a flank they suffered 6 K & 24 wounded. We suffered from shrapnel	OR 1 K. 3 wounded

1577 Wt. W10791/1773 500,000 1/15 D. D. & L. A.D.S.S./Forms/C. 2118.

Army Form C. 2118.

WAR DIARY
or
INTELLIGENCE SUMMARY.
(Erase heading not required.)

Instructions regarding War Diaries and Intelligence Summaries are contained in F. S. Regs., Part II. and the Staff Manual respectively. Title pages will be prepared in manuscript.

1/4 Leic Rgt — 138th Inf Bde 46th Div

Place	Date 1915 Sept	Hour	Summary of Events and Information	Remarks and references to Appendices
Trenches	25.		Enemy somewhat perturbed – a good deal of rifle & mac gun fire came over – no damage	
			Capt FIELDSEND 1/5 Linc Rgt i/c mac guns in 41 seriously wounded in head looking over p/p	
		8 am	Situation becoming normal. Raining steadily	
			Various reports during day indicate some success by 3rd Div – 14th unable to main[tain] any advantage gained. About 150 Ger' prisoners reported going by ZILLEBEKE	
6.15 am. Our [illegible] bombs appeared to upset Ger – [illegible]			LAKE to K'STRAAT. Our 1st Army reported going strong in S & also French	
			on front of 25K. Bde Brigadier visited Bn HQ about 2 pm.	1 OR. killed
[illegible] damage 4 pm			CO & Adj visited fire trenches in p.m. very bad state after rain	5 OR. wounded (1 returned to duty)
Ger' shelled [illegible] 5 pm			Some enemy shelling of 41/S & CT 40 to SQ WOOD.	
our [illegible] line (in error) [illegible]			Quiet evening & night. Patrol under 2/Lt SCHOLES (from 41) to endeavour to rouse Germans to indicate strength by rifle fire – no result of importance, but patrol did its work well. Ger' trenches apparently v. lightly held at night.	[initials]
			Information rec'd indicates distinct progress by French & ourselves in the South	
	26.		Quiet day – fine & hot. All energies concentrated on cleaning up. CO & Adj visited all fire trenches	
		9.40 pm	Relief by 1/5 Linc Rgt completed.	
		10 pm	Sudden outburst of bombing – quickly followed by heavy rifle fire & gun fire – this appeared to come from HOOGE neighbourhood. Coys by this time en route for DICKEBUSCH HUTS. Situation normal by 11 pm	[initials]

1577 Wt. W10791/1773 500,000 1/15 D. D. & L. A.D.S.S./Forms/C. 2118.

10.

Army Form C. 2118.

Instructions regarding War Diaries and Intelligence Summaries are contained in F. S. Regs., Part II. and the Staff Manual respectively. Title pages will be prepared in manuscript.

WAR DIARY
or
INTELLIGENCE SUMMARY.
(Erase heading not required.)

1/4 LEIC. RGT. 138TH INF BDE 46th Divn

Place	Date 1915 Sept	Hour	Summary of Events and Information	Remarks and references to Appendices
HUTS	26		2 Lt T.F. O'CALLAGHAN & servant joined for duty from entrenching Bn. "B" Coy.	3 OR wounded / 1 to F.A. Sick. R.S.B.
	27.		Quiet day - cold - some rain. Information rec^d that Captain J. MILNE sick - to be struck off.	Nil R.S.B.
	28.		Quiet - cold - heavy rain in evening. Draft of 35 arrived. Instructions received to prepare to give up present trench line on or about evening of 30/Oct. Divn likely to move elsewhere. All leave cancelled. 2Lt F.C. BLUNT joined for duty - "C" Coy & to take Mac Gun	2 to F.A. Sick R.S.B.
	29.		Very wet almost entire day. Coys devoted day to interior economy. A.D.M.S. inspected new draft. Found same v. poor - mostly "old hands" returned & quite unfit. 4/10 found unfit & others to be re-examined.	2/Lt HOBBS to F.A. 10 to F.A. R.S.B.
	30.		C.O. inspected all Coys in F.S.M.O. Four ptes tried by F.G.C.M. 2. sleeping on post, (both cases due to overfatigue) 1. Drunkenness on 2 occasions & 1. insubordination. Orders rec^d to withdraw Mac Guns from trenches - this arranged for but not carried out. Germans exploded mines under 40 & 47 Barricade - no serious damage. G.O.C. visited Bn in huts unofficially. Orders re Trench Reliefs & movement of Bn to Transport lines on 1st rec^d. Wet & cold day - Situation normal in Div^l Reserve. Fighting in HOOGE area	1 sick to F.A. R.S.B. R.S. [illegible] Capt & Adj 1/4 Leic Rgt 30.9.15

1577 Wt. W10791/1773 500,000 1/15 D. D. & L. A.D.S.S./Forms/C. 2118.

138th Inf.Bde.
46th Div.

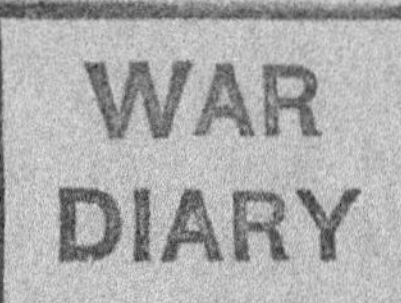

4th BATTN. THE LEICESTERSHIRE REGIMENT.

O C T O B E R

(1/26.10.15)

1 9 1 5

Instructions regarding War Diaries and Intelligence Summaries are contained in F. S. Regs., Part II. and the Staff Manual respectively. Title pages will be prepared in manuscript.

or

INTELLIGENCE SUMMARY.

(*Erase heading not required.*)

1/4 Leic Regt — 138th Inf Bde — 46th Div

Place	Date 1915 Oct	Hour	Summary of Events and Information	Remarks and references to Appendices
Huts				FA [illegible] "S13h"
DICKEBUSCH	1	a.m. 10.30	CO addressed Bn on parade re movement to VI Corps. Importance of discipline & smartness impressed on men now showing signs of wear after 6 months trench warfare.	G.R. GFA
		1.45 pm	Ad parties to new area. Windmill Fm, Transport Fm & Field.	
		2.30 pm	Bn moved to new area – 'A' & part of 'B' in barns – remainder in 2 man Blanket bivouacs. HQ Trans Fm.	
Windmill & Transport Fm		5 pm	Bn settled in – Bde informed.	
			Mac Guns in trench area relieved midnight.	
N. of OUDERDOM (1500x)		6.30 pm	O.O. 11. Copy S.	
			2/Lt G.E.R. RUSSELL returned from Div Rest Stn – not yet fit for duty.	
			Ordered to send Lt BIRKINGTON & 2/Lt WAGSTAFFE to 3rd Div to join Tunnelling Co.	
	2	a.m. 1.30	Amendments as to times & place of entrainment of Inf of Bde recd from Bde	G.R. GFA
		a.m. 4	Reveille – Blankets rolled & taken to Qm's Store by 5 am	
		6 am	Blankets & surplus stores to 7th Line Trans lines to meet lorries – Lorries not there till 9.30 am	
			*VIth Corps Commander & G.O.C. 46th Div saw all officers – *Major Gen ALLENBY congratulated CO on work of Bn & wished all ranks good luck	
		pm 1.30	M.G. Section under 2 Lt F.C. BLUNT moved by road to entrain at GODEWAERSVELDE (7.32 pm)	
			Capt [illegible] Capt. B.F. [illegible]	

Instructions regarding War Diaries and Intelligence Summaries are contained in F. S. Regs., Part II. and the Staff Manual respectively. Title pages will be prepared in manuscript.

or

INTELLIGENCE SUMMARY.

(*Erase heading not required.*)

Place	1915 Date Oct.	Hour	Summary of Events and Information	Remarks and references to Appendices
Farms & Bivouacs as p.1	2nd	pm 1.45	Remainder of 1st Line Trans less S.A.A. carts not with M.G. moved under Captain W.B. JARVIS to VIEUX BERQUIN	
		2.35	Bn marched to ABEELE - march discipline good - no men fell out.	
		6.5	- reached ABEELE - cooked teas in 10 mins halt before proceeding to entrain which was done in v. hurried fashion - 8 per carriage - not usual "boxes"	
		6.55	Train left ABEELE	
		9.0.	- reached FOUQUEREUIL - detrained. Large amount of surplus baggage & blankets of various regts in Bde. Bn sent on billeting party to GONNEHEM - arriving there about midnight.	
GONNEHEM.	3rd	1 am	Coys billeted - as per attached rough plan. 2 men fell out but rejoined - sprained ankles.	
		am 3.30	M.G. Section with S.A.A. Carts arrived.	FA. Nil.
			CO. 2nd in C visited billets with Bde Commander - Adj & billeting Officer after transport lines & billets. Coys washing & inspecting rifles feet etc.	
		5 pm	Transport under Capt JARVIS arrived 1 "cooker" broken down - axle gone - fetched in on G.S. wagon	
		6.30 pm	CO. saw all Os.C. Coys re. working in rest - physical training - marching - handling of arms & musketry. ~~Routes for R.A. given~~	

1577 Wt. W10791/1773 500,000 1/15 D. D. & L. A.D.S.S./Forms/C. 2118.

Instructions regarding War Diaries and Intelligence Summaries are contained in F. S. Regs., Part II. and the Staff Manual respectively. Title pages will be prepared in manuscript.

~~WAR DIARY~~ or INTELLIGENCE ~~SUMMARY.~~

(Erase heading not required.)

1/4 Leic Rgt. 138th Inf Bde / 46th Div.

Place	Date 1915 Oct	Hour	Summary of Events and Information	Remarks and references to Appendices
GONNEHEM	4th	7 am	Reveille – 20 mins p. training before b'fast. 8 miles R. march (no packs) for Coys before dinners – M. G. under M. G. O. – Signallers under Sgt Major. CO & 2nd in C – visited Coys on march.	2Lt G. D. [illegible] & 3 O.R. [illegible] 97 O.R. return [illegible] F.A. [illegible] [illegible] before [illegible] back
		2.30 pm	COs & Adjts 138th Inf Bde attended conference at Bde HQ – G.O.C. addressed them on situation locally & work to be done. Gen. Sir Douglas Haig came in. Coys bayonet fighting, musketry etc – Bombers practising throwing.	
		6.30	CO saw Os. C. Coys re work done.	
	5th	7 am	Reveille & parades for day as on 4th. R. M. with packs. CO to conference at Bde. 2nd in C & Adj to C & D Coys on march.	
		2.15 pm	CO & Adjt to Bde HQ to meet Corps (XI) Commander – who did not materialise.	
		4.15	Billeting party [illegible] Staff Captain to go to HESDIGNEUL – [illegible] under Lt HARVEY. Bn ordered to be prepared to move this night – this finally cancelled at [illegible] 7 pm after everything ready – without getting on road. Bde states will not move before [illegible] tomorrow probably.	

1577 Wt. W10791/1773 500,000 1/15 D. D. & L. A.D.S.S./Forms/C. 2118.

Instructions regarding War Diaries and Intelligence Summaries are contained in F. S. Regs., Part II. and the Staff Manual respectively. Title pages will be prepared in manuscript.

or INTELLIGENCE SUMMARY.

(Erase heading not required.)

1/4 Leic Rgt 138th Inf Bde 46th Divn

Place	Date 1915 Oct.	Hour	Summary of Events and Information	Remarks and references to Appendices
GONNEHEM	6th	7.am	Reveille	
		7.10am	Adj warned by Bde Major on telephone that Bde marches 8.45am [illegible] 4th Line, 4/Leic, 4/Linc, 5/Leic Rgt. Transport [illegible]	
		8.55am	Bn passed S.P. 600x S. of ~~[illegible]~~ Bn HQ 5 mins late owing to [illegible] discussion [illegible] returning to Qm's stores at WHITTINGHAM [illegible] billets. Route CHOCQUES – FOUQUEREUIL. 5/Leic Rgt were some 10–15 mins in rear.	
HESDIGNEUL		11.25am	Bn arrived at billeting area – no casualties. Distance about 5½ miles.	
		1.pm	Bn billets [illegible] "C" Coy & remainder "D" Coy billets [illegible]	
		7pm	60 men of "A" to Bde HQ. billet & "C" moved into old billets – a more satisfactory arrangement.	
	7th	7.am	Reveille & same training throughout day as at GONNEHEM. Captain ABELL sick	
		3.30pm	COs & Adj to Bde HQ. to meet Bdr re proposed retaking of HOHENZOLLERN Redoubt by 138th Bde.	
		6.30pm	CO saw Coy ~~officers~~ commanders re this attack.	
	8th	7.am	Reveille – later 1½ Route marching & remainder of a.m. bombing for all ranks.	
		8.am	CO., 2nd in C., Adj., A O's C. Coys & Bomb Officer with others of Bde to the trenches – by motor lorry to VERMELLES & thence on foot.	

1577 Wt. W10791/1773 500,000 1/15 D. D. & L. A.D.S.S./Forms/C. 2118.

Instructions regarding War Diaries and Intelligence Summaries are contained in F. S. Regs., Part II. and the Staff Manual respectively. Title pages will be prepared in manuscript.

~~WAR DIARY~~ or INTELLIGENCE SUMMARY.

(Erase heading not required.)

1/4 Leic. Rgt. 138th Inf Bde — 46th Div.

Place	Date 1915 Oct	Hour	Summary of Events and Information	Remarks and references to Appendices
HESDIGNEUL	8th		By means of periscopes - all were enabled to see limited amount of Redoubt - Dump & FOSSE No 8. No rifle fire - slight shelling by Germans - our artillery fair	
		11.30 am	Party returned to just E of VERMELLES - which was slightly shelled for an hour.	
		1.45 pm	" " " HESDIGNEUL.	
			Heavy gun fire continuous throughout afternoon.	
		5.20.	Message from Bde followed immediately on visit from Staff Captain who had stated Germans attacking ~~message~~ & Bde next to move up if wanted - message said - prepare to move at once - don't fall in. All coys warned - M.G.O., T.O., & Bomb Officer.	
		5.45.	Message from Bde that Germans attacking all along XI Corps line - Bde to be ready to move at [illegible] hr's notice with 1st Line T. Wagons not to be packed.	
		7.56.	CO saw Coy commanders and Bomb Officer re: visit to trenches & attack.	
		7.50	Message from Bde re. Bus at 8 a.m. as for 8th - to take 6 officers this [illegible] to trenches if state of readiness cancelled before 7 a.m. 9th.	
		11.15	"State of readiness" cancelled". Germans reported to have made attack on BIG WILLIE Trench & been repulsed with [illegible] loss.	[illegible]

1577 Wt. W10791/1773 500,000 1/15 D. D. & L. A.D.S.S./Forms/C. 2118.

or

INTELLIGENCE SUMMARY.

Instructions regarding War Diaries and Intelligence Summaries are contained in F.S. Regs., Part II. and the Staff Manual respectively. Title pages will be prepared in manuscript.

1/4 Leic. Rgt (*Erase heading not required.*) 138th Inf Bde, 46th Div

Place	1915 Date	Hour, Date, Place Hour	Summary of Events and Information	Remarks and references to Appendices
	Oct			
HESDIGNEUL	9th	8. am.	Coy commanders and 2nd-in-C to trenches as on 8th	
		9 am.	Lt. FORSELL ~~C.S.~~ major's & platoon commanders to Divl HQ to see RE re-versing parapet of captured trench	
		9.30 am	CO. & Adj to Divl HQ. to see RE. etc as above & to conference on proposed operations	
			Work for Coys as previously – all ranks practising with live Mills bombs.	
		2.30 pm to 3.30	Bn practising attack in 4 lines of platoons extended to 1 pace at 50x interval.	
		6 pm.	CO. & Adj to Bde for conference.	
		9 pm.	CO. saw O's C. Coys, M.G. & Grenade Officers.	
"	10th	8. am.	5 officers to trenches – 4 officers & sig cpl at 10.30 am	
		9–11 am.	Training	
		12 noon	C. of E. Divine Service & H.C. celebration afterwards	
		2.45 pm.	Co. & Adj conference with OC 1/5 Leic Rgt	
		5.15 pm.	COs, 2nds in C, Adjs, O's C. Coys met Gen HAKING at Divl HQ. (Corps Commander)	
		6.15 pm.	Conference for Coy commanders.	

(9 29 6) W 3332—1107 100,000 10/13 H W V Forms/C. 2118/10.

Instructions regarding War Diaries and Intelligence Summaries are contained in F. S. Regs., Part II. and the Staff Manual respectively. Title pages will be prepared in manuscript.

or

INTELLIGENCE SUMMARY.

1/4 Leic Rgt (~~Erase heading not required.~~) 138th Inf Bde. 46th Div

Place	Date	Hour	Summary of Events and Information	Remarks and references to Appendices
	1915. Oct.		Usual training	
HESDIGNEUL	11.	11.15 am	G.O.C. Saw Bombers throwing "live" Mills - No 5 grenade.	
		2.45 pm	C.O. spoke to Bn on parade of operation coming off	Adv. Copy of Bde O.O. No 14 rec'd 2.5 pm. No 4 Copy
		3.30 pm	C.O. & Adjt to 1/5 Leic Rgt HQ. for conference with 1/4 Leic & 1/5 Leic Rgt	
		5 pm	Bde conference. Captain ABELL returned from Hospital. BETHUNE but too unfit for duty & sent to F.A. again	
		9 pm	Bn Officers Conference	
		9.30 pm	Bde O.O. No 15 Copy No 5. received.	
				[initials]
	12th	9 am	Bn marched to Sailly-Labourse. Dinners & teas were cooked here. Rations for 13th were issued	
		5-15 PM	Bn marched to Vermelles where stores were taken up	
		11 PM	Bn arrived at Trenches.	
TRENCHES	13th	Noon	Our artillery started to Bombard	
		1 PM	Our smoke & gas started	
		1-50 PM	Smoke & gas stopped	
		2 PM	Artillery lifted & Bn assaulted the Hohenzollern Redoubt. Lt Col R.E. Martin was wounded early but remained in the fire trench directing operations for nearly 22 hours & until relieved	

(9 29 6) W 3332—1107 100,000 10/13 H W V Forms/C. 2118/10.

Instructions regarding War Diaries and Intelligence Summaries are contained in F.S. Regs., Part II. and the Staff Manual respectively. Title pages will be prepared in manuscript.

or INTELLIGENCE SUMMARY.

(*Erase heading not required.*)

Hour, Date, Place	Summary of Events and Information	Remarks and references to Appendices
Trenches Oct 13th Contd	to the dressing station by Brig Gen Kemp. All the Officers of the Bn were either killed or wounded.	
Oct 14th	In the evening the Bn was relieved by part of the 139th Brigade & went back to the Lancashire Trench. Roll call revealed that 188 N.C.O. & men returned.	
Oct 15th	In the afternoon the Bn returned to billets at Hesdigneul	
Oct 16th Noon	Major W S N Toller 5th Leicestershire Regt on the orders of Brig Gen Kemp assumed Command of the Bn.	
Oct 17th 10 AM	Divine Service Conducted by Canon Hunt	
2 30 PM	Lt Gen R C B Haking inspected the Bn & spoke to every man who had been in the fight. He also inspected two reinforcements which had arrived.	
Oct 18th	Sergt Major Davenport went to Hpl. 4½ hrs were spent in Coy Training, Route marching etc.	
Oct 19th 10 30 AM	Major Gen Stuart Wortley inspected & addressed the Bn. The remainder of the day was spent in kit inspection & Coy training.	
Oct 26th	The Bn ~~marched~~ to rest billets at VERQUIN.	M
Oct 24th	The following officers joined the Battalion. Capt R Evans. 2/Lt A.J. Wakerly, 2/Lt A.J. TYLER, 2/Lt G. BOLUS, 2/Lt C.F. Wright, 2/Lt A.S. NEALE, 2/Lt M.S. HOLDEN, 2/Lt A.V. Coleman, 2/Lt A.G. HYSLOP, 2/Lt L.R.E. JACKSON	

138th Inf.Bde.
46th Div.

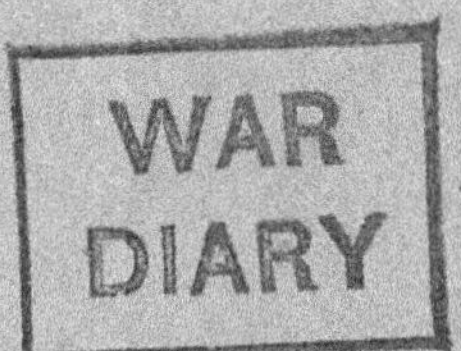

4th BATTN. THE LEICESTERSHIRE REGIMENT.

N O V E M B E R

1 9 1 5

Instructions regarding War Diaries and Intelligence Summaries are contained in F. S. Regs., Part II. and the Staff Manual respectively. Title pages will be prepared in manuscript.

WAR DIARY
or
INTELLIGENCE SUMMARY.
(Erase heading not required.)

Army Form C. 2118.

Volume II Page I

Hour, Date, Place	Summary of Events and Information	Remarks and references to Appendices
~~Verquin~~ Oct 21st	Lt L. G. Barton arrived.	[initials]
Verquin Nov 2nd	2/Lt H. L. Pochin & 2/Lt B. J. C. Gilbert & 108 men arrived to join the Battalion	[initials]
Nov 3rd	10 men arrived to join the Battn.	
	Major B. F. Clarke arrived from 6th Bn Leicestershire Regt to assume command of the Battn vice Major W. S. N. Toller.	[initials]
VERQUIN. Nov 6th	The Brigade moved by march route to ROBECQ PAS-DE-CALAIS & went into billets.	[initials]
Robecq. Nov 7th to ~~12th~~	The time was employed in Musketry Training, Company training, & training of new personnel to replace casualties sustained amongst stretcher bearers, machine gunners, bombers, signallers etc.	[initials]
Nov 10th	~~Pte~~ L/Cpl Cor F. H. 2227 accidentally wounded whilst on machine Gun Instruction.	Conveyed to F.A. 10 11 15

(9 29 6) W 3332—1107 100,000 10/13 H W V Forms/C. 2118/10.

Army Form C. 2118.

WAR DIARY

or

INTELLIGENCE SUMMARY.

(Erase heading not required.)

Instructions regarding War Diaries and Intelligence Summaries are contained in F. S. Regs., Part II. and the Staff Manual respectively. Title pages will be prepared in manuscript.

Hour, Date, Place		Summary of Events and Information	Remarks and references to Appendices
ROBECQ	Nov 12th	The Battalion moved from ROBECQ to RICHBOURG ST. VAAST where they were billeted for one night.	
	Nov 13th 9 am	Officers went into trenches for instructional purposes.	
	3.30 pm	Battalion took over new line of trenches from 3rd London Regt with the 5th Leicesters on our right and the 139th Brigade on our left. Sector occupied opposite Rue du Bois about 1000 yards from the village of Richbourg l'Avoue.	Trenches in very bad condition. Very wet.
	Nov 15th	Pte Harding 6/4210 Killed whilst going up to front line on relief	
	Nov 16th	Pte Corfield 4/2185 wounded. Shot through head in front line. Died of wounds 19.11.15.	
	Nov 26th 6 pm	The Battn. left this sector of trenches and moved to rest billets at Le Touret	
	Nov 30th 3.30 pm	The Battalion moved to new sector of trenches to relieve the 5th Lincolns period of occupation 6 days in and 6 days rest, with the Indians on our right and the 5th Leicesters on our left	Trenches in much better condition than last although very wet. ASN

138th Inf.Bde.
46th Div.

WAR
DIARY

4th BATTN. THE LEICESTERSHIRE REGIMENT.

D E C E M B E R

1 9 1 5

Army Form C. 2118

WAR DIARY

or

INTELLIGENCE SUMMARY

(Erase heading not required.)

Instructions regarding War Diaries and Intelligence Summaries are contained in F. S. Regs., Part II. and the Staff Manual respectively. Title Pages will be prepared in manuscript.

4th Leicestershire — 138th Inf Bde 46th Division — Volume II page 1

Place	Date	Hour	Summary of Events and Information	Remarks and references to Appendices
	Dec 1st 15		Major L.E. Pelley of the 4th Battalion Lincolnshire Regt attached to the Battalion from this date as 2nd in command.	[illegible]

1875 Wt. W593/826 1,000,000 4/15 J.B.C. & A. A.D.S.S./Forms/C. 2118.

Instructions regarding War Diaries and Intelligence Summaries are contained in F. S. Regs., Part II. and the Staff Manual respectively. Title Pages will be prepared in manuscript.

WAR DIARY
or
INTELLIGENCE SUMMARY
(Erase heading not required.)

4th Leic: Regt — 138th Inf Bde 46th Division — Volume III page 7

Place	Date	Hour	Summary of Events and Information	Remarks and references to Appendices
	3.12.15.	7.30pm	Battalion relieved by 9th Battalion Welsh Regiment at 7.30pm. and proceeded to billets at Le Touret preparatory to moving to Merville. "C" Coy's relief lost their way, in consequence this Coy had to stay in trenches (front line) till 7.30pm 4.12.15. when it proceeded to join the Battalion at Merville in motor omnibuses.	
	4.12.15	10 AM.	Battalion left Le Touret for Merville and marched 12 miles with very little rest D Coy not having arrived at billets previous night till 4 AM. 4.12.15. The behaviour of all ranks was excellent no men falling out. Dinners were served on the road.	
		3.30pm	Arrived at billets Le Sart just outside Merville, Lincoln band played us through the town.	
	5.12.15 – 9.12.15		Companies did Company training, musketry, Physical training & route marching.	
	10.12.15		Battalion was inspected by Brigadier General G. C. Kemp comdg. 138th Inf. Brigade.	
	11.12.15 to 18.12.15		Battalion carried on with Coy training as above.	
	19.12.15	9.40 AM.	Left Le Sart for Le Tannay arrived 1.30pm.	
	18.12.15		Capt R.S. Dyer Bennett rejoined Battalion from England	

WAR DIARY
or
INTELLIGENCE SUMMARY

(Erase heading not required.)

Instructions regarding *War Diaries* and *Intelligence Summaries* are contained in F. S. Regs., Part II. and the Staff Manual respectively. Title Pages will be prepared in manuscript.

4th Leic: Regt. 138th Infantry Bde 46th Division

Volume III page 3

Place	Date Dec.	Hour	Summary of Events and Information	Remarks and references to Appendices
LE TANNAY	19/12/15	to	Company training, physical drill and route marching, with one afternoons Tactical scheme (Outposts) 24.12.15.	
	21/12/15			
	22/12/15		A draft of 92 NCO's and men joined the Battalion on this date from 3/4 Leic: R. (Belton Park Grantham) 2/Lieut A S Neale appointed Acting Adjutant vice Capt R.S. Dyer Bennett.	
	26/12/15		Training as above.	
	28/12/15	2.30 pm	Draft inspected by Brigadier General G. C. Kemp.	
	29/12/15		Brigade Tactical scheme, advanced, flank and rear guards Battalion arrived back in billets at 2 pm.	
	30/12/15	31/12/15	Company training as above.	

B. Clarke Lieut Colonel
cmdg 4 / Leic: Regt

1875 Wt. W593/826 1,000,000 4/15 J.B.C. & A. A.D.S.S./Forms/C. 2118.

46/15

1/4 Leicester Regt

Jan

Vol XI

Instructions regarding War Diaries and Intelligence Summaries are contained in F. S. Regs., Part II. and the Staff Manual respectively. Title Pages will be prepared in manuscript.

WAR DIARY
or
INTELLIGENCE SUMMARY
(Erase heading not required.)

Army Form C. 2118

4th Leic. Regt   138th Brigade   46th Division   Volume IV Page 1

Place	Date 1916 JAN	Hour	Summary of Events and Information	Remarks and references to Appendices
LE TANNAY	1.		Major F. E. Lilley, 4th Battalion Lincolnshire Regt transferred to 4th Battalion Leicestershire Regt and taken on the strength from this date	
"	1-4		Training continued in Musketry, Physical training, Route marching and	
"	6	10 AM	Battalion left LE TANNAY for BERGUETTE where they entrained for Marseilles at 1.45 P.M. Wagons travelled with Battalion, horses followed 3 days later.	
	8	11 pm	Battalion arrived at Marseilles and proceeded to Santi camp Carcassone.	
	9. 20		Spent at Marseilles. Battalion doing training in Coy drill, Route marching, Physical training, Musketry, Bombing. N.C.O's classes under Regimental Sergt. Major. Draft joined the Battalion at Marseilles. 111 N.C.O's and men from 3/4th Leic: R. Nottingham.	
	21	7.30 AM	Battalion embarked on "H.M.T. Andania preparing for Sailing for Egypt.	
	22	7.AM	Received orders to disembark and return to Santi Camp.	
	27	8 48 am	Battalion entrained to return to the. Transport accompanied.	

1875 Wt. W593/826 1,000,000 4/15 J.B.C. & A. A.D.S.S./Forms/C. 2118.

Instructions regarding War Diaries and Intelligence Summaries are contained in F. S. Regs., Part II. and the Staff Manual respectively. Title Pages will be prepared in manuscript.

WAR DIARY
or
INTELLIGENCE SUMMARY
(Erase heading not required.)

Army Form C. 2118

Place	Date Jan 1916	Hour	Summary of Events and Information	Remarks and references to Appendices
Pont Remy	30	6.30 Am	Battalion arrived Pont Remy and detrained, left station for billets at 9 A.m.	
BUIGNY L'ABBÉ	"	11 AM	Arrived here about 11 A.m. 2/Lt H.R. Pochin preceding the Batt. with a billeting party. A Battalion canteen was opened on this day.	
N.B	14.		2/Lts. C S Bubby, G.L. Lea, H.H. Clifford and L. Paddon joined the Battalion from 3/4 Leic. R.	

Marshall [illegible]
Comdg 4/Leic. Regt

Army Form C. 2118

Instructions regarding War Diaries and Intelligence Summaries are contained in F. S. Regs., Part II. and the Staff Manual respectively. Title Pages will be prepared in manuscript.

WAR DIARY
or
INTELLIGENCE SUMMARY
(Erase heading not required.)

Place	Date	Hour	Summary of Events and Information	Remarks and references to Appendices
BUIGNY L'ABBÉ	FEB 1st TO 11th		Battalion carried out Coy. + Battalion Training. Two companies fired on range. Machine Gun fired short course. New classes of Machine Gunners, Bombers, + Signallers were started.	
PUCHEVILLERS	12th		The Battalion left BUIGNY L'ABBÉ at 7 A.M. in motor lorries + proceeded to PUCHEVILLERS arriving at 12 NOON. Transport arrived by march route at 6.30 p.m.	
	13th		Battalion finding 400 men for work on railway. Machine Gun, Bombing, + Signalling classes continue.	
	14th–19th		Battalion continued fatigue duties on railway.	
FIENVILLERS	20th		The Battalion left PUCHEVILLERS at 9.15 A.M. and marched to FIENVILLERS, arriving at 2 P.M.	
	21st – 23rd		Battalion + company training was carried out.	
MONTRELET	24th		Battalion left FIENVILLERS at 8.30 A.M. + marched to MONTRELET, arriving about 10. A.M.	
	27th		Lt.-Col. B. Clarke proceeded to School of Instruction at FLIXECOURT. Major A.C. Tetley assumed command in his place.	

1875 Wt. W593/826 1,000,000 4/15 J.B.C. & A. A.D.S.S./Forms/C. 2118.

Army Form C. 2118

Instructions regarding War Diaries and Intelligence Summaries are contained in F. S. Regs., Part II. and the Staff Manual respectively. Title Pages will be prepared in manuscript.

WAR DIARY
or
INTELLIGENCE SUMMARY
(Erase heading not required.)

Place	Date	Hour	Summary of Events and Information	Remarks and references to Appendices
GEZAINCOURT	FEB 29		Battalion marched to GEZAINCOURT, arriving about 1. P.M.	
			J Eric Pedley Major for O.C. 4th Leicestershire Reg	

1875 Wt. W593/826 1,000,000 4/15 J.B.C. & A. A.D.S.S./Forms/C. 2118.

Instructions regarding War Diaries and Intelligence Summaries are contained in F. S. Regs., Part II. and the Staff Manual respectively. Title Pages will be prepared in manuscript.

WAR DIARY
or
INTELLIGENCE SUMMARY
(Erase heading not required.)

Army Form C. 2118

Part I

4th Battn. The Leicestershire Regt.

Place	Date	Hour	Summary of Events and Information	Remarks and references to Appendices
GEZAINCOURT	1/3/16	2-30pm	Battalion moved to DOULLENS, arriving about 4-pm.	
DOULLENS	2/3/16	9-15am to 12-30pm	Battn Training	
		2-30pm to 3-30pm	Practice with smoke helmets, Rifle exercises and Musketry.	
	3/3/16	8-30am	Battn Training ("Company in the Attack") practice tube helmets used. Transport Route March under Bdge arrangements	
	4/3/16	9-am to 12-30pm	Interior Economy Bathing etc 162 Steel helmets issued and worn for the first time	
	5/3/16	9-am to 12-30pm	Battn Route March. R.Cs and Nonconformists church parade. 60 men attended divine service at the protestant church RUETHELU. RUE d'ARRAS Comdg Officer (Major [illegible]) Adjutant (2Lt. S.F. [illegible]) Lewis Gun Officer (2Lt [illegible]) and Sigly Sergt visited the A line of trenches at SOUCHEZ (a French Division in occupation)	

1875 Wt. W593/826 1,000,000 4/15 J.B.C. & A. A.D.S.S./Forms/C. 2118.

Sheet 2

Army Form C. 2118

Instructions regarding War Diaries and Intelligence Summaries are contained in F. S. Regs., Part II. and the Staff Manual respectively. Title Pages will be prepared in manuscript.

WAR DIARY
or
INTELLIGENCE SUMMARY
(Erase heading not required.)

Place	Date	Hour	Summary of Events and Information	Remarks and references to Appendices
			afterwards taken over by this Battn. Comndg Officer (Lt. Col. B.F. Clarke) returned from course at III Army Schools.	
	6/3/16	8-30am	Battalion moved (Brigaded) to new billeting area SERICOURT distance about 11 miles arrived about 1-pm	
SERICOURT.	7/3/16	11-am	Comndg Officer lectured Officers and N.C.Os in SERICOURT Schools.	
	8/3/16	9-30am to 12-30pm	Battn Training	
	9/3/16	10-15am.	Battalion moved to new area GUOY-EN-TERNOIS arrived at [illegible] Distance about 6 miles.	
GUOY-EN-TERNOIS	10/3/16		Interior Economy. Bombers [illegible] for practice	
	11/3/16		Battalion moved into Brigade reserve billets CAMBLAIN L'ABBE. distance about 12 miles	

Sheet 3

Instructions regarding War Diaries and Intelligence Summaries are contained in F. S. Regs., Part II. and the Staff Manual respectively. Title Pages will be prepared in manuscript.

WAR DIARY
or
INTELLIGENCE SUMMARY
(Erase heading not required.)

Army Form C. 2118

Place	Date	Hour	Summary of Events and Information	Remarks and references to Appendices
	12/3/16		Morning devoted to cleaning billeting area	
	13/3/16	9-30 am to 10-3 am	Cleaning up huts etc.	
		10-40 am to 11-30 am	Drill under Coy arrangements	
		11-30 am to 12-30 pm	Musketry.	
	14/3/16	9-30 - 11-30 am	Coy arrangements, mens feet rubbed well with oil	
			Various working found.	
			2/Lt W. Cross joined the Battn from the line	
	15/3/16		Battalion left billets passing through VILLERS au BOIS en route for trenches to relieve 5th Battn Lincolnshire Regiment in Right Sector of Brigade frontage opposite Givenchy and Vimy Ridge. Relief completed 9-35 pm. Battalion went on for 6 days marking out and digging new support line of trenches also using same.	
	21/3/16		Battalion relieved on the night 21/22 by 5th Lincolnshire Regt and went into support trenches at TALUS - des - ZOUAVES for 6 days.	
			2/Lt W. Cross and 2/Lt Wagstaff also a draft of 165 Other Ranks joined 16/3/16.	
			Lt J. Grundy joined 17/3/16.	

1875 Wt. W593/826 1,000,000 4/15 J.B.C. & A. A.D.S.S./Forms/C. 2118.

Sheet 4

Instructions regarding War Diaries and Intelligence Summaries are contained in F. S. Regs., Part II. and the Staff Manual respectively. Title Pages will be prepared in manuscript.

WAR DIARY
or
INTELLIGENCE SUMMARY
(Erase heading not required.)

Army Form C. 2118

Place	Date	Hour	Summary of Events and Information	Remarks and references to Appendices
	22/3/16		Draft of 145 Other Ranks joined the Battalion in the trenches from 3/4th Leics Regt.	
	27/3/16		Battn relieved the 5th Battn Lincolnshire Regt in front line trenches, relief completed 10 pm	
	28/3/16		2/Lt C. H. Cox joined from 3/4 Leics Regt.	
			Casualties one other Rank Killed.	
	29/3/16		Casualties:– three other Ranks ~~killed~~ Wounded.	
			2/Lt. C. Paddon and one N.C.O. commenced a course of instruction at 46th Div Schools	
	30/3/16		Casualties:– 2/Lt. A. F. Gerrard Killed in Action also one N.C.O and 1 man. Two Other Ranks Wounded.	
	31/3/16		Casualties:– Two Other Ranks Killed in Action One Other Rank Wounded.	

R S Neale Lieut Col.
17806. 4th Leics Regt
8/4/16

1875 Wt. W593/826 1,000,000 4/15 J.B.C. & A. A.D.S.S./Forms/C. 2118.

Instructions regarding War Diaries and Intelligence Summaries are contained in F.S. Regs., Part II. and the Staff Manual respectively. Title pages will be prepared in manuscript.

WAR DIARY
or
INTELLIGENCE SUMMARY.
(Erase heading not required.)

Army Form C. 2118.

138/46

Hour, Date, Place	Summary of Events and Information	Remarks and references to Appendices
CAMBLAIN L'ABBÉ. APRIL 2ND 10·30 P.M.	Battalion relieved by 5th Lincs Regt, relief completed 10·30 P.M. Coys marched home seperately last Coy arriving at the huts at 4 AM 3rd inst. Out for 6 days rest. Major H.E. Tetley took over command of the 5th Lincs Regt temporarily.	
5TH. 10·30 A.M.	Battalion less transport inspected by Major Gen. The Hon E. Montagu-Stuart-Wortley C.B.; C.M.G.; M.V.O. G.O.C. 46th Division and he expressed his appreciation of the particularly smart and soldierly appearance and bearing.	
6TH 9–12·30	Short Batt. route march through Camblain L'abbé – Estrée Cauchie – Cambligneul.	
7TH 6 P.M.	Inter Coy tug-o-war judged by the G.O.C. 46th Division	
8TH 5 P.M.	Battalion left huts at Camblain L'abbé to proceed to relieve 5th Lincs Regt accompanied by cookers. [illegible] in N. end of Bois des Alleux. Relief completed 10.15 pm. Night very quiet	

(9 29 6) W 3332—1107 100,000 10/13 H W V Forms/C. 2118/10.

Instructions regarding War Diaries and Intelligence Summaries are contained in F. S. Regs., Part II. and the Staff Manual respectively. Title pages will be prepared in manuscript.

WAR DIARY
or
INTELLIGENCE SUMMARY.
(Erase heading not required.)

Army Form C. 2118.

Hour, Date, Place	Summary of Events and Information	Remarks and references to Appendices
CAMBLAIN L'ABBÉ APRIL 2ND 10.30 P.M.	Battalion relieved by 5th Lincs Regt, relief completed 10.30 P.M. Coys marched home seperately last Coy arriving at the huts at 4 AM 3rd inst. Out for 6 days rest.	
	Major F.G. Fuller took over command of the 5th Lincs Regt temporarily.	
5TH 10.30 AM	Battalion less transport inspected by Major Gen The Hon E. Montague Stuart Wortley. C.B., C.M.G. M.V.O. G.O.C. 46th Division and he expressed his appreciation of the particularly smart and soldierly appearance and bearing.	
6TH 9 – 12.30	Short Batt route march through Camblain L'abbé – Estrée Cauchie – Cambligneul.	
7TH 6 P.M.	Inter Coy tug-o-war judged by the G.O.C. 46th Division.	
8TH 5 P.M.	Battalion left huts at Camblain L'abbé to proceed & relieve 5th Lincs Regt accompanied by [illegible] Sub sector N. end of Bois des Alleux. Relief completed 10.15 pm. Night very quiet	

(9 29 6) W 3332—1107 100,000 10/13 H W V Forms/C. 2118/10

Instructions regarding War Diaries and Intelligence Summaries are contained in F. S. Regs., Part II. and the Staff Manual respectively. Title pages will be prepared in manuscript.

WAR DIARY
or
INTELLIGENCE SUMMARY.

(Erase heading not required.)

Army Form C. 2118.

Hour, Date, Place	Summary of Events and Information	Remarks and references to Appendices
12TH 2.30 – 6.30pm TALUS DES ZOUAVES	Enemy bombarded our trenches very heavily, but with not much success beyond damaging our trenches. They dropped over 1,000 heavy calibre shells in the Talus des Zouaves doing no damage. Our artillery replied with good effect.	
13TH 2.30 – 5	A repetition of the 12TH on our front trenches without much success and very few casualties.	
14TH 6 P.M.	Battalion relieved by the 5th Lincs Regt in the front line relief complete about 8.30pm. Battalion went into support in the TALUS DES ZOUAVES.	
16TH 9.30P.	Very intense bombardment by the enemy which lasted about 2 hours. Gas shells were used by the enemy.	
18TH	Battalion relieved from front line by 5th Lincs Regt for 4 days.	
19TH.	Our miners blew a big mine opposite 4th Lincs Regt on our left front.	
20TH 6.30	Enemy blew a mine on our left in retaliation for our mine of previous night	
22ND.	Battalion should have been relieved by 2nd Royal Irish Rifles at 10.30 pm but relief delayed through two of the relieving Coys losing their way. Relief finally	

(9 29 6) W 3332—1107 100,000 10/13 H W V Forms/C. 2118/10

Instructions regarding War Diaries and Intelligence Summaries are contained in F.S. Regs., Part II. and the Staff Manual respectively. Title pages will be prepared in manuscript.

WAR DIARY
or
INTELLIGENCE SUMMARY.
(*Erase heading not required.*)

Army Form C. 2118.

Hour, Date, Place	Summary of Events and Information	Remarks and references to Appendices
12TH 2.30 – 6.30 pm TALUS DES ZOUAVES	Enemy bombarded our trenches very heavily but without much success beyond damaging our trenches. They dropped over 1,000 heavy calibre shells in the Talus des Zouaves doing no damage. Our artillery replied with good effect.	
13TH 2.30 – 5	A repetition of the 12TH on our front trenches without much success and very few casualties.	
14TH 6 PM.	Battalion relieved by the 5th Lincs Regt in the front line relief complete about 8.30 pm. Battalion went into support in the TALUS DES ZOUAVES.	
16TH 9.30 P.	Very intense bombardment by the enemy which lasted about 2 hours. Gas shells were used by the enemy.	
18TH	Battalion relieved from front line by 5th Lincs Regt for 4 days.	
19TH.	Our miners blew a big mine opposite 4th Lincs Regt on our left front.	
20TH 6.30	Enemy blew a mine on our left in retaliation for our mine of previous night	
22ND.	Battalion should have been relieved by 2nd Royal Irish Rifles at 10.30 pm. but relief delayed through two of the relieving coys losing their way. Relief finally	

Army Form C. 2118.

Instructions regarding War Diaries and Intelligence Summaries are contained in F. S. Regs., Part II. and the Staff Manual respectively. Title pages will be prepared in manuscript.

WAR DIARY
or
INTELLIGENCE SUMMARY.
(Erase heading not required.)

Hour, Date, Place	Summary of Events and Information	Remarks and references to Appendices
22ND	Relief finally completed about 6 AM on the 23rd Inst.	
23RD 10.A M. MAIZIERES	Battalion brought to billets at MAIZIERES by motor lorries arriving 12 Noon.	
	A draft of 93 men joined the Battalion here from 3/4TH Leicestershire Regt, Nottingham.	
25TH	Time spent in rest and cleaning up.	
26TH 9.30 – 12.30	Battalion route march MAIZIERES – PENIN.	
27TH – 29TH	Battalion in training by Coys. Bombers, Machine Gunners, Scouts, Snipers continued training.	
30TH 10.30 AM MAIZIERES.	Church parade taken by the Commanding Officer.	
	The casualties during the Battalions tour from ~~April 2?~~ March 16th to April 23rd were 20 Killed 76 wounded including 2/Lieut S. F. Lennard Killed in action.	

B. Clarke Lieut Colonel
Comdg 4th Leicestershire Regt

(9 29 6) W 3332—1107 100,000 10/13 H W V Forms/C. 2118/10.

Instructions regarding War Diaries and Intelligence Summaries are contained in F. S. Regs., Part II. and the Staff Manual respectively. Title pages will be prepared in manuscript.

WAR DIARY
or
INTELLIGENCE SUMMARY.
(Erase heading not required.)

Army Form C. 2118.

Hour, Date, Place	Summary of Events and Information	Remarks and references to Appendices
22nd	Relief finally completed about 6 pm on the 23rd Inst.	
23rd 10. A.M. MAIZIERES.	Battalion brought to billets at MAIZIERES by motor lorries arriving 12 Noon	
	A draft of 93 men joined the Battalion here from 3/4th Leicestershire Regt, Nottingham.	
25th	Time spent in rest and cleaning up.	
26th 9.30 - 12.30	Battalion route march MAIZIERES - PENIN.	
27th - 29th	Battalion in training by coys, Bombers, Machine Gunners, Scouts, Snipers continued training.	
30th 10.30 A.M. MAIZIERES	Church parade taken by the Commanding Officer.	
	The casualties during the Battalions tour from ~~April 2nd~~ March 26th to April 23rd were 20 Killed 76 wounded including 2/Lieut S. J. Leonard killed in action.	
	R Clarke	Lieut Colonel Comdg 4th Leicestershire R.

(9 29 6) W 3332—1107 100,000 10/13 H W V Forms/C. 2118/10

Instructions regarding War Diaries and Intelligence Summaries are contained in F.S. Regs., Part II. and the Staff Manual respectively. Title pages will be prepared in manuscript.

WAR DIARY
or
INTELLIGENCE SUMMARY.
(Erase heading not required.)

Army Form C. 2118.

46

Hour, Date, Place	Summary of Events and Information	Remarks and references to Appendices
MAIZIERES MAY. 1ST	A draft of 120 N.C.Os and men joined the Batt on this date from 3/4th Leicestershire Regt.	
9 30 AM	The C.O. inspected this draft and the previous one	
2ND 9 30 AM	The Battalion inspected by Brigadier General G.C. Kemp Comdg 138th Inf. Bde.	
3RD 2 30 pm	The Battalion held some Regimental Sports on this day attended by the Brigadier.	
2.45 pm	Orders received from Brigade to hold Battalion in readiness to move at short notice.	
SAVY 4TH 9 AM	Battalion moved to SAVY, to be in Corps Reserve (17th Corps) and bivouaced in field S. of the town	
5TH. 6 8TH	Company training, bombers, Lewis gunners, signallers, snipers, scouts and Stretcher Bearers continued training.	

(9 29 6) W 3332—1107 100,000 10/13 H W V Forms/C. 2118/10.

Instructions regarding War Diaries and Intelligence Summaries are contained in F. S. Regs., Part II. and the Staff Manual respectively. Title pages will be prepared in manuscript.

WAR DIARY
or
INTELLIGENCE SUMMARY.
(*Erase heading not required.*)

Army Form C. 2118.

Hour, Date, Place		Summary of Events and Information	Remarks and references to Appendices
SAVY. LE SOUICH	9TH 9AM	Battalion left SAVY and marched to Le Souich in billets. Brigade at Lucheux.	
	10TH	9AM – 4.30. 200 hundred men making hurdles under R.E. Supervision, cutting brushwood, making and clearing in Lucheux Wood.	
	11TH	9AM – 4.30pm 200 men doing work as above.	
	13TH 9.30 AM	Battalion drill for an hour and a half under Commanding Officer.	
	3PM.	Four new officers joined the Batt. as follows:- 2/Lieut. E. Tubberne, A J Fletcher, H JA Parkinson, and AW. Fergusson from 3/4th Leicestershire Regt.	
	14TH 3pm	2/Lieut H.N. Salter joined the Battalion from 3/4 Leicestershire Regt.	
	9AM–4.30	Working parties of 200 men on R.E. Wood fatigue	
	15TH	As above. Wood fatigue.	
	16TH 9AM.	C.O and Adjutant went to Souastre to visit new area with the Brigadier and Staff	RL
	1.30 pm	2/Lieut C.B. Knight joined the Battalion from 3/4 Leicestershire Regt	

Instructions regarding War Diaries and Intelligence Summaries are contained in F.S. Regs., Part II. and the Staff Manual respectively. Title pages will be prepared in manuscript.

WAR DIARY
or
INTELLIGENCE SUMMARY.
(*Erase heading not required.*)

Army Form C. 2118.

Hour, Date, Place		Summary of Events and Information	Remarks and references to Appendices
LE SOUICH	17TH. 11AM	The G.O.C. came to see the Battalion at work. 200 men on wood fatigue, the remainder attacking through a wood.	
	3pm	The VIITH Corps Commander Lieut Gen Sir T D'O Snow KCB visited the Battalion.	
	18TH 9.30 – 4.30	Battalion found all wood working parties as previously mentioned but 500 strong.	
	19TH 9AM	Party of Officers visited new area at Humbercamps.	
	3 P.M.	Battalion found a Guard for Corps Headquarters 1 Sgt & 23 other ranks.	
HUMBERCAMP	20TH 3P.M.	Battalion moved to new area at HUMBERCAMP. ~~[illegible]~~. Arrived at Humbercamps 9.30pm. Transport Bivouaced at La Bazeque Ferme.	
	21ST.	Church parade 4th Lincs & 4th Leics with the Bde band.	
	22ND	Fatigues in rear of trenches, digging gun emplacements, communication trenches etc	[initials]

Instructions regarding War Diaries and Intelligence Summaries are contained in F. S. Regs., Part II. and the Staff Manual respectively. Title pages will be prepared in manuscript.

WAR DIARY
or
INTELLIGENCE SUMMARY.
(Erase heading not required.)

Army Form C. 2118.

Hour, Date, Place	Summary of Events and Information	Remarks and references to Appendices
HUMBERCAMP 23rd	Brigade fatigues on gun emplacements, burying cables etc.	
24th		
25th	As above.	
26th 3pm	The Battalion was inspected by General Sir Douglas Haig, Commander-in-Chief of the British Army in France. C.O. congratulated on smart turn out and soldierly appearance of the men.	
27th	Fatigues as above.	
28th 10.30pm	Church parade 4 Lincs and 4th Leics. The G.O.C. present. After the Service the G.O.C. presented 2984 Pte Bennett H with the ribbon of the [illegible] medal for bravery at Souchez.	
29-31.	Day and night fatigues of 450 men continued digging trenches, gun pits etc.	

B. Clarke Lieut Colonel.
Cmndg 4th Leicestershire Regt.
31.5.16.

46

Army Form C. 2118.

1/4 Leicester Regt

Vol 16

Instructions regarding War Diaries and Intelligence Summaries are contained in F. S. Regs., Part II. and the Staff Manual respectively. Title pages will be prepared in manuscript.

WAR DIARY
or
INTELLIGENCE SUMMARY.
(Erase heading not required.)

Hour, Date, Place	Summary of Events and Information	Remarks and references to Appendices
JUNE 1ST – 4TH HUMBERCAMP	Working parties found of 500 men daily for working at FONCQUEVILLERS digging cable trenches.	
5TH	Battalion relieved 8TH Sherwood Foresters in Centre Sector at FONCQUEVILLERS. Relief completed at 11.15 pm. Headquarters at the Brasserie. A+C Coys in front line B+D in support.	
6TH – 16TH	Battalion in the line during this period working very hard on front line, making saps, clearing damaged front line & rebuilding throughout. Ammunition, bomb stores & RE dumps made the length of the trench. On the 11TH Inst B+D Coys relieved A+C Coys in front line. Enemy very quiet but working hard all along GOMMECOURT PARK. Our artillery did very good & effective work on enemy works especially our Heavy Guns.	
9TH	Lieut C B P. Peake and 2/Lieuts J D Thomson, A B. P[illegible], C A. Payne ~~Atn.~~ joined the Battn on this date.	

(9 29 6) W 3332—1107 100,000 10/13 H W V Forms/C. 2118/10

Instructions regarding War Diaries and Intelligence Summaries are contained in F.S. Regs., Part II. and the Staff Manual respectively. Title pages will be prepared in manuscript.

WAR DIARY
or
INTELLIGENCE SUMMARY.
(Erase heading not required.)

Army Form C. 2118.

Hour, Date, Place		Summary of Events and Information	Remarks and references to Appendices
FONCQUEVILLERS	12TH	2/Lieut M. G.R. Elliott joined Battalion from 3/4 Leic R.	
	15TH	" A.N. Jewitt, A.N. Leslie " " " "	
	19TH	" E.C. Doudney " " " " "	
	16TH	The Battalion were relieved from Centre Sector by 6th N. Staffs Regt. Relief complete 5 pm. Battalion went into huts at HUMBERCAMP.	
	18TH to 21ST.	Battalion relieved 6th N. Staffordshire Regt in Centre Sector Foncquevillers left Humbercamp 7.30 pm relief complete 11.30 pm.	
WARLINCOURT	21ST	Battalion relieved by 5th North Staffs Regt relief complete 1.5 Am 22nd. Battalion found working party of 400 men digging new line. Batt. marched back by cycle to WARLINCOURT. last party arrived in huts 8 Am.	
	24TH	The bombardment of GOMMECOURT commenced. This was divided into 5 days, the 24th being U day, 25th V day and so on.	
FONCQUEVILLERS	26TH	Battalion marched to FONCQUEVILLERS and relieved 5th N. Staffs in the line owing to bad weather, relief completed 2.50 A.m. Attack on GOMMECOURT postponed for 24 hours owing to very bad weather.	

(9 29 6) W 3332—1107 100,000 10/13 H W V Forms/C. 2118/10.

Instructions regarding War Diaries and Intelligence Summaries are contained in F.S. Regs., Part II. and the Staff Manual respectively. Title pages will be prepared in manuscript.

WAR DIARY
or
INTELLIGENCE SUMMARY.
(Erase heading not required.)

Army Form C. 2118.

Hour, Date, Place	Summary of Events and Information	Remarks and references to Appendices
FONCQUEVILLERS 27TH to 30TH	In front line trenches during original X, Y and Z days 2 days afterwards altered to July 1st. Relieved by 5TH South Staffs in front line from GOMMECOURT Rd to Stafford Avenue and by 5th N. Staffs thence to Lincoln Lane. Relief complete 5.30 pm. Battalion marched	
ST. AMAND 6 pm.	back to billets at St. Amand preparatory for the attack by 137th and 139th Inf Brigades, 138th Bde being in reserve. The attacks due to commence July 1st 1916 7.30 A.m.	[illegible] Lt Colonel Comd 4/ Leic Regt

(9 29 6) W 3332—1107 100,000 10/13 H W V Forms/C. 2118/10

138/46

1/4 Leicester R

Vol 20 17

Instructions regarding War Diaries and Intelligence Summaries are contained in F. S. Regs., Part II. and the Staff Manual respectively. Title pages will be prepared in manuscript.

WAR DIARY
or
INTELLIGENCE SUMMARY.

(Erase heading not required.)

Army Form C. 2118.

Hour, Date, Place	Summary of Events and Information	Remarks and references to Appendices
JULY 1ST 6.25AM	Bombardment (very intense) commenced on GOMMECOURT WOOD and PARK by our artillery.	
GOMMECOURT WOOD 7.30AM	137th and 139th Inf Bdes left their trenches to take the German lines opposite that is in front of Wood.	
Map 57D 1/40,000	This Battalion moved to field D.9 c. , as reserve Battalion, of reserve Brigade. At 6pm orders were received from Brigade for the Battalion to move up to Corps line behind FONCQUEVILLERS, in reserve to 138th Bde. D.24 d to E13 c. at 10pm orders were received to move to	
Map 57D 1/40,000	MIDLAND TRENCH in rear of FONCQUEVILLERS at E 26 b 4/2 to E 15 c 85/35. where the Battalion remained for the night 1/2 July.	
2ND 6pm. 57D NE 1&2. Map FONCQUEVILLERS 1/10,000 & 57C SE MONCHY 3&4 1/10,000	Orders received from 138th Bde for Battalion to move to HANNESCAMPS to relieve 10TH Batt Loyal North Lancs Regt. On right Sector from ~~W 28 a~~ to E 5 c to W 29 a. Relief completed 1 Am 3rd Inst.	
3RD	Enemy shelled us heavily at 4 pm with [illegible] of special design.	
4TH	Heavy rains from night of 3rd Inst. Trenches in a terrible state.	
7TH – 9TH	Cylinders of gas carried up to front line preparatory to giving the enemy a dose of Gas without an attack.	
10TH	2/Lieut. J Douglas joined the Battalion from 3/4th Leicestershire Regt.	

Instructions regarding War Diaries and Intelligence Summaries are contained in F. S. Regs., Part II. and the Staff Manual respectively. Title pages will be prepared in manuscript.

WAR DIARY
or
INTELLIGENCE SUMMARY.
(Erase heading not required.)

Army Form C. 2118.

Hour, Date, Place	Summary of Events and Information	Remarks and references to Appendices
July 11TH 5 P.M.	Battalion relieved in right sector of Brigade by 10th Yorks Lancs R. relief complete 7.15pm and marched to billets at SAULTY. Arriving there 10 P.M.	+ 10th Batt Northumberland Fusiliers trenches 72 to 90 inclusive
SAULTY 12TH	Day spent in rest, cleaning of equipment etc and interior economy.	
13TH 10.30 AM	Battalion inspected by Major General W. Thwaites General Officer Commanding 46th Division. Battalion congratulated by the G.O.C. on work done at FONCQUEVILLERS prior to July 1st.	
BIENVILLERS 14TH	Battalion left Saulty and marched to BIENVILLERS as Batt. in Brigade reserve, arrived Bienvillers 8.30pm	
15TH	A combined gas and smoke attack sent over at 10.40pm with artillery co-operation. BIENVILLERS heavily shelled	
9–10 AM	between 9 and 11 A.m.	
to 17TH	Working parties found for Naked Street and carrying of Gas cylinders. Intense bombardment of enemy lines and Gas attack	
18TH	Battalion relieved 5th Batt Leic. Regt in right sector 76–89 relief complete 7.15pm. Our own bombardment of enemy	(inclusive)
to	lines, roads and MONCHY village and transport.	
24TH	Completed tour of six days in right sector, doing much work on the whole of front line, support and building dugouts. Relieved by 5th Batt Leic. Regt relief complete 9.20pm. Battalion marched to billets at POMMIER.	76 – 89 inclusive

(9 29 6) W 3332—1107 100,000 10/13 H W V Forms/C. 2118/10.

Instructions regarding War Diaries and Intelligence Summaries are contained in F. S. Regs., Part II. and the Staff Manual respectively. Title pages will be prepared in manuscript.

WAR DIARY
or
INTELLIGENCE SUMMARY.
(Erase heading not required.)

Army Form C. 2118.

Hour, Date, Place	Summary of Events and Information	Remarks and references to Appendices
POMMIER 25TH to 29TH	Divisional reserve. Spent in training of Companies bombers, Signallers, Scouts and Snipers etc. Two companies using the range for a day each in addition to Lewis Gunners and Snipers. Working parties of 200 men found daily for Railway construction at Point D 6 Central (Cheminée de Fours).	
30TH 11.30 AM	Battalion inspected by Brigadier General G. G. Kemp C.B. who expressed satisfaction on the turn out.	
5 P.M.	Battalion relieved 5th Leic. Regt in the right sector.× relief completed 9.30 pm.	×Trenches. 76 - 89 inclusive
31ST.	Spent in general improvement of trenches, building up by sandbagging to narrow and excavating for deep dug-outs	

J. Eric Jelley
Major
Commanding
4th Batt Leicestershire Regt

31. 4. 16

(9 29 6) W 3332—1107 100,000 10/13 H W V Forms/C. 2118/10.

Instructions regarding War Diaries and Intelligence Summaries are contained in F. S. Regs., Part II. and the Staff Manual respectively. Title Pages will be prepared in manuscript.

WAR DIARY
or
INTELLIGENCE SUMMARY
(Erase heading not required.)

Army Form C. 2118

1/4 Leicester Reg^t

Vol 218

Place	Date	Hour	Summary of Events and Information	Remarks and references to Appendices
MONCHY TRENCHES	AUGUST 1-3.		Battalion in front line trenches opposite Monchy with 169th Inf Bde on our right and 4th Lincolns on our left.	
	3/4TH		Batt relieved on this night by 5th Bn Leicestershire Regt relief completed at 3.5pm	
		3.15am	Enemy shelled us very heavily at centre sector.	
BIENVILLERS.	4TH		Anniversary of declaration of war. Enemy attempted a raid on our lines. S.O.S	
		3-4am	given very heavy gunfire. Battalion stood to for an hour in billets	
	5TH.	11.25pm	5th Batt Leic: Regt made a raid on enemy trenches opposite Monchy, wire found to be very strong and insufficiently cut. Party had to retire. Very heavy and accurate firing by our guns on enemy lines and communications.	
	6TH		Voluntary Church parade in bath House 5.30pm.	
	7TH & 8TH		Nothing of importance to report.	
	9TH		Battalion relieved 5th Batt Leic. Regt in right sector relief complete 9.30pm	
			Relief delayed owing to our heavy and medium trench mortars firing on enemy lines.	
	to		Enemy shelled Bienvillers very heavily for about 3 hours.	
	15TH		Six days tour in right sector, very quiet, hardly any shelling or activity taking place. Batt. working on defences, especially front line wire & entanglements. Much good work done.	
			Relieved in right sector by 5th Batt Leicestershire Regt. Batt went back for five days rest to POMMIER	
POMMIER	16TH to 21ST.		These six days spent in training and Sports etc. Details such as Signallers Bombers, Scouts, Lewis Gunners, Snipers all brought up to strength and new details commenced training. Battalion	

1875 Wt. W593/826 1,000,000 4/15 J.B.C. & A. A.D.S.S./Forms/C. 2118.

Instructions regarding War Diaries and Intelligence Summaries are contained in F. S. Regs., Part II. and the Staff Manual respectively. Title Pages will be prepared in manuscript.

WAR DIARY
or
INTELLIGENCE SUMMARY
(Erase heading not required.)

Army Form C. 2118

Place	Date	Hour	Summary of Events and Information	Remarks and references to Appendices
POMMIER.	16TH to 21ST		Carried on with close order drill (Special attention being paid to accuracy and smartness of movement), musketry, bombing, Physical training, Guard drill and firing on range. The Senior N.C.O's taken in special class of bayonet fighting under Sergt Major Bentley. The officers also had a 2 hours course under this N.C.O.	
	20TH	2.30pm	The Brigadier inspected the Battalion by companies in the afternoon and was pleased with the turn out.	
	21ST.	5P.M.	Battalion left POMMIER to relieve the 5TH Battalion in the right sector of Bde line. Relief completed 7.30.	
	22ND		Day quiet no shelling on either side. Bosch caught cutting our wire opposite 89. Trench dispersed by L/Gun fire.	
	24TH to 27TH		Enemy shelled POMMIER heavily but did no material damage. and also put about 200 5.9 in shell in FONCQUEVILLERS - BIENVILLERS ROAD. Battalion working very hard in front and support lines improving trenches both in front line and support much good and valuable work done. Relieved at 5pm by 5th Battalion relief completed at 7.35pm. Battalion went back to billets at BIENVILLERS. This tour of 6 days was extraordinarily quiet, only one casualty being reported and that being from a shell splinter which came from HANNESCAMP.	
	31ST		Battalion in Brigade reserve at BIENVILLERS. Issue of gas from Left Section of Brigade front at 10P.M. on 30TH INST.	

J. Eric Jelley Major
Comdg 4th Bn Leicestershire Regt.

1875 Wt. W593/826 1,000,000 4/15 J.B.C. & A. A.D.S.S./Forms/C. 2118.

WAR DIARY
or
INTELLIGENCE SUMMARY
(Erase heading not required.)

Instructions regarding War Diaries and Intelligence Summaries are contained in F. S. Regs., Part II. and the Staff Manual respectively. Title Pages will be prepared in manuscript.

Army Form C. 2118

Vol 19

Place	Date	Hour	Summary of Events and Information	Remarks and references to Appendices
B.E.F. BIENVILLERS AU-BOIS.	SEPT.	1ST	Battalion in Brigade Reserve. Training carried on with as follows, Musketry with use of the range. Physical Training, Bomb throwing & manual drill. All specialists doing training as such.	
	2ND	5PM	Battalion left billets for trenches where they relieved the 5th Battalion in the Right Sector of Bde area opposite MONCHY. Relief completed at 6.45 P.M. Our artillery shelled the enemy lines behind MONCHY with apparent good effect. The 17th DIVISION were on our right and 5th Lancs Regt. on our left during this time.	
POMMIER.	8TH.		Battalion relieved by 5th Leics Regt in the Right Sector. Relief completed at 7.15 pm. Battalion went into DIVISIONAL RESERVE at POMMIER. Received orders that we should move to new area.	
LACAUCHIE.	10TH	10.30 Am.	Battalion left billets at 10.30 Am for new area at LA CAUCHIE.	
	11TH.	2 PM.	The 138TH INFANTRY BRIGADE SPORTS held at LA BADIQUE FERME. Battalion did well.	
	12TH	11 Am.	The Battalion marched to La Banque and did Battalion drill.	
	14TH to 20TH	[illegible]	Battalion relieved the 5th Battalion in the right Sector, relief completed 4.45 pm. Coys carried on with the repairs to front line trenches, and general improvement of front and support line. Battalion relieved by the 5th Leic. Regt relief completed 7 pm.	
BIENVILLERS	21ST. to 26TH		In Brigade Reserve, time spent in training and working parties. 4 Bn[illegible] Battalion Bombers, Signallers, Scouts and Snipers all underwent special training. The Companies were under training in Guard duties. Bayonet fighting, Manual Drill, special attention being paid to Bayonet fighting and Bombing.	

1875 Wt. W593/826 1,000,000 4/15 J.B.C. & A. A.D.S.S./Forms/C. 2118.

Instructions regarding War Diaries and Intelligence Summaries are contained in F. S. Regs., Part II. and the Staff Manual respectively. Title Pages will be prepared in manuscript.

WAR DIARY
or
INTELLIGENCE SUMMARY
(Erase heading not required.)

Army Form C. 2118

Place	Date	Hour	Summary of Events and Information	Remarks and references to Appendices
BIENVILLERS & MONCHY.	SEPTEMBER 26TH to 30TH	1916	Battalion relieved the 5th Battalion in the Right Sector opposite the village of MONCHY. Relief completed 7.30 PM. Delayed owing to shelling of HANNESCAMPS. NEWS RECEIVED OF THE FALL OF THIEPVAL. The enemy ~~[illegible]~~ displayed more activity than usual sending over quite a number of trench mortars and rifle grenades, also showing himself more especially on patrol.	
			30/9/16	
			J. Eric Petley	
			[illegible] Lt Col Comdg. 4th Bn Leicestershire Regt	

1875 Wt. W593/826 1,000,000 4/15 J.B.C. & A. A.D.S.S./Forms/C. 2118.

46/138

Instructions regarding War Diaries and Intelligence Summaries are contained in F. S. Regs., Part II. and the Staff Manual respectively. Title pages will be prepared in manuscript.

WAR DIARY
or
~~INTELLIGENCE SUMMARY.~~
(Erase heading not required.)

4th Leicesters — 4 Leic. Regt — 138th I.B. 46th DIVISION. Vol 20

Army Form C. 2118.

Hour, Date, Place	Summary of Events and Information	Remarks and references to Appendices
OCTOBER 1ST TRENCHES MONCHY SECTOR	This was the last day of 6 days tour in the line.	
2ND	Battalion relieved by 5th Bn Leic: Regt. Relief complete 5.30 P.M. Marched back to billets at LA CAUCHIE arriving there 7 P.M. Transport at BAVINCOURT.	
LACAUCHIE. 3RD – 7TH	These 5 days spent in training by Companies including Bombing, Physical training, Musketry, Manual and close order drill.	
6TH 10.30 A.M. LA CAUCHIE	Battalion inspected by Major General W. Thwaites G.O.C. 46th Division. No transport.	
8TH – 14TH	Battalion marched from LA CAUCHIE to take over the MONCHY Sector from 5th Battalion. Relief completed 7.30 P.M. Six days tour. Very quiet no casualties.	
14TH 6.30 P.M. BIENVILLERS-AU-BOIS	Relieved in front line by 5th Battalion Leic: Regt & marched back to BIENVILLERS to billets in Brigade Reserve.	
18TH	Raid carried out by 5th Lincolnshire Regt in which this Battalion were to have co-operated. Our orders were cancelled reason unknown. to Cnl (Capt ? J Magee) [illegible] should have made this raid	
20TH BIENVILLERS	Battalion left billets 4 pm to relieve right section of Brigade front. Relief completed 5.30 P.M. G.O.C. inspected Brigade transport. Most satisfactory report on this Battalion.	

(9 29 6) W 3332—1107 100,000 10/13 H W V Forms/C. 2118/10.

Instructions regarding War Diaries and Intelligence Summaries are contained in F.S. Regs., Part II. and the Staff Manual respectively. Title pages will be prepared in manuscript.

WAR DIARY
or
~~INTELLIGENCE SUMMARY.~~
(Erase heading not required.)

Army Form C. 2118.

4th Leicesters 46 Div.

Hour, Date, Place	Summary of Events and Information	Remarks and references to Appendices
20th to 25th 5PM	Battalion received orders that they would be relieved by the 5th Battalion on the day following their usual	
25th 6.30P.M.	Relief completed 5.45 P.M. Battalion marched back to billets at POMMIER into Divisional Reserve. Companies training.	
26th 27th POMMIER		
28th 6.35PM. HALLOY	Battalion left POMMIER en route for new area, marched via HUMBERCAMP - LABAZIQUE - ARRAS ROAD - MONDICOURT - POMMERA to HALLOY, where the Battalion arrived at 11PM. Billeted in huts. The men stood the march very well, no casualties en route.	
29th. 30th ~~[illegible]~~	Battalion in strict training, doing close order drill, Bayonet Fighting, route marching, scouting etc.	
31st. 10A.M. 12.30 NOON	Battalion moved from huts at HALLOY to billets at BOUQUEMAISON. Arrived new billets 12.30. Distance 8 miles. Transport followed the Battalion. Route taken HALLOY ~~BOUQUEMAISON~~ - LUCHEUX - BOUQUEMAISON. During this marching the Battalion did exceedingly well no man falling out or going sick.	
	31.10.16.	

J. Eric Petley Lieut Colonel.
Comdg. 4th BN LEICESTERSHIRE REGT. T.F.

(9 29 6) W 3332—1107 100,000 10/13 H W V Forms/C. 2118/10.

Instructions regarding War Diaries and Intelligence Summaries are contained in F.S. Regs., Part II. and the Staff Manual respectively. Title pages will be prepared in manuscript.

WAR DIARY
or
INTELLIGENCE SUMMARY.
(Erase heading not required.)

Army Form C. 2118.

4th Leicesters
Vol 21

Hour, Date, Place	Summary of Events and Information	Remarks and references to Appendices
BOUQUEMAISON NOV 1ST 7.Am	The Battalion left Bouquemaison at 7Am and marched to billets at NOEUX en route for ABBEVILLE training area, where we arrived at 11Am.	8½ miles
NOEUX. 2ND 8.15Am	Battalion left billets in Noeux for ONEUX where it arrived at 1.45P.M. Battalion led the Brigade march, marched past the G.O.C. who highly complimented the C.O. on the marching and transport turn outs.	12½ miles
ONEUX 3RD 9Am	Battalion left billets at Oneux for DRUCAT where it arrived at 12.15 Noon. this was our village for training area.	6 miles.
DRUCAT 4TH	Spent in rest, interior economy and cleaning	
5TH	Church Parade and rest.	
6TH 7TH	Training in close order, arms drill and Physical training Specialist continued training.	
8TH	Received orders at 12.35Am for Battalion to move to a new area at DOMVAST arrived in billets 1pm.	
DOMVAST.		5 miles.
9TH 10TH	Battalion in training on area.	
11TH	Orders received to return to previous billets at DRUCAT. where we arrived at 1.30pm.	5 miles
12TH	Brigade church parade on training area. G.O.C. present.	

(9 29 6) W 3332–1107 100,000 10/13 H W V Forms/C. 2118/10.

Instructions regarding War Diaries and Intelligence Summaries are contained in F.S. Regs., Part II. and the Staff Manual respectively. Title pages will be prepared in manuscript.

WAR DIARY
or
INTELLIGENCE SUMMARY.
(Erase heading not required.)

Army Form C. 2118.

4th Leicesters.

Hour, Date, Place		Summary of Events and Information	Remarks and references to Appendices
DRUCAT.	13TH	Battalion in training on area. Night operations.	~~Drummalcap~~ Battn played 138th Bde Bay won 12-1 v 5 Lincs. 2-0 v 5 Leic. 4-0 Semi final v 5th Sherwoods 2-0 Final to be played Dec 2nd.
	14TH	A draft of 220 Ranks arrived from 12 Inf Base Depot.	
6-10pm.	15TH 16TH	Battalion training on area. Night operations	
	17TH & 18TH	arrived back in billets 10pm.	
	19TH	Church parade. A lecture was given at St RIQUIER to all Officers by Lieut Colonel Weber 30th Division.	
	20TH	Brigade attacks over the open	
	21ST	Training and night operations which turned out very satisfactorily.	
DOMQUEVR.	22ND	Battalion moved from Drucat to Lucheux area + arrived in billets at DOMQUEVR via St Riquier arrived billets 12 50pm (12 miles)	During the marching to and from the training areas the Battn was many times highly praised for good march discipline + bearing
BONNIERES	23RD	Battalion moved to BONNIERES leaving billets at 7 15Am arrived billets (noon 1.30pm) (15 miles)	
	24TH	Day spent in rest, cleaning and interior economy.	
MONDICOURT	25	Battalion moved to new billets at MONDICOURT. Left Bonnieres 9 20Am arrived billets 2 30pm. (13½ miles)	
	26TH.	Spent in rest, cleaning and interior economy.	
	27TH	Training on training area	
	28TH 29TH	" "	
	30TH.	46th Divisional Cross country run 2¾ miles open to all Battalions of the Division Won by 4th Leicestershire Regt number home 304 all ranks.	

J. Eric Jessop Lieut Colonel 4 Leic. Regt.

1/12/16

(9 29 6) W 3332—1107 100,000 10/13 H W V Forms/C. 2118/10.

Instructions regarding War Diaries and Intelligence Summaries are contained in F.S. Regs., Part II. and the Staff Manual respectively. Title pages will be prepared in manuscript.

WAR DIARY
or
~~INTELLIGENCE SUMMARY.~~
(Erase heading not required.)

Army Form C. 2118.

Vol 22

Hour, Date, Place	Summary of Events and Information	Remarks and references to Appendices
December 1st 1916. Mondicourt 2 p.m.	The Corps Commander Lieutenant General Sir T. D'O. Snow K.C.B. inspected the Brigade. Both the Corps Commander and the G.O.C. of the Division spoke in high terms of the smartness of the Battalion turn out especially complimenting the Company Commanders.	
2nd. 9 AM - 12 Noon	Battalion practising Trench attack, consolidating captured position etc.	
3rd.	Battalion played 5th N. Staffs in the final for the Divisional Cup at La Folie Ferme, Lucheux. Result 5th N Staffs 3 goals, 4th Leic 1 goal.	
4th. 5th	The Battalion left Mondicourt for Bienvillers to relieve the 6th Bn W. Yorks Regt in Brigade reserve.	
6th Bienvillers.	The Battalion relieved the 5th Bn W. Yorks in the Hannescamps Sector (ie E 11 a 4/9 to E 17 a 3/3 map ref. Foncquevillers 57 D.N.E. 1/10,000.	
10th Hannescamps Area.	Relief completed 12.30 Noon. Six days tour. Major B. F. Newill rejoined Bn from 3rd line.	
11th	Battalion relieved by 5th Bn Leicestershire Regiment in left subsector of the Brigade frontage. Relief completed 4.30 p.m. Went back to billets in Bienvillers.	
Bienvillers 13th	Very intense bombardment by Divisional & Corps Artillery on Monchy au Bois. Bn lived in cellars all day and night.	
14th	Lieut Colonel B. F. Clarke rejoined Battalion & took over command.	
17th Hannescamps Area	Battalion relieved 5th Bn, Leic. Rgt in Left Subsector of Brigade frontage relief complete 3.15 p.m.	

(9 29 6) W 3332—1107 100,000 10/13 H W V Forms/C. 2118/10.

Instructions regarding War Diaries and Intelligence Summaries are contained in F. S. Regs., Part II. and the Staff Manual respectively. Title pages will be prepared in manuscript.

WAR DIARY
or
INTELLIGENCE SUMMARY.
(*Erase heading not required.*)

Army Form C. 2118.

4th Leicesters

Hour, Date, Place	Summary of Events and Information	Remarks and references to Appendices
Dec. 21st SOUASTRE	Battalion relieved by 5th Bn Lin. Regt relief completed 3.30 p.m. [illegible] SOUASTRE	
23rd FONQ[illegible]	Battalion [illegible] relieve 5th [illegible] left sector relief completed 1.45 p.m.	
to 29th [illegible] Area	Battalion completed [illegible] days [illegible] Battalion headquarters [illegible] relief	
	Battalion relieved by 5th Bn Linc. Regt. Relief completed 1.25 p.m.	
	The Battalion [illegible] by the G.O.C. [illegible] held November 30th.	
30th & 31st BIENVILLERS	Battalion in Brigade Reserve in Bienvillers.	
	[illegible]	
	December 30th 1916	[signature] Lieut Colonel Commdg. 4th Bn Leicestershire Regt B.E.F.

(9 29 6) W 3332—1107 100,000 10/13 H W V Forms/C. 2118/10.

Instructions regarding War Diaries and Intelligence Summaries are contained in F. S. Regs., Part II. and the Staff Manual respectively. Title pages will be prepared in manuscript.

WAR DIARY
or
INTELLIGENCE SUMMARY.
(Erase heading not required.)

Army Form C. 2118.

1/4 Leicester Reg[?] Vol 23

Place	Date	Hour	Summary of Events and Information	Remarks and references to Appendices
Bienvillers	January 1st		Battalion in cellars at Bienvillers in Brigade Reserve for HANNESCAMPS sector.	
		12 MN	Enemy artillery very active at midnight. One salvo caused some casualties in "D" Coy. [illegible]	
	2nd	10 AM	The Battalion relieved the 5th Battn in the HANNESCAMP sector leaving billets at 10 Am and completing the relief at 12.45 Noon.	
	3rd		Work of draining and revetting trenches carried on night and day. Enemy artillery very active on the remains of Bienvillers.	
	4th		A patrol was sent out from Battalion right sector under Lieut A. G. Heploss[?], consisting of 12 other ranks. Two enemy came and immediately surrendered. Our patrol captured one of these men a Corporal of the 55th R.I.R. The prisoner to Corps Intelligence branch.	
SOUASTRE	6th		Relieved in the Hannescamps sector by 5th Battalion and went into billets at SOUASTRE in Divisional Reserve. Relief complete by 12.15 Noon.	
	7th	10 Am	Church parade.	
	8th		Battalion found a Guard of honour of 3 Officers and 100 other ranks for the presentation of medal ribbons by Gen Sir Edmund Allenby K.C.B. G.O.C. 3rd Army.	
	9th			
HANNESCAMPS	10th		Relieved the 5th Battalion in the line. Relief complete 12 Noon.	
	11th		Work continued on whole of Battalion sector day and night.	
	12th		A draft of 32 other ranks arrived from the Brigade Depot. (3rd line).	
Bienvillers.	14th		Relieved by 5th Battalion. Relief complete 12.15 Noon. Enemy artillery very active at night.	
	17th		Very heavy snowfall 6" deep much delayed our parties working. 2/Lts J B. Lumber[?] R. Hopworth[?] rejoined the Bn.	
Hannescamps	18th	10 A.M.	Relieved 5th Bn in front line trenches. Relief completed 12 Noon. [illegible]	
SOUASTRE	22nd	10 AM	Relieved by 5th Bn in Hannescamps sector. Relief complete 11.30 Am. 2/Lt R F Wagstaffe rejoined the Bn.	
	23rd		A draft of 22 other ranks arrived from the Brigade Depot. (3rd Line) 2/Lts G S ANDERSON R S PROVIS G P CLAY joined the Battalion from the 4th Res. Battalion.	

Instructions regarding War Diaries and Intelligence Summaries are contained in F. S. Regs., Part II. and the Staff Manual respectively. Title pages will be prepared in manuscript.

WAR DIARY
or
INTELLIGENCE SUMMARY.
(Erase heading not required.)

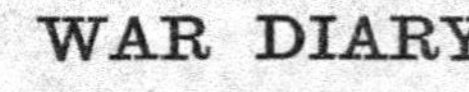

Army Form C. 2118.

Place	Date	Hour	Summary of Events and Information	Remarks and references to Appendices
SOUASTRE	24th	11 Am	The Commanding Officer inspected the draft which arrived on the previous day.	
	25th	11.15 Am	Church Parade.	
	26th	10 Am	Battalion relieved the 5th Battalion in Hannescamps sector. Relief completed 12.15 Noon.	
	27th	11.15	One of our Nieuport machines came down between Hannescamps and Foncquevillers at 11.15 Am. Enemy shelled it heavily all day and night to prevent salvage.	
	29th		A draft of 58 other ranks arrived from Brigade Depot.	
	30th		Relieved in Hannescamps sector by 5th Battalion for good in view of moving to a line further North.	
	31st		Spent by Battalion in working parties, Rest, cleaning and interior economy.	

1.1.17

B. Clarke Lieut Colonel.
Comdg 4th Battn Leicestershire Regt

A5834 Wt. W4973/M687 750,000 8/16 D. D. & L. Ltd. Forms/C.2118/13.

Instructions regarding War Diaries and Intelligence Summaries are contained in F. S. Regs., Part II. and the Staff Manual respectively. Title pages will be prepared in manuscript.

WAR DIARY
or
INTELLIGENCE SUMMARY.
(Erase heading not required.)

Army Form C. 2118.

Vol 24

Place	Date	Hour	Summary of Events and Information	Remarks and references to Appendices
BIENVILLERS	1917 1 Feby.	-	Battalion in Brigade reserve. Instructions received to take over new line in front of MONCHY-AU-BOIS on the 3rd inst. C.O. inspected new front then occupied by the 5th Sth Staffs.	
do.	2 "	-	Battalion in Brigade reserve.	
Trenches	4-6	-	Relieved 5th Battn. who had taken over from the 6th Sth Staffs the previous day in the new sector. Second line London Regt. were attached for instruction.	
	7th	-	Relieved by 5th Battn. & proceeded to rest camp at SOUASTRE	
SOUASTRE	8-9.	-	Rest billets. Battalion training.	
	10th	-	Relieved 5th Battn. in trenches in the evening.	
Trenches	11-13	-	Enemy active with trench mortars intermittently during the tour. 2nd Line London Regiment were attached for instruction. The severe weather which at times during the previous month had registered 22° of frost showed signs of thaw.	
BIENVILLERS	14th.	-	Relieved by 5th & went to Brigade Reserve in BIENVILLERS.	
	15th	-	Private Harry Bray (A Coy.) awarded the Croix de Guerre (other ranks) for bravery in the field.	
	16-18th	-	Brigade reserve	
	19th	-	Relieved 5th and 8th Sherwood Foresters then occupying the 139th Brigade frontage in trenches opposite GOMMECOURT: Headquarters in FONQUEVILLERS	
Trenches	20th	-	Trenches	
	21st	3 am	Enemy opened a very heavy bombardment with trench mortars and shells on front line trenches occupied by A or Captain Wright's company opposite the Z and barraged the approaches thereto and main road of FONQUEVILLERS with shrapnel & shells of all calibres for 1½ hours either for the purpose of attempting a raid or getting rid of surplus ammunition with a view to withdrawing from GOMMECOURT. Three platoons occupying the front line under Lt. Rodhin, Mantle & Wordsworth withdrew or thinned their line and blocked communication trenches leaving Lewis Guns in position.	

Instructions regarding War Diaries and Intelligence Summaries are contained in F. S. Regs., Part II. and the Staff Manual respectively. Title pages will be prepared in manuscript.

WAR DIARY
or
INTELLIGENCE SUMMARY.
(Erase heading not required.)

Army Form C. 2118.

4 Leicesters

Place	Date	Hour	Summary of Events and Information	Remarks and references to Appendices
Trenches	1917 Feby 21	3am	Our artillery replied to the assist call within four minutes. If a raid was attempted none of the enemy succeeded in reaching our lines. All ranks behaved well under very trying circumstances and two runners of A coy Pte. H. Bradshaw and Pte C. Coley were later awarded the military medal. The B.G.C. complimented the battalion on its work. Later in the morning A coy was relieved by B. who were in support.	
	23rd	-	Relieved by 5th Battn & proceeded to new billets in SOUASTRE	
SOUASTRE	24–26	-	Divisional reserve. Battalion training.	
do.	27th	-	Relieved 5th Battn. in trenches during the morning leaving SOUASTRE 8.30 am	
Trenches	27th	9.55pm Zero Hour	Taking of GOMMECOURT. C & D coys. under Capts. Vergee and Pilkington without artillery preparation, advanced from our front line by platoons and occupied a line of trenches in GOMMECOURT on a semi-circular front of about 350 yards with the enemy's front line as a base without a casualty. Shortly afterwards the line was advanced 200 yards and extended along the SE lisière of the village.	
	28th	8 am	At 8 am C & D coys. again advanced 500 yards and occupied bombing posts at the junctions of communication trenches with the German third line on a frontage of about 1500 yds. along the STEIN WEG to the cemetery getting in touch with the D.L.I. on our right.	
	28th	8am	A & B coys moved up in support under cover of the mist and the 4th Lincolns during the night dug a C.T. between the two old front line about 200 yds long parallel to the FONQUEVILLERS–GOMMECOURT Road.	

A5834 Wt. W4973/M687 750,000 8/16 D. D. & L. Ltd. Forms/C.2118/13.

Instructions regarding War Diaries and Intelligence Summaries are contained in F. S. Regs., Part II. and the Staff Manual respectively. Title pages will be prepared in manuscript.

WAR DIARY
or
INTELLIGENCE SUMMARY.
(Erase heading not required.)

Army Form C. 2118.

4 Leicesters.

Place	Date	Hour	Summary of Events and Information	Remarks and references to Appendices
GOMMECOURT	28th	–	During the afternoon the mist lifted and the enemy opened a heavy fire on the whole of GOMMECOURT and the new C.T. inflicting several casualties and at the same time attacked the junctions of trenches recently occupied by us in one or two cases causing us slightly to withdraw. During the night of the 28th/1st March the battalion regained their positions at the head of the C.T. junctions by bombing actions and held them till relieved at 7 am by the 5th Leicestershire Regt. All ranks behaved very well during these operations and the Commanding Officer received the congratulations of the Divisional Commander for the work of the battalion. [signature] Lt Col Cmd 4/Leic Regt	

A5834 Wt. W4973/M687 750,000 8/16 D. D. & L. Ltd. Forms/C.2118/13.

C/56/W.O.

Instructions regarding War Diaries and Intelligence Summaries are contained in F. S. Regs., Part II. and the Staff Manual respectively. Title pages will be prepared in manuscript.

WAR DIARY
or
INTELLIGENCE SUMMARY.
(Erase heading not required.)

Army Form C. 2118.

4th Leicester Regt

Vol 25

Place	Date	Hour	Summary of Events and Information	Remarks and references to Appendices
FONQUVILLERS	March 1st 1917	5AM	Battalion relieved in trenches by GOMMECOURT by 5th Battalion and proceeded to billets at SOUASTRE	
SOUASTRE	2nd to 6th		Battalion in training. Attack practice and route marching.	
	7th to 9th	2-5pm	Relieved 7th SHERWOODS in front line trenches from Lulu Lane (HANNESCAMPS - MONCHY ROAD to LA BRAYELLE RD (3000x Battalion frontage)	
	10th		Lieut Colonel [illegible] Clarke left the Battalion sick permanently. Major [illegible] 4th Lincs Regt appointed to command from that date.	
	11th		Battalion relieved in above sector by 5th Battalion relief complete 5pm. Marched back to billets at Souastre.	
	12th		C.O and Company Commanders reconnoitred ground round ROSSIGNOL WOOD in view of Divisional operations.	
	13th		Orders received from the Brigade to hold the Battalion in readiness for an attack. 137th Inf Bde attacked BUCQUOY GRABEN between RETTEMOY FME and BUCQUOY. 138th Bde in Reserve.	
	14th	11AM	C.O and O.C Coys reconnoitred ground and trenches round RETTEMOY FARM in view of taking over trenches from 5th SHERWOODS. Cancelled owing to enemy vacating Bucquoy and surrounding district [illegible]	
	15th to 16th		Practice attack on Bucquoy. News received that pending attack was cancelled.	
	17th		Battalion received orders to relieve 8th Sherwoods in Gommecourt, proceeded to [illegible] [illegible] found the enemy retiring, [illegible] H.Q in PIGEON WOOD with 2 Coys in ESSARTS under O.C 4th Lincs Rgt. Enemy seen burning ABLAINZEVILLE and DOUCHY les AYETTE etc.	
	18th	10AM	Orders received from Bde to move Battalion up to ESSARTS. [illegible] Stood by all day expecting to move forward.	

A5834 Wt. W4973/M687 750,000 8/16 D. D. & L. Ltd. Forms/C.2118/13.

Instructions regarding War Diaries and Intelligence Summaries are contained in F. S. Regs., Part II. and the Staff Manual respectively. Title pages will be prepared in manuscript.

WAR DIARY
or
INTELLIGENCE SUMMARY.
(Erase heading not required.)

Army Form C. 2118

4th Leicester Rgt.

Place	Date	Hour	Summary of Events and Information	Remarks and references to Appendices
ESSARTS	19th	2pm	Battalion left ESSARTS and proceeded to take over right Outpost line of Bde [illegible] from 5th Lincs' Regt.	
AYETTE	20th	11am	Battalion left AYETTE for St. Amand where we arrived in billets [illegible] marched through ESSARTS – HANNESCAMPS ~~[illegible]~~ across NO MANS LAND [illegible] old sector of trenches.	
	21st	1.30AM	Received train from Bde [illegible].	
ST. AMAND	22nd		Moved from ST. AMAND to BERTRANCOURT by Bde formation via COUIN. Transport Brigaded	
BERTRANCOURT	23rd		Battalion moved from BERTRANCOURT to RAINCHEVAL with transport at 200' interval between Coys and transport arrived at Raincheval 5pm.	
RAINCHEVAL	24th		Left Raincheval for PIERREGOT 9.30Am arrived Pierregot at 2pm. with transport	
	25th		Half Bde moved to SALEUX area. Church parade.	
	26th		Battalion marched from Pierregot to [illegible] Amiens Rd where they embussed at 1pm for SALEUX. Debussed at DURY and marched SALEUX, where we arrived 5.30p.m.	
	27th		Battalion standing by at SALEUX prior to entraining.	
	28th	6am	The Battalion and transport commenced entraining at SALEUX en route for LILLERS via MONTIERES, DOULLENS, FREVANT + ST POL arrived [illegible] at 6Am 29th.	
	29th	6Am	Arrived at LILLERS detrained and had breakfast in [illegible] Station. Left LILLERS 10.30Am for [illegible] at FLECHIN arrived FLECHIN 3P.m. march about 15 miles.	
	30th + 31st		Spent in Interior economy cleaning and training. Close order drill, bayonet fighting etc. The [illegible] [illegible] by Corps Commander Gen Sir Claude Jacob Commanding II Army Corps.	

J. Eric Petley
Lieut Colonel
O.C. 4th Leicestershire Rgt

A5834 Wt. W4973/M687 750,000 8/16 D. D. & L. Ltd. Forms/C.2118/13.

Instructions regarding War Diaries and Intelligence Summaries are contained in F. S. Regs., Part II. and the Staff Manual respectively. Title pages will be prepared in manuscript.

WAR DIARY
or
INTELLIGENCE SUMMARY.
(*Erase heading not required.*)

1/4 Leicester Regt R4

Army Form C. 2118.

Vol 26

Place	Date	Hour	Summary of Events and Information	Remarks and references to Appendices
Flechin.	April. 1st	9.15AM.	Church Parade. Battalion in Corps Reserve. The Commanding Officer addressed the Battalion, congratulating the Officers and men on their turn-out and marching.	
	2nd + 3rd		Battalion in training in Physical Training, Bayonet Fighting, Musketry etc.	
Evry St. Julien	4th	9-1pm	Practice battalion in the attack in Trench to Trench system.	
	5th	9-2pm	Bde Scheme. This Battalion formed the advanced guard. Route Flechin - Febvin Palfart - Cuhem - Lires. Operation very successful.	
	6th		Battalion training one day on the range.	
	7th	9-1pm	Training continued. Battalion attacked through wood in artillery formation.	
	8th	9.15pm	Church Parade.	
	9th	8.30AM	Divisional route march route via Febvin Palfart - Westrehem - Rely - Estree Blanche - Flechin. Drums on the march. Marched past Lt Gen Sir Claude Jacob commanding the 1st Army Corps, who expressed his satisfaction on the turn out which exceptionally good.	
Flechin.	10th		Battalion parade cancelled owing to inclement weather. Companies lectured by O.C. Coys.	
	11th 12th		Battalion training in Physical Training, Bayonet Fighting, Bomb Throwing, Musketry, Range, + close order drill. Bad weather.	
	13th		Left FLECHIN for L'ECLEME via St HILAIRE and LILLERS arrived at L'Ecleme at 5pm.	13 miles
	14th		Battalion resting with a half parade by platoons for Physical Exercise	
	15th	11.15AM	Church Parade (cancelled bad weather). Battalion quite close to Gonnehem the village where the Battalion rested prior to the Hohenzollern Battle Oct 1915.	
	16th	10.30AM	Battalion left L'ECLEME for VENDIN LEZ BETHUNE arriving there at 1.30pm. Companies very scattered in billets at Oblinghem + Vendin.	5 miles

A5834 Wt. W4973/M687 750,000 8/16 D. D. & L. Ltd. Forms/C.2118/13.

Instructions regarding War Diaries and Intelligence Summaries are contained in F. S. Regs., Part II. and the Staff Manual respectively. Title pages will be prepared in manuscript.

WAR DIARY
or
INTELLIGENCE SUMMARY.
(*Erase heading not required.*)

Army Form C. 2118.

Place	Date	Hour	Summary of Events and Information	Remarks and references to Appendices
Vendin lez Bethune	17th	9pm	Received orders that the Brigade would relieve the 72nd I.B in the line opposite LENS.	
	18th	9am	Battalion left billets at Vendin for MAROC to relieve above Brigade. Dinners on the march. Route: Bethune – NOEUX les MINES BULLY GRENAY – MAROC. Took over support line in front of LENS from 8th Bn Royal West Kent Regiment. Relief complete 12 midnight.	
	19th		Relieved 1st Bn North Staffs Regt in sector N W of LENS [illegible] through CITE ST LAURENT. Relief complete 12 midnight. A & C Coys in front line. The line was a series of Posts & trenches. Enemy holding houses and cellars.	A Capt Vaughan? C.F. B Capt J Nagea?
	20th		Heavy shelling by the enemy on our men all day.	
	21st		C Company attacked enemy trench ~~NARVAL~~ COOPER with two platoons Nos 9 & 12 commanded by 2/Lt J A Dickinson & Lt Dodney. Objective gained without loss. Ten prisoners taken of 93rd Regt. Trench ran N1d to N7b on edge of Cite St Laurent. 2/Lt A W LESLIE (D Coy) killed whilst carrying trench mortar ammunition to the line.	LENS 8a 36c S.W 1
	22nd		One platoon of A Coy (2/Lt Whitcher) one platoon of B Coy (2/Lt J B Lambie) made flank attack on NARVAL trench, which they captured but were forced to retire owing to their being largely outnumbered and meeting a German counter attack on the 14th D L I on our left. 2/Lt Whitcher killed & 2/Lt J B Lambie missing believed killed and 60 other ranks. 2/Lts C D BROWN & J GEMMILL (A Coy) both wounded going up to reinforce. LT B T C GILBERT on Staff 138th I.B. killed whilst making a reconnaissance for the Brigade. All the officers NCO's & men of these Coys displayed magnificent courage all through the operations.	
	23rd		Relieved by 5th Battalion at 9pm. relief complete 12 30 am Marched back to billets at BULLY GRENAY. Bosch shelled B.H.Q so badly that it had to be vacated in a hurry.	

A5834 Wt. W4973/M687 750,000 8/16 D. D. & L. Ltd. Forms/C.2118/13.

Instructions regarding War Diaries and Intelligence Summaries are contained in F. S. Regs., Part II. and the Staff Manual respectively. Title pages will be prepared in manuscript.

WAR DIARY
or
INTELLIGENCE SUMMARY.

(Erase heading not required.)

Army Form C. 2118.

Place	Date	Hour	Summary of Events and Information	Remarks and references to Appendices
BULLY GRENAY.	24th	11AM	Received orders from the Brigade that we should relieve the 5th Lincs. Regt in Bde Support at ~~MAROC~~ CITE ST PIERRE. whence we moved from billets at 8.40pm and took over from that Regiment completing the relief at 10.45pm. Fairly quiet night. Battalion in cellars at above place.	Lens ## 8a 1/10,000 36cSW1
	25th		Fairly quiet day except for a lively bombardment of the enemy artillery on Battalion Headquarters.	
	26th		Quiet day with sharp bursts of artillery fire on both sides. Great aerial activity over LENS where huge fires and explosions were going on all day.	
	27th		Enemy shelled Battalion H.Qrs & that area rather heavily. Big artillery duel just South of the Bde front, i.e. South West of LENS.	
	28th		Quieter day than usual. Our artillery shelled tracks and communications of enemy east of LENS. This continued all day.	
			The whole Battalion were carrying on 27th & 28th Special R.E. Emplacements (9ins)	
	29th	9pm	Battalion relieved the 5th Bn in the front line trenches N.W. of LENS. D & B Coys in line. Enemy artillery very active over whole area. Gas discharged [illegible]	A & C in support
	30th	8.30pm	Quiet day enemy artillery fairly active. Enemy opened heavy barrage on whole of the front line, silenced very effectually by retaliation from our field Batteries and heavy groups. Capt J. Bennett (5th Bn) joined for duty posted temporarily to A Coy. The latter part of the month has been ~~very~~ rather trying the Battalion have lost several fine officers and a great number of rank and file. A Coy suffering most heavily.	

J. Eric Petley Lt Colonel

A5834 Wt. W4973/M687 750,000 8/16 D. D. & L. Ltd. Forms/C.2118/13.

Instructions regarding War Diaries and Intelligence Summaries are contained in F. S. Regs., Part II. and the Staff Manual respectively. Title pages will be prepared in manuscript.

WAR DIARY
or
INTELLIGENCE SUMMARY.
(Erase heading not required.)

Army Form C. 2118.

Vol 27

Place	Date	Hour	Summary of Events and Information	Remarks and references to Appendices
Front line trenches St Pierre Sector W of LENS	MAY 1st		Battalion in the line 3rd day of tour. Quiet day. Enemy shelled Battalion H.Q. no damage.	Trench map LENS 36c S.W.1 edition 8a 1/10,000
	2nd		Very quiet day, very little artillery fire on either side.	
	3rd		Relieved by the 5th Battalion in the front line, relief complete 11 pm. Battalion went into support in St. Pierre.	
	5th		Billeting party left the line for Quartermaster Stores prior to relief	
	6th		Battalion relieved by 5th Battalion SHERWOOD FORESTERS in support, relief	
NOEUX les MINES			complete 12 midnight. Marched back to billets at NOEUX les MINES arriving there 3 am. Billeted in huts.	
	7th		Spent in rest, cleaning, baths and interior economy. Enemy shelled the town.	
	8th		Battalion training on areas West of Noeux les Mines.	
	9th		The C.O. and O.C. Coys reconnoitred route to Bois de RIAUMONT with a view to relief.	
	10th		Battalion training 9th and 10th. The General Officer Commanding the Division rode over to see training.	
	11th		G.O.C. Division presented medals to officers and men of the Brigade at Petit Sains 2 pm. Eight other ranks from this Battalion receiving decorations.	
LIEVIN	12th	6 p.m.	Battalion left Noeux les Mines by platoons at 6 pm to relieve the 6th N. Staffs R. in the LIEVIN Sector, marching via Petit Sains, Aix Noulette and Angres. Relief complete 12.30 am. Canadian Corps being on our right and the 4th Lincs Rgt on our left. 1500 yard Battalion frontage. Battalion Headquarters in ~~old~~ evacuated enemy gun position at M28b 30/12. Enemy shelling very intense.	138th I.B.

A5834 Wt. W4973/M687 750,000 8/16 D. D. & L. Ltd. Forms/C.2118/13.

Instructions regarding War Diaries and Intelligence Summaries are contained in F. S. Regs., Part II. and the Staff Manual respectively. Title pages will be prepared in manuscript.

WAR DIARY
or
INTELLIGENCE SUMMARY.

(Erase heading not required.)

Army Form C. 2118.

Place	Date	Hour	Summary of Events and Information	Remarks and references to Appendices
LIEVIN	13th		Quiet day, nothing of interest occurred.	
	14th		2/LT W.A. FERGUSSON seriously wounded. This officer died of wounds 15th inst.	
	15th		Received a report that the enemy were massing south of the Souchez River informed artillery who did excellent work. Relieved in front line by 5th Leics Regt. Went into Reserve at the Red Mill LIEVIN. Relief complete 11.50 pm.	
	16th		Working parties found at night for digging cable trenches.	
	17th		..	
	18th		Enemy planes very active. Relieved the 5th Battalion in the front line. Relief complete 11.50 pm.	
	19th		Nothing of interest occurred.	
	20th		Enemy shelled night by very heavily. Knocked in Coy H.Qrs. Nominal damage being done.	
	21st		Battalion relieved by 5th Battalion, relief complete 12.15 am. Went into Reserve at the Red Mill.	
	22nd		Enemy shelled heavily at night. Our gunners replied. Party of six other ranks left for the rest camp Boulogne.	
	23rd		Nothing of importance. Found large working parties to work on front line etc.	
	24th		Digging new trenches. Diggers complimented on their good work.	
	25th		Battalion relieved by 5th Battn Sherwood Foresters. Relief complete 12.15 am. Marched back to billets at Fosse 10. arriving there 2 am 26th.	

A5834 Wt. W4973/M687 750,000 8/16 D. D. & L. Ltd. Forms/C.2118/13.

Instructions regarding War Diaries and Intelligence Summaries are contained in F. S. Regs., Part II. and the Staff Manual respectively. Title pages will be prepared in manuscript.

WAR DIARY
or
INTELLIGENCE SUMMARY.
(Erase heading not required.)

Army Form C. 2118.

4th Leic Regt

Vol 28

Place	Date	Hour	Summary of Events and Information	Remarks and references to Appendices
JUNE	1st		The Battalion engaged practicing the Attack on a flagged course at MARQUEFFLES FARM. Three companies as "moppers up" to the 5th Leicestershire Regt & 4th Lincolnshire Regt. "A" Company as a rapid wiring party. Bombing, rapid digging & musketry in afternoon.	
	2nd		The same as on the 1st	
	3rd		The same as yesterday except that the whole Brigade practiced the Attack under the eye of the Major General. Afterwards there was a Church Parade. Dinners in the field followed by Company training. At night 4 parties of an Officer & 40 OR were carrying Trench Mortars to dumps in front line. These parties were out from 8.30 pm to 4.30 am.	
	~~4th~~ 4th		Attack practice at MARQUEFFLES FARM by the whole Brigade under the eyes of the Corps Commander (Lt Gen l Holland) and Major General W. Thwaites CB. A contact aeroplane called for signals.	
	5th		Rest day for the Brigade. Plans for the Attack changed, the operation to be a raid on a large scale.	
	6th		Went up to the trenches, the companies billetted in cellars in LIEVIN. Quiet night except for our own guns. Lieut M. S. Holden slightly wounded about the ankle.	
	7th		Day spent in issuing bombs etc. and making final preparations for the raid. Very hot day	
	8th		Heavy artillery bombardment of enemy positions commencing at 5 a.m. and continuing until Zero hour (8.30 pm) + 3 minutes. Companies ~~comm~~ begin to assemble in trenches in the CITÉ du RIAUMONT at 5 pm under orders of Lt Col TRIMBLE 5th Leicestershire Regt (2 Companies B & C) and Lt Col Yool, 4th Lincolnshire Regt (D Company). The assembly was complete at 7.45 p.	

A5834 Wt. W4973/M687 750,000 8/16 D. D. & L. Ltd. Forms/C.2118/13.

Instructions regarding War Diaries and Intelligence Summaries are contained in F. S. Regs., Part II. and the Staff Manual respectively. Title pages will be prepared in manuscript.

WAR DIARY
or
INTELLIGENCE SUMMARY.
(Erase heading not required.)

Army Form C. 2118.

Place	Date	Hour	Summary of Events and Information	Remarks and references to Appendices
8th	8th June		and at 8 pm the enemy barraged the position of assembly though fortunately little harm resulted. At 8.30 pm the assault commenced under cover of Heavy Artillery. At Zero + 3 the Field Artillery put down a shrapnel barrage which crept forward on to HILL 65. On the right progress was good troops reaching their objectives in ALMANAC TRENCH and "B & C" Companies under Captain G Abell (B) and Lieut Hyslop (C) commenced "mopping up". They found a large number of enemy in FOSSE 3 where there were 11 Buildings with many dugouts. These were dealt with with bombs and mobile charges. Heavy casualties were inflicted upon the enemy and 2 officers & 12 OR taken prisoners. "C" Company were greatly impeded by uncut wire which prevented them silencing a machine gun which was troublesome. The whole operation was a great success in that destruction was caused to enemy dugouts & casualties inflicted. On the left "D" Company under Capt A J Wakerley "mopping up" for the 4th Lincolnshire Regt met with more serious opposition in AHEAD Trench and suffered many casualties Captain Wakerley being killed and 2/Lt R G Wagstaff slightly wounded. The trenches were entered and many dugouts bombed & many casualties inflicted upon the enemy. The withdrawal commenced at 1 am 9th June and all companies were back in cellars by 3 am. "A" Company had specially training for wiring but were not called upon. 2/Lieuts E C Doudney, 2/Lieut J Douglas, 2/Lt D T Sleeper, 2/Lt H J A Parkinson were wounded and there were 70 OR killed & wounded.	
	9th		Battalion in Support in LIEVIN. Recommendations for bravery & good work forwarded to Brigade. 2/Lieut R Provis recommended for the Military Cross.	

A5834 Wt. W4973/M687 750,000 8/16 D. D. & L. Ltd. Forms/C.2118/13.

Instructions regarding War Diaries and Intelligence Summaries are contained in F. S. Regs., Part II. and the Staff Manual respectively. Title pages will be prepared in manuscript.

WAR DIARY
or
INTELLIGENCE SUMMARY.
(Erase heading not required.)

Army Form C. 2118.

Place	Date	Hour	Summary of Events and Information	Remarks and references to Appendices
JUNE	10		Battalion relieved 8th Sherwood Foresters in the Left Sector (CITE JEANNE D'ARC) W of LENS from railway M18 b 40.60 to road M24a 90.25 (MAP 36c S W.1)	
	11		G.O.C. visited most of Battalion front.	
			2/Lieuts Paddon, Cheeseman, Rodgers reported for duty.	
	12 to 13		Nothing to report	
	13		The Battn relieved in the line by 4th Lincolnshire Regt after four days tour.	
			Captain S. Pilkington rejoined from the Base.	
	15 to 18		In Brigade Support in cellars in LIEVIN. All available men digging new trenches each night in preparation for further advance.	
			Lieut Suckley reported for duty.	
	19 to 22		In the line as on the 10th. Artillery & trench mortars active during the whole of this tour.	
	22nd		Relieved by the 6th South Staffordshire Regt at night & proceeded to billets in BOUVIGNY BOYEFFLES	
	23rd		Bathing, interior economy & rest. Fine hot weather.	
	24th		G.O.C. congratulated the battalion on its work on the night of the 8/9th June	
	25		Attack practice at MARQUEFFLES FARM in preparation of an attack on HILL 65 W of LENS	
	26th		Same as yesterday. Ribbon presentations by G.O.C. to Sergt H. DIXON, L/Cpl BRADSHAW (Military Medal) Pte PRICE a bar to M. Medal for gallant conduct on the night 8/9th June	

A5834 Wt. W4973/M687 750,000 8/16 D. D. & L. Ltd. Forms/C.2118/13.

Instructions regarding War Diaries and Intelligence Summaries are contained in F. S. Regs., Part II. and the Staff Manual respectively. Title pages will be prepared in manuscript.

WAR DIARY
or
INTELLIGENCE SUMMARY.
(Erase heading not required.)

Army Form C. 2118.

Place	Date	Hour	Summary of Events and Information	Remarks and references to Appendices
JUNE	27		Battalion relieved 5th Lincolnshire Regt in the trenches at the foot of HILL 65 W of LENS 5th Leicestershire Regt on our right 5th South Staffordshire Regt on our left. This was the position of assembly for the attack tomorrow.	
	28		Final preparations for the assault. Collections of bombs, SAA etc. ZERO hour was 7.10 pm at which time rain descended very heavily. Under heavy barrage the attacking waves advanced over the hill in splendid order and gained their objectives with practically no opposition. A few enemy were seen running away from ADJUNCT & ADJACENT Trenches. "A" Coy under Capt C. F. Wright and "C" Coy under Capt F. J. Nugee were the assaulting companies. "B" Coy under 2/Lieut. R. Pron's carried stores for both companies. "D" Company under 2/Lieut A. B. Pick was in support. The trenches were found to be almost destroyed so posts were organised & the companies dug themselves in for protection against shell fire which continued day & night. Communication to B.H.Q was very difficult & information scarce and quite impossible during daylight.	
	29		Position the same. Heavy shelling at intervals.	
	30		The battalion relieved by 5th Lincolnshire Regt who were assembling for an attack at 2.47 am July 1st. A difficult relief satisfactorily accomplished.	

1/7/17

J. Eric Tetley Lt Colonel
Cmdg 4th Leicestershire Regt

A5834 Wt. W4973/M687 750,000 8/16 D. D. & L. Ltd. Forms/C.2118/13.

Instructions regarding War Diaries and Intelligence Summaries are contained in F. S. Regs., Part II. and the Staff Manual respectively. Title pages will be prepared in manuscript.

WAR DIARY
or
INTELLIGENCE SUMMARY.
(Erase heading not required.)

4 Leicester Rgt

Army Form C. 2118.

Vol 29

Place	Date	Hour	Summary of Events and Information	Remarks and references to Appendices
JULY 1917	1st	2.47 am.	138th Infantry Brigade holding line S.W. of LENS. Canadians on the right, 6th Division on the left.	
Cité de Riaumont			Small attack by 46th Division in conjunction with Canadian operation involved the 4th & 5th Lincoln Regt who were in the front line. 4th & 5th Leic Regts in support.	
W. of LENS	1st	10 pm.	The Battalion relieved the 5th Lincs Regt in the newly won position on the outskirts of Cité du Moulin, this was the most difficult relief that the Battalion has taken part in but despite these facts the Battalion did very well. Relief complete 2 am 2nd inst.	
	2nd		Quiet day but Headquarters cut off from Coys except by runner & all the runners behaved splendidly & did excellent work. No signals possible. Capt S. Pilkington killed.	8 am
		9.30 pm	Battalion relief commenced by 25th Canadians.	
	3rd	2 am	Relief completed. 2/Lt R.S.H. Bowell and platoon not relieved. This party remained in the line another two days. Behaviour of all this party was magnificent.	(D Coy) (1.4 platoon)
		8 am	Battalion on relief embussed at Aix Noulette and proceeded to Billets at MONCHY-BRETTON and ORLENCOURT.	C & D at Monchy Bretton A & B at Orlencourt with B.H.Q.
	4th		Spent in rest, cleaning & interior economy.	
	5th		2/Lt Bowell and platoon rejoined Battalion. Companies reorganising.	
	6th		Company training, platoon, arms and physical drill. Training soldiers at their subjects. Live Bomb throwing.	
	7th	6 am 7 pm	Battalion on the range at ROCOURT all day firing preliminary practice for Divisional Rifle meeting.	
	8th	10 am	Brigade church parade on training area Rocourt. G.O.C. 46th Division attended. Medal Ribbon presentations after service 2/Lt R.S. PROVIS received Military Cross for gallantry on June 8th S.W. of LENS. Football.	
	9th		Company training. B.G.C. 138th Bde inspected Battalion transport. very smart turn out.	Transport Officer Lieut J. H. Tyler

(A7092). Wt. W12839/M1293. 750,000. 1/17. D. D. & L., Ltd. Forms/C.2118/14.

Army Form C. 2118.

WAR DIARY
or
INTELLIGENCE SUMMARY.
(Erase heading not required.)

Instructions regarding War Diaries and Intelligence Summaries are contained in F. S. Regs., Part II. and the Staff Manual respectively. Title pages will be prepared in manuscript.

Place	Date	Hour	Summary of Events and Information	Remarks and references to Appendices
JULY. Monchy Breton	10th		Battalion training. Skilled soldiers at their subjects.	
	11th	4 am	Range. All companies firing practice for Divisional Meeting.	
		12 Noon	The Battalion held Athletic Sports at ORLENCOURT. Very great success. Prizes presented by Brigadier General F Rowley CMG comdg 138th I Bde.	
	12th		Battalion training in area. Ceremonial drill Company and Battalion.	
	13th	2 pm	Battalion inspection in football field Roconit by Brigadier Gen F Rowley	C.M.G.
	14th		Range and Battalion training in the "Attack".	
	15th	9.15 am	Church Parade.	
	16th	2 pm	Brigade practice Ceremonial parade preparatory for G.O.C's inspection.	
	17th	10.30	Brigade inspected by the I Army Commander, General Sir H. S. HORNE K.C.B. accompanied by the Major Gen. W Thwaites CB. comdg 46th Division. After the inspection the Army Commander addressed the Brigade and spoke of the excellent work it had done opposite LENS.	
	18th		Parades cancelled owing to weather.	
	19th	20th	Divisional rifle meeting.	
	21st	9 am	Battalion left Monchy Breton area for DROUVIN area. Arrived billets VAUDRICOURT 2 pm.	12 miles
VAUDRICOURT	22nd	11 am	Left above for NOEUX les MINES where Battalion was in Bde Reserve.	Billeted in C Camp (huts)
	23rd		Officers reconnoitred Village Line opposite HULLUCH in case of alarm. Battalion carried out platoon company training.	

(A7092). Wt. W12839/M1293. 750,000. 1/17. D. D. & L., Ltd. Forms/C.2118/14.

Instructions regarding War Diaries and Intelligence Summaries are contained in F. S. Regs., Part II. and the Staff Manual respectively. Title pages will be prepared in manuscript.

WAR DIARY
or
INTELLIGENCE SUMMARY.
(Erase heading not required.)

Army Form C. 2118.

Place	Date	Hour	Summary of Events and Information	Remarks and references to Appendices
Noeux les mines	24th		Battalion ceremonial Drill company and platoon training.	
	25th	9 am.	Route march via Hesdigneul.	
	26th		C.O and O.C. Coys visited trenches opposite HULLUCH with a view to taking over from 5th Battalion. Companies practising the Trench to trench attack.	Tunnel System.
	27th		Platoon commanders reconnoitred new line. Battalion route march.	
HULLUCH	28th	6pm	Battalion left billets at Noeux les mines to relieve 5th Battalion by march route via NOYELLES*, where teas were served. Left Noyelles for the line 9.20 pm via PHILOSOPHE	
		1.30am	Relief complete (29th). C & D Coys in the line, A & B in support. Sector from ESSEX LANE to HULLUCH Rd; 5th Lincoln Regt on right, 5th Sherwoods on the left.	Ref map LOOS 1/10000
	29th		Quiet day	36c N.W. 3
	30th		Enemy artillery very active on Battalion sector especially right sector & support line.	
	31st		Artillery active, our artillery were active with view to operations on our right by Canadians	
			The sector mentioned above is known as the HULLUCH Tunnel system, the name being given in view of the fact that the Coy & Battalion in actual front line and posts consist of tunnel entrances only. By night the trenches surrounding these are manned. The right sector is held as in the ordinary trench systems.	
			J. P. Robertson LIEUT. COLONEL, O.C. 4th BN. LEICESTERSHIRE REGT.	

6 AUG 1917

(A7092). Wt. W12839/M1293. 750,000. 1/17. D. D. & L., Ltd. Forms/C.2118/14.

Instructions regarding War Diaries and Intelligence Summaries are contained in F. S. Regs., Part II. and the Staff Manual respectively. Title pages will be prepared in manuscript.

WAR DIARY
or
~~INTELLIGENCE~~ SUMMARY.
(*Erase heading not required.*)

Army Form C. 2118.

1/4 Leicester Rg

Vol 30

Place	Date 1917	Hour	Summary of Events and Information	Remarks and references to Appendices
In the field.	Aug 1 to Aug 2		The battalion occupied trenches opposite HULLUCH. In this sector tunnels have in a measure taken the place of communication trenches. The casualties during the tour were slight.	
	Night Aug 2nd/3rd		Relieved by 6th NORTH STAFFS REGT. and marched out to VAUDRICOURT.	
	Aug 3rd to Aug 16th		138th Brigade was in Divisional Reserve. The battalion carried out training. The battalion drums were reformed during this period.	
	Aug 6th		Lt Col J. R. Robertson took over the command.	
	11th		Battalion attended a Bde Church parade. The GOC presented military medals to 5 NCOs & men of the battalion	
	Night Aug 16th/17th		Battalion relieved 7th SHERWOOD FORESTERS. on the left of ST ELIE SECTOR	
	" 17/18th		The 5th battalion made a raid on enemies trenches opposite HULLUCH	
	Aug 18th		The Canadians attacked HILL 70 at 4-35 am.	

(A7092). Wt. W12839/M1293 750,000. 1/17. D. D. & L., Ltd. Forms/C.2118/14.

Instructions regarding War Diaries and Intelligence Summaries are contained in F. S. Regs., Part II. and the Staff Manual respectively. Title pages will be prepared in manuscript.

WAR DIARY
or
INTELLIGENCE SUMMARY.
(Erase heading not required.)

Army Form C. 2118.

Place	Date	Hour	Summary of Events and Information	Remarks and references to Appendices
	Aug 18th		Capt Hyslop was wounded.	
	19th		Major B. F. Tewill was wounded by Trench bomb the C.O was also slightly wounded but remained at duty.	
Night	Aug 21/22nd		The battalion was relieved by 5th LEIC REGT and went to PHILOSOPHE to Brigade support.	
	Aug 22nd to Aug 29th		The battalion was occupied on working parties etc.	
	Aug 26th		The Adjt Capt A. S. Teale left for England on special leave.	
	Aug 27th		The enemy shelled PHILOSOPHE with 5.9" & 8" shells but did little damage.	
Night	Aug 29/30th		Battalion relieved 5th Leic Regt.	
	Aug 30th to Sept 3rd		The battalion occupied the line.	

[illegible signature] Capt & A/Adjt.
for O.C. 4th Leic Regt.

(A7092). Wt. W12839/M1293. 750,000. 1/17. D. D. & L., Ltd. Forms/C.2118/14.

Instructions regarding War Diaries and Intelligence Summaries are contained in F. S. Regs., Part II. and the Staff Manual respectively. Title pages will be prepared in manuscript.

WAR DIARY
or
INTELLIGENCE SUMMARY.
(Erase heading not required.)

Army Form C. 2118.

R52

Vol 31

Place	Date	Hour	Summary of Events and Information	Remarks and references to Appendices
	1917 Sept 1st.		The battalion was holding trench system ST ELIE LEFT SUBSECTOR.	
			A trench raid to be carried out by A & B Coys on night 1st/2nd cancelled.	
	Sept 3rd.		The battalion relieved by 5th LEIC & marched to Div reserve at FOUQUIÈRE.	
			The drums led the battalion for the first time since their renaissance	
	4th		Cleaning up.	
	5th to 7th		Training.	
	8th.		Church parade	
	Sept 9th.		Relieved 5th Leicester Regt in same sector.	
			Col Robertson sent to Hospital sick. Major Beckett in command.	
			The Adjutant Capt A S Tew[?] goes to Brigade as Staff Learner.	
	9th to		Normal trench tour. Enemy moderately inoffensive.	
	15th.		Relieved by 5th Leicesters. Go into Brigade Reserve at PHILOSOPHE.	
	Sept 16th		Working parties.	
	17th to 21st		"	
	Sept 22nd		Relieved 5th Leicester Regt in same sector.	

DP.

A5834 Wt. W4973/M687 750,000 8/16 D. D. & L. Ltd. Forms/C.2118/13.

Army Form C. 2118.

Instructions regarding War Diaries and Intelligence Summaries are contained in F. S. Regs., Part II. and the Staff Manual respectively. Title pages will be prepared in manuscript.

WAR DIARY
or
INTELLIGENCE SUMMARY.
(Erase heading not required.)

Place	Date	Hour	Summary of Events and Information	Remarks and references to Appendices
Sept	23rd to 25th		Quiet. We kept enemy well supplied with stokes shells & rifle grenades. He was rather unresponsive. Our 60 pdr. T.M.s bombarded him severely.	
Night	26th/27th		P Coy Special R.E. bombarded enemy trenches round Fosse 8 with 4" Stokes Gas shells, putting over 1000 in 8 minutes. The enemy made no reply.	
	27th		Relieved by 5th Leicester Regt. Marched to Fouquieres. Col Robertson assumed command on returning from Rest Station.	
	28th to 30th		Training. Capt Mugee appointed Battalion Sports Officer.	

[Signature] Capt & Adjt.

834 Wt. W4973/M687 750,000 8/16 D. D. & L. Ltd. Forms/C.2118/13.

Army Form C. 2118.

WAR DIARY
or
INTELLIGENCE SUMMARY.
(Erase heading not required.)

Instructions regarding War Diaries and Intelligence Summaries are contained in F. S. Regs., Part II. and the Staff Manual respectively. Title pages will be prepared in manuscript.

1/4 Leicester Rgt

Ref MAP 36B N.W 1/10000

Vol 32

Place	Date	Hour	Summary of Events and Information	Remarks and references to Appendices
1917 OCTOBER		1st 2nd 3rd	Battalion in Divisional Reserve at FOUQUIÉRES. A & B Coys training for raid.	
	night 3rd/4th		Relieved 5th Bn the Leicestershire Regt in ST ELIE LEFT SUBSECTOR	
		4th	Trenches. Normal. Active patrolling. Enemy quiet.	
		5th	do	
		6th	do	
	night 6th/7th		At 10 pm A & B Coys raided enemy line under an 18 pdr barrage. The operation had been carefully worked out and no hitch occurred. Our party penetrated to 2nd line but no enemy were encountered. Sundry dugouts & MG emplacements were destroyed with ammonal charges. Lieut LEA was O.C Raiding Party. 2 Lt. C.F SAUNDERS took over the leading wave. 2Lt. G.B. TAYLOR took over the 2nd. Our casualties were 1 Killed 4 wounded. Enemy retaliation was not heavy.	
		7th	Normal	
		8th	Normal	

Army Form C. 2118.

Instructions regarding War Diaries and Intelligence Summaries are contained in F. S. Regs., Part II. and the Staff Manual respectively. Title pages will be prepared in manuscript.

WAR DIARY
or
INTELLIGENCE SUMMARY.
(Erase heading not required.)

Place	Date	Hour	Summary of Events and Information	Remarks and references to Appendices
1917				
OCTOBER	9th		Normal	
Night	9th/10th		The battn was relieved by 5th LEIC REGT and went back to Bde Support, with B.H.Q at PHILOSOPHE.	
	10th to 15th		Working parties.	
Night	15th/16th		Relieved 5th LEIC in line. At about 4-50 am enemy attempted silent raid on one of our BORDER CRATERS posts. He was driven off leaving one wounded man in front of our wire. 2Lt J.H. WATSON & No 200555 Pt WORTH fetched him in at considerable risk. About the same time a Hun walked up to FARMERS LANE post. He was challenged & quite cheerfully surrendered. He gave much useful information & stated that his division was being relieved on the 18th.	
	16th		Normal.	
	17th		Normal	
	18th		Our artillery harrassed enemy tracks etc with night fire.	

(A7092). Wt. W12839/M1293. 750,000. 1/17. D. D. & L., Ltd. Forms/C.2118/14.

Instructions regarding War Diaries and Intelligence Summaries are contained in F. S. Regs., Part II. and the Staff Manual respectively. Title pages will be prepared in manuscript.

WAR DIARY
or
INTELLIGENCE SUMMARY.
(Erase heading not required.)

Army Form C. 2118.

Place	Date	Hour	Summary of Events and Information	Remarks and references to Appendices
OCTOBER	19th		Normal	
	night 19th/20th		Much movement of transport heard behind enemy line. Our field guns fired with good effect.	
	20th		Normal.	
	night 20/21st		Relieved by 5th LEIC Regt. marched back to rest billets at FONCQUIÈRES	
	21st to 27th		Training	
	night 27/28th		Relieved 5th LEIC. in trenches	
	28th 29th 30 31st		Normal.	

[signature] Capt & Adjt
for C.O. 4th Leicestershire Regt

(A7092). Wt. W12839/M1293. 750,000. 1/17. D. D. & L., Ltd. Forms/C.2118/14.

Army Form C. 2118.

1/4 Leicester Rgt
Vol 33

Instructions regarding War Diaries and Intelligence Summaries are contained in F. S. Regs., Part II. and the Staff Manual respectively. Title pages will be prepared in manuscript.

WAR DIARY
or
INTELLIGENCE SUMMARY.
(Erase heading not required.)

Place	Date	Hour	Summary of Events and Information	Remarks and references to Appendices
In the Field.	1917 NOVEMBER: 1st		The battn is holding the line in ST ELIE LEFT SUBSECTOR. Normal.	
	2nd		No change. At 7.30 pm Btn moves into Bde SUPPORT in PHILOSOPHE.	
	3rd to 8th		Working parties etc.	
	8th		At 6pm Bn again takes over line in ST ELIE LEFT SUBSECTOR.	
	9th to 15th		Line. Normal activity	
	15th		At 6pm the battn is relieved by the ROBIN HOODS 139th Bde. The battn moves to MAZINGARBE. 139th Bde takes over H.Q. at PHILOSOPHE & 138th Bde. H.Q. moves to PREVITE CASTLE and takes over the HILL 70 Sector.	
	16th to 21st		The battn is billetted in huts in MAZINGARBE.	
	21st		Relieve the 5th Bn Leic Regt in HILL 70 Left subsector. Trenches where they existed ~~were~~ fairly dry.	
	22nd		At 6 am the enemy opened an intense bombardment of our line with shells of all calibre & kept it up till 6.50 am, during which	

R70

Army Form C. 2118.

Instructions regarding War Diaries and Intelligence Summaries are contained in F. S. Regs., Part II. and the Staff Manual respectively. Title pages will be prepared in manuscript.

WAR DIARY
or
INTELLIGENCE SUMMARY.

(Erase heading not required.)

Place	Date	Hour	Summary of Events and Information	Remarks and references to Appendices
	Nov. 1917			
	22nd		~~The~~ a party of the enemy rushed one of our Lewis gun posts. Every man on the post was wounded & the enemy succeeded in getting away with one man and a Lewis gun. Our artillery and MGs put a heavy barrage on enemy front line & must have caused the returning raiders heavy casualties. Our casualties 1 missing 3 killed 22 wounded. The remainder of the day quiet, except for some shelling.	
	23rd 24th 25th 26th		Normal activity	
	26th		Bn is relieved by the 6th Bn YORK and LANCS and moves to huts in NOEUX LES MINES. The whole of 138th Inf Bde goes into rest billets handing over HILL 70 sector to 32nd Bde.	
	27th 28th		Cleaning & training.	
	29th		The B.G.C inspects the Bde.	
	30th		Training.	

[signature] Capt & Adjt.
for Lt Col. Comdg 4th Leic Regt.

(A7092). Wt. W12839/M1293. 75,000. 1/17. D. D. & L., Ltd. Forms/C.2118/14.

R 237

1/4th BATTN
LEIC REGT
Vol 34

Army Form C. 2118.

WAR DIARY
or
INTELLIGENCE SUMMARY.
(Erase heading not required.)

Instructions regarding War Diaries and Intelligence Summaries are contained in F. S. Regs., Part II. and the Staff Manual respectively. Title pages will be prepared in manuscript.

Place	Date	Hour	Summary of Events and Information	Remarks and references to Appendices
NOEUX-LES MINES	1917 December 1st		Brigade in Divisional Reserve at NOEUX-LES-MINES. The GOC's inspection of the Brigade due on the 2nd cancelled on the night of 31st owing to the Brigade being ordered to take over the CAMBRIN SECTOR 24 hours earlier than originally ordered. As the battn moves into CAMBRIN SUPPORT area early in the morrow, reconnoitring parties are sent up today to make arrangements. CAMBRIN SECTOR at present occupied by 74th Inf Bde 25th Division	
	December 2nd		At 8.30am the battn left NOEUX and marched by platoons to CAMBRIN SECTOR Support billets. Two coys B Coy (LEA) and C Coy (NUGEE) in village of ANNEQUIN and two Coys in immediate support, A Coy (PICK) on right in FACTORY DUGOUTS and D Coy (JACKSON) on left in MAISON ROUGE Dugouts. Relief completed by 10am without incident. The QM Stores & Transport Lines remain at SAILLY LABOURSE. LT.COL. T.P. FIELDING JOHNSON joins from 4th LINES and takes over command from LT.COL. G.R.A. BECKETT	
	December 3rd		The two coys in ANNEQUIN occupied in training and working parties, those in forward support in working, carrying & general improvement of their quarters.	
	December 4th to December 7th		Occupied as for 3rd inst. Enemy becoming very active in bombing raids on the back areas. On 6th inst at 6-30pm several bombs were dropped in SAILLY LABOURSE wounding 4 transport drivers of this battn, but missing our stores & horse lines. Enemy in line opposite quiet and weather cold but dry. On morning of 7th a number of the officers & NCOs reconnoitre the line in CAMBRIN RIGHT SUBSECTION, which we take over on the morrow.	

(A7092). Wt. W12839/M1293. 750,000. 1/17. D. D. & L., Ltd. Forms/C.2118/14.

Instructions regarding War Diaries and Intelligence Summaries are contained in F. S. Regs., Part II. and the Staff Manual respectively. Title pages will be prepared in manuscript.

WAR DIARY
or
INTELLIGENCE SUMMARY.
(Erase heading not required.)

Army Form C. 2118.

PAGE II

Place	Date	Hour	Summary of Events and Information	Remarks and references to Appendices
ANNEQUIN	1917 December 8th.		At 8-30 am the battn moved off to relieve the 5th Bn, now under command of Lt Col CURRIN, in the CAMBRIN RIGHT SUBSECTION. This section adjoins the ST ELIE LEFT SUBSECTION, occupied by this battn from Aug to Nov 1917, and includes that portion known as the HOHENZOLLERN REDOUBT, where the battn fought so gallantly & lost so heavily on Oct 13th 1915. Relief completed without incident by 11-15 am. Trench strength 25 officers and 445 O.R. Dispositions A Coy (PICK) Right Front Line D Coy (JACKSON) Left Front Line B Coy (LEA) Right Support, C Coy (MUGEE) Left Support.	
CAMBRIN RIGHT SUBSECTION	December 9th		Enemy trench mortars shew signs of increased activity. At 5.25 pm a heavy barrage of T Ms, all calibres, 77 mm, 105 mm & 150 mm shells, was dropped by enemy onto our front & support lines. The artillery 61st Batty C.F.A. on being appealed to, promptly put a counter barrage on enemy line. Fire seemed most intense on our left Coy front and at 5.35 pm O.C Coy on our left reported that he thought he was being raided. The left Lewis gun post of our left Coy opened an enfilade fire to the left and the Artillery converged their fire onto the threatened spot MAD POINT. At about 6-15 pm the enemy fire died down, without his infantry having effected an entrance into our trenches. Our casualties 1 man wounded.	

(A7092). Wt. W12839/M1293. 750,000. 1/17. D. D. & L., Ltd. Forms/C.2118/14.

Army Form C. 2118.

Instructions regarding War Diaries and Intelligence Summaries are contained in F. S. Regs., Part II. and the Staff Manual respectively. Title pages will be prepared in manuscript.

WAR DIARY
or
INTELLIGENCE SUMMARY.
(Erase heading not required.)

Place	Date 1917	Hour	Summary of Events and Information	Remarks and references to Appendices
CAMBRIN RIGHT SUBSECTOR	December 10th		Enemy trench mortars continued active, but otherwise quiet.	
	December 11th		At 1 am the enemy projected gas on to this front dropping some 700 projectiles into the Pony [illegible] sector. The alarm was speedily given and respirators donned, with result that our casualties were one man slightly gassed. Owing to the wind the concentration was highest round Battn H.Q. A blind shell was dug up behind the reserve line & was sent back to Army H.Q. Upon examination it was found to contain phosgene. This is the first time the Germans have ever used the projector method of producing a gas cloud. A reorganization of the Battn sector, which had been under consideration for several days, took place today. The distribution is now 3 Coys in the line each with a platoon in the reserve line for counter attack purposes. A Coy (PICK) on Rt. B Coy (LEA) Centre D Coy (JACKSON) on left & C Coy (NUGEE) in Reserve. At 3.40 pm the 5th SHERWOOD FORESTERS of 139th Inf Bde on our right raided to the enemies 3rd line in the vicinity of the Quarries. A dummy barrage and smoke screen was put down on either flank just prior	

(A7092). Wt. W12839/M1293. 750,000. 1/17. D. D. & L., Ltd. Forms/C.2118/14.

Instructions regarding War Diaries and Intelligence Summaries are contained in F. S. Regs., Part II. and the Staff Manual respectively. Title pages will be prepared in manuscript.

WAR DIARY
or
INTELLIGENCE SUMMARY.
(Erase heading not required.)

Page IV

Army Form C. 2118.

Place	Date 1917	Hour	Summary of Events and Information	Remarks and references to Appendices
	Dec 11th continued.		which successfully diverted the enemies fire from the raided spot. The raiders returned with 5 prisoners. Our sector came in for some retaliation, but no casualties resulted. The night was quiet	
	December 12th.		Quiet day except for some T.M. activity on part of the enemy. At 8.30 pm we projected gas onto Fosse 8 accompanied by a bombardment by the C.F.A. covering our front. An gas officer of the American Army was present during the operation At about 10 pm the enemy opened up with a heavy bombardment of our right & centre coy sectors with artillery & T.Ms. The tunnels which in the right & left coy sectors, have taken the place of the forward communication trenches were too shallow to withstand such a bombardment and most of the entrances & in several places the galleries were smashed in. All communications were cut & Rt Coy H. Qrs was isolated from the 3 left hand posts. At the same time the enemy vigorously bombarded the rear with mustard gas. Bn H Qrs was so far affected by this latter that respirators were worn for two hours. The bombardment on the front line was by no means confined to this Battn front, as the "attack" signal was sent by the two Bttns on either flank. Our artillery responded splendidly to our own attack signal.	

Instructions regarding War Diaries and Intelligence Summaries are contained in F. S. Regs., Part II. and the Staff Manual respectively. Title pages will be prepared in manuscript.

WAR DIARY
or
INTELLIGENCE SUMMARY.
(Erase heading not required.)

Page V

Army Form C. 2118.

Place	Date	Hour	Summary of Events and Information	Remarks and references to Appendices
	1917 Dec. 12 continued		The activity lasted about 1¾ hours & died away without the German infantry making any attack	
	December 13th.		At 3.30 am the enemy repeated his bombardment of the front line. The fire became so intense and all forward communications having broken down ~~that~~ the SOS signal was sent up from Centre Coy & repeated from H.Qrs. The bombardment slackened at 3.45 am & stopped at 4-15 am. The enemy were reported to have been seen in NO MANS LAND, but nowhere effected an entrance into our trenches, thanks to the prompt response of our artillery. The day was exceedingly quiet & the work of digging out the trenches & reopening the tunnels was proceeded with. The 170th Tunnelling Coy had throughout each bombardment, behaved splendidly, sparing no effort to keep the tunnels open. A company of 1st MONMOUTH (PIONEER) Bn was sent up and did good work on the battered trenches.	Casualties for night 12th/13th 1 Killed 3 wounded.
BEUVRY.	December 14.		The battn relieved by 5th Bn & marched back to Div Reserve at BEUVRY Relief complete by 11 am without incident, although hostile artillery was somewhat active. The afternoon devoted to rest & cleaning up.	

A5834 Wt. W4973/M687 750,000 8/16 D. D. & L. Ltd. Forms/C.2118/13.

Instructions regarding War Diaries and Intelligence Summaries are contained in F. S. Regs., Part II. and the Staff Manual respectively. Title pages will be prepared in manuscript.

WAR DIARY
or
INTELLIGENCE SUMMARY.
(Erase heading not required.)

Army Form C. 2118.

Page VI

Place	Date	Hour	Summary of Events and Information	Remarks and references to Appendices
	1917			
BEUVRY	December 15th to December 19th		In Divisional Reserve at BEUVRY. Time spent in training and recreational training. The drums who, as usual had been sent to the Div Depot Bn while the 6th was in the line rejoined. On Dec 19th the 6th football team, played the SPRINGBOKS (Div Supply Column) beating them by 2 goals to one. Weather cold & frosty.	
	December 20th		At 8.30 am battn marched to the line to relieve 5th Bn. Relief complete by 12 noon. The morning was remarkable for a very thick fog. Since the battn was last in the line the enemy had been exceedingly quiet and the 5th bn had made good headway with the work of clearing the trenches. Dispositions C Right B Centre D Left A Reserve.	
	December 21st		Very little hostile activity. An odd priester bomb falling on one of our posts, unfortunately killed 1 man & wounded 1 Sgt & 2 O.R the Sgt dying of wounds next morning. At 11-10 pm 2Lt H. MARKHAM took a patrol of 7 O.R. out on the left Coy (JACKSON) front, to endeavour to rush a German post opposite. The party unfortunately came upon the post earlier than expected & was met with a fusilade of bombs & rifle shots. They however threw all their bombs into the post and 2Lt MARKHAM having been shot through the foot	

Army Form C. 2118.

Instructions regarding War Diaries and Intelligence Summaries are contained in F. S. Regs., Part II. and the Staff Manual respectively. Title pages will be prepared in manuscript.

WAR DIARY
or
INTELLIGENCE SUMMARY.
(Erase heading not required.)

Place	Date	Hour	Summary of Events and Information	Remarks and references to Appendices
			the patrol withdrew in good order, with the exception of No 201503 Pte J HERBERT, who asserted that they were returning in the wrong direction. He broke away from the patrol & ran towards the enemy lines. A search was made for him later, without success. All identifications had been removed from him before the patrol left our lines. With exception of above incident the night was quiet.	
	December 22nd		no event of importance	
	December 23rd.		An uneventful day, the weather continuing frosty. The 14th CFA Bde relieved by the 58th Bde RFA (Lt Col D de L. WINTER. CMG. DSO. RFA.	
	December 24th.		From 12 noon to 3 pm our artillery subjected enemy to harassing fire on roads & tracks. No immediate retaliation followed. The division on our left (42nd) at 6·30 pm bombarded the enemy with gas & H.E, repeating the dose at intervals. The Brigade on our right (139th) projected gas at 9 pm. The combination of the two operations raised the anger of the Bosche to such an extent that he treated this Bn HQs & those of the Left Bn to a liberal dose of 77 mm & 10 5 mm shells. Which operation he thought fit to repeat at 12 midnight & 5 am.	

Instructions regarding War Diaries and Intelligence Summaries are contained in F. S. Regs., Part II. and the Staff Manual respectively. Title pages will be prepared in manuscript.

WAR DIARY
or
INTELLIGENCE SUMMARY.
(Erase heading not required.)

Army Form C. 2118.

Place	Date	Hour	Summary of Events and Information	Remarks and references to Appendices
	1917			
	December 25th		Christmas Day was not marked by any important events. A few shells fell on the sector during the day. Snow fell during the afternoon & by 7 pm was about 2" deep. The night was exceptionally quiet. No attempt was made by the enemy to fraternise, ~~[illegible]~~ & the hearty & carefully arranged reception which our artillery had ready, was not needed.	
	December 26th		Relieved by 5th Bn. Relief completed without incident by 12·30 pm. Marched back to Bde Support, B Coy in FACTORY TRENCH, C Coy in MAISON ROUGE & A & D Coys in ANNEQUIN. Bn HQs in ANNEQUIN	
ANNEQUIN	December 27th		Bn engaged in carrying & working parties. Enemy shelled batteries on East side of ANNEQUIN, inflicting 5 or 6 casualties, one being a civilian, who are also still allowed in CAMBRIN. As yet no prospect of a thaw & the roads are very slippery.	
	December 28th		Nothing of importance. Light snowfall at 8 pm.	

A5834 Wt. W4973/M687 750,000 8/16 D. D. & L. Ltd. Forms/C.2118/13.

Army Form C. 2118.

Instructions regarding War Diaries and Intelligence Summaries are contained in F. S. Regs., Part II. and the Staff Manual respectively. Title pages will be prepared in manuscript.

WAR DIARY
or
INTELLIGENCE SUMMARY.
(Erase heading not required.)

Place	Date	Hour	Summary of Events and Information	Remarks and references to Appendices
	1917			
ANNEQUIN	December 29th		Nothing to report. Thaw sets in about 7 pm.	
	December 30th		Nothing to report.	
	December 31st		Nothing to report. The battn moves into the line early on the morrow. Lt Col. J.P. Fielding Johnson entrains for 14 days leave to U.K. Major G.R.A. Beckett takes command.	

G.R.A. Beckett Major.

Commanding 1/4th Bn. Leicestershire Rgt.

A5834 Wt. W4973/M687 750,000 8/16 D. D. & L. Ltd. Forms/C.2118/13.

Instructions regarding War Diaries and Intelligence Summaries are contained in F. S. Regs., Part II. and the Staff Manual respectively. Title pages will be prepared in manuscript.

WAR DIARY
or
INTELLIGENCE SUMMARY.
(Erase heading not required.)

Army Form C. 2118.

APPENDIX A.

Casualties for month of December.

Place	Date	Hour	Sick	Wounded	Killed	Remarks and references to Appendices
Dec	1		4	–		
	2		3	–		
	3		1	–		
	5		–	4		
	7		2	–		
	9th		.	1		
	11th		1	1		
	12		–	3	1	
	13		3	–	–	
	14		1	–	1	
	15		–			
	16		2	–	–	
	18		1			
	19		5			
	20		2			
	21		–	2	1	
	22		–	2Lt H. MARKHAM.	1 missing.	
	23		2			
	24		2			
	26		1			
	27		2		1	
	28		1			
	31		4	–		
			37	1 Off 11 OR	4 1 missing	

Strengths

Date.	Ration Off	Ration OR	Effective Offs	Effective O.R.
Dec 1	33	684	42	793
Dec 8	30	609	43	805
15	30	598	43	791
22nd	28	580	41	782
" 31st	28	576	42	804

A5834 Wt. W4973/M687 750,000 8/16 D. D. & L. Ltd. Forms/C.2118/13.

Instructions regarding War Diaries and Intelligence Summaries are contained in F. S. Regs., Part II. and the Staff Manual respectively. Title pages will be prepared in manuscript.

WAR DIARY
or
INTELLIGENCE SUMMARY.
(Erase heading not required.)

Army Form C. 2118.

1/4 Leicestershire Regt

Vol 35

Place	Date	Hour	Summary of Events and Information	Remarks and references to Appendices
	1918			
ANNEQUIN	January	1st.	The battalion in Bde Reserve. Weather clear & frosty, snow still on the ground. At 9·30 am marched to trenches and relieved 5th Bn in CAMBRIN RIGHT Subsection, relief being completed 12 noon. Dispositions C Coy (MUGEE) Right, B Coy (LEA) Centre, A Coy (PICK) Left, D Coy (JACKSON) Reserve. An Officer of U.S.A. Army, Capt BOWDEN is attached to us for instruction. At 5am this morning, before Bn left Reserve, the enemy showed considerable activity with artillery and T.Ms. on the front of Bde on our Right.	
		2nd.	Day quiet. At 9-20 pm enemy attempted raids at 3 points on Bde front on our right, to the accompaniment of a heavy bombardment which embraced not only our sector but also CAMBRIN LEFT. RAILWAY ALLEY our chief rearward C.T. was shelled at the same time. No casualties resulted. Major BECKETT is commanding Bn during absence on leave of Lt Col T.P. FIELDING JOHNSON. CAMBRIN RIGHT and LEFT Subsections are in future to be known as CAMBRIN SOUTH and NORTH Subsections.	

A5834 Wt. W4973/M687 750,000 8/16 D. D. & L. Ltd. Forms/C.2118/13

Instructions regarding War Diaries and Intelligence Summaries are contained in F. S. Regs., Part II. and the Staff Manual respectively. Title pages will be prepared in manuscript.

WAR DIARY
or
INTELLIGENCE SUMMARY.
(Erase heading not required.)

Army Form C. 2118.

Place	Date	Hour	Summary of Events and Information	Remarks and references to Appendices
	1918 January 3rd.		Quiet day & night. Light snow fall during day. During the evening the 5th Bn put another belt of wire in front of reserve line in bn sector. Capt BOWDEN returns to Bde H.Q. Major BECKETT hears through the gazette that he has been awarded the Military Cross in the New Year Honours List.	
	January 4th.		Quiet day & night. Still freezing.	
	5th		400 men of 5th LEIC REGT wired the reserve line of battalion sector on our left. Capt MAGEE is in the gazette for Military Cross	
	6th		Normal. During afternoon our heavies shelled enemy line on our left. From 3pm to 6pm enemy artillery and trench mortars were active in a mild way but the shooting was very scattered.	
	7th		Relieved by the 5 Leic Regt. (CURRIN). Relief uninterrupted by enemy. Marched to BEUVRY to Divisional Reserve, arriving at billets by 12.30pm.	

A5834 Wt. W4973/M687 750,000 8/16 D. D. & L. Ltd. Forms/C.2118/13

Instructions regarding War Diaries and Intelligence Summaries are contained in F. S. Regs., Part II. and the Staff Manual respectively. Title pages will be prepared in manuscript.

WAR DIARY
or
INTELLIGENCE SUMMARY.
(Erase heading not required.)

Army Form C. 2118.

Place	Date	Hour	Summary of Events and Information	Remarks and references to Appendices
	1918			
BEUVRY	January 8th.		Bathing, cleaning up and resting.	
	9th.		At 9-45 am the battalion marched to VAUDRICOURT CHATEAU grounds to practise for Army Commanders inspection on the 10th. The B.G.C. was not pleased with the turn out.	
			Lt & Q.M. M.F. SHEPHERD, very busy during the morning arranging for mens Christmas dinner.	
			At 5 pm the men sat down to their Christmas dinner consisting of roast pork, brussels sprouts & potatoes followed by plum pudding & rum sauce, oranges apples etc, the whole washed down with a liberal supply of beer. Two companies A (PICK) & B (LEA) were accomodated in BEUVRY SCHOOLS and two companies C (HUGEE) & D (JACKSON) in DOU DOU Camp. The G.O.C Div ~~Major~~ Gen W. THWAITES and the B.G.C. Brig Gen. F. ROWLEY visited all Companies ~~and~~	
			Snowed hard during afternoon & evening	

A5834 Wt. W4973/M687 750,000 8/16 D. D. & L. Ltd. Forms/C.2118/13

Instructions regarding War Diaries and Intelligence Summaries are contained in F. S. Regs., Part II. and the Staff Manual respectively. Title pages will be prepared in manuscript.

WAR DIARY
or
INTELLIGENCE SUMMARY.
(Erase heading not required.)

Army Form C. 2118.

Place	Date	Hour	Summary of Events and Information	Remarks and references to Appendices
	1918			
BEUVRY	Jan	10th	Training from 9-30 am to 12-30 pm, which is very much hampered by snow. At 5 pm the Sgts of the battalion held their Christmas dinner at DON DON Camp, followed by a "smoker", at which the officers attended. Thaw commenced at 6 pm. Sgts collected 800 frs for St Dunstans Hostel	
		11th	Training. During afternoon CO (Major Beckett) & Adjt reconnoitred the TOURBIERE district defences. The officers held Christmas dinner at 8 pm. Major ~~F.B.~~ TETLEY, the late commanding officer was present. Freezing again.	
		12th	Training.	
		13th	Relieved the 5th Battn in CAMBRIN SOUTH. Enemy dropped a 5·9" about every 2 mins throughout relief, just short of CAMBRIN CHURCH but as the range was very consistent, the spot was avoided and though relief was slightly delayed, no casualties occurred. Remainder of day quiet. More snow.	

A5834 Wt. W4973/M687 750,000 8/16 D. D. & L. Ltd. Forms/C.2118/13

Army Form C. 2118.

WAR DIARY
or
INTELLIGENCE SUMMARY.
(Erase heading not required.)

Instructions regarding War Diaries and Intelligence Summaries are contained in F. S. Regs., Part II. and the Staff Manual respectively. Title pages will be prepared in manuscript.

Place	Date	Hour	Summary of Events and Information	Remarks and references to Appendices
	1918 January 14th		Day quiet. The thaw set in, in earnest. Trenches commence falling in, and every available man turned to, to keep communication trenches open. The Intelligence Officer of 6th YORK. REGT. (11th Div) ~~att~~ who are to relieve us in a few days, is attached to us to learn the sector.	
	15th		Rain throughout the day. The trenches in a very bad state. The enemy apparently too busy on his own trenches to worry us. Every available man ~~[illegible]~~ in the battalion working his hardest, for fear lest the Divnl relief should have to be postponed.	
	16th		Weather continues bad. Trenches continue to fall in. RAILWAY ALLEY the only C.T back to CAMBRIN quite impassable. The relief by the 11th Div postponed owing to state of the roads.	

A5834 Wt. W4973/M687 750,000 8/16 D. D. & L. Ltd. Forms/C.2118/13

6

Army Form C. 2118.

WAR DIARY
or
INTELLIGENCE SUMMARY.
(Erase heading not required.)

Instructions regarding War Diaries and Intelligence Summaries are contained in F. S. Regs., Part II. and the Staff Manual respectively. Title pages will be prepared in manuscript.

Place	Date 1918	Hour	Summary of Events and Information	Remarks and references to Appendices
	January	17th	Enemy very quiet. Owing to the state of the trenches, the B.G.C. decided that relief of front line troops was necessary. Owing to the state of communication trenches daylight relief impossible. The 5th Bn Leic Regt relieved us, at dusk, relief completed by 8 pm both incoming & outgoing troops proceeding on the top.	
			The bn goes into Bde Support at ANNEQUIN, ~~B & C~~ B (LEA) & C (MUGEE) in the village A (PICK) in FACTORY DUGOUTS D (JACKSON) in MAISON ROUGE	
		~~18th~~	Lt Col FIELDING JOHNSON returned from leave & resumes command.	
ANNEQUIN		18th.	Working parties on clearing communication trenches. Remainder of bn cleaning & resting.	
		19th.	The bn relieved in Bde Support, CAMBRIN Sector by the 6th Bn the YORK and LANCS (LAVIE). Completed about 4 pm without incident. On relief bn marched to billets at the TOBACCO FACTORY BETHUNE. This relief is the commencement of Bde relief by 32nd Inf Bde.	

A5834 Wt. W4973/M687 750,000 8/16 D. D. & L. Ltd. Forms/C.2118/13

7

Instructions regarding War Diaries and Intelligence Summaries are contained in F. S. Regs., Part II. and the Staff Manual respectively. Title pages will be prepared in manuscript.

WAR DIARY
or
INTELLIGENCE SUMMARY.
(Erase heading not required.)

Army Form C. 2118.

Place	Date	Hour	Summary of Events and Information	Remarks and references to Appendices
	1918			
BETHUNE	January 20th.		At 10-30 am the bn marched from BETHUNE to MT BERNENCHON W1.b and Q31.c. (Map BETHUNE Combined). Owing to danger from long range guns movement through BETHUNE was by platoons, but on getting clear of the town bn formed up to Coys at 100 yds. The G.O.C Divn watched the bn march by. He seemed pleased with the turn out. The command of the CAMBRIN sector passed to G.O.C 32nd In Bde at 1 pm and 138th Inf Bde HQ moved to BUSNE CHATEAU.	
MT. BERNENCHON.	January 21st.		Interior economy, cleaning up etc. The total amount collected by the bn for ST DUNSTANS HOSTEL for BLINDED SOLDIERS was 1668-50 francs.	
	22nd.		As the ground around MT BERNENCHON is all under cultivation or water training on any scale was impossible, however a certain amount of smartening arms drill, musketry & P.T. was carried out. The bn received orders to work under the O.C. 419th Field Coy R.E. (RUSSELL) 55th Divn. the work to consist of wiring the "BROWN" line. Major G.R.A. BECKETT proceeded on leave to U.K	

A5834 Wt. W4973/M687 750,000 8/16 D. D. & L. Ltd. Forms/C.2118/13

8

Army Form C. 2118.

Instructions regarding War Diaries and Intelligence Summaries are contained in F. S. Regs., Part II. and the Staff Manual respectively. Title pages will be prepared in manuscript.

WAR DIARY
or
INTELLIGENCE SUMMARY.
(Erase heading not required.)

Place	Date	Hour	Summary of Events and Information	Remarks and references to Appendices
	1918 January 23rd		Unable to carry on with wiring as no materials yet received. Companies carry out usual training	
	24th		No materials yet. Training as usual.	
	25th		Wiring commenced at various points between OBLINGHEM MILL and LE PLOUY FME. (nr HINGES). Type of wire, standard double apron fence. During the day the C.O & Adjt reconnoitred the back areas of the PORTUGESE CORPS in company with the Brigadier, OC 5th LINCS & 5 LEIC and their adjutants. A line of strong posts between FOSSE and LACOUTRE is to be occupied by this Bn in event of a determined attack on our gallant allies. During the evening the Hun carried out a large bombing raid on BETHUNE. Our planes went up, after the raiders, but the latter appeared to get away without loss.	

A5834 Wt. W4973/M687 750,000 8/16 D. D. & L. Ltd. Forms/C.2118/13

Instructions regarding War Diaries and Intelligence Summaries are contained in F. S. Regs., Part II. and the Staff Manual respectively. Title pages will be prepared in manuscript.

WAR DIARY
or
INTELLIGENCE SUMMARY.
(Erase heading not required.)

Army Form C. 2118.

Place	Date	Hour	Summary of Events and Information	Remarks and references to Appendices
MT BERNENCHON	Jun. 26th		A. B & C Coys continue the wiring under R.E supervision. D Coy training in vicinity of billets. Draft of 10 men from Divn depot.	
	27th		Sunday. No wiring owing to lack of material. C of E Parade service by Rev R. G. Lowndes C.F. on battalion parade ground. The Bn drums played the hymns. Weather very cold. The C.O. inspected the new draft. The GOC has ordered all Bns to wear a distinguishing mark, this Bn's to be a 1¾" yellow square on each shoulder.	
	28th		A Coy bathing at GONNEHEM. B. C & D occupied in wiring or unloading barges on the canal	
	29th		B Coy bathing. D C & A Coys wiring.	
	30th		No wiring again owing to lack of materials. Coys train in vicinity of billets.	

A5834 Wt. W4973/M687 750,000 8/16 D. D. & L. Ltd. Forms/C.2118/13

Instructions regarding War Diaries and Intelligence Summaries are contained in F. S. Regs., Part II. and the Staff Manual respectively. Title pages will be prepared in manuscript.

WAR DIARY
or
INTELLIGENCE SUMMARY.
(Erase heading not required.)

Army Form C. 2118.

Place	Date	Hour	Summary of Events and Information	Remarks and references to Appendices
	1918			
MONT BERNENCHON			A, B & D Coys working under R.E. C Coy training.	
	January 31st		Orders received to move to BUSNES on 1st Feb, our place to be taken by the 5th Lincs Regt.	
			From the 30th inst the 138th Inf Bde is to consist of 3 bns only. The 1/4th LINCS Regt is being broken up and reformed as such in the Second Line Linc & Leic Bde.	
			The 2/5th Leic Regt is also being broken up but is losing its identity, being used to reinforce this bn, the 2/4th bn and the 1/5th bn. 9 officers & 200 O.R. were posted to this bn, of which 5 officers & 153 OR joined on the 30th.	
			J. P. Fielding Johnson Lt. Col Comdg 1/4th Leicestershire Regt	

A5834 Wt. W4973/M687 750,000 8/16 D. D. & L. Ltd. Forms/C.2118/13

Strength of Unit for month of JANUARY, 1918, as per A.F.B.213.

	Effective Strength of Unit.		Rations Strength of Unit.	
	Officers	Other Ranks	Officers	Other Ranks
5th January, 1918.	40	795	30	542
12th -do-	41	797	28	572
19th -do-	42	815	29	591
26th -do-	41	827	31	615

(1)

Army Form C. 2118.

Instructions regarding War Diaries and Intelligence Summaries are contained in F. S. Regs., Part II, and the Staff Manual respectively. Title pages will be prepared in manuscript.

WAR DIARY
or
INTELLIGENCE SUMMARY.

(Erase heading not required.)

February 1918

1/4th LEICESTERSHIRE REGT

Vol 36

Place	Date	Hour	Summary of Events and Information	Remarks and references to Appendices
	1918.			
MONT BERNENCHON.	1st FEBY		Battalion employed on "Wiring & Carrying" under 419th Field Coy. R.E in HINGES Area. Returned to billets at 2.30 pm – Eight Platoon Commanders from the battalion proceeded on horseback to ALLOUAGNE to witness demonstration by "Model" platoon at 46th Divisional Training Depôt 10.30 am – On completion of wiring the battalion had dinners and marched by Companies independently to BUSNES – all Companies reported in billets 6pm.	
BUSNES.	2nd		Day spent in bathing, interior economy & reorganization in conjunction with new draft which reached us 2 days ago from 2/5th LEICS. REGT.	
	3rd		Sunday. Two parade services in CINEMA HALL, BUSNES, Church of England and Nonconformists. – The day further allotted to a continuance of interior economy, bathing, medical inspection and reorganization.	
	4th		No. 3 Range ALLOUAGNE allotted to 3 Companies A (PICK) B (LAWSON) D (JACKSON), for firing & practice of A.R.A. platoon Competition.	

(A7092). Wt. W12839/M1293. 75,000. 1/17. D. D. & L., Ltd. Forms/C.2118/14.

(2)

WAR DIARY
or
INTELLIGENCE SUMMARY.
(*Erase heading not required.*)

FEBRUARY 1918 — Army Form C. 2118.

Instructions regarding War Diaries and Intelligence Summaries are contained in F. S. Regs., Part II. and the Staff Manual respectively. Title pages will be prepared in manuscript.

1/4 LEICS. REGT.

Place	Date	Hour	Summary of Events and Information	Remarks and references to Appendices
BUSNES.	4th	(Cont'd)	Sergt Instructor KIMBER at our disposal. "C" Coy (NUGEE) spent day in bathing and platoon training near billets. Eight platoon Commanders from battalion walked to ALLOUAGNE to witness a further demonstration by the "model" platoon at Div. Training Depot 10.30 am. 1 Sergt & 3 privates left this morning to accompany Brigade advance party to the new (BOMY) area.	
	5th		The battalion, less "D" Coy (JACKSON) marched to No. 16 area CHOCQUES today to carry out 'PRELIMINARY' Firing Practices and to practice over the Assault Courses – Companies at 100 yards distance preceded by Drums. "D" Coy carried out Company training near billets particularly Musketry, Rapid loading and Fire Discipline. All Coy Gas N.C.O's attended lecture in CINEMA HALL, BUSNES at 10.30 am by Div Gas Officer. In view of forthcoming marches a careful foot inspection was carried out after Companies returned from training.	

(A7092). Wt. W12839/M1293. 750,000. 1/17. D. D. & L., Ltd. Forms/C.2118/14.

(3)

Instructions regarding War Diaries and Intelligence Summaries are contained in F. S. Regs., Part II. and the Staff Manual respectively. Title pages will be prepared in manuscript.

WAR DIARY
or
INTELLIGENCE SUMMARY.
(*Erase heading not required.*)

FEBRUARY 1918

1/4 LEICS. REGT.

Army Form C. 2118.

Place	Date	Hour	Summary of Events and Information	Remarks and references to Appendices
BUSNES	5th	(Cont'd)	No 200689 Sergt S WATSON is awarded the Belgian decoration of the Croix de Guerre - During the afternoon an inspection of the Transport of the battalion was carried out by the B.G.C (Brig. Gen. F. ROWLEY) on the BUSNES - L'ECLEME Road. - weather bright and springlike.	
	6th		Training under Company arrangements. The Commanding Officer (Lt Col. FIELDING JOHNSON) inspected Companies in full marching order.	
	7th		Training under Company arrangements. At 2 15pm the Brigade Commander (Brig Gen F. ROWLEY) inspected the battalion - dress, full marching order - weather wet.	
	8th		The Brigade moved to the WESTREHEM area today. The battalion left BUSNES at 9 15am and marched to billets in WESTREHEM which was reached at 2pm - Companies marched at 100 yards distance - weather very wet.	

A5834 Wt. W4973/M687 750,000 8/16 D. D. & L. Ltd. Forms/C.2118/13

(4)

Army Form C. 2118.

Instructions regarding War Diaries and Intelligence Summaries are contained in F. S. Regs., Part II. and the Staff Manual respectively. Title pages will be prepared in manuscript.

WAR DIARY or INTELLIGENCE SUMMARY.

(Erase heading not required.)

FEBRUARY 1918

1/4 LEICS REGT.

Place	Date	Hour	Summary of Events and Information	Remarks and references to Appendices
WESTREHEM	9th		Tactical Scheme. Information received that a BLUE Force is marching on BRUAY from N.W. A Division of Cavalry is holding Crossing of River AA, between BLENDECQUES and VERCHOCQ - The 46th Division has been ordered to hold Crossing of River LYS, between DELETTE and DENNEBROEUCQ. - The 138th Inf Bde. (under Lt. Coln. WARING) is ordered to march to BOMY today as 'Advance Guard' to 46th DIV. - This battalion formed the VAN GUARD - The Corps Commander (1st Corps) (LIEUT. GEN. HOLLAND) and Divisional Commander (Maj. Gen. THWAITES watched the Brigade pass the starting point at FEBVIN-PALFART. - On reaching FLECHIN at 11.30 am a halt was made till 1pm for dinners. At 12.53 pm 138th Inf Bde Order 194 received - This battalion (Van Guard) ordered to move at 1pm and to seize the Crossing of the River LYS from DELETTE to DENNEBROEUCQ both inclusive - not to be withdrawn till the outpost line has been taken up. - at 4.20 pm the battalion had made good all Crossings on River LYS as ordered - No signs of enemy.	

A5834 Wt. W4973/M687 750,000 8/16 D. D. & L. Ltd. Forms/C.2118/13

(5)

Instructions regarding War Diaries and Intelligence Summaries are contained in F. S. Regs., Part II. and the Staff Manual respectively. Title pages will be prepared in manuscript.

WAR DIARY or INTELLIGENCE SUMMARY.

(Erase heading not required.)

FEBRUARY 1918

Army Form C. 2118.

1/4 LEICS REGT.

Place	Date	Hour	Summary of Events and Information	Remarks and references to Appendices
Tactical Scheme	9th	(Contd)	Dispositions were as follows:- D Coy (JACKSON) DELETTE (inclusive) to COYECQUE (exclusive) - B Coy (LEA) COYECQUE (inclusive) to GLEM (exclusive) - C Coy (NUGEE) GLEM (inclusive) to DENNEBROEUCQ (inclusive) - A Coy (PICK) reserve - Bn Hdqrs in PONCHÉ Q17d.4.4. At 5.0 pm Companies withdrew and marched to billets in COYECQUE - Casualties for the two day march. 1. O.R.	
COYECQUE	10th		Sunday - Devoted to rest & cleaning up. Church of England parade service ordered for 11.0 am. Owing to unfavourable weather this was held in School, COYECQUE. Maj. BECKETT proceeded to a Course at 1st Army Musketry Camp. MATRINGHEM	
	11th		Companies carried out platoon training during the morning.	
	12th		Companies fired Preliminary Course on Miniature Ranges - Practised Bayonet fighting Musketry and A.R.A. Competition - In the afternoon all men put back for further instruction attended special Musketry Class. A Riding Class was held for Company Commanders & Seconds in Command of Companys under the R.S.M.	

A5834 Wt. W4973/M687 750,000 8/16 D. D. & L. Ltd. Forms/C.2118/13

(6)

Instructions regarding War Diaries and Intelligence Summaries are contained in F. S. Regs., Part II. and the Staff Manual respectively. Title pages will be prepared in manuscript.

WAR DIARY
or
INTELLIGENCE SUMMARY.
(Erase heading not required.)

FEBRUARY 1918.

Army Form C. 2118.

1/4 LEICS. REGT.

Place	Date	Hour	Summary of Events and Information	Remarks and references to Appendices
COYECQUE	(Cont'd) 13th		During morning Companies fired Preliminary Course on Miniature Range. Owing to inclement weather it was impossible to practise A.R.A Competition. All platoon Commanders and 6 Senior N.C.O's per Company received instruction in A.R.A. Competition under Sergt Instructor KIMBER. Officers Riding Class for platoon Commanders under R.S.M	
	14th		C. B and D Coys on Gallery Range for firing practises 4, 5 & 6 of Divisional Course. When not on Range Companies carried out musketry training & practice of A.R.A Competition. During afternoon C & D Coys had use of Gallery Range for practice of this. Lecture for Officers & N.C.O's in the School, COYECQUE at 5pm by Major DELANEY P & B.T. Superintendent 1st Army. The Adjutant, Captain H.R. POCHIN proceeded on 14 days leave. LIEUT F M MANTLE took over his duties.	
	15th		A & B Companies on Gallery Range for practises 4, 5 & 6 Divisional Course. Companies when not engaged on Range carried out Bayonet training, musketry & A.R.A Competition. During the afternoon A & B Coys practised A.R.A. Competition. C & D Coys Football	

A5834 Wt. W4973/M687 750,000 8/16 D. D. & L. Ltd. Forms/C.2118/13

(7)

Army Form C. 2118.

WAR DIARY
or
INTELLIGENCE SUMMARY.
(Erase heading not required.)

FEBRUARY 1918

1/4 LEICS. REGT.

Instructions regarding War Diaries and Intelligence Summaries are contained in F. S. Regs., Part II. and the Staff Manual respectively. Title pages will be prepared in manuscript.

Place	Date	Hour	Summary of Events and Information	Remarks and references to Appendices
COYECQUE	15th	(Contd)	All Subaltern Officers attended 'Compass March' under Major G R A BECKETT - Lecture to Corporals & Lance Corporals by R.S.M. - Platoon football Competition 9 platoon V 12 platoon. Latter victorious.	
	16th		C & D Companies on Gallery Range - When not on Range all Companies carried out Musketry & Bayonet training - each platoon went over the Assault Course - Afternoon spent in football & games - Weather Clear & frosty	
	17th		Sunday. Parade Services in Schools - Church of England and Nonconformists - Roman Catholics attended Mass in Village Church. Medical inspection of battalion by Medical Officer.	
	18th		Morning - Watched demonstration by "Divisional Training Depot "Demonstration" platoon in :- Rapid Fire, A.R.A. Competition, Platoon in the Open Attack, Assault Course - after the demonstration C Coy had use of gallery range for a final practice in A.R.A. Competition. In the afternoon ~~A & B~~ Coys. Continued Part II Divisional Course on Gallery Range - Musketry, bayonet training & platoon in the attack also carried out -	

A5834 Wt. W4973/M687 750,000 8/16 D. D. & L. Ltd. Forms/C.2118/13

(8)

Instructions regarding War Diaries and Intelligence Summaries are contained in F. S. Regs., Part II. and the Staff Manual respectively. Title pages will be prepared in manuscript.

WAR DIARY *or* INTELLIGENCE SUMMARY.

(Erase heading not required.)

FEBRUARY 1918

1/4 LEICS. REGT.

Army Form C. 2118.

Place	Date	Hour	Summary of Events and Information	Remarks and references to Appendices
COYECQUE	18th	(Contd)	A lecture was given in the Schools to Senior NCO's & 2 Selected Corporals per Company by the Intelligence Officer (HORNABROOK). Officers Conference at 5.30 pm - all P.H. Helmets were handed in today.	
	19th		A.R.A. Competition Company Eliminations - When not on Range Companies carried out Musketry & platoon training. In the afternoon A Coy carried out further firing of Part II. Lecture by the R.S.M. for all Sergeants. The first of the Inter-Company football matches was played off this afternoon for the "Rowley" Cup Competition - D Coy v. B Coy - B Coy were victorious.	
	20th		A Coy (Pick) practiced Company in Open attack in all stages up to & including Outposts. Area Q18 & R.19 (BOMY 1/20000) C, D & B Coys further firing of Part II during the day. Company Conferences for Officers & N.C.O's on S.S.143. Intelligence Officer gave a further lecture to Senior NCO's. Inoculation started on - 98 throughout the unit. The Second of the "Rowley" Cup matches was played. A v. C Coy: A Coy were victorious.	

(9)

Instructions regarding War Diaries and Intelligence Summaries are contained in F. S. Regs., Part II. and the Staff Manual respectively. Title pages will be prepared in manuscript.

WAR DIARY
or
INTELLIGENCE SUMMARY.
(Erase heading not required.)

FEBRUARY 1918

Army Form C. 2118.

1/4 LEICS. REGT.

Place	Date	Hour	Summary of Events and Information	Remarks and references to Appendices
COYECQUE	21st		A.R.A. Competition, Battalion Elimination, on Gallery Range. No. 9 Platoon, 2Lt. W.L. BARBER in Command, total points 314. A & B Coys platoon and Company in open attack. C & D Coys Completion of Part II Musketry. In the afternoon A & B Coys football & games. Scouts & Snipers trained under Intelligence Officer. Capt. F.J. NUGEE proceeded to England for 6 months tour of duty.	
	22nd		Company training, included Company in the open attack. Scouts & Snipers & Signallers paraded for special instruction under their respective Officers. – Lewis Gunners and all skilled soldiers did their special training during the afternoon.	
	23rd		Company training, Company in the Attack, all stages. 9 am to 10.30 am Snipers on Gallery Range. 10.30 am to 1 pm all Casuals fired on Range. Signallers special training under Signal Officer (FOXON). – Capt. G.L. LEA assumed Command of "C" Coy as from the 22nd. – Battalion Final of the "Rowley" Cup Competition A versus B resulted in draw. Will be played off again tomorrow.	

(10)

Instructions regarding War Diaries and Intelligence Summaries are contained in F. S. Regs., Part II. and the Staff Manual respectively. Title pages will be prepared in manuscript.

WAR DIARY
or
INTELLIGENCE SUMMARY.
(*Erase heading not required.*)

FEBRUARY 1918

Army Form C. 2118.

1/4 LEICS. REGT.

Place	Date	Hour	Summary of Events and Information	Remarks and references to Appendices
COYECQUE	24th		Sunday. Church of England parade services in the schools. Baths at Ponche allotted to the battalion – all Coys. were enabled to complete. Officers Commanding Companies met the Commanding Officer to reconnoitre ground for a battalion attack arranged for tomorrow.	
	25th		Weather very wet – Operations for today cancelled – platoon training lectures etc instead. At 2pm all Officers met the B.G.C. (Brig Gen F. ROWLEY) to discuss the Brigade Operations for 26th & to reconnoitre the ground – Baths allotted to details to complete the battalion. The men carried out football & games during the afternoon. – Steel helmets, having been painted & marked with battalion sign, were re-issued to Companies.	
	26th		Brigade Counter attack Scheme.	
	27th		8.30AM – 1P.M. Battalion gas drill through test chamber – Platoon drill + Scouts & signallers under their respective officers, near billets COYECQUE. 10 AM Bgde ARA competition No 9 Platoon representing this (Battn)	

A5834 Wt. W4973/M687 750,000 8/16 D. D. & L. Ltd. Forms/C.2118/13

Instructions regarding War Diaries and Intelligence Summaries are contained in F. S. Regs., Part II. and the Staff Manual respectively. Title pages will be prepared in manuscript.

WAR DIARY
or
INTELLIGENCE SUMMARY.
(*Erase heading not required.*)

Army Form C. 2118.

Place	Date	Hour	Summary of Events and Information	Remarks and references to Appendices
	Feb 27.		Batt'n against the 1/5 BN Leicestershire Reg't, on range RECLINGHEM.	
		2:30 PM.	Bgde Semi Final football match, This Battalion playing 1/4 BN Leicestershire Reg't at RECLINGHEM. Remainder football + games if not at above match.	
	28	8.3 AM. to 2.15 PM.	Divisional Counter attack scheme carried out by 138th Inf Bgde under Brig Gen. F ROWLEY. Lt. Col. T.P FIELDING JOHNSON in command of this Battalion.	

T. P. Fielding Johnson Lt. Col
Comdg 1/4th Leicestershire Regt

A5834 Wt. W4973/M687 750,000 8/16 D. D. & L. Ltd. Forms/C.2118/13

138/4 6

Instructions regarding War Diaries and Intelligence Summaries are contained in F. S. Regs., Part II. and the Staff Manual respectively. Title pages will be prepared in manuscript.

WAR DIARY
or
INTELLIGENCE SUMMARY.
(Erase heading not required.)

R745.

1/4th Bn. Leicestershire R. Army Form C. 2118. 1

Vol 37

Place	Date	Hour	Summary of Events and Information	Remarks and references to Appendices
	1918			
COYECQUE	MARCH 1st.		Battalion under command of Lt Col. ~~TEP~~ FIELDING JOHNSON. Move from COYECQUE at 9-30 am. marched through BOMY, CUHEM to FLECHIN and billeted for the night. No man fell out on the line o march.	
FLECHIN	2nd.		At 9 am the C.O left by motor to reconnoitre the line in CAMBRIN SOUTH At 10.0 am, the Bn under Major G.R.A BECKETT. M.C. marched via WESTREHEM – ST HILAIRE to MANQUEVILLE (near LILLERS). No men fell out. Capt H.R. POCHIN returned from leave, and took over Adjutants duties from 2 Lt L C HORNABROOK. ~~Capt~~ Lieut TYLER (Transport) returned from leave. The CO. rejoined Bn the same night.	
MANQUE-VILLE	3rd		Left at 9.0 am and marched to NOEUX-LES-MINES, billeting there in huts. None fell out on march.	
NOEUX-LES-MINES	4th.		At 1 pm Bn left NOEUX and marched into the trenches of CAMBRIN SOUTH SECTOR, taking over from 9th WEST. YORKS REGT 11th DIVN.	

A5834 Wt. W4973/M687 750,000 8/16 D. D. & L. Ltd. Forms/C.2118/13

Army Form C. 2118. 2

Instructions regarding War Diaries and Intelligence Summaries are contained in F. S. Regs., Part II. and the Staff Manual respectively. Title pages will be prepared in manuscript.

WAR DIARY
or
INTELLIGENCE SUMMARY.
(Erase heading not required.)

Place	Date	Hour	Summary of Events and Information	Remarks and references to Appendices
	1918 MARCH 4th (Cont.)		Bn Boundaries (Right) GORDON ALLEY (exclusive) to (Left) RAILWAY ALLEY (exclusive). Dispositions C Coy (LEA) Right Front. D Coy (FLYNN) Left Front. A Coy (BROWN) Support. B Coy (CASHMORE) Reserve Coy in New FACTORY DUGOUTS.	
CAMBRIN TRENCH SECTOR	5th		Very quiet day. Weather fine & no casualties.	
	6th		Again quiet. Good visibility. Aerial activity on both sides above normal. Nothing of interest reported by patrols. Casualties 1 wounded C Coy	
	7th		Quiet day. Enemy propaganda balloon, shot down by our Lewis guns contained copy of GAZETTE DES ARDENNES	
	8th		Relieved at 12 noon by 5th Bn LEIC REGT. and moved out into Bde Support. H.Qs & 2 Coys ~~at~~ A Coy (BROWN) and B Coy (CASHMORE) at ANNEQUIN and 2 Coys C Coy (LEA) & D Coy (FLYNN) at SAILLY LABOURSE.	

A5834 Wt. W4973/M687 750,000 8/16 D. D. & L. Ltd. Forms/C.2118/13

Army Form C. 2118.

Instructions regarding War Diaries and Intelligence Summaries are contained in F. S. Regs., Part II. and the Staff Manual respectively. Title pages will be prepared in manuscript.

WAR DIARY
or
INTELLIGENCE SUMMARY.
(Erase heading not required.)

Place	Date	Hour	Summary of Events and Information	Remarks and references to Appendices
	8th (cont)		2 casualties by shell fire just prior to relief 1 killed 1 wounded.	
	9th.		Coys in ANNEQUIN supplied working parties for RESERVE LINE. ANNEQUIN shelled with 4.2" & 5.9" during afternoon. One fell in Orderly room yard. Orderly Room moved. No casualties. Summer time in force at midnight 9th/10th.	
	10th. 11th		Training & working parties. Some shelling in ANNEQUIN & SAILLY LABOURSE.	
	12th.		Relieved 1/5th LINCS REGT in CAMBRIN NORTH SUBSECTION. Right Coy A (BROWN) Left Coy B (CASHMORE), Support Coy D (FLYNN) Reserve Coy C (LEA). Enemy artillery active during relief no casualties. Bn HQ shelled with fast 77 mm shell from noon till 2 pm.	
	13th.		Enemy artillery again active. In the course of a patrol, carried out in day light by 2 LT. F. W. HUSSEY, he found a Lewis gun 20 yards	

A5834 Wt. W4973/M687 750,000 8/16 D. D. & L. Ltd. Forms/C.2118/13

Instructions regarding War Diaries and Intelligence Summaries are contained in F. S. Regs., Part II. and the Staff Manual respectively. Title pages will be prepared in manuscript.

WAR DIARY
or
INTELLIGENCE SUMMARY.
(Erase heading not required.)

Army Form C. 2118. 4

Place	Date	Hour	Summary of Events and Information	Remarks and references to Appendices
			from the enemy wire, wrapped in a waterproof sheet and in good condition. Apparently a gun lost by a previous battalion during a hostile raid. Human remains beside the gun shews that at least one of the raiders paid the penalty. This find, in a measure balances up our loss of a gun at HILL 70, the memory of which has rankled ever since.	
	14th.		Relieved by 1/5th LEIC. REGT. and move into Bde Support 2 Coys A Coy (BROWN) and B Coy (CASHMORE) in FACTORY DUGOUTS under 2nd i/c Major G.R.A. BECKETT. M.C. Bn HQ C Coy (LEA) & D Coy (FLYNN) in SAILLY LABOURSE.	
	15th.		Capt L.R.E. JACKSON returned from leave & resumed command of D Coy. Working parties & interior economy.	
	16th.		Relieved in Bde Support by 1/5th LEIC REGT. and move into Divisional Reserve at BEUVRY. Good billets but of late somewhat shelled.	
BEUVRY	17th.		Church parade by Rev H.K. DAVIS. C.F. Bathing.	

Instructions regarding War Diaries and Intelligence Summaries are contained in F. S. Regs., Part II. and the Staff Manual respectively. Title pages will be prepared in manuscript.

WAR DIARY
or
INTELLIGENCE SUMMARY.
(Erase heading not required.)

Army Form C. 2118. 5

Place	Date	Hour	Summary of Events and Information	Remarks and references to Appendices
BEUVRY	18th 19th		Platoon training. Weather fine. No hostile shelling in BEUVRY.	
	20th		Relieve 1/5th LINCS in HOHENZOLLERN SECTOR, a composite sector, formed by amalgamating CAMBRIN SOUTH SECTOR and Rt Coy of CAMBRIN NORTH. Quiet relief. Disposition C Coy (LEA) Right, D Coy (JACKSON) ~~Centre~~ Centre B Coy (BROWN) Left, A Coy (PICK) Support.	
	21st		Normal day, but heavy gas shell bombardment of batteries in rear about 4-45 am, caused Bn HQ + Reserve line to don their SBRs for some 35 minutes. No casualties.	
	22nd		At 12-20 am enemy ~~[illegible]~~ opened a heavy T.M + artillery barrage on this sector + the ones on the right + left. The artillery responded promptly + well to our call for assistance. All communications went down almost immediately, except for telephone to Centre Coy.	

A5834 Wt. W4973/M687 750,000 8/16 D. D. & L. Ltd. Forms/C.2118/13

Army Form C. 2118. 6

Instructions regarding War Diaries and Intelligence Summaries are contained in F. S. Regs., Part II. and the Staff Manual respectively. Title pages will be prepared in manuscript.

WAR DIARY
or
INTELLIGENCE SUMMARY.
(Erase heading not required.)

Place	Date	Hour	Summary of Events and Information	Remarks and references to Appendices
			who reported no infantry attack on his front. Hostile fire ceased at 1-30 am.	
			It afterwards transpired that enemy had endeavoured to enter our left Coy line and been repulsed with rifle & Lewis gun fire	
			The main attack directed at 8th SHERWOOD FORESTERS succeeded in overcoming the front line and entering their Reserve Line, from whence he endeavoured to bomb along our Reserve Line. He did not get far. His casualties were very heavy as the 9 dead Bosche in NO MANS LAND and 2 prisoners left in our hands testify. Valuable identification was obtained	362 I.R
			Our casualties 2 missing & 8 wounded.	
			Remainder of day quiet.	
	23rd.		Nothing to report Major G R A BECKETT MC to Field Amb sick.	
	24th.		Relieved in HOHENZOLLERN SECTOR by 1/5th LEICS REGT. at 10 am.	
			Moved into Bde Support. Bn HQ A & B Coys in SAILLY LABOURSE	

A5834 Wt. W4973/M687 750,000 8/16 D. D. & L. Ltd. Forms/C.2118/13

Instructions regarding War Diaries and Intelligence Summaries are contained in F. S. Regs., Part II. and the Staff Manual respectively. Title pages will be prepared in manuscript.

WAR DIARY
or
INTELLIGENCE SUMMARY.
(Erase heading not required.)

Army Form C. 2118.

Place	Date	Hour	Summary of Events and Information	Remarks and references to Appendices
			C. & D Coys Village Line. Prisoner taken on 23rd stated that enemy would attack between HILL 70 & LA BASSEE CANAL with 3 Divisions. As this in a measure confirmed reports of ground & air observers that an attack was impending Bn HQ A & B Coys moved up to the NOYELLES – GRENAY LINE at 8 pm.	on 25th
	25th.		Bn HQ, A & B Coys returned to SAILLY at 8.30 a.m. Battns. again ordered to occupy NOYELLES – GRENAY LINE but order cancelled at 6-30 pm.	
	26th		Quiet day. C.O & Adjt summoned to Bde HQ at 4 pm. Told we shall be relieved by Canadians, who proceeded to reconnoitre our areas. Probably march out on 27th and move South to battle area	
	27th		Orders altered. Bde is moving to HILL 70 Sector to hold the line. Bn moved out of SAILLY at dusk to LES BREBIS. QM stores to NOEUX-LES-MINES.	

A5834 Wt. W4973/M687 750,000 8/16 D. D. & L. Ltd. Forms/C.2118/13

Army Form C. 2118. 8

WAR DIARY
or
INTELLIGENCE SUMMARY.
(*Erase heading not required.*)

Instructions regarding War Diaries and Intelligence Summaries are contained in F. S. Regs., Part II. and the Staff Manual respectively. Title pages will be prepared in manuscript.

Place	Date	Hour	Summary of Events and Information	Remarks and references to Appendices
LES BREBIS	28th		C.O. O.C. Coys Intelligence & Signal Officers reconnoitre trenches of HILL 70 Left sector during morning	
			Bn relieved 50th Canadian Bn in this sector by 10-20 pm	
			Relief quiet, but very wet.	
			Disposition A Right, B Left C Right Support D Left Suppt.	
			The sector is same as held by Bn Nov 23rd 1917 except left flank 100yds More S	
	29th		Very quiet. Major G R A BECKETT rejoined from No 1 CCS.	
	30th		At 4.0 am. an enterprising enemy patrol attempted to bomb one of our advanced posts, but was driven off by rifle fire	
	31st		Enemy very quiet	

J. R. Fielding Johnson Lt Col.
Cmdg 4th Bn LEICESTERSHIRE REGT.

A5834 Wt. W4973/M687 750,000 8/16 D. D. & L. Ltd. Forms/C.2118/13

138th Brigade.
46th Division.

1/4th BATTALION

LEICESTERSHIRE REGIMENT

A P R I L 1918.

Instructions regarding War Diaries and Intelligence Summaries are contained in F. S. Regs., Part II. and the Staff Manual respectively. Title pages will be prepared in manuscript.

WAR DIARY
or
INTELLIGENCE SUMMARY.
(Erase heading not required.)

Army Form C. 2118.

138/4/6 1/4 Leicester Regt. Vol 38

Place	Date	Hour	Summary of Events and Information	Remarks and references to Appendices
TRENCHES	1918 April 1st.		Bn in trenches in HILL 70 Left Subsection. Day quiet, though enemy aircraft shewed an increased activity	
	2nd		At 8 am the bn on our left 9th NOTTS & DERBYS. 11th Divn carried out a raid on enemy line. Our left support Coy saw a party of Germans endeavouring to enfilade raiding party from South with a light M.G. and frustrated their attempt with Lewis gun and rifle fire. A certain amount of retaliation for the raid, which was well screened with smoke was delivered on to this sector, shells of 77 mm & 105 mm being liberally plastered on support & communication trenches. By 10 am all was quiet and remained so for remainder of day.	
	3rd		During a dusk patrol 2Lt F. W. HUSSEY discovered a concrete pillbox in NO-MANS-LAND about 30 yds from the enemy wire. Inside was a vertical shaft, which appeared to communicate by tunnel with the Hun front line.	

A5834 Wt. W4973/M687 750,000 8/16 D. D. & L. Ltd. Forms/C.2118/13

Instructions regarding War Diaries and Intelligence Summaries are contained in F. S. Regs., Part II. and the Staff Manual respectively. Title pages will be prepared in manuscript.

WAR DIARY
or
INTELLIGENCE SUMMARY.
(Erase heading not required.)

Army Form C. 2118.

Place	Date	Hour	Summary of Events and Information	Remarks and references to Appendices
	1918 April 4th		Quiet day. Enemy's aerial activity still high.	
	5th.		2Lt F.W. HASSEY again took out a patrol to enemy pill box and lowering a 25lb. ammonal charge down on a wire successfully wrecked it. The noise of the patrols preliminary efforts evidently attracted the enemies attention as he kept up a brisk rifle and M.G. fire throughout the operation. For the remainder the day was quiet.	
	6th.		Soon after dusk the 1/5th Bn LINCS Regt (Col WARING) moved into the sector in relief to this bn. On completion of relief about 9 pm the bn moved into Bde Support. During the afternoon 5 officers and 80 ORs proceeded to QM Stores at LES BREBIS for 3 days rest.	
	7th.		Bn employed on working parties	

A5834 Wt. W4973/M687 750,000 8/16 D. D. & L. Ltd. Forms/C.2118/13

Instructions regarding War Diaries and Intelligence Summaries are contained in F. S. Regs., Part II. and the Staff Manual respectively. Title pages will be prepared in manuscript.

WAR DIARY
or
INTELLIGENCE SUMMARY.
(Erase heading not required.)

Army Form C. 2118.

Place	Date	Hour	Summary of Events and Information	Remarks and references to Appendices
April Bde Support HILL 70	8th.		Occupied as on 7th. During night of 7th/8th enemy shelled batteries in rear with Yellow Cross gas shell. Fortunately owing tho the wind the bn was not affected.	
	9th.		At about 5 am the enemy commenced a gas shell bombardment of the batteries and back areas. ~~The air~~ A thick fog entirely obscured all visibility, and there was hardly a breath of wind, what little there was being from the North. Gas masks were donned and not until 1 pm was it possible to move above ground without them. ~~[illegible]~~ Fortunately ~~[illegible]~~ some of the dugouts occupied by the bn were gas proof and afforded some relief from the continual wearing of the masks. Some 20 men were sent to hospital as a result of gas, but almost everyone in the bn was more or less affected as, the gas continued to hang about in patches for many hours after.	

A5834 Wt. W4973/M687 750,000 8/16 D. D. & L. Ltd. Forms/C.2118/13

Instructions regarding War Diaries and Intelligence Summaries are contained in F. S. Regs., Part II. and the Staff Manual respectively. Title pages will be prepared in manuscript.

WAR DIARY
or
INTELLIGENCE SUMMARY.
(*Erase heading not required.*)

Army Form C. 2118.

Place	Date	Hour	Summary of Events and Information	Remarks and references to Appendices
	April 9th		(continued) At dusk the Bn moved up in relief to 1/5th Bn LEIC REGT in HILL 70 RIGHT. Relief completed without incident by 11 pm. B Cy (BROWN) Right Front A Cy (PICK) Left Front C Cy (MYLIUS) Right Support D Cy (JACKSON) Left Support.	
	10th		Enemy very quiet; his efforts at FESTUBERT and RICHEBOURG seem to be taking all his attention	
	11th		Quiet day. Hints of an early relief.	
	12th		Bn relieved in the line by 1st Bn CANADIAN MOUNTED RIFLES. Relief, without incident, completed at 1-15 pm. Bn marched out to FOSSE 10 SAINS EN GOHELLE, arriving in billets by 4 am. 13th. Transport & stores moved to NOEUX LES MINES.	
SAINS EN GOHELLE.	13th		At 4.0 pm the bn marched to HERSIN, billetted in hutment near BOIS de FROISSART. Bn is placed at 4 hours notice. Transport and stores move to HERSIN.	
HERSIN	14th.		Church Parade in YMCA. Medical inspections etc.	
	15th		Training for open warfare, platoon schemes etc.	

A5834 Wt. W4973/M687 750,000 8/16 D. D. & L. Ltd. Forms/C.2118/13

Instructions regarding War Diaries and Intelligence Summaries are contained in F. S. Regs., Part II. and the Staff Manual respectively. Title pages will be prepared in manuscript.

WAR DIARY
or
INTELLIGENCE SUMMARY.
(Erase heading not required.)

Army Form C. 2118.

Place	Date / Hour 1918	Summary of Events and Information	Remarks and references to Appendices
FROISSART CAMP. HERSIN.	April 16th.	Bn bathed at BARLIN. All men through gas chamber. (A Coy (PICK) practise field firing.	
	17th.	Training.	
	18th.	9am Muster parade. Bn put at 1 hours notice. Sudden orders to move to billets in HERSIN. All in by 4 pm.	
HERSIN.	19th	Bn again at 4 hrs notice. Training.	
	20th.	Training.	
	21st	Church services in HERSIN.	
	22nd	Bn under 2 hours notice to move. (Bathing at NOEUX LES MINES.) Training	
	23rd	Training. From the 18th inst a large number of high temperature cases have had to be sent to hospital. The malady lasts for about 4 days and is unlike ordinary influenza. The medical men attribute it largely to the effects of the gas bombardment of 9th inst. The 5th Leic Regt have a larger number of cases than we have, sending away sometimes 100 per day	

A5834 Wt. W4973/M687 750,000 8/16 D. D. & L. Ltd. Forms/C.2118/13

Army Form C. 2118.

WAR DIARY
or
INTELLIGENCE SUMMARY.
(*Erase heading not required.*)

Instructions regarding War Diaries and Intelligence Summaries are contained in F. S. Regs., Part II. and the Staff Manual respectively. Title pages will be prepared in manuscript.

Place	Date 1918	Hour	Summary of Events and Information	Remarks and references to Appendices
HERSIN	April 24th		At 8.30 am orders received to move to DIVION at 2 pm. Marched via BARLIN & HOUDAIN and arrived in billets at 5-30 pm.	
DIVION.	25		At 5 pm Bn marched to FOUQUIERES arriving at 8.30 pm. The Bde is now in divisional reserve, the other two brigades being in the line. Bn billetted in what used to be I Corps Rest Station.	
FOUQUIERES	26th		A large number of 5·9" shells fell between FOUQUIERES & BETHUNE. One hit a tree in the camp and killed one man, wounding eleven others of this unit	
	27th		Some shelling. C.O, 2Lt Howarth (as acting adjutant) & 4 OC Coys reconnoitred the line.	
	28th		The Bde moves into the line and becomes the Left Bde of the Division This Bn is in Bde support, in the vicinity of ESSARS. Relieving 5th Bn SHERWOOD FORESTERS. Relief completed by 12.20 am 29th. Bn HQ. ESSARS CHURCH shelled. Major G R A BECKETT and a proportion of officers and men remain out of line and march to billets in BRUAY.	

A5834 Wt. W4973/M687 750,000 8/16 D. D. & L. Ltd. Forms/C.2118/13

Instructions regarding War Diaries and Intelligence Summaries are contained in F. S. Regs., Part II. and the Staff Manual respectively. Title pages will be prepared in manuscript.

WAR DIARY
or
INTELLIGENCE SUMMARY.
(Erase heading not required.)

Army Form C. 2118.

Place	Date	Hour	Summary of Events and Information	Remarks and references to Appendices
TRENCHES.	1918 April 29th		B'N disposed over large area; men in breastworks & shelters. B'N. H.Q. in a house in ESSARS. No movement allowed by day. ESSARS & CHURCH heavily shelled this morning.	
	30th		ESSARS again shelled this morning, several direct hits on Church & tower; Afternoon quiet with exception of some shelling of bridges over LAWE CANAL.	

J. P. Fielding Johnson Lt Col
Cmdg 1/4th Battn Leicestershire Rgt.

A5834 Wt. W4973/M687 750,000 8/16 D. D. & L. Ltd. Forms/C.2118/13

Instructions regarding War Diaries and Intelligence Summaries are contained in F. S. Regs., Part II. and the Staff Manual respectively. Title pages will be prepared in manuscript.

WAR DIARY
or
~~INTELLIGENCE SUMMARY.~~
(Erase heading not required.)

Army Form C. 2118.

Vol 39

Place	Date 1918	Hour	Summary of Events and Information	Remarks and references to Appendices
Trenches	1st May		Quiet during the morning. Some shelling by 5.9's of ESSARS and our Coy (B) during the afternoon. Orders were issued for relieving the 5th LINCOLNSHIRE Regt in the LEFT SUBSECTOR to take place on the night 2nd/3rd May 1918.	
Do	2nd May		The day was quiet. The Bn relieved the 5th LINCOLNSHIRE REGT in the LEFT SUBSECTOR OF ESSARS. The relief was complete by 1 a.m. on the 3rd MAY.	
Do	3rd May		As movement was impossible by day the men were allowed to sleep in their shelters. During the night the front was actively patrolled and working parties were out connecting the isolated shell holes. The trenches were dug to a depth of two feet. Additional wire was also put out on our front.	
Do	4th May		Between 5 a.m and 5.50 a.m. the enemy put down a heavy barrage on our LEFT COY FRONT. The C.O. rendered a full report to the brigade. No infantry action followed. Our casualties were 2 O.R's killed and 1 O.R. wounded – ~~all~~ from B & "D" Coys. Enemy M.G's were active throughout the night.	

A5834 Wt. W4973/M687 750,000 8/16 D. D. & L. Ltd. Forms/C.2118/13

Instructions regarding War Diaries and Intelligence Summaries are contained in F. S. Regs., Part II. and the Staff Manual respectively. Title pages will be prepared in manuscript.

WAR DIARY
or
~~INTELLIGENCE SUMMARY.~~

(Erase heading not required.)

Army Form C. 2118.

Place	Date	Hour	Summary of Events and Information	Remarks and references to Appendices
	1918.			
TRENCHES.	5th May		Considerable activity took place on our LEFT FLANK but our sector was not unduly worried. A few salvoes of 4·2s fell on B.HQ and RESERVE COY (A) during the evening. M.G's active during the night. Enemy aircraft patrolled over our sector between 5.45 p.m. and 6.20 p.m. Operation orders were issued stating that the Bn would be relieved by the 5th SOUTH STAFFORDSHIRE REGT on the night 6th/7th May.	
do	6th May		The day was very quiet. Relief commenced at 9.20 p.m. and was complete by 10.30 p.m. The Bn marched to VAUDRICOURT and took over bivouacs from the 6th NORTH STAFFORDS. On the way out we sustained four casualties on the outskirts of ESSARS. The Bn was accommodated in bivouacs by 2 A.m.	
Vaudricourt	7th May		The day was devoted to rest, cleaning up and bathing.	
do	8th May		As many men as possible attended the workshops for repairs of clothing and boots. The Bn was medically inspected and all rifles were examined by the armourer sergeant	

A5834 Wt. W4973/M687 750,000 8/16 D. D. & L. Ltd. Forms/C.2118/13.

Instructions regarding War Diaries and Intelligence Summaries are contained in F. S. Regs., Part II. and the Staff Manual respectively. Title pages will be prepared in manuscript.

WAR DIARY
or
~~INTELLIGENCE SUMMARY.~~
(Erase heading not required.)

Army Form C. 2118.

Place	Date	Hour	Summary of Events and Information	Remarks and references to Appendices
Vaudricourt	1918 9th May		The C.O. inspected one platoon per Coy on the ground in front of CHATEAU at 10 a.m. Platoons were equipped as for battle. A church service was held at 12 noon on the same ground. A service for Roman Catholics took place at VERQUIN CHURCH at 11 a.m. The Armourer Sergeant inspected the Lewis Guns of "C" & "D" Coys during the afternoon. Exchange of personnel at Divisional Wing (BRUAY). As an attack was expected to take place on FIRST ARMY FRONT early on morning of the 10th May, the brigade was placed in Divisional Reserve. This Bn moved into position in the BETHUNE locality, N. of BEUVRY-BETHUNE RD. Except for occasional shelling of our positions with Gas Shells nothing occurred and the expected infantry action did not take place.	
Do	10th May		The Bn returned to billets previously occupied in Vaudricourt. The day was devoted to rest and operation orders were issued for the Bn to relieve 1/6 SHERWOOD FORESTERS in GORRE LEFT SUB-SECTOR. The Bn left billets at 8.30 p.m. & relief was complete at 11.30 p.m.	

A5834 Wt. W4973/M687 750,000 8/16 D. D. & L. Ltd. Forms/C.2118/13.

Instructions regarding War Diaries and Intelligence Summaries are contained in F. S. Regs., Part II. and the Staff Manual respectively. Title pages will be prepared in manuscript.

WAR DIARY
or
~~INTELLIGENCE SUMMARY.~~
(Erase heading not required.)

Army Form C. 2118.

Place	Date	Hour	Summary of Events and Information	Remarks and references to Appendices
TRENCHES	1918 11	May	This was extremely quiet. Patrols were sent out at night and at dawn. Working parties were employed in strengthening their defences and connecting up posts during the night and much wire was put out	
	12	"		
	13	"		
	14	"		
"	15	May	The day was quiet. An inter-company relief took place at 9 p.m. on the night 15/16 May "B" and "C" Companies relieving "A" and "D". Platoons moved up to the front line at ½ hour intervals. The relief was complete by 12.30 a.m. (16th May)	
"	16	May	It was very quiet. The usual working parties were busy during the night	
"	17	May	Repeated bombardment of B.HQ at GORRE CHATEAU with 4.2s and Gas Shells during the whole of the day. The bombardment increased in intensity during the evening and some of "A" Coy left their positions and join the SUPPORT Company (D).	

A5834 Wt. W4973/M687 750,000 8/16 D. D. & L. Ltd. Forms/C.2118/13.

Instructions regarding War Diaries and Intelligence Summaries are contained in F. S. Regs., Part II. and the Staff Manual respectively. Title pages will be prepared in manuscript.

WAR DIARY

~~or~~

~~INTELLIGENCE SUMMARY.~~

(*Erase heading not required.*)

Army Form C. 2118.

Place	Date	Hour	Summary of Events and Information	Remarks and references to Appendices
TRENCHES	1918 May. 18		As a result of the heavy Gas Bombardment of last night and during the morning in GORRE Chateau & wood the Commanding Officer, Adjt Intelligence Officer, Signal Officer & M.O became casualties, in addition to about 34 Other ranks of Bn. H.Q details. The Reserve Company (A) also had several gas casualties. In consequence of the above no Officers were left on B.H.Q. Capt. PICK (A) company took command of the Bn. and the Bde: Int: Officer came up to act as Adjt. During the evening Major G.R.A. BECKETT M.C & arrived to take over the command of the Bn and 2/Lt. D.W. HOWARTH assumed the duties of Adjt. having been sent for from Q.M. Stores. The Battalion was relieved during the night by the 6th NORTH STAFFORDS and marched to bivouacs in VAUDRICOURT WOOD	
VAUDRICOURT	May. 19.		Bn. in bivouacs. Day devoted to rest and cleaning up. Men who had been in contact with gas marched to F.A. for purpose of having clothes disinfected in Thresh Disinfector. Several more men sent to hospital as a result of gas mentioned above.	

Army Form C. 2118.

WAR DIARY
or
~~INTELLIGENCE SUMMARY.~~
(Erase heading not required.)

Instructions regarding War Diaries and Intelligence Summaries are contained in F. S. Regs., Part II. and the Staff Manual respectively. Title pages will be prepared in manuscript.

Place	Date	Hour	Summary of Events and Information	Remarks and references to Appendices
VAUDRICOURT	1918 May. 20.		Bathing and Medical Inspection during the day. Good weather with plenty of sunshine. A few more cases of delayed Gas sent to F.A. Personnel left out of line at commencement of last tour in the trenches returned to Bn. and new personnel sent to BRUAY. Capt. J.C. LEDWARD joined Bn. from BRUAY & took command of 'A' company in place of Capt. A.B PICK sent to F.A. as gas casualty.	
do:	May 21.		Morning occupied with Gas Lectures by Div: Gas Officer & Gas Drill with test in Gas Chamber. All companys inspected by C.O. Conference of Officers to discuss next tour in the line.	
do	May 22.		Training under company arrangements. Orders issued for relief of SHERWOOD FORESTERS in Support in ESSARS Sector. At 3-30pm Bde: Operation Order cancelled & warning order for relief of 137 Bde in GORRE Sector issued. C.O. & Adjt. attended Brigadiers conference to discuss relief. Appeared that 137 Bde: had suffered heavy casualties through Gas, hence their relief before due. Battalion relieved 1/6th S. STAFFORDS in Support, GORRE Sector. Quick relief. Relief completed about 1-40 ~~pm~~ a.m.	

A5834 Wt. W4973/M687 750,000 8/16 D. D. & L. Ltd. Forms/C.2118/13

Army Form C. 2118.

WAR DIARY
or
~~INTELLIGENCE SUMMARY.~~

(Erase heading not required.)

Instructions regarding War Diaries and Intelligence Summaries are contained in F. S. Regs., Part II. and the Staff Manual respectively. Title pages will be prepared in manuscript.

Place	Date	Hour	Summary of Events and Information	Remarks and references to Appendices
Trenches	May	23.	Battalion in Support GORRE SECTOR. Artillery comparatively quiet. Slight shelling of GORRE, a few gas shells falling on our right company front. As no movement was possible by day, men slept in during the night wiring parties were provided, the remainder of the men utilising the time in improving their positions. Capt Dickinson reported to the battalion from 177 L.T.M.B and was posted to 'A' Coy.	
do	May	24.	Hostile artillery was very quiet and weather conditions were adverse owing to rain. Wiring parties were provided to strengthen our defences at night and also 270 YDS of wire were put out by our SUPPORT Coy to complete the defence of LOISNE.	
do	May	25.	During the day, hostile artillery was slightly more active around GORRE. Gas shells fell every two or three mins in the neighbourhood of QUESNOY and the men were compelled to wear their gas masks. At night working parties were provided by the	

Instructions regarding War Diaries and Intelligence Summaries are contained in F. S. Regs., Part II. and the Staff Manual respectively. Title pages will be prepared in manuscript.

WAR DIARY
or
~~INTELLIGENCE~~ SUMMARY.

(Erase heading not required.)

Army Form C. 2118.

Place	Date	Hour	Summary of Events and Information	Remarks and references to Appendices
TRENCHES	May 25 (continued)		Coys to work with the R.E's. News reached battalion headquarters that Lt Col T.P. Fielding Johnson, Capt H.R. Pochin and 2/Lt W.L. Bass had been mentioned in Sir D. Haig's Despatch of April 7 (London Gazette Supplement May 23.) One O.R slightly wounded in right leg by M.G bullet.	
do	May 26.		During the morning the G.O.C visited B.HQ. It was quiet during the day with occasional shelling of GORRE with gas shells. The battalion relieved the 1/5 Leicesters in front line GORRE sector. Speedy and quiet relief completed at 11.50 p.m.	
do	May 27.		At 6 a.m. the T.M's on our right fired 20 rounds at hostile posts. At 12.15 p.m about 15 18" enemy shells fell around our R.A.P at LOISNE apparently in retaliation. Wind N.W. At 6.30 p.m E.A flew over SUPPORT Coy but were driven back to their own lines by our A.A fire. The night was spent in improving defences and wiring. Patrols were sent out but no identifications were obtained.	

A5834 Wt. W4973/M687 750,000 8/16 D. D. & L. Ltd. Forms/C.2118/13

Instructions regarding War Diaries and Intelligence Summaries are contained in F. S. Regs., Part II. and the Staff Manual respectively. Title pages will be prepared in manuscript.

WAR DIARY
or
~~INTELLIGENCE SUMMARY.~~
(Erase heading not required.)

Army Form C. 2118.

Place	Date	Hour	Summary of Events and Information	Remarks and references to Appendices
TRENCHES	28	May.	During the day 60 shells fell on the Bn front, the major portion being directed towards LOISNE + our right coy (B). A few gas shells also fell around BHQ. The wind was N E. Throughout the day E A were very busy over our sector and often came under close range of our M.Gs. During the night the B.G.C was round the front accompanied by MAJOR BECKETT M.C. Working parties were out all night wiring + improving positions. Four patrols were out during the night.	
Do	29	May	Bursts of Enemy 4.2's fell around BHQ and RESERVE LINE at intervals during the day and at 9.30 p.m. a number of gas shells dropped in the same area. But for this shelling the day was quiet. Wind was N.E. Wiring parties were working during the night on our right coy front + the whole Bn front was patrolled continuously	
Do	30	May.	At 2.30 a.m. the enemy opened a heavy T M. barrage on our right and followed it up with heavy M.G fire some of which fell on our front. At 2.45 a.m. our front line coys (B + C) reported everything O.K. on our front. The rest of the day was quiet + during the night	

A5834 Wt. W4973/M687 750,000 8/16 D. D. & L. Ltd. Forms/C.2118/13

Instructions regarding War Diaries and Intelligence Summaries are contained in F. S. Regs., Part II. and the Staff Manual respectively. Title pages will be prepared in manuscript.

WAR DIARY
or
~~INTELLIGENCE SUMMARY.~~
(Erase heading not required.)

Army Form C. 2118.

Place	Date	Hour	Summary of Events and Information	Remarks and references to Appendices
TRENCHES	30 May (continued)		The 1/6 SHERWOOD FORESTERS relieved the Bn in GORRE Sector. The relief was quiet and was completed by 11.30 p.m. During this tour 2/Lt L H Busby (B Coy) and three O.Rs were wounded. On relief the Bn marched to VAUDRICOURT.	
VAUDRICOURT	31 May		Bn in bivouac at VAUDRICOURT. Bathing and Medical Inspection during the day. The weather was good and the remainder of the day was spent in cleaning equipment & tidying up the camp. During the evening Lt Col. F. W. Foster M.C. arrived and took over command of the Bn.	

[signature] Lt Col.
Cmdg 1/4th Bn Leicestershire Regt

A5834 Wt. W4973/M687 750,000 8/16 D. D. & L. Ltd. Forms/C.2118/13

Instructions regarding War Diaries and Intelligence Summaries are contained in F. S. Regs., Part II. and the Staff Manual respectively. Title pages will be prepared in manuscript.

WAR DIARY
or
~~INTELLIGENCE SUMMARY.~~
(Erase heading not required.)

Army Form C. 2118.

1/4 Leicester Rgt

Vol 40

Place	Date	Hour	Summary of Events and Information	Remarks and references to Appendices
VAUDRICOURT	1918 1 June		The Bn took over the bivouacs usually occupied by them when out of the line. Reveille was at 7 a m and breakfast at 7.30 a m. During the day all companies bathed at FOUQUIERES and the Armourer Sergeant inspected all rifles. The companies were at the disposal of Company Commanders when not on bathing or Armourer's inspection parades. The time was utilised in cleaning up and preparing for the Brigade Ceremonial Service which took place on the following day. No 200404 Sergt. A Parker was appointed Provost Sergeant.	
do	2 June		A Brigade Ceremonial Church Parade took place at 10 a m in VAUDRICOURT PARK outside the CHATEAU and the G O C was present. The dress for this parade was drill order, with rifles & soft caps. The drums formed up immediately in rear of the Bn. The service was conducted by the Rev. R K DAVIS M.A. At the conclusion of the service, the Brigade marched past in column of route. The Drums preceeded the Bn and played them off the parade ground as far as the saluting base. After reaching the saluting base the Drums played the Bn 'March Past'. The remainder of the day was spent resting.	

(A7092). Wt. W12839/M1293. 750,000. 1/17. D. D. & L., Ltd. Forms/C.2118/14

Instructions regarding War Diaries and Intelligence Summaries are contained in F. S. Regs., Part II. and the Staff Manual respectively. Title pages will be prepared in manuscript.

WAR DIARY
or
~~INTELLIGENCE SUMMARY.~~
(Erase heading not required.)

Army Form C. 2118.

Place	Date	Hour	Summary of Events and Information	Remarks and references to Appendices
	1918			
Vaudricourt.	3 June		At 3 a.m a draft of 108 O.R's arrived from CALONNE RICOUART. At 9.15 a.m they were paraded & posted to their various companies. The C.O interviewed all Company Commanders at 10.30 a.m concerning the relief to take place on the night 3/4 June. Operation Orders were issued for the Bn to relieve 1/6th SOUTH STAFFORDS in the ESSARS LEFT SUB-SECTOR. The Coys were at the disposal of Company commanders.	
TRENCHES	4 June		The Bn relieved the 1/6th South Staffords and relief was complete at 12.55 a.m. A few gas shells fell on the ESSARS ROAD during the relief. Movement by day in the line was impossible as the men rested during the day. At night wiring parties were out also carrying parties. The Brigade Major proceeded round the line with the C.O. and visited all the posts at 10.15 p.m. The night was very quiet & two patrols were sent out. Wind W.N.W.	
do	5 June		The day was quiet & there was no artillery activity. Wind N.W. At night wiring was continued also revetting of parts of	

(A7092). Wt. W12839/M1293. 750,000. 1/17. D. D. & L., Ltd. Forms/C.2118 14.

Instructions regarding War Diaries and Intelligence Summaries are contained in F. S. Regs., Part II. and the Staff Manual respectively. Title pages will be prepared in manuscript.

WAR DIARY
or
~~INTELLIGENCE~~ SUMMARY.

(*Erase heading not required.*)

Army Form C. 2118.

Place	Date	Hour	Summary of Events and Information	Remarks and references to Appendices
Trenches	5 June (contd)		LIVERPOOL LINE. Except for occasional bursts of M G fire, the night was quiet.	
do.	6	"	The morning was very quiet except for intermittent shelling on the right of LIVERPOOL LINE. In the afternoon BLUE CROSS GAS SHELLS fell around our RIGHT FORWARD COY HQ. & also a few 4.2s fell on our left company front killing two O.R's and wounding 2 O.Rs. During the evening OPERATION ORDERS were issued ordering the Bn to relieve the 5th LINCOLN REGT in the ESSARS LEFT SUB-SECTOR on the night 7/8th June 1918. On relief the Bn. to move into BRIGADE SUPPORT. Wiring parties were busy during the night strengthening their defences & Some working parties improved & revetted part of the LIVERPOOL LINE. Except for occasional shelling of the RUE DE BOIS, the night was quiet.	
do	7 June		At 1 a.m. the brigade on our right carried out a minor operation & captured a light M G but obtained no identification. No shells fell on our right front coy during this operation. The day was quiet wind W.N.W. The Bn was relieved by the 5th LINCOLNS and relief was complete by 12.5 a.m. Quiet & speedy relief.	

Instructions regarding War Diaries and Intelligence Summaries are contained in F. S. Regs., Part II. and the Staff Manual respectively. Title pages will be prepared in manuscript.

WAR DIARY
or
~~INTELLIGENCE SUMMARY.~~
(Erase heading not required.)

Army Form C. 2118.

Place	Date	Hour	Summary of Events and Information	Remarks and references to Appendices
TRENCHES	8th	June	The battn in Brigade support. "C" Coy the forward coy & the remainder in support. No work was carried out by day as no movement was permissible. The day was quiet except for occasional gas shelling on our right coy (A) front. During the night salvage parties were out salving corrugated iron and wire & a working party was busy repairing the light railway.	
Do.	9th	June	The Bn remained in the trenches during the day & rested. The day was quiet & during the night the usual working parties were provided. The men not employed on working parties improved their positions.	
Do	10	June	Up to this time, the weather has been very good during the present tour but it rained during the morning. Artillery on both sides was very quiet. Towards the evening E.A. became more active and from 9pm until 12.30am Gas Shells were fired at intervals on the localities around LE QUESNOY, GORRE and ESSARS. Operation orders were issued for the relief of the Bn by the 1/6 SHERWOOD FORESTERS on the night of the 11/12 inst.	
Do	11	June	The day was bright & the front was very quiet. Very little E.A. The Bn was relieved by the 1/6 SHERWOOD FORESTERS and the	

D. D. & L., London, E.C.
(A8001) Wt. W1-71/M2031 750,000 5/17 Sch. 52 Forms/C2118/14

Instructions regarding War Diaries and Intelligence Summaries are contained in F. S. Regs., Part II. and the Staff Manual respectively. Title pages will be prepared in manuscript.

WAR DIARY
or
~~INTELLIGENCE SUMMARY.~~

(Erase heading not required.)

Army Form C. 2118.

Place	Date	Hour	Summary of Events and Information	Remarks and references to Appendices
TRENCHES	11 June (contd)		relief was complete by 11.55pm Very quiet & speedy relief. The Bn proceeded to usual billets at VAUDRICOURT PARK	
Vaudricourt	12 June		Reveille was at 9am. All the men bathed during the day & a medical inspection was held during the afternoon. The Armourer Sergt inspected two Coys rifles & the workshops were kept busy repairing boots and clothing. A programme was drawn up & published announcing a "Sports and Horse Show" to take place near the Transport lines on June 14th 1918. All officers reconnoitred a system of reserve trenches SOUTH of the BETHUNE-BEUVRY Road during the day.	
do	13 June		Reveille was at 6am. During the day all box respirators were tested at the GAS HUT, VERQUIN. During the morning 1 platoon from the Bn & all the signallers carried out a signalling practice with a Contact Aeroplane. The CO & Adjutant visited this display. During the evening a march of one hour's duration, wearing box respirators was carried out. In the afternoon the Brigade Band played selections in the Bn lines.	
do	14 June		All coys fired on the range between the hours of 8am and 12noon. The afternoon was devoted to a "Sports & Horse Show" and a very	

D. D. & L., London, E.C.
(A5001) Wt. W1 71/M2031 750,000 5/17 Sch. 52 Forms/C2118/14

Instructions regarding War Diaries and Intelligence Summaries are contained in F. S. Regs., Part II. and the Staff Manual respectively. Title pages will be prepared in manuscript.

WAR DIARY

or

~~INTELLIGENCE SUMMARY.~~

(Erase heading not required.)

Army Form C. 2118.

Place	Date	Hour	Summary of Events and Information	Remarks and references to Appendices
Vaudricourt	14 (contd)	June	excellent programme was arranged. The B.G.C. attended & presented the prizes to the successful competitors.	
"	15	June	Voluntary Church Services were held during the morning & orders were issued for relief by the Bn of the 6th NORTH STAFFORDS in the GORRE LEFT sub-sector on the night 15/16 JUNE 1918. The ~~Bn~~ C.O. held a Coy Commanders Conference at 9 a.m. At 8.45 p.m. the Bn left VAUDRICOURT for the line. The relief was complete by 12.25 a.m. (16th June). A speedy & quiet relief.	
TRENCHES	16	June	There has not been a great amount [of] shelling during the day. The majority fell on our RIGHT FRONT Coy (B). From 12 noon until 8 p.m. enemy artillery was particularly quiet. During the night four patrols were sent out & the remainder of the men were employed in improving their positions throughout Bn front.	
"	17	June	An enemy aeroplane flew very low over B.HQ and reserve coy (A) lines at 4.30 a.m. The LOISNE Area was occasionally shelled with 4.2s from 6 a.m. to 8 a.m. The wind was N.E. The night was quiet but enemy M.Gs were active. The usual working parties were busy during the night.	

D. D. & L., London, E.C. (A8004) Wt W1771/M2031 750,000 5/17 Sch. 52 Forms/C2118/14

Instructions regarding War Diaries and Intelligence Summaries are contained in F. S. Regs., Part II. and the Staff Manual respectively. Title pages will be prepared in manuscript.

WAR DIARY
or
~~INTELLIGENCE SUMMARY.~~
(Erase heading not required.)

Army Form C. 2118.

Place	Date	Hour	Summary of Events and Information	Remarks and references to Appendices
TRENCHES.	18	June	Between 4.30 am & 5 am a few Gas shells fell in the LOISNE Area. One shell hit the Signal Office in SUPPORT LINE (D Coy) but caused no casualties. It was quiet during the day but towards evening both our aeroplanes and those of the enemy were active. ~~The wind was S.W.~~ The night was quiet until 12 mid & the usual working parties were out.	
do	19	June	At 12.35 am the Bn on our left performed a minor operation. As a result of this the Bn front was subject to intermittent shelling by 4.2s, 77mm & 5.9s until 3.20 a.m. After this time the situation again became normal and remained so during the day. A few 4.2s fell on Bn front between 11.30 pm & midnight. An inter-company took place at 11 p.m. A Coy relieved B Coy in the RIGHT FRONT LINE and B Coy went into RESERVE. D Coy relieved C Coy & C Coy went into SUPPORT, D Coy taking over the LEFT FRONT LINE. A quiet and speedy relief. The usual working parties were provided and patrols were sent out.	
do	20	June	About 12 mid 4.2s fell in LOISNE Area between 2 am and 2.30 am. Our artillery retaliated. Wind S.SE. The day was very quiet. Occasional 4.2s fell on Bn front during the afternoon. Patrols were sent out during the night & working parties were busy improving their defences.	

D. D. & L., London, E.C.
(A8004) Wt W1771/M2031 750,000 5/17 Sch. 52 Forms/C2118/14

Army Form C. 2118.

WAR DIARY
or
~~INTELLIGENCE~~ SUMMARY.
(Erase heading not required.)

Instructions regarding War Diaries and Intelligence Summaries are contained in F. S. Regs., Part II. and the Staff Manual respectively. Title pages will be prepared in manuscript.

Place	Date	Hour	Summary of Events and Information	Remarks and references to Appendices
Trenches	21 June.		The situation was generally quiet throughout the day. Between 6.30pm & 7pm BLUE CROSS GAS SHELLS fell in LOISNE AREA. During the period 11pm till midnight the Bn front was subject to intermittent shelling by 4.2's & 77mm. Rain fell during the evening making conditions bad for front line coys. Wiring & revetting parties were busy improving defences & patrols were sent out on both company fronts.	
Do	22 June		The day was very quiet except for the usual occasional bursts of artillery on the Bn sector. The wind was W.S.W. Operation Orders were issued for the relief of the Bn on the night 23/24 June 1918 by the 8th SHERWOOD FORESTERS. Wiring parties were out until midnight but were withdrawn at that time owing to MINOR OPERATION on our right.	
Do	23 June		The day was quiet and there is nothing of importance to report. Three enemy aeroplanes flew over our sector at 6.50 pm. The Bn was relieved by the 8th SHERWOOD FORESTERS and relief was complete by 12.35 a.m. A speedy and quiet relief. On relief being complete the Bn marched to VAUDRICOURT PARK and took over billets there.	

D. D. & L., London, E.C.
(A8004) Wt W1771/M2031 750,000 5/17 Sch. 52 Forms/C2118/14

Instructions regarding War Diaries and Intelligence Summaries are contained in F. S. Regs., Part II. and the Staff Manual respectively. Title pages will be prepared in manuscript.

WAR DIARY
or
~~INTELLIGENCE SUMMARY.~~
(Erase heading not required.)

Army Form C. 2118.

Place	Date	Hour	Summary of Events and Information	Remarks and references to Appendices
VAUDRICOURT	24	June	Bn at rest in billets. Reveille was at 9.30 a.m and breakfast at 10 a.m. The day was devoted to cleaning up & inspections. 'A' & 'C' Companies utilised the baths at FOUQUIERES and clothing and boots were repaired at the workshops. The day was overcast & inclined to rain. The Bn band played selections in the afternoon. The Brigade Band played at Officers' Mess.	
"	25	June	Reveille was at 6.30 a.m. Box respirators were tested and inspected by the Gas Officer at VERQUIN during the morning and B & D Companies used the baths at FOUQUIERES. The rifle range was allotted to C Coy from 2 p.m – 5 p.m. A party of officers from the Bn visited the Corps Driving School to witness a tank demonstration in the afternoon.	
"	26	June	The C.O. inspected the Bn by companies during the morning. The dress was Fighting Order. The coys were at the disposal of Company Commanders for remainder of the morning. During the afternoon a competition in Signalling was held & the signallers from 'A' Coy were successful in winning the prize offered.	

D. D. & L., London, E.C.
(A8004) Wt W1771/M2031 750,000 5/17 Sch. 52 Forms/C2118/14

Instructions regarding War Diaries and Intelligence Summaries are contained in F. S. Regs., Part II. and the Staff Manual respectively. Title pages will be prepared in manuscript.

WAR DIARY
or
~~INTELLIGENCE SUMMARY.~~
(*Erase heading not required.*)

Army Form C. 2118.

Place	Date	Hour	Summary of Events and Information	Remarks and references to Appendices
Vaudricourt.	27 June.		The C.O held a Coy Commanders Conference in the morning & the Brigade Band played in our lines until 12.30 p.m. The Bn left VAUDRICOURT at 8.45 p.m & proceeded to relieve the 6th S. STAFFORDS in Brigade Support. Essars Sector. Relief passed off without incident & was complete at 12.35 a.m 28 June 1918.	
Trenches.	28 June		The day was quiet & owing to restriction of movement by day, the men rested. Working parties were provided for the forward Bns during the night & salvage parties were also busy. The remainder of the men improved the breastworks in front of their positions. E.A. were active throughout the night.	
do	29 June.		BLUE CROSS shells fell on Bn area during the early hours of the morning. The rest of the day was quiet. The Coy officers reconnoitred the RIGHT FRONT ESSARS sub sector preparatory to taking over of this line. The usual working & salvage parties were provided.	
do	30 June		Hostile artillery was fairly active & ESSARS CHURCH & RUE DE BOIS were shelled intermittently during the day. The night was very quiet except for the usual harassing fire. Operation Orders were issued for the relief of the 5th Leicesters by the Bn in	

Instructions regarding War Diaries and Intelligence Summaries are contained in F. S. Regs., Part II. and the Staff Manual respectively. Title pages will be prepared in manuscript.

WAR DIARY
or
~~INTELLIGENCE SUMMARY.~~
(Erase heading not required.)

Army Form C. 2118.

Place	Date	Hour	Summary of Events and Information	Remarks and references to Appendices
TRENCHES	30 June (contd)		the ESSARS RIGHT SUB-SECTOR to take place on the night 1/2nd July.	
			[illegible signature] Lieut Colonel Cmdg 1/4th Bn Leicestershire Regiment.	

D. D. & L., London, E.C.
(A8co4) Wt W1771/M2031 750,000 5/17 Sch. 52 Forms/C2118/14

Instructions regarding War Diaries and Intelligence Summaries are contained in F. S. Regs., Part II. and the Staff Manual respectively. Title pages will be prepared in manuscript.

WAR DIARY

or

~~INTELLIGENCE SUMMARY.~~

(Erase heading not required.)

Army Form C. 2118.

1/4 Leicester Rg

41

Place	Date	Hour	Summary of Events and Information	Remarks and references to Appendices
TRENCHES.	1st	July.	Bn relieved the 1/5 LEICESTERS in the ESSARS RIGHT SUBSECTOR on night 1/2 July.	O.O. 83.
"	2nd	"	Nothing to report except the usual harassing fire from 9 pm until 12 midnight.	
"	3rd	"	The day was quiet. The usual working parties + patrols were active during the night.	
"	4th	"	Operation orders issued for relief of Bn by 5th SHERWOOD FORESTERS.	O.O. 84.
"	5th	"	The Bn was relieved by the 5th SHERWOOD FORESTERS. Relief complete 11.51 pm.	O.O. 84.
VAUDRICOURT	6th	"	Medical Inspection and bathing. Coy Commanders reconnoitre CANAL BRIDGE-HEADLINE.	
"	7th	"	The C.O. inspected all Companies.	
"	8th	"	The Bn formed part of the Brigade Guard of Honour to the Corps Commander who visited GOSNAY and presented the M.S.M. to R.Q.M.S. W ROBERTSON, Sgt J WATTS. and L/Cpl R.H. PEXTON.	
"	9th	"	Companies at disposal of Coy Commanders. C.O's conference in morning. Bn relieved by 5th South Staffords in GORRE LEFT Subsector.	O.O. 35
TRENCHES.	10th	"	The day was quiet. Enemy artillery was active from 11.45 pm to 12.30 am in GORRE AREA.	
"	11th	"	Nothing of importance to report.	
"	12th	"	Operation Orders issued for relief of Bn by the 5th LINCOLNSHIRE REGT.	O.O. 86.
"	13th	"	Bn relieved by 5th LINCOLNSHIRE REGT at 12-10 am. Bn goes into Brigade Support.	O.O. 86.
"	14th	"	Bn provides working + carrying parties for forward Bn. The day was quiet.	
"	15	"	} Working parties provided for RIGHT FORWARD BN also for forward Coys.	
"	16			
	17	"	Operation orders issued for relief of 5th LEICESTERSHIRE REGT by Bn in GORRE RIGHT Subsector.	O.O. 87
	18	"	During night 17/18 July Bn relieved 5th LEICESTERSHIRE REGT. Relief complete 12-20 am.	

D. D. & L., London, E.C.
(A8c04) Wt W1771/M2031 750,000 5/17 Sch. 52 Forms/C2118/14

Instructions regarding War Diaries and Intelligence Summaries are contained in F. S. Regs., Part II. and the Staff Manual respectively. Title pages will be prepared in manuscript.

Army Form C. 2118.

WAR DIARY

or

~~INTELLIGENCE SUMMARY.~~

(Erase heading not required.)

Place	Date	Hour	Summary of Events and Information	Remarks and references to Appendices
TRENCHES	19th	July.	The day was quiet, usual working parties and patrols.	
"	20th	"	Operation Orders were issued for relief of Bn. in GORRE RIGHT Subsector on the night 21/22 July	0028.
			Patrol under 2Lt G Cashmore succeeded in rushing a post and obtaining identification	
"	21st	"	Battalion Relieved as above.	
VAUDRICOURT.	22nd	"	Day spent cleaning up and at rest.	
"	23	"	Bn bathed and clothes were disinfected.	
"	24	"	A C & D Companies at Range and on Training Ground. B Company wiring at GORRE.	
"	25	"	All officers reconnoitred forward area positions on 3rd Divisional Front. G.O.C. & B.G.C visited Brigade Sports in afternoon. Working party provided at Essars.	
"	26	"	Officers not on working party attended R.E. Demonstration & lecture at Hesdigneul Aerodrome. Rear areas of 3rd Division Front reconnoitred.	
"	27	"	Companies at disposal of Company Commanders. Church Parade 10-30 am. Operation Orders issued for relief of 1/6th SOUTH STAFFS by the Battn. Bn relieved in GORRE RIGHT subsector. Relief Complete 1 am 28/7/18.	0029.
TRENCHES	28	"	Occasional fire by enemies 4.2 and 5.9 batteries on Tuning FORK WOOD SWITCH and B.H.Q areas	
"	29	"	The usual patrols were out and working parties for revetting purposes supplied.	
"	30	"	Operation Orders for inter company relief were published. A successful patrol under Cpl Aston secured a prisoner.	0090.
"	31	"	Inter-company relief took place during the night. Up to date it has been quiet in the sector and the weather has been very good.	

J M Emler Lieut Col.
Comdg 1/4 Leicestershire Regt.

D. D. & L., London, E.C.
(A8c04) Wt W1771/M2031 750,000 5/17 Sch. 52 Forms/C2118/14

"SECRET."

1/4th Bn. Leicestershire Regiment. Copy. No. 1
Operation Order. No. 83
1st July 1918

Ref Maps GORRE & VIEILLE CHAPELLE 1/20000.

1. RELIEF The Battalion will relieve the 5th LEICESTERS in ESSARS RIGHT Subsector tonight 1st/2nd July 1918.

2. DISPOSITIONS.

C. Coy 4th LEICS relieves A. Coy 5th LEICS in RIGHT front
B " " " D " " " LEFT front.
A " " " B " " " RIGHT Support.
D " " " C " " " LEFT Support.

3. GUIDES. Guides for B & D Coys 4th LEICS will arrive at Coy. H.Q by dawn of the 1st July.
Guides for A Coy 4th LEICS will be at Right Support Coy. H.Q; X 27 a 80.80 at 10.30pm.
Guides for C. Coy 4th LEICS. Nil.

4. MOVE Companies will move as follows:-
C & B. Coys at 10-30pm
A & D Coys at 10-40pm
B. H. Q at 10-30pm.
Platoons at 200 yards.

5. STORES. Companies will arrange to carry own mess kit to new Company H.Q.
Cooking utensils of all Companies to be carried under Company arrangements to Cookhouse near RIGHT Bn. H.Q.
Mess kit & stores of B H Q will be loaded on to light trucks at ESSARS dump by the Police & pushed up with rations to Rt Bn H.Q

6. RATIONS. Will be pushed up from ESSARS Dump by Police.
A. Coy will send ration parties for own Company & C. Coy to Rt Bn H.Q after relief. C Coy will send guide to Rt Bn. H.Q to meet ration party.
D Coy will send ration parties for own Company & B. Coy to RIGHT Bn H.Q after relief. B. Coy will send guide to Rt Bn H.Q to meet ration party

7. COOKING. For all Companies is done at Cookhouse near Rt Bn H.Q
A Coy will supply hot tea carrying party of 8 men for C Coy, and D Coy will supply same number for B. Coy to be at Cookhouse by 1-15 am, 2nd inst. On subsequent nights these parties will report twice nightly at Cookhouse, at 10-30pm & 1-15am.

8. HANDING & TAKING OVER LISTS. Lists of stores taken over, & lists of stores handed over, will be sent to Orderly Room by 11 pm on the 2nd.

9. REPORTS. "Relief Complete" will be sent to Orderly Room by runner.

PTO

10. GENERAL. The Companies of 5th LEICS coming into Brigade Support will be disposed as follows:-

A Coy 5th LEICS	takes over from	A Coy 4th LEICS.
B "	" " "	C "
C "	" " "	D "
D "	" " "	B "

(Sd) DW Howarth 2/Lieut + A/Adjt

Issued to:-

Copy No 1 Adjt for C.O.
2 3 4 + 5 All Companies
6 Trans. Off. + Q.M.
7. R.S.M.
8 C.O. 5th Leics
9 138 Inf Bde
10. File

SECRET.

1/4th Bn Leicestershire Regiment
Operation Order No 84
4th July 1918.

Copy No: 10

---

1. RELIEF. The Battalion will be relieved in the ESSARS RIGHT Subsector on the night of 5th/6th July by the 5th Bn. SHERWOOD FORESTERS.
Companies will be relieved as follows:-
C Coy 4th Leics will be relieved by A Coy 5th SHERWOODS
B . . . . . B
A C
D . . . . . D

2. GUIDES. 1 guide per platoon, + 1 for Bn. H.Q. will meet incoming Bn. at road junction X 29 c 20.70 at 10-15 pm.
All guides to be at B.H.Q. by dawn of the 5th, where they will remain during the day, & report to 2/Lieut. W.L. BASS at 9-45 pm.

3. MARCH. Incoming Bn. will march to bivouacs in VAUDRICOURT WOOD via MIDLAND BRIDGE thence along Railway.
Companies will draw Box Respirators from E18 d 50.60 to end of march.

4. LEWIS GUNS & STRETCHERS. These will be carried to MIDLAND BRIDGE and dumped on N. side of Canal under charge of Sgt PARK + 1 man per Company. Transport Officer will collect from this point at 1-30 am.

5. STORES. All Bn. + Company stores, cooking utensils, mess kits to be at Bn. dump by 10-30 pm. Police rounds will load on to trucks & push to them at ESSARS.
All petrol tins supplied to those taken over by Companies from HINGE, belonging to H.Q. stores, will be sent to B.H.Q. by 10-30 pm.

6. HANDING OVER LISTS. All trench stores, secret trench maps, etc will be handed over. Handing over lists to be sent to Orderly Room by 4 pm 6th July.

7. REPORTS. "Relief complete" to be sent to B. H.Q. by runner.

8. RESERVE. Action in case of attack. On command "MOVE RESERVES" Bn. will take up defence of Bridgehead line between Right Division Boundary, & junction of this line with Newcastle line about F 2 a, and be disposed as follows:-
A + C on RIGHT. B + D on LEFT.
C Coy will be on Canal line between Rt. Division Bdy + F 3 c 9.2.
A Coy from F 3 c 9.2 to Newcastle line.
B Coy RIGHT SUPPORT about F 8 a
D Coy LEFT SUPPORT about F 8 central
Bn. H.Q. will be in house at LE QUESNOY at F 8. b. 6. 8
All Officers + N.C.Os to reconnoitre positions during afternoon + evening of 6th inst.
Particular attention to be directed to covering approaches to GORRE Bridge with Lewis gun fire.
Sketch maps showing dispositions of platoons with Company H.Q. to be rendered to B.H.Q. on night of 6th inst.

(Sd) D.W. Howard 2/Lt a/Adjt.

10. GENERAL. The Companies of 5th LEICS coming into Brigade Support will be disposed as follows:-

A Coy 5th LEICS takes over from A Coy 4th LEICS.
B " " " " " C " " "
C " " " " " D " " "
D " " " " " B " " "

(Sd) D.W. Howarth 2/Lieut + A/Adjt

Issued to:-
Copy No 1 Adjt for CO
2 3 4 + 5 All Companies
6 Trans. Off. + Q.M.
7. R.S.M.
8 OC 5th Leics
9 138 Inf Bde
10. File

SECRET.

4th Bn. Leicestershire Regiment
Operation Order No. 84
4th July 1918

Copy No. 10

1. RELIEF. The Battalion will be relieved in the ESSARS RIGHT Subsector on the night of 5th/6th July by the 5th Bn. SHERWOOD FORESTERS. Companies will be relieved as follows:-

C Coy 4th Leics will be relieved by A Coy 5th SHERWOODS
B — B
A — C
D — D

2. GUIDES. 1 guide per platoon, + 1 for Bn. H.Q. will meet incoming Bn. at road junction X 27c 20.70 at 10-15 pm.
All guides to be at B.H.Q. by dawn of the 5th, where they will remain during the day, & report to Adjt. W.L. PASS at 9-45 pm.

3. MARCH. The relieved Bn. will march to bivouacs in VAUDRICOURT WOOD, via MIDLAND BRIDGE thence along Railway.
Companies will wear Box Respirators from E18a 50.60 to end of march.

4. LEWIS GUNS & STRETCHERS. These will be carried to MIDLAND BRIDGE and dumped on N. side of Canal under charge of Sgt PARK & 1 Lewis Gunner per Company. Transport Officer will collect from this point at 1-30 am.

5. STORES. All Bn. & Company stores, cooking utensils, mess kit to be at Bn. dump by 10-30 pm. Platoon [illegible] will load on to trucks & push to train at ESSARS.
All patrol [illegible] surplus to those taken over by Companies from H.Q., belonging to H.Q. stores, will be sent to B.H.Q. by 10-30 pm.

6. HANDING OVER LISTS. All trench stores, secret trench maps etc. will be handed over. Handing over lists to be sent to Orderly Room by 4 pm 6th July.

7. REPORTS. "Relief complete" to be sent to B.H.Q. by runner.

8. RESERVE. Action in case of attack. On command "MOVE RESERVES" Bn. will take up defence of Bridgehead line between Right Division Boundary & junction of this line with Newcastle line about F2.a, & will be disposed as follows:-

A + C on RIGHT. B + D on LEFT.
C Coy will be on Canal line between Rt Division Bdy & F3c 9.2.
A Coy from F3c 9.2 to Newcastle Line.
B Coy RIGHT SUPPORT about F8a
D Coy LEFT SUPPORT about F8 central.
Bn. H.Q. will be in House at LE QUESNOY at F8.b.6.8.
All Officers & N.C.Os to reconnoitre positions during afternoon & evening of 6th inst.
Particular attention to be directed to covering approaches to GORRE Bridge with Lewis gun fire.
Sketch maps showing dispositions of platoons with Company H.Q. to be rendered to B.H.Q. on night of 6th inst.

(Sd) G.W. Howarth 2/Lt. A/Adjt.

10. GENERAL. The Companies of 5th LEICS coming into Brigade Support will be disposed as follows:-

A Coy 5th LEICS takes over from A Coy 4th LEICS.
B " " " " " C " "
C " " " " " D " "
D " " " " " B " "

(Sd) D W Stoworth 2/Lieut + A/Adjt

Issued to:-
Copy No 1 Adjt for CO
2 3 4 + 5 All Companies
6 Trans. Off. + Q M.
7. R S M
8 OC 5th Leics
9 138 Inf Bde
10 File

SECRET. 4th Bn Leicestershire Regiment Copy No 10

Operation Order No 84

4th July 1918

1. RELIEF. The Battalion will be relieved in the ESSARS RIGHT Subsector on the night of 5th/6th July by the 5th Bn. SHERWOOD FORESTERS.
Companies will be relieved as follows:-

C Coy 4th LEICS will be relieved by A Coy 5th SHERWOODS
A [illegible] B
B [illegible] C
D [illegible] D

2. GUIDES. 1 guide per platoon, + 1 for Bn. H.Q. will meet incoming Bn. at road junction X 27c 20.70 at 10-15 pm.
All guides to be at B.H.Q. by dawn of the 5th, where they will remain during the day, & report to Adjutant W.L. PASS at 9-45 pm.

3. MARCH. Incoming Bn. will march to [illegible] via VAUDRICOURT WOOD and MIDLAND BRIDGE thence along Railway.
Companies will [illegible] Bn's Respectively from E18 a 50.60 to end of march.

4. LEWIS GUNS & STRETCHERS. These will be carried to MIDLAND BRIDGE and dumped on N. side of Canal under charge of Sgt PARK & 1 Lewis Gunner per Company. Transport Officer will collect from this point at 1-30 am.

5. STORES. All Bn. & Company stores, cooking utensils, mess kit to be at Bn. H.Q. by 10-30 pm. These [illegible] will load on to trucks & push to [illegible] at ESSARS.
All petrol tins & surplus to those taken over by Companies from HOME, belonging to H.Q. stores must be sent to B.H.Q. by 10-30 pm.

6. HANDING OVER LISTS. All trench stores, [illegible] trench maps etc will be handed over. Handing over lists to be sent to Orderly Room by 4 pm 6th July.

7. REPORTS. "Relief complete" to be sent to B. H.Q. by runner.

8. RESERVE. Action in case of attack. On command "MOVE RESERVES" Bn will take up defence of Bridgehead line between Right Division Boundary & junction of this line with Newcastle line about F2.a, and be disposed as follows:-

A + C on RIGHT. B + D on LEFT.
C Coy will be on Canal line between Rt. Division Bdy & F3c 9.2.
A Coy from F3c 9.2 to Newcastle line.
B Coy RIGHT SUPPORT about F8d
D Coy LEFT SUPPORT about F8 central.
Bn. H.Q. will be in House at LE QUESNOY at F8. b.6.8
All Officers & N.C.O.'s to reconnoitre positions during afternoon & evening of 6th inst.
Particular attention to be directed to covering approaches to GORRE Bridge with Lewis gun fire.
Sketch maps showing dispositions of platoons with Company H.Q. to be rendered to B.H.Q. on night of 6th inst.

(Sd) D.W. Howard[illegible] 2/Lt. [illegible]

Issued to —

Copy No. 1. Brigade Comd

2–5 O.C. All Companies

6 T.O. & Q.M.

7 R.S.M.

8 O.C. 5th Bn. [illegible]

9 13th Inf. Bde

10 War Diary

11 File.

S E C R E T. 1/4th Bn. Leicestershire Regiment. Copy No....13.

OPERATION ORDER No. 85

9th July 1918.

Ref. Maps GORRE and VIEILLE CHAPELLE 1/20000

---

1. RELIEF. The Battalion will relieve the 5th South STAFFS. in the LEFT Sub-sector of the GORRE sector tonight, 9th/10th July 1918.
2. DISPOSITIONS.
   A.Coy LEICS. relieves D.Coy STAFFS. on RIGHT front
   D " " " C " " " LEFT front
   C " " " B " " in SUPPORT
   B " " " A " " in RESERVE
   Bn.H.Q. at GORRE BREWERY.
   R.A.P. at LOISNE FARM.
3. GUIDES.Nil.
4. MARCH. Battalion will pass starting point - R.A.P. - at 8.45 pm in following order - A - D - C - B. Platoons at 200 yards.
   Route - VERQUIN - usual route to E.18.d.50,70, thence along RAILWAY and over MIDLAND BRIDGE.
   H.Q.Coy will proceed by train from LA PIERRETTE Siding, E,22c 2.6, and must entrain by 8.45 pm.
5. LEWIS GUNS AND STRETCHERS. Transport Officer will arrange to convey these to MIDLAND BRIDGE, where they will be dumped on N. side of Canal under charge of Cpl.PALMER and one lewis gunner per Company.
6. STORES. Valises and packs will be dumped alongside Drive by 4 pm. Mess kit and cooking utensils will be collected at 8 pm. They will be taken to line by train. Cooks and Police will accompany.H.Q.Stores will be off loaded at SUPPORT Bn. Dump. Company Stores will be pushed by Police up to dump near LOISNE, B.Coy's stores being off loaded where Railway crosses Reserve line.
   Companies will arrange to carry own stores and rations from dump.
7. TAKING OVER LISTS. All trench stores, etc, will be taken over, and lists sent to Orderly Room by 11pm, 10th inst.
8. REPORTS. "Relief Complete" will be sent to Orderly Room by runner.

(sd) D.W.HOWARTH, 2/Lieut & A/Adjt.

Issued to;-
Copy No. 1 Adjt. for C.O.
2,3,4 and 5 All Companies.
6 Transport Officer
7 Quartermaster
8 R.S.M.
9 I.O and M.O.
10 O.C. 5th S.Staffs.
11 H.Q. 138th Inf.Bde
12 File
13 War Diary

SECRET.

1/4 Battn Leicester Regt. Copy No. 10

Operation Order No 86.

12 July 1918

Ref Maps GORRE & VIEILLE CHAPELLE 1/20000

1/. RELIEF The Battalion will be relieved in the GORRE LEFT Subsector on the night 13/14th July by the 5th LINCOLNSHIRE Regt. Relief will commence about 10-15 pm.

Incoming Bn will be disposed as follows:-

A Coy LINCOLNS relieve	A Coy LEICESTERS	on Right.
B ..	D ..	LEFT.
C	C	in Support
D	B	in RESERVE.

2/. GUIDES Runners from B.H.Q. will report at each Company H.Q tonight to take 1 guide per platoon & 1 per Company H.Q. to H.Q of relieving Company of LINCOLNS. These guides will guide LINCOLN Companies in, & on completion of relief will guide own Companies to SUPPORT positions. Rations should be taken

3/. MOVE. On relief the Bn will move into Brigade Support & will be disposed as follows:-

A Company will take over from A Coy LINCOLNS		about F 3a 40.40.
D	B	in LE QUESNAY
C	C	about F 4c 4 0.
B ..	D	in LIVERPOOL TRENCH

4/. ADVANCE PARTIES 1 NCO per company will accompany guides as above to relieving Company H.Q. to take over stores.

5/. WORKING PARTIES. Companies will find working parties whilst in Support as found by the Companies relieving them. Details of these parties should be carefully taken over from relieving Companies

6/. STORES. Companies will make own arrangements to carry down stores cooking utensils etc.

7/ RATIONS Companies will send carrying parties to Bn Dump near Support B.H.Q. for rations

8/. LISTS Lists of stores taken over & handed over to reach Orderly Room by 10 pm 14th July.

9/ REPORTS "Relief Complete" will be sent to B.H.Q. by runner

(Sd) D.W. Haworth 2/Lt & A/Adjt.

Issued to:-

Copy No 1. Adjt for CO
2 3 4 & 5 All Companies.
6 Trans Off & Q.M.
7 R.S.M.
8 O.C. 5th Lincolns
9 138 Inf Bde
10 War Diary
11. File.

[illegible] Regt [illegible] 11

[illegible]

17 July 1918

Ref. [illegible] CHAPELLE [illegible]

1. RELIEF. The Battalion will relieve the 5 LEICESTERS in [illegible] RIGHT subsector the night 17/18 July

2. DISPOSITIONS.

C Coy 4 Leicesters relieves A Coy 5 Leicesters in		RIGHT
B	D	LEFT
D	C	SUPPORT
A	B	RESERVE

After 11 pm B.H.Q will be about F[illegible] 80.
RAP at [illegible].

3. GUIDES. Guides at the rate of one per platoon will arrive at respective Coy H.Q. before dawn today and will remain with Coys during day and guide platoons up at night.

4. MOVE. Companies will move at following times

B + C Coys at 10.20 pm.
A + D at 10.30 pm.

5. STORES. Companies will arrange to carry own [illegible] cooking utensils etc to line.

6. RATIONS. Rations for Coys will come up on limbers to Reserve Coy H.Q. about F 8c 15.95. Companies will each send 1 man to B.H.Q. by 10 pm who will meet limbers, accompany them to dump & then act as guard over rations. Coys will each send guide to Reserve Coy H.Q who will guide ration carrying parties. Ration carrying parties will be found by Reserve Coy (A) as soon after completion of relief as possible each night.

7. WATER. Water and tea will be carried for front companies by Reserve Coy. [illegible] tea will be carried from Reserve Coy cookhouse at [illegible] a.m. forward coys having first attention. Support Coy will carry own water & [illegible]

8. LISTS. All trench stores etc will be taken over. 5th Leicesters will send 1 NCO to each Coy before dawn of 17th to take over stores of support positions. Handing & taking over lists to be at B.H.Q. by dawn of the 18th.

9. REPORTS. Relief Complete will be sent to B.H.Q. by runner.

Issued to:

(Sd) [illegible] Capt & A/Adjt

Copy No 1 Adjt for C.O.
2-5 [illegible] Coys
6 [illegible]
7 R.S.M.
8. [illegible]
9 [illegible] Inf Bde
10 File
11 War Diary.

SECRET.

1/4TH. Bn. Leicestershire Regiment
Operation Order No. 88
20th July 1918

Copy No. 11

Ref Maps. GORRE + VIEILLE CHAPELLE 1/20000

1. RELIEF. The Bn. will be relieved in the GORRE RIGHT Subsector by the 6th SOUTH STAFFORDS on the night 21st/22nd July 1918. Relief will commence about 12.15 am.
The incoming Bn will be disposed as follows:-

A. Coy	STAFFS. will relieve	C. Coy. LEICS	on the	RIGHT.
D "	" " "	B "	" "	LEFT.
B "	" " "	D "	" in	SUPPORT
C "	" " "	A "	" "	RESERVE

2. GUIDES. 1 guide per platoon, 1 for Coy. H.Q, + 2 for B.H.Q will meet incoming unit as follows:-
Guides for C. Coy. STAFFS at F3.b.40.40 (entrance to GORRE CHATEAU) at 11-45 pm.
Guides for A.B + D Coys + B.H.Q of STAFFS at N. side of MIDLAND BRIDGE at 11-45 pm.
All guides should be furnished with a chit showing their Company + No. of Platoon, + the Company they are to guide.
Company Commanders will arrange for guides to reconnoitre routes before dawn.

3. ADVANCE PARTIES. A small advance party will arrive at Company + B.H.Q. about 10 pm on the 21st.

4. MARCH. On relief Bn. will move to bivouacs in VAUDRICOURT WOOD. Details of route, etc, will be notified separately later.

5. LEWIS GUNS. Arrangements will be notified later.

6. STORES. Arrangements for conveyance of cooking utensils, mess Kit, etc, will be notified later.

7. WORK. Details of work in progress, priority, etc, will be carefully handed over.
All H.Q's, Trenches, etc, will be handed over in a scrupulously clean condition, + certificates to this effect will be forwarded to B.H.Q by runner bringing "Relief complete"

8. LISTS. Lists of Stores, Maps, etc handed over will be sent to Orderly Room by 4 pm, 22nd inst.

9. REPORTS. "Relief complete" will be sent to B.H.Q. by runner.

(Sd) DW Howarth, Capt + A/Adjt.

Issued to:-
Copy No 1 Adjt for CO.
2 3, 4 5 All Companies
6 Trans. Off. + Q.M.
7. R.S.M.
8 O.C. 6th S Staffs
9 138 Inf Bde.
10 File
11 War Diary

SECRET. 1/4th Leicestershire Regiment Copy No 11

21st July 1918

To all recipients of Op. Order No 88.

1. MARCH. It is hoped to be able to arrange for trains to convey the Bn. to VAUDRICOURT. If this cannot be arranged Companies will be wired "NO ROADS"
If trains are available, detailed instructions will be sent after dark.

2. STORES. Cooking Utensils & mess Kit must be at Reserve Coy Dump at 10 pm. If O's/C. B, C & D. Coys think light will not permit of this, as much as possible should be sent to Reserve Coy. Dump by dawn today, & remainder carried out.
Stores will be loaded on two T.M. handcarts at Reserve Coy Dump, (Capt. SILVER being responsible,) & pushed to Light Railway at SUPPORT Bn. Dump. All stores must arrive at SUPPORT Bn. Dump by 10.40 pm.
Police & Cooks will accompany stores from SUPPORT Bn. Dump.

3. LEWIS GUNS & STRETCHERS. These will be carried to GORRE Brewery & dumped alongside the wall by the Bathing place under charge of Cpl PALMER & one Lewis Gunner per Company. Transport Officer will arrange to convey from this point at 2.30 am.
Companies will be notified if any change is made in this arrangement by reason of trains being available.

(Sd) D W Howarth, Capt & a/a.

While the Bn is in Divisional Reserve the following positions are selected for Companies in the event of order "Move Reserves" being issued.

A Coy. under cover in rear of that portion of the BEUVRY – ANNEQUIN line included in the squares F14b and F8d with one platoon in the trench itself, & to get in touch with the Right Flank Bn.

B Coy. under cover in rear of the BEUVRY – ANNEQUIN line included in the square F8c with one platoon pushed forward into the trench itself to make liaison with A Coy and the Flank Bn in DOCK [illegible] ~~=~~ the latter by patrols.

C and D Companies in Bn Reserve in the BETHUNE locality North of the main BETHUNE – BEUVRY Road as per sketch map attached.

Company Commanders will arrange for all Officers and N.C.Os of their Companies who have not already reconnoitred these areas to do so during the afternoon & evening of the 22nd inst.

Bn H.Q. will be in the Quarry at F8d 15.05 and Companies will send two runners each to report to above H.Q.

Quartermaster & Transport Officer will report to Bn H.Q. before the Bn leaves VAUDRICOURT WOOD if it has moved, then to the above new position in the Quarry.

Companies will report by 10pm on the 22nd whether they have or have not reconnoitred the reorganised their position as per above orders.

A and B Coys will first move their troops into the fighting position in the trenches, afterwards withdrawing three platoons to billets.

C and D Coys will first billet their troops then take their Officers + NCOs once again over the trenches allotted to them in the attached sketch.

J M Foster Lt Col
21-7-18 Comdg 9th Leicestershire Regt.

Copies to All Companies
Transport Officer
Quartermaster
110 Inf Bde
War Diary
File.

SECRET. **1/4th Lancashire Regt.** Copy No. 11.

To recipients of Op. Order No 88.

TRAIN ARRANGEMENTS

Two trains each capable of holding 175 men will be at KANTARA Siding at 1 am on 22nd. These trains will be filled as relieved personnel arrive, & as soon as each train is filled it will proceed to HAIRPIN Siding at F19a/2 & troops will there detrain. The two trains will then return to MUSHROOM Siding, F13a 8.0 arriving about 2am, & again fill with troops.

After the first two trains have left KANTARA relieved troops should proceed to MUSHROOM Siding & entrain. The trains will carry them to SPRINGWELL SPUR where troops will detrain. Trains will then return to MUSHROOM Siding & take remaining troops.

LEWIS GUNS. Arrangements notified last night for dumping guns at BREWERY will stand.

21-7-18. Lt. J C [illegible] Capt. A/Adjt

S E C R E T. 1/4th Bn. LEICESTERSHIRE REGIMENT. Copy No.....13

O P E R A T I O N   O R D E R No 89

27th July 1918.

Ref. Maps GORRE 1/20000 and LOCON 1/10000.

---

1. RELIEF. The Battalion will relieve the 6th SOUTH STAFFS. in the RIGHT Subsector of the GORRE Sector tonight, 27th/28th July 1918.

2. DISPOSITIONS.
A.Coy LEICS relieves C.Coy SOUTH STAFFS on RIGHT front.
D.Coy " " B Coy " " on LEFT front
B Coy " " D Coy " " in SUPPORT
C.Coy " " A.Coy " " in RESERVE.
Bn. H.Q. at F.10.a.45.85
R.A.P at GORRE BREWERY

3. GUIDES. 1 per platoon will be at GORRE BRIDGE at 9.30 pm. The Canal will not be crossed before 9.30 pm.

4. MARCH. B. and C. Companies and H.Q.Details in that order, will pass starting point, R.A.P., at 7.30 pm. Platoons at 200 yards.
Route - VERQUIN - usual route to E.18.d.30.70, thence along Railway and over GORRE BRIDGE.
A. and D. Companies will proceed by train from LA PIERRETTE, E.21.d.9.5
Three trains will leave siding at 9.0 pm. Half A.Coy will entrain on second train from MUSHROOM SPUR. Rest of A.Coy and D. Coy on third train for KANTARA.

5. TAKING OVER LISTS. All trench stores, etc , will be taken over and lists sent to Orderly Room by 10 pm on 28th inst.

6. LEWIS GUNS AND STRETCHERS. Transport Officer will arrange to convey these to wall of GORRE BREWERY adjoining Canal, where they will be dumped under charge of Sergt. PARK and one lewis gunner per Company.

7. STORES. Valises and packs will be dumped alongside drive by 4 pm. They will be collected by 7.45 pm. Mess kit and cooking utensils will be collected by 7.45 pm. They will be taken to line by train. Cooks and Police will accompany. All train stores will be off loaded at F.3.●.35.30 and conveyed thence by limber to Reserve Company dump. Ration arrangements as formerly in this sector. Reserve Company will provide carrying parties for forward Companies.

8. CAMP. To be ready for inspection 30 minutes before the first Company moves off. Lines and bivouacs to be left scrupulously clean.

9. REPORTS. Relief complete to be reported to Orderly Room by fullerphone (code words "Ref.A.K.7 Two required") and confirmed by two runners.

(Sd) J.C.LEDWARD, Capt. & A/Adjt.

Issued to :-
Copy No. 1 Adjt. for C.O.
2,3,4,5, All Companies
6 Transport Officer
7 Q.M.
8 R.S.M.
9 I.O. and M.O.
10 O.C. 6th S.Staffs.
11 H.Q. 138th Inf.Bde.
12 File
13 War Diary

SECRET

1/4th Bn. Leicestershire Regiment

Operation Order No. 90

30th July 1915.

Copy No. 9.

1. RELIEF. There will be an inter-company relief in the RIGHT Sub-sector of the GORRE sector tomorrow night 31st July/1st Aug 1915. Relief will commence about 10 pm.

2. DISPOSITIONS

C. Coy	will relieve	A. Coy	on	RIGHT front
B	" "	D	"	LEFT "
D	" "	B	in	SUPPORT
A	" "	C	"	RESERVE

3. GUIDES. to be arranged between Companies.

4. TAKING and HANDING OVER LISTS. All trench stores etc will be taken over & both taking over & handing over lists will be sent to Orderly Room before dawn, Aug 1st.

5. WORK. Work in hand to be properly explained & understood by relieving Company & platoon Commanders, & work is to be carried on immediately relief is complete.

6. STORES. Mess kit & cooking utensils will be moved under Company arrangements.

7. REPORTS. Relief complete to be reported to Orderly Room by runner.

(Sd) J.C. Ledward. Capt & Adjt.

Issued to:-

Copy No. 1 Adjt for C.O.
2, 3, 4, 5 All Companies
6 Q.M. & T.O.
7 R.S.M.
8 File
9 War Diary.

Instructions regarding War Diaries and Intelligence Summaries are contained in F. S. Regs., Part II. and the Staff Manual respectively. Title pages will be prepared in manuscript.

WAR DIARY
or
~~INTELLIGENCE SUMMARY.~~

(Erase heading not required.)

Army Form C. 2118.

D103. 4 Leicester Regt. VR 42

Place	Date	Hour	Summary of Events and Information	Remarks and references to Appendices
TRENCHES	1st	Aug	Usual artillery and machine gun activity. Patrols out by day and night.	
"	2nd	"	A very wet day. Snipers were out but rain and mist made observation difficult.	
"	3rd	"	Harassing fire in vicinity of canal and B.H.Q. during the day.	
"	4th	"	Operation Orders issued for relief of Bn. by 1/5 LEICESTERS. on night 4/5th Aug. Relief complete at 11-30 pm. Bn in BRIGADE SUPPORT. (LEQUESNOY)	0.0.91
"	5th	"	Salvage parties worked during the day. Working parties supplied at night for forward Bns. Shelling by 4.2 around B.H.Q.	
"	6th 7th 8th	"	Companies improve their battle positions by day. Salvage parties busy in LA QUESNOY. Parties supplied for the R.E.S. also carrying parties. At night working parties supplied to front line Battalions. Operation issued 8th for relief of Bn by 8th SHERWOOD FORESTERS. Bn relieved night of 8th/9th.	0.0.92.
VAUDRICOURT	9th	"	Bn at rest cleaning up. Medical and armourer's inspections	
"	10th	"	Commanding Officer goes to GRANTHAM. Major GRA BECKET MC. commands Bn. Bathing parade and C.O's inspection of Bn.	
"	11th	"	Church parade. Camp inspected by C.O.	
"	12th	"	Battalion on working party. Corps Sports.	
"	13th	"	During the morning Bn occupied on the range and training ground at HESDIGNEUL. Preliminary rounds of Bde Boxing competition fought during afternoon.	
"	14th	"	Operation Orders issued for relief of 5th SHERWOOD FORESTERS. by the Bn. in BDE SUPPORT GORRE Sector on night 14th/15th August.	0.0.93.
TRENCHES	15th	"	Bn provide working parties for R.E.s. during the day and for forward Battns at night. Left forward Coy (B) & B.H.Q. shelled during morning.	

D. D & L., London, E.C. (A8c04) Wt W.771/M2031 750,000 5/17 Sch. 52 Forms/C2118/14

Instructions regarding War Diaries and Intelligence Summaries are contained in F. S. Regs., Part II. and the Staff Manual respectively. Title pages will be prepared in manuscript.

WAR DIARY
or
~~INTELLIGENCE SUMMARY.~~
(Erase heading not required.)

Army Form C. 2118.

Place	Date	Hour	Summary of Events and Information	Remarks and references to Appendices
TRENCHES.	16th	Aug	Bn in Brigade Support.	
"	17th	"	Usual working and carrying parties provided. Salvage work carried on.	
"	18th	"	Night of 18th/19th Bn relieved 1/5th Leicesters in GORRE RIGHT Subsector.	
"	19th	"	Active patrolling throughout day & night. Touch maintained with enemy.	
"	20th	"	Enemy commence to retire on left Bn front. Companies in line moved forward and established liason posts with the Division on our Right.	
"	21st	"	By 4am Bn occupy line running from Route B along Western side Rue de L'Epinette where we were in touch with Division on Right. Bn took over Brigade outpost line and two companies relieved 1/5 Leicesters in front line outposts. B.H.Q. were moved forward to Loisne Chateau.	
"	22	"	Left flank of Battn pushed forward N.W of LE TOURET where liason was established with Staffords. During the day and throughout the night left flank positions were improved N of RUE DE BOIS.	
"	23	"	Right flank pushed forward and by night had established positions E of RUE DE L'EPINETTE and N of Route B. The outpost line held by the Bn now ran from NW LE TOURET. N of RUE DE BOIS to ROUTE B then South along Eastern side of RUE DE L'EPINETTE. Liason established with 55th Division SW RUE DE LEPINETTE. Night of 23rd/24th Bn relieved by 1/5 Leicesters.	
"	24	"	Bn in Support. Day was quiet.	
"	25	"	" "	
"	26	"	Relieved by 8th Sherwood Foresters. 1/2 Batt. & B.HQ to Fouquières. 1/2 Batt under Major Beckett to Newcastle Line on Divisional left.	
	27	"	Batt. training.	
	28	"	" "	
	29	"	" "	
	30	"		
	31	"	" "	

[illegible] Lt Col
4th Leicesters.

SECRET

1/4 Bn Leicestershire Regiment.
Operation Order No 91.
3rd August 1918.

Copy No. 12.

Ref Maps. GORRE 1/20,000 & LOCON 1/10,000

1. RELIEF The Battalion will be relieved by the 1/5 LEICESTERS in the RIGHT Subsector of the GORRE sector tomorrow night 4/5 Aug 1918.

2. DISPOSITIONS

C Coy 4th Leics will be relieved by A Coy 5th LEICS on RIGHT front.
B .. .. D .. .. .. LEFT ..
D .. .. C .. .. in SUPPORT
A .. .. B .. .. .. RESERVE.

$. On completion of relief Companies will move to positions held when last in Support.

C Coy to WOOD SWITCH
B .. .. LIVERPOOL LINE
A .. .. GORRE FARM. F3d 58.62.
D .. .. LE QUESNOY.

B.H.Q. at F3c 25.20.
R.A.P. at F9a 32.76.

3. GUIDES No guides will be required, but relief will commence about 9-30 pm.

4. TAKING OVER Companies will send one officer per Company & one N.C.O. per platoon for taking over. Personnel from B and C Coys will leave trenches at dawn. All will take rations with them & report direct to the Company in the position they are taking over.
Intelligence Officer & R.S.M. will take over for B.H.Q.
All lists of stores taken over, & handed over, & billet receipts will reach these H.Q. by 9am Aug 5th.

5. STORES. Mess Kit, cooking utensils etc will be moved under Company arrangements.

6. TRENCHES and BILLETS. will be handed over to incoming Bn in a scrupulously clean & tidy condition.
Companies will satisfy themselves that the trenches & billets they take over are in the same condition & any complaints must be made or received at the time of taking over.
Clean billets etc receipts will be given and taken.

7 RATIONS & WATER. Arrangements as before.
The pump at GORRE FARM is not to be used. 30 water tins are available & will be handed over by B Coy 5th Leics to A Coy 4th Leics.

8. REPORTS. Relief complete to be reported to B.H.Q. by runners.

(Sd) J.C. Ledward. Capt & A/Adjt.

Issued to
Copy No 1. Adjt for C.O.
2.3.4 & 5. All Companies.
6 Quartermaster & Trans Off.
7. R.S.M.
8 I.O. & M.O.
9. O.C. 1/5 Leicesters
10 HQ 138 Inf Bde
11 File
12 War Diary.

SECRET. 1/4 Bn Leicestershire Regt. Copy No. 12

Operation Order No 92.

8 August 1918

Ref Maps GORRE 1/10000 and LOCON 1/10000

1. RELIEF. The Bn will be relieved by the 1/ NORTH STAFFS Regt in SUPPORT in the GORRE Sector [illegible] 8th/9th August 1918.

2. DISPOSITIONS

C Coy 4 LEICS will be relieved by	C Coy NORTH STAFFS in	RIGHT FRONT
B	A	LEFT
A	B	SUPPORT
D	D	RESERVE

3. GUIDES. No guides will be required, but the relief is expected to commence about midnight.

4. MARCH. On completion of relief, Coys will proceed to their usual billets in VAUDRICOURT PARK. Platoons to move at 200 yds interval. Route under Company arrangements.

5. TRAIN. One detachment exceeding 50 men proceed to HARTARA CAMP at 11 pm and then entrain for HAIRPIN SIDING. [illegible] will take charge of the party.

6. LISTS. All [illegible] trench maps, defence schemes, trench stores etc will be handed over. For the present [illegible] will be regarded as trench stores & handed over as such. Handing over lists & billet receipts etc to reach Orderly Room by 12 noon [illegible].

7. Lewis Guns & Stretchers. will be dumped on the E side of the road opposite old B.H.Q. under charge of Cpl PALMER and one Lewis Gunner per Company by 2am. Transport Officer will arrange for limbers to collect.

8. STORES. [illegible] stores & cooking utensils will be brought down to Bn Salvage Dump (where Light Railway [illegible] in LE QUESNOY) by 9 pm. Police & Cooks will accompany.

9. BILLETS etc. All trenches, posts, billets and Headquarters will be handed over in a scrupulously clean condition. O.C. Coys will obtain certificates to this effect from incoming Bn.

10. RESERVE. When in Divisional Reserve at VAUDRICOURT PARK the Bn will be held ready to move at 4 hours notice (from 8am – 8 pm) & 1 hours notice (from 8 pm – 8 am). Upon the order "MOVE RESERVES" being received the Bn will move to position B as previously reconnoitred. All Officers & Platoon Commanders who have not already done so will reconnoitre this position at the earliest possible moment. O.C. Coys can obtain copy of special orders from Orderly Room on application.

11. REPORTS. "Relief Complete" to be reported by runner and ALL IN BILLETS as soon as possible after reaching VAUDRICOURT PARK.

[illegible]

Issued to:

Copy No 1 [illegible] C.O.

2–5 All Companies

6 Transport Offr [illegible]

7 R.S.M.

8 I.O. [illegible]

9 G.S. 46th N. Staffs

10 138 Inf Bde

11 File

12 War Diary

SECRET.

AFTER Order 1
Operation Order No 92

Message received that [illegible] will relieve [illegible] tonight instead of [illegible].

Operation order No 92 will be followed except as regards dispositions and unit relieving.

Further details later.

(Sd) [illegible]
Capt & Adjt.

SECRET.

Additions and Corrections
TO
Operation Order No. 92
8 August 1918

Copy No. 12

PARA 1. For "1/6 NORTH STAFFS." substitute "8th SHERWOOD FORESTERS"

PARA 2. Dispositions will now read.

C Coy 4 Lincs will be relieved by C Coy 8th Sherwoods.
B .. .. .. A ..
A .. .. .. B ..
D .. .. .. D

Relief to commence about 10 pm.

PARA 3. Substitute the following:-

"Guides 1 per platoon, 1 for C.H.Q. & 1 for B.H.Q. will meet incoming Bn. at junction of railway tracks about F.1.d.40.03. at 9.15 pm"

PARA 5. Instructions notified later.

PARA 7. For "2 AM" read "11-30 pm"

(Sd) J.C. Tedward Capt 1/a/Adjt

Issued to all recipients of O.O. 92.

S E C R E T. 1/4th Bn. Leicestershire Regiment. Copy No. 13

O P E R A T I O N O R D E R No. 96

14th August 1918.

Ref: Maps GORRE and VIEILLE CHAPELLE.

1. RELIEF. The Battalion will relieve the 5th SHERWOOD FORESTERS in SUPPORT in the GORRE Sector on the night 14th/15th August 1918.
2. DISPOSITIONS.
A.Coy 4th LEICS. relieves A.Coy 5th SHERWOODS in GORRE FARM.
B. " " " " C. " " " " LIVERPOOL LINE
C. " " " " B " " " " WOOD SWITCH
D " " " " D " " " " LE QUESNOY
3. GUIDES. NIL.
4. ADVANCE PARTIES. Sgt. A PARKER D.C.M. and 2 Signallers for H.Q., and 1 N.CO. and 1 Signaller per Company will proceed to line at 6 pm as advance parties to take over stores, etc.
5. MARCH. Battalion will pass starting point, R.A.P., at 7.25 pm in following order:- B, C, A, D, H.Q. Platoons at 200 yards.
Route - VERQUINe Cross Roads, BEUVRY F.14.c.45.50 - Road Junction F.14.c.82.30, thence as follows :-
D.Coy to LE QUESNOY.
A, B, and C.Coys - F.14.b.78.85 - STAFFORD BRIDGE - F.3.d.50.05
6. LEWIS GUNS. Transport Officer will arrange to convey lewis guns as follows:-
D.Coy to F.8.b.90.45. Limber to leave with first platoon of Company.
A, B, and C.Coys to F.9.b.20.85 (Road le ading to Bridge).
These guns will be dumped here in charge of Cpl. PALMER and one lewis gunner per A, B, and C Coys by 8.45 pm.
7. STORES. Officers valises and men's packs will be collected at 5.30 pm. Stores, officers personal kit, cooking utensils and mess kit for the line will be collected at 7 pm. Police a nd Cooks will accompany these stores.
Stores not for the line will be collected at 7.30 pm.
8. TAKING OVER LISTS. All trench stores, e tc, will be taken over. List duly signed to be sent to Orderly Room by 9 am, 15th inst.
9. REPORTS. "Relief complete" will be sent to Orderly Room by Runner and by Fullerphone, using code, "Ref. your G.S.72 (NO.) required".
10. GENERAL. The Camp will be thoroughly clean and ready for inspection by 7 pm.

(Sd) D.W.HOWARTH, Capt. & Adjt.

Issued to :-
Copy No. 1 Adjt. for C.O.
2,3,4,5 All Companies
6 Transport Officer
7 Quartermaster
8 R.S.M.
9 I.O. and M.O.
10 O.C. 5th Sherwoods
11 H.Q., 138th Inf. Bde
12 File
13 War Diary.

SECRET.

1/4th Bn. Leicestershire Regiment.
Operation Order No. 94
18th August 1918

Copy No. 12.

Ref. Maps GORRE and VIEILLE CHAPELLE 1/20,000

1. RELIEF. The Battalion will relieve the 5th LEICESTERS in GORRE RIGHT Subsector on the night 18th/19th Aug 1918.

2. DISPOSITIONS.

A Coy. 4th LEICS relieves B Coy. 5th LEICS. on RIGHT
D " " " C " " " LEFT.
B " " " D " " " in SUPPORT.
C " " " A " " " RESERVE.

3. GUIDES. Nil.

4. MOVE. Companies will move at following times:-

A. & D Coys at 8.45 pm.
B & C " 9.15 pm.
Platoons to move at 2 minute intervals.
B.H.Q. will move at 9-30 pm.

5. ADVANCE PARTIES. 1 N.C.O. and 1 Signaller per Company will move as advance parties to take over stores ½ hour before above times.

6. STORES. Companies will make own arrangements for carrying stores, and for carrying utensils to Cook House at Reserve Company.

7. RATIONS. For Companies, will come up by limber to Reserve Company H.Q. Each Company will have 2 men at Reserve Coy. Dump at 8.30 pm to take over rations from limbers. They will stand by rations until carrying parties arrive for them.

Support & Reserve Companies will carry own rations.

Reserve Company will detail 1 section per Company, to carry rations to each of two forward Companies.

B.H.Q. rations will come up by Mess Cart to point on Road along S. side of Canal opposite CORK BRIDGE.

2 Police will be at this point at 8.30 pm to take over rations.

8. WATER. Will be carried to two forward Companies by Reserve Coy. Returning ration parties should bring back empty petrol tins, & take them back filled.

9. TAKING OVER LISTS. Copies of taking over, & handing over lists to reach Orderly Room by 10 pm, 19th Aug.

10. WORK. All details of work should be very carefully taken over.

11. REPORTS. "Relief Complete" will be fullerphoned by the code words "D1. received, (state number) required," & confirmed by runner.

(Sd) D.W. Howarth, Capt. & Adjt.

Issued to:- Copy No 1. Adjt for C.O.
2, 3, 4, 5 All Companies.
6 Q.M. & T.O.
7 R.S.M.
8. S.O. & M.O.
9 O.C. 5th Leics.
10. H.Q. 138 Inf Bde
11 File
12 War Diary.

SECRET

1/4 Bn Leicestershire Regt.
Operation Orders No 95
23 August 1918.

Copy No. 12

Ref maps GORRE & VIEILLE CHAPELLE 1/20000

1 **RELIEF.** The Battn will be relieved in Brigade Outpost Line tonight 23rd/24th inst by the 5th Leicesters.

2. **DISPOSITIONS.**

A Coy 5th Leicesters relieves C Coy 4th Leicesters on RIGHT.
D " " " " B " " " LEFT
B " " " " A " " " in RIGHT SUPPORT
C " " " " D " " " " LEFT SUPPORT.

3. **GUIDES.** 1 guide for Company HQ. and 1 per platoon will meet incoming companies as follows:-
Guides from A & C Coys for A and B Coys 5 Leics at A Coy HQ. at 10-30 P.M.
" " B & D " " D and C " " " Bn HQ. at 10.30 pm
B Company of the 5th relieving A Company has only 3 platoons.

4 **MOVE.** On relief Bn will move into Brigade Support RIGHT. and be disposed as follows:-
A Coy in TUNING FORK LINE (old Support Coy position recently held by B Coy) (position held by B Coy when in old Brigade Support
B " " WOOD SWITCH.
C " " old position in RESERVE LINE.
D " " LIVERPOOL LINE. (position held by B Coy when in old Brigade Support)
B.H.Q. on Canal Bank (old position)
ADVANCE PARTIES Coy Cdrs to use own discretion as to sending of small advance parties during the afternoon to take over accomodation and guide coys in after relief. One N.C.O. per coy will be left behind by 5th Leicesters to hand over stores. O.C B & C Coys will report personally at present B.H.Q. LOISNE CHATEAU on relief.

5. **HANDING OVER LISTS.** All trench stores etc. will be handed over and signed handing over lists sent to O.R. by 12 noon 24th inst.

6. **STORES COOKS UTENSILS etc.** Coys will carry own stores.
The cook N.C.O. will arrange for coy cooking utensils to be taken to Coy cookhouses. R.S.M. will arrange for conveyance of H.Q stores to B.H.Q.

7. **RATIONS** will come up by limbers. 6 H.Q. Scouts will report to Adjt at 9 pm to receive instructions for guiding limbers & standing by rations until coys can send for them.
Rations for B & D Coys will be dumped at F4a 55.25.
" " A Coy " " " " F5a 10.65. (Road junction)
" " C " " " " Coy H.Q.
Coys will send parties for rations as soon after arrival in Support positions as possible.

8. **WATER TINS.** Coys should send down as many empty water tins as possible to H.Q. for B & D & old Reserve Coy cookhouse for A & C Coys before 7-30pm.

REPORTS. "Relief Complete" to be Fullerphoned by code words "water required" and confirmed by runner.
B.H.Q. to be notified as soon as Coys are in Support positions

Sd [illegible] Capt & Adjt.

Issued to:-
No 1. Adjt for C.O.
2.3.4.5. All Coys
6. QM & T.O.
7. R S M
8 M.O.
9 S. Lewis
10 138 Inf Bde
11 War Diary
12 File

1:20,000
NOTE CHANGE OF COLOUR.
Enemy Trenches in Blue.
American Corps
A
B
C
138 Inf Brigade
Staffords
29.9.18

SECRET

1/4 Battn Leicestershire Regt.
Operation Order No 96.
25 August 1918.

Copy No. 14

Ref Maps GORRE + VIEILLE CHAPELLE 1/20,000

1. RELIEF. The Bn will be relieved in GORRE RIGHT SUPPORT on the night 26th/27th August by the 8th SHERWOOD FORRESTERS.
Dispositions of incoming Bn will be as follows:-

C Coy SHERWOODS relieves A Coy LEICESTERS in TUNING FORK LINE.
B " " " C " " RESERVE LINE
A " " " B " " WOOD SWITCH.
D " " " D " " LIVERPOOL LINE.

2. GUIDES 1 per platoon + 1 per Coy H.Q. will meet incoming Bn at GORRE BRIDGE at 9 pm. 2/Lt A.F. CASTLE will be in charge of guides.

3 HANDING OVER LISTS. All trench stores, trench maps etc, will be carefully handed over and signed copies of handing over lists sent to Bn H.Q. by 12 noon 27th.

4. CLEANLINESS Company Commanders will ensure that all trenches, billets, Cookhouses Headquarters etc are handed over scrupulously clean.
A certificate to this effect signed by the Officer taking over will be sent to Orderly Room by the runner bringing the "Relief Complete".

5. REPORTS. "Relief Complete" to be sent to H.Q. by runner.

6. MOVE. On relief the Bn will move into Divisional Reserve, and will be disposed as follows:-
Bn H.Q. and B and D Coys in FOUQUIERES with Bn H.Q. at old Corps Rest Stn.
A + C Coys will move to NEWCASTLE LINE and come under G.O.C. Supp Brigade. A Coy in NEWCASTLE LINE — C Coy in NEWCASTLE LINE SUPPORT.
Major G.R.A. Baker D.S.O. will be in command of A and C Coys with H.Q. at X 25c.9.9.

7. ADVANCE PARTIES 2/Lt W.G. BASS. 1 Scout and 1 signaller for Bn H.Q. and one officer per coy with 1 N.C.O. and 1 guide per platoon will proceed as advance parties at 2 pm on the 26th as follows:-
(a) Bn H.Q. B + D Coys to report at Bn H.Q. FOUQUIERES.
This party will take over accommodation and will meet platoons on LA PIERRETTE siding about E 22c.10.50. at 11.15 pm.
2/Lt BASS will, if possible, arrange for a H.Q. Bn mess.
(b) A and C Coys to report at ½ Bn H.Q. ESSARS X 25c 9.9 where they will be provided with guides by 8th SHERWOOD FORESTERS, and proceed to take over stores + details of accommodation. They will then return to own companies, + guide own platoons after relief.

8 ROUTES. (a) A + C Coys will take own routes to Newcastle Line
(b) 4 trains will be at KANTARA SIDING from 10 pm. These will be used by Bn H.Q. and B + D Coys. Trains will move off as filled and troops will be detrained at LA PIERRETTE siding where guides will meet.

9. LEWIS GUNS. A + C Coys will each send Lewis Gun N.C.O. with their advance party to reconnoitre road for gun limbers from present position to new positions.
Lewis Guns and magazines will be collected as follows:-
A Coy to dump guns under L.G. N.C.O. at F 5a 05 50.
They will be collected by limbers at 11 pm. L.G. N.C.O. will guide limbers to new position of Company.

P.T.O.

9. LEWIS GUNS (Contd) C Coy will dump guns at their Company H.Q. Limber will collect at 11 pm and be guided by Sgt & S.O. to the Coys new position.

B and D Coys will dump guns under Cpl PALMER at F3c 60,50. along Railway wall. Limber will collect at 11 pm.

10 RATIONS A & C Coys will each send 1 runner to Bn H.Q. by 9 a.m. Runners will accompany Major BECKETT. MC. to reconnoitre ration dumps. These runners will meet ration limber at 9 pm at E6a 30,85. and guide to dumps. Storeman will remain with rations until companies send for them. A & C Coys will be given position of dumps later.

11 STORES Mess kit of A [illegible] Coys and cooking utensils will be collected from Coy H.Q. by limber at 9 pm & conveyed to 1/2 Bn H.Q. ESSARD. X25c 7.9. Cooks will accompany.

Mess kit and personal kit of Major Beckett M.C. will be dumped at F4a 55,25. by 9 pm & collected by above limber on passing. Mess kit and stores of Bn H.Q. B and D Coys to be on KANTARA Siding by 8-30 pm. Provost Sergt and Police will take charge and accompany stores out of line on returning ration train.

12. DIVISIONAL RESERVE Bn will come into Div Reserve after relief & be at 6 hours notice (from 8am to 8pm) and 2 hours notice (from 8 pm to 8 am)

On Order "move Reserves" Bn (less the 2 Coys in [illegible] Line who remain under G.O.C. (Left Brigade.) will take up position B. being disposed as follows:-

Bn H.Q. in Quarry. F8.d00.20.

B (or C during last 3 days) in Reserve along line F15a 0.0- F15a 15.75 to F8d 10.50. Company H.Q. F15a 10.80.

D (or A during last 3 days in Reserve) along line F8c 10.50.- F8c 50-20. to F7d 85.30 Company H.Q. in trench about F8c 80.40 Any Officer or N.C.O.s who have not reconnoitred these positions will do so during morning of 26th

Sd (P W [illegible] Capt Adjt.

Issued to.

Copy No 1 Adjt for C.O.

2 Major G.K. Beckett. M.C.

3-4.5-6 All Companies

7. T.O. & Q.M.

8 R.S.M.

9 I.O. & S.O.

10 [illegible] Reserve.

11 do Adv.

12 13?th Inf Brigade

13 File

14 War Diary.

Instructions regarding War Diaries and Intelligence Summaries are contained in F. S. Regs., Part II. and the Staff Manual respectively. Title pages will be prepared in manuscript.

WAR DIARY
or
~~INTELLIGENCE SUMMARY.~~
(Erase heading not required.)

Army Form C. 2118.

1/4 Leicester R.

Vol 43

Place	Date	Hour	Summary of Events and Information	Remarks and references to Appendices
	1-9-18		Battalion left FOUQUIERES to go into support at GORRE RIGHT SUB SECTOR. 1st Platoon left at 4-30 pm, last left at 5-10 pm. Battalion in position by 7 pm.	
	2-9-18		Copies of August Diary despatched at 9 am.	
	3-9-18		Operation carried out by 19th Div on our left in conjunction with 46th Div. Attack proved successfull, 50 prisoners being taken. 5th Lincolns advanced their line one coy of the 1/4 Leicesters being attached to them.	
	4-9-18		1/5 Leicesters pushed forward this morning at 5-30 am. Objective reached with little opposition. Patrols pushed forward into OLD BRITISH LINE and DU BOIS FARM. "B" Coy front shelled during the morning. 4 pm orders to move forward. Troops in position and communication established to signals at 6 pm.	
	5-9-18		7 am 2 hostile planes flew over flying very low. 12-15 pm orders received to move back to old position in support owing to alteration in line of resistance. Batt in position by 1-30 pm. 9 pm Batt moved to billets in FOUQUIERES. Batt in billets 12 midnight.	
	6-9-18		Cleaning. MO inspection and repairs.	
	7-9-18		Batt bathing. G.O.C. 46th Div saw all officers at 5 pm	
	8-9-18		Training carried out as per programme.	
	9-9-18		— do — do — do — do — do —	
	10-9-18		— do — do — do — do — do —	
	11-9-18		Order received to proceed to another area. Batt left FOUQUIERES at 10-15 pm marching to CHOCQUES to entrain arriving there at 11-35 pm.	
	12-9-18		Batt entrained at 12-5 am train leaving at 1-25 am arriving at MERICOURT L'ABBE at 3-15 pm. All in billets by 3.50 pm	
	13-9-18		Day spent in cleaning up billets.	
	14-9-18		Training carried out as per programme.	
	15-9-18		— do — do — do — do —	
	16-9-18		— do — do — do — do —	
	17-9-18		Carried out Tactical Scheme as per [illegible] programme.	
	18-9-18		Training carried out as per programme. Left MERICOURT L'ABBE at 7 pm. Embussed at 11-15 pm from SUGAR FACTORY RIBEMONT.	
	19-9-18		Arrived at debussing point cross roads ESTREES 5-30 am. Arrived at TERTRY 6-30 am. Battalion bivouaced and rested.	
	20-9-18		Training carried out as per programme. Advance party left for the line at 5 pm. 5 officers 38 O.R.	
	21-9-18		Battalion left for line at 2-30 pm. Battalion in position west of PIKE WOOD by 9-30 pm. Badly bombed by hostile planes. 10 Casualties O.R.	
	22-9-18		Day was quiet except for a little shelling carried out on our front line on two occasions.	
	23-9-18		Harrassing fire from enemy between 11 am and 12-30 pm at different intervals. Casualties 7 O.R. Killed 1 wounded 6.	
	24-9-18		5th Leicesters attacked PONTRUET in conjunction with 1st Div. 40 men and 2 officers attached to Trench Mortars. Attack was made at dawn. 12 prisoners were taken by our detachment. Lt HUSSEY was killed in this attack. 4 missing.	
	25-9-18		5 am to 7 am enemy placed approx 1000 rds mixed calibre on our front. Generally quiet throughout day.	
	26-9-18		5 am our artillery harrassed the enemy with High Explosive and gas.	
	27-9-18		Bn attacked PIKE WOOD at 7-15 pm and succeeded in taking the objective & capturing 2 officers & 150 O.R. Bn relieved by the Staffordshire Regt (2 Bns).	
	28-9-18		Bn at rest in rear area around PING-POST.	
	29-9-18		Bn in attack on BELLENGLISE and MAGNY LA FOSSE. Full report of operations attached	
	30-9-18		Bn hold objective captured on previous day. B.H.Q. situated in dugout near BARACQUE - JONCOURT ROAD.	

G R H Bircket [illegible] Major.
Commanding 1/4 Bn Leicestershire Regiment.

D. D. & L., London E.C
(10342) W1 W5300/P713 750,000 3/18 E 688 Forms/C2118/16

SECRET. 4th Leicestershire Regiment Copy No
Operation Order No 104
28th Sept 1918

Ref Map OMISSY 1/20000
THORIGNY 1/20000

1. At hour and date to be notified later 46th Division as part of larger operation will cross St. QUENTIN CANAL, capture the HINDENBURG LINE, and advance to the GREEN Line.

2. 30th AMERICAN Div. will be operating on left.

3. 137th Infantry Brigade will capture first and second objectives 'BROWN Line', after which 139th Infantry Brigade on RIGHT and 138th Infantry Brigade on LEFT will pass through to final objective.

4. On completion of capture of GREEN Line, 32nd Division passes through to RED Line.

5. Objectives and approximate times are shown on Map 'A' and Appendix 'A'

6. One Battalion Tanks is allotted to Division, half Battalion to 138th Inf. Bde. They will join Brigade before advance to YELLOW LINE.

7. Watches will be synchronised by Signal Officer on morning of 'Z' day.

8. 137th Infantry Bde. will advance from their trenches under barrage at Zero hour.

This Battalion will advance from position 'A' at Zero minus 55 minutes in order to reach position 'B' at Zero minus 30 minutes.

Companies will form up in position 'B' in rear
A.

Artillery formation. All four Coys. in line, each Coy on two platoon frontage, with two platoons in support. Coy. front approximately 440 yards. Order of battle from Right; A - B - C - D - Coys. Distance between lines 50 to 100 yards. These dispositions will be maintained throughout. B. H. Q. details will march under 2/Lt FOX, approximately 200 yards in rear of Battalion.

Coy. boundaries, objectives and B. H. Q. are marked on Coy. Commanders map "A" by I. O. Coy. Commanders will see that all officers maps are marked similarly.

9. At Zero Battalion will advance to arrive at position "C" at Zero plus 10. Companies will not advance from this point until further orders are received.

10. These orders will be issued in time to get Battalion at BROWN LINE at Zero plus 5 hours 30 minutes. Attack will then be carried out under a barrage, Coys. objectives being YELLOW LINE as shown on Map "A".

When objective reached 5th LINCS and 5th LEICS will leap frog to ~~[illegible] line~~, ~~and~~ DOTTED BLUE and GREEN LINE respectively.

On reaching objective each Coy. will at once re-organise and will consolidate and defend its position at all costs against enemy counter attack.

Should 137th Inf. Brigade require assistance in mopping up and repelling enemy counter attack beyond eastern bank of CANAL, 4th LEICS Regt. must be prepared to re-inforce. For this purpose, C. Coy will provide an officer patrol to be in close touch with 137th Inf. Bde. to inform B. H. Q exact position of this Brigade after its crossing of CANAL. Positions will be sent to B. H. Q. on message maps.

11. TANKS. will meet Battalion on BROWN LINE. They will

carry S.A.A. and Lewis Gun Ammunition. In addition one supply Tank will probably be available to carry S.A.A. and L.G. Ammunition and Grenades which will be dumped at G.35 a 9.9

12. GUIDES. Each Company will provide guides to keep in touch with preceding Battalions. These men must be carefully selected and must be prepared to guide their Coys the shortest route to the crossings of the CANAL

13. Battalion H.Q. will be marked by Battn. flag. After crossing CANAL B.H.Q. will be at junction of Sunken Road and trench at G 39 b 1.2. On reaching YELLOW LINE, at junction of sunken road and sap at G.30 b. 2.6

14. SIGNAL COMMUNICATIONS. (a) Once advance has commenced communications will be maintained by visual, etc

(b) Red flares, discs and rifles placed three in a row and parallel to each other, muzzles to enemy will be used to signal position to aircraft

(c) 1. Success signal (which will be sent up by B.H.Q.) will be WHITE over WHITE over WHITE

2. S.O.S. RED RED RED.

15. LIASON. A Company must keep touch with 139th Inf Bde. on RIGHT and D Coy with 30th AMERICAN Div on LEFT, touch to be gained before Coys leave BROWN LINE. Exceptionally capable N.C.O's to be placed on flanks of Battn. to keep direction and touch.

16. DRESS. Attack order, no greatcoats – 140 rounds S.A.A. – 2 – 36 Grenades per man – 20 L.G. Magazines per gun – Rifle Grenadiers 12 grenades each. – 2 water bottles per man, 1 in haversack with remainder of day's rations and iron ration – 1 box No 27 smoke grenades per platoon

(Sd) D W Horsnell, Capt. + Adjt.

1/4th Leicestershire Regiment.
Administrative Instructions.

Sept 28th 1918.

1. DRESS. Necessary Grenades, Ammunition, Water Bottles, etc. will come up tonight to B.H.Q. Each Company will send one platoon to draw same at 7-30 pm. They must be issued to Coys by 2 am.

2. RATIONS for Coys. will come up to GRAND PRIEL Farm tonight. Rations will be carried on the man tomorrow, together with iron rations.
For B.H.Q. will come up to B.H.Q.

3. WATER. Will come to same point as rations. All men must commence the attack with ~~bottle~~ both water bottles filled. Water tins will first be used for filling bottles & men must be instructed not to touch water before attack. Empty tins can then be refilled at water cart which will be at L30 a 40.10 until 4 am tomorrow.
Coys will send all empty petrol tins to ration dump tonight by 7.15 pm.

4. GREATCOATS. These will be dumped by Coys. at L30 c 60.20 at time to be notified later under charge of 2 Regtl. Police.

5. MEDICAL ARRANGEMENTS. Positions of R.M.O. and R.A.P. will be near Bn. H.Q.

6. COMMUNICATIONS. Coy. Commanders must send back reports to Bn. H.Q.
Contact Aeroplanes will be marked with black rectangular board hanging from rear of 'plane.
Flares and discs will be called for at:-

Zero plus 3 hours
" " 5 "
" " 7 " 30 mins.
" 9

Only front line troops will show flares & discs.

7. HEADQUARTERS. Bn. will mark position of B.H.Q. as it moves forward by laying out white tape.

8. TANKS. Troops are to be reminded that great assistance can be given tanks by firing smoke grenades to blind Anti-Tank guns & strong points.
46th Div. Tanks will carry a flag of Div. Colour.

(Sd) D.W. Howarth,
Capt & Adjt.

— 2 —

took over command from Capt G.L.LEA when YELLOW LINE was reached, and handed over to Major G.R.A. BECKETT M.C. on his arrival at 8 0 p.m.

[illegible]

10 GEFE

(SD) Major G.R.A BECKETT M.C

D205

Operations carried out by 1/4th Leicestershire Regt on Sept 29th 1918.

At 5 am the Battn occupied 'A' position

At Zero minus 5·5 minutes (4·55 am) the Battn less B coy, advanced and took up a position in ASCENSION VALLEY; B coy occupied the Front line trench in position 'C'. This coy followed up the STAFFORD Brigade and occupied PIKE COPSE; the coy was distributed by Platoons from this position, in Rear of the STAFFORDS, along the Brigade front. They collected prisoners and 'Mopped up' the area WEST of the St QUENTIN CANAL.

A, C, and D coys occupied position 'C' at Zero plus 18 mins, A and D coys occupying Front line trench; C coy in Support.

In taking up this position Lt Col F W FOSTER MC and A/Capt + Adjt D W HOWARTH became casualties.

2/Lt W.L. BASS established Bn HQ at G29 d 80·75 and handed over to Capt G.L. LEA on his arrival.

Orders were issued for the Battn to advance at 10 15 am and occupy the HINDENBURG LINE, reorganise, and take up a position in the BROWN LINE by 11 20 am. This was done according to Barrage table

The YELLOW LINE was attacked, and captured, very little resistance was encountered.

This operation was carried out by A C + D coys, B coy following up in Support.

The Trench running from G24 d 20 99 to G30 b 40 80 was occupied by D coy; C coy occupying line from G30 b 40 80 to G30 d 50 60. A coy held Trench from G30 d 50·60 to G36 a 58·80. Battn HQ were established at G29 d 80 68, the R A P. adjoining Bn HQ.

The Front line ~~companies~~ coys pushed out Outposts from their positions and held the YELLOW LINE, this was completed by 2·30 PM. Capt J C LEDWARD

O.C. Coys

Operation Order No. 66

Information.
The 137th Inf Bde have had little difficulty in reaching the BROWN LINE

Intention
The Battalion will move forward & occupy the BROWN Line attacking the YELLOW LINE according to Barrage table.

A. C. & D Coys will move off at 10 am this will give them time to reorganise before they attack at 11-20 AM

B Coy will advance as Battn passes through them

29-9-18 (Sd.) W.L. Bass A/K

SECRET. 1/4th Bn. Leicestershire Regiment Copy No

Operation Order No 107

30th Sept. 1918

Ref Map THORIGNY [illegible]

1. INFORMATION. Enemy hold JONCOURT and LEVERGIES the hill NAUROY and the WEST and SOUTH of NAUROY and LEVERGIES.
The 32nd Division are in front of us.

2. INTENTION. The Battn. will take up an Outpost line from corner of FOSSE WOOD G.30.d.4.0 to G.30.c.5.8 (the latter exclusive.) The GREEN LINE through these points will be the main line of resistance.

3. DISPOSITIONS. C Coy from RIGHT Boundary to 20 central (inclusive)
D Coy from 20 central to LEFT Boundary (exclusive)
Each Outpost Coy will furnish its own Supports & must dig themselves in where necessary.
A and B. Coys will be in Bn. Reserve in cellars in MAGNY LA FOSSE or trench through H.25.a & b.
A Coy on RIGHT B Coy on LEFT.
B.H.Q. & R.A.P. at gun pits in H.26.a

4. RATIONS etc. Rations and water & overcoats will be brought to new B.H.Q. & will be carried from there by Coys.
Outpost Coys will draw 50 shovels each from dump at LA BARAQUE

5. DISPOSITIONS. Dispositions of Coys & map reference of Coy H.Q. to be sent to B.H.Q. as soon as possible.

6. MOVE. Move to be completed [illegible] Relief complete to be notified to B.H.Q. by runner.

(Sd) J.C. [illegible] Capt. & Adjt.

AFTER ORDER

(a) Coys will send forward 1 Officer per Coy & 1 N.C.O. per platoon & Coy H.Q. in advance to reconnoitre position [illegible]. They will return [illegible] to their [illegible]. O.C. Coys will arrange rendezvous where guides will meet the Coy. These parties [illegible] move at once.

Over.

3/

(a) DISPOSITIONS

C Coy will relieve 2 RIGHT platoons D Coy 5th LEICS
D " " " 2 LEFT " D Coy

A & B Coys will be ready to occupy DOTTED BLUE LINE from H25 c 6.0 to H19 b 2.0, but can accommodate their Coys in MAGNY LA FOSSE if desired.

36751 McQUINN. M. R
241919 BOULBY E

138/46

Instructions regarding War Diaries and Intelligence Summaries are contained in F. S. Regs., Part II. and the Staff Manual respectively. Title pages will be prepared in manuscript.

WAR DIARY
or
INTELLIGENCE SUMMARY.
(Erase heading not required.)

Army Form C. 2118.

Vol 44

Place	Date 1918	Hour	Summary of Events and Information	Remarks and references to Appendices
	Oct 1st		Battalion took over left sector of 5th LEICESTERS front before MAGNY la FOSSE. Bn HQ in [illegible] FOSSE WOOD	
	Oct 2nd		Bn hold line	
	Oct 3rd		Divisional attack on FONSOMME LINE, RAMICOURT, and MONTBREHAIN. 138th Brigade in support. 4 LEICESTERS take over left front before MONTBREHAIN with ANZACS on the left	
	Oct 4th		Bn hold line before MONTBREHAIN and is relieved by Australian Division. (Pioneer Bn)	
	Oct 5th		Bn rest in trenches running between [illegible] and MAGNY LA FOSSE. Bn move to western side of ST QUENTIN CANAL and take over billets in trenches adjoining [illegible]	
	Oct 6th		Bn resting in billets.	
	Oct 7th		Day devoted to interior economy and bathing.	
	Oct 8th		Bn moves forward to area around [illegible] CROSE. In support to [illegible] in the line.	
	Oct 9th		Bn [illegible] FRESNOY and hold line running along railway cutting [illegible] N.E. of FRESNOY.	
	Oct 10th		Bn continue to advance and "leapfrog" 5th LINCOLNS who hold [illegible] BOHAIN - [illegible] R d. Bn take up line along BOHAIN, LA M[illegible]ETTE Road and pushed forward [illegible] S.W. of BOIS DE RIQUERVAL. Bn relieved on night 10th-11th by 6 SOUTH Staffs in Support. 5th Leics holding front line	
	Oct 11th		Bn in billets in FRESNOY. Lieut Colonel F.H. EDWARDS MC 1st BEDFORDSHIRE REGT [illegible] command of Bn.	
	Oct 12th		Day devoted to interior economy, reorganisation, cleaning of billets and bathing	
	Oct 13th		Brigade church parade at theatre FRESNOY. [illegible] conference at 12.30 pm.	
	Oct 14		Training under Coy. arrangements. Commanding Officer inspects billets	
	Oct 15		Training under Coy. arrangements.	
	Oct 16		Day devoted to making preparations for Battalion taking part in attack. 10.15 Battalion marches [illegible] to take up position of attack in VALLEY HESSARD. H.E.C. BOHAIN.	
	Oct 17		Battalion as part of major operation attacks at 05.20. 5th LINCOLN REGT on left and 8th SHERWOOD FORESTERS on right. Battn secures all objectives REGNICOURT being taken in addition and handed over to SHERWOODS	
	Oct 18		Battn relieved in front line by 5th LEICESTERS moves back to old German front line. Battn moves back to billets in FRESNOY LE GRAND [illegible] BOHAIN and marches [illegible] Brigadier General [illegible]	
	Oct 19		Day devoted to cleaning up and re-organisation	
	Oct 20		Divisional Church Parade in FRESNOY	
	Oct 21		Training under Coy. arrangements. Company Commanders conference at 11.00	

D. D. & L., London E.C.
(10342) Wt W5300/P713 750,000 3/18 E 688 Forms/C2118/16.

Instructions regarding War Diaries and Intelligence Summaries are contained in F. S. Regs., Part II. and the Staff Manual respectively. Title pages will be prepared in manuscript.

WAR DIARY

or

~~INTELLIGENCE SUMMARY.~~

(Erase heading not required.)

Army Form C. 2118.

Place	Date	Hour	Summary of Events and Information	Remarks and references to Appendices
	Oct	22	Training under Coy arrangements. Work commenced on NEW RIFLE RANGE in I 23 c.	Etaves 1/20,000
	"	23	Training under Coy arrangements. Work on range continued. Demonstration by Model Platoon.	
	"	24	Training under Coy arrangements. Gas lecture by D.G.O. at Cinema, Fresnoy at 14.00. Afternoon devoted to Recreational Tr.	
	"	25	Training continued. Firing on miniature range.	
	"	26	Bn formed part of the Guard of Honour to the Divisional Commander commanding the French Division who presented medals to officers & N.C.Os entitled to the "CROIX DE GUERRE" award.	
	"	27	Church parade inspection of billets by C.O and recreational training.	
	"	28	Bathing parades and training. C.O inspects Bn in MARCHING ORDER in afternoon.	
	"	29	Training continued. Range practices on the long range. Lectures by Platoon Commanders in the afternoon.	
	"	30	As for 29th.	
	"	31	Training continued. C.O. inspects Bn during the afternoon.	

[signature] Major,
Comdg. [illegible]

D. D. & L., London E.C.
(19342) Wt W5300/P713 750,000 3/18 E 688 Forms/C2118/16.

SECRET. 1/4th Bn. Leicestershire Regiment. Copy No. 12

OPERATION ORDER No.114

30th October 1918.

Ref.Map.ETAVES 1/40,000

1. Battalion will move to BUSIGNY ~~tomorrow, 31st inst.~~ 1st Nov/18
2. Battalion will form up ready to move off, outside Bn.H.Q. at 09.00 in the following order;-

Drums -H.Q.Details - A - B - C - D.

Dress - Marching Order. Jerkins to be rolled on top of packs; steel helmets underneath valise straps. Soft caps will be worn. No sandbags to be carried.

3. Transport under Transport Officer will move off in time to reach a point about J.2.c.0.0 at 09.50.
4. Route - FRESNOY - BOHAIN - BUSIGNY.
5. Stores. Gramaphones and spare mess kit should be sent to Q.M.Stores before Retreat ~~tonight~~. 31st inst.

Lewis Guns. Lewis gun limbers will be loaded by Retreat ~~tonight~~. 31st inst. Sgt.Park will accompany these on ~~31st inst.~~ 1st Nov/18.

Officers valises to be dumped at Q.M.Stores by 07.45, ~~31st.~~ 1st Nov/18

Bn.H.Q., A. and B. Coys will be collected by mess cart. C. and D. Coys to be carried under Company arrangements.

Mess kit must be ready by 07.50, to be collected at 08.00.

Blankets will be tied in bundles of 10's and dumped at Q.M.Stores at 07.00.

Drums - Packs and rifles will be dumped at Q.M.Stores by 07.45.

Medical Cart - will be packed by 08.00.

6 Cleanliness. All billets will be left scrupulously clean, and must be inspected by an officer of each Company. Certificates will be handed in to the Adjutant on parade, stating that this order has been complied with.

7. Marching Out States. Transport Officer, Companies, and Bn.H.Q. will send marching out states, shewing officers and other ranks, to Orderly Room by 08.30.

8. Reports. All Companies will send exact position of their Company H.Q. to Bn.H.Q., at same time that "All in billets" is reported.

(Sd) W.L.BASS, 2/Lieut. & A/Adjt.

Issued to ;-

Copy No.1 Adjt for C.O.
2,3,4,5, All Companies
6 Transport Officer
7 R.Q.M.S.
8 R.S.M.
9 M.O.
10 H.Q., 138th Inf. Bde.
11 File
12 War Diary.

ORIGINAL

EF5243

Army Form C. 2118.

WAR DIARY
or
~~INTELLIGENCE SUMMARY.~~
(Erase heading not required.)

1/4 Leicester Regt

Instructions regarding War Diaries and Intelligence Summaries are contained in F. S. Regs., Part II. and the Staff Manual respectively. Title pages will be prepared in manuscript.

95 45

Place	Date 1918	Hour	Summary of Events and Information	Remarks and references to Appendices
	1st Nov		Bn left FRESNOY le GRAND at 0900 and proceeded to billets at BUSIGNY	
BUSIGNY	2nd		Bn in billets at BUSIGNY. Training carried out under Coy arrangements.	
MOLAIN	3rd		Left BUSIGNY at 1900 and proceeded to MOLAIN area. The Bn spent the night under [illegible]	
In the line	4th		Bn proceeded to RIBEAUVILLE – L'ARBRE de GUISE area and [illegible] assembly position. [illegible] went forward to MAZINGHEIM – LA LOUVIERE area & relieved the CAMERONS of the 1st Bde in the line on the night of the 4th/5th.	
La GROISE	5th		Bn in the line. Relieved by the Staffords 137 Bde. Bn remained in the La GROISE area.	
Cartignies	6th		Bn marched via Prisches to CARTIGNIES & took over billets for the night.	
	7th		Bn marched via [illegible] on AVESNES. Two companies of the Bn were attached to Bn in support to Bde marching on AVESNES. The 5th Bn Leicestershire Rgt.	
	8th		Two coys still attached; advance still in progress. Remaining two coys & details proceeded to CARTIGNIES to take over billets & remained there for the night	
Cartignies	9th		Remaining two coys & details left Cartignies at 0700 & proceeded to SAINS DU NORD arriving there at 1230. Two Coys still with 5th Leicestershire Rgt.	
	10th		Billets were taken over [illegible]	
SAINS DU NORD	11th		Bn took over Outpost line E of SAINS DU NORD. Two Coys on outpost, two in support in SAINS DU NORD. Wire from Bde to say that hostilities were to cease at 1100.	
	12th		Position of outpost as for 11th	
AVESNELLES	13th		Outpost withdrawn at 1100. Bn proceeded to billets at AVESNELLES arriving at 1600.	
BOUSIES	14th		Bn marched to BOUSIES to billets arriving at 1645	
"	15th, 16th		Bn training under Coy arrangements.	
"	17th		Church Parade at LANDRECIES. G.O.C. 46 Div presented medals	
	18th		Training under Coy arrangements. League Football [illegible]	
	19th		B, C, D Coys [illegible] A Coy carry out training	2/Lt H.G. FAIRALL, 2/Lt C. H. WOOD
	20th		A, B, D [illegible] C	
			2/Lt F. H. WILLS awarded the M.C.	
	21st		Bn [illegible] Recreational training in afternoon.	
	22nd		Bn billets at BOUSIES. 2/Lt SEXTON appointed Education Officer	

D. D. & L., London E.C
(10342) Wt W5300/P713 750,000 3/18 E 688 Forms/C2118/16.

WAR DIARY

~~or~~

~~INTELLIGENCE SUMMARY.~~

(Erase heading not required.)

Army Form C. 2118.

Instructions regarding War Diaries and Intelligence Summaries are contained in F. S. Regs., Part II. and the Staff Manual respectively. Title pages will be prepared in manuscript.

Place	Date 1918.	Hour	Summary of Events and Information	Remarks and references to Appendices
BOUSIES	23 Nov		Bn clearing up area. Lt T.R. Flynn awarded M.C.	
"	24		Church parade at BOUSIES	
"	25.		Bn cleaning up area	
"	26		Bn medically inspected. Coy training. League matches.	
"	27		Bn clear ~~[illegible]~~ up evacuated area. Recreational training during afternoon	
"	28		Bn baths at BOUSIES	
"	29			
"	30		Bn clean up area. Major G.S. BROWN and 2/Lt PARTRIDGE awarded the M.C. Cpl C WINFIELD, Cpl H.W. HARDY + Pte H. MOWBRAY awarded D.C.M.	

W.L. Bass
Capt & A/Adj
for O.C.
1/4 Leicestershire Regt

D. D. & L., London E.C
(1034e) Wt W5300/P713 750,000 3/18 E 688 Forms/C2118/16.

REPORT ON OPERATIONS E. OF THE CANAL DE LA SAMBRE, from 1st to 11th November 1918.

=*=*=*=*=*=*=*=*=*=*=*=*=*=

Reference Maps 62.C. & 57.A. 1/40,000.

1st. The Brigade, which had been resting at FRESNOY-LE-GRAND since 18th October moved to the BUSIGNY Area. Orders were then received the same day that the Division would shortly be in Reserve to an attack by the 1st and 32nd Divisions across the Canal de la Sambre and be prepared to exploit success.

The area about W. bank of Canal and routes thereto from BUSIGNY were therefore reconnoitred the following day by all Officers.

At 17.00. hours on the 3rd the Brigade, to which "B" Coy, 46th Bn: M.G.C. had been attached, moved up to the area N. & E. of MOLAIN, and camped there for the night. Brigade Headquarters remained at BUSIGNY.

4th The following morning the Brigade moved to assembly positions in the triangle L'ARBRE DE GUISE - MAZINGHIEN - RIBEAUVILLE, with Brigade Headquarters in the first named village. This move was completed by 08.00. hours.

At 10.15. hours the Brigade was ordered to move forward and take up positions N. of REJET-DE-BEAULIEU, the head of the column to rest on the road junction X.4.d. New positions were taken up at 13.00. hours.

At 13.30. hours the Brigade was ordered to move one Battalion across the Canal in Support to the 2nd Infantry Brigade; the 5th LEICESTERSHIRE REGIMENT was accordingly detailed for this duty and took up a position in S.2.b. at 15.30. hours.

At 15.55. hours orders were received to relieve the 1st Infantry Brigade in the line between HAUTREVE and LA-GROISE. This sector had not been reconnoitred, as provisional orders had been received to relieve the 2nd Infantry Brigade. Relief was complete at 23.30. hours, when dispositions were :-

Right Front	...	4th LEICESTERSHIRE REGT.
Left Front.	...	5th LINCOLNSHIRE REGT.
Support (in BOIS-DE-L'ABBAYE)		5th LEICESTERSHIRE REGT.

Brigade Headquarters in BOIS-DE-L'ABBAYE.

Two sections of Cyclists were attached to the Brigade.

5th Orders were then received that the advance would be continued the following morning at 08.00. hours by the 137th. Infantry Brigade and the 139th. Infantry Brigade, the former passing through our line. As soon as it was light our forward Battalions pushed on to the line Gd TOAILLON FARM-ZOBEAU, without encountering any opposition. The 5th LINCOLNSHIRE REGT captured 4 77 mm and 3 10.5 cm guns as well as 4 M.G's in this operation.

When the 137th. Infantry Brigade had passed through, the Brigade concentrated in the MEZIERES-LA-GROISE Area, Brigade Headquarters remaining at BOIS-DE-L'ABBAYE.

6th The following day the advance was continued, and the Brigade moved forward in Support, the head of the column passing the Cross Roads M.28.b. at 06.45 hours. A halt was made on the ERROAT Area until 14.00 hours when orders were received to relieve the 139th. and 137th. Infantry Brigades in the line along W. side of the PETIT HELPE River.

/2.

Relief was complete at 18.00 hours when dispositions were :-

5th LEICESTERSHIRE REGT on Right in O.17. and O.23.
5th LINCOLNSHIRE REGT on Left E. of CARTIGNIES.
4th LEICESTERSHIRE REGT in Support in the W. end of village.

Brigade Headquarters was at HAYETTES FARM.

A troop of Scots Greys was attached to the Brigade and used for patrolling in front of the Infantry.

The Brigade was ordered to continue the advance the following morning and reach a line along high ground Q.13.a. - Q.17.d. - Q.8.a. - Q.7.c. - K.33. - K.27.d.

All bridges across the PETIT HELPE had been destroyed by the enemy and owing to heavy rain the river was in flood, about 30' foot wide and 10' deep.

The 5th LINCOLNSHIRE REGT, however, succeeded in constructing a temporary bridge by running carts into the stream. Half an hour later the detachment of the 468th Fld Coy R.E. with the Brigade had constructed a pontoon bridge across. The whole Brigade was over by 09.00. hours. Considerable resistance was encountered in the close country S.W. of AVESNES, and along the AVESNES - ETROEUNGT Road. The 5th LEICESTERSHIRE REGT gained the line of the Road in P.19.a., capturing a 4 - gun battery and 16 prisoners. The French on their right were counter-attacked and compelled to retire; our right flank being thus exposed our men withdrew slightly and were compelled to abandon 3 of the guns.

At 15.15. hours the situation was as follows :-

5th LEICESTERSHIRE REGT on Right, not in touch with French, holding a line P.17.c. & a. - P.11.c. & a. - P.5.c. (in touch with 5th LINCOLNSHIRE REGT).

5th LINCOLNSHIRE REGT on Left holding a line through P.5.c. - P.5.d. & a. - R.34.c. & a. in touch with 32nd Division in R.28.c.

To protect our right flank 2 Companies of the Support Battn (4th LEICESTERSHIRE REGT) were attached to the 5th LEICS REGT, 1 holding a defensive flank in P.17.c. and 1 being kept in Reserve. The remainder of the Support Battn was concentrated in the area P.2.a.

8th inst. The Brigade was ordered to push on to Final Objective, and to establish an 'Outpost Objective' E. of it along the ZOREES-SEMERIES Road.

A Squadron of 20th Hussars was attached to the Brigade and used for patrol work.

Cavalry and Cyclist patrols sent out at dawn reported the enemy holding approximately the same positions as before.

The chief points of resistance were QUART-DE-ROUTE (P.24.a.) Cross Roads (P.12.a.) Houses (P.35.c.). Artillery concentrations were put down at 08.30. hours and 11.00. hours on these points, and the 60 pdrs co-operated, engaging the high ground in Q.7.

The Armoured Car attached to the Brigade was sent up, but 'ditched' behind our lines and did not recover in time to take part in the operation.

After heavy fighting for some hours, the enemy's resistance completely broke down, and at 13.50. hours our troops advanced without opposition and reached their final objectives (line Q.7.d. B.0.- K.28. central) at 18.00. hours. Patrols were at once pushed out and the outpost objective established before dawn the following day.

Brigade Headquarters which had moved to CARTIGNIES on the 7th was brought forward to P.3. central on the afternoon of the 8th.

During the operations on the 7th and 8th the Brigade captured over 30 prisoners and 1 77 mm gun.

/3.

Orders were received that the Brigade would be relieved by the 137th. Infantry Brigade on the 9th and move back to the CARTIGNIES Area. Relief was already in progress and 2 Coys and Headquarters of the 4th LEICESTERSHIRE REGT were already in CARTIGNIES when this order was cancelled.

The Brigade was then ordered to take up an Outpost Line E. of SAINS-DU-NORD and SEMERIES.

At 16.30. hours dispositions were :-

5th LEICS REGT (with 2 Coys 4th LEICS REGT attached) in SAINS-DU-NORD with 2 Coys holding an Outpost Line in R.7. and R.1.

5th LINCS REGT in SEMERIES, with 2 Coys holding an Outpost Line in K.36. and K.30.

The following day the remainder of the 4th LEICESTERSHIRE REGT moved up to SAINS-DU-NORD, and on the 11th took over the whole of the Outpost Line.

Brig-General,

Commanding 138th. Infantry Brigade.

15th November 1918.

Instructions regarding War Diaries and Intelligence Summaries are contained in F. S. Regs., Part II. and the Staff Manual respectively. Title pages will be prepared in manuscript.

WAR DIARY
or
INTELLIGENCE SUMMARY.
(Erase heading not required.)

1/4 Leicester Rg

Army Form C. 2118.

98 46

Place	Date 1918	Hour	Summary of Events and Information	Remarks and references to Appendices
BOUSIES	Dec 1		Battⁿ marched to LANDRECIES to see H.M. The King	
"	" 2 to " 9		Garrison duty. Clearing & filling in area	
"	" 10 to " 20		Capt Jackson & 2Lt Millington rejoined the Battⁿ. Garrison duty. Clearing & filling in area. Colours arrived from England on 20th	
"	" 21		Do Do	
"	" 22		Do Do	
"	" 23		Do Do	
"	" 24		Battⁿ parade for reception of Colours.	
"	" 25		XMAS DAY.	
"	" 26 – " 27		Garrison duty.	
"	" 28		Capt W.L. Bass awarded M.C.	
"	" 29 – " 30		Garrison duty.	
"	" 31		" " Lt A.B. Pick. " J.A. Tyler. Cpl T. Heward. Pte Dobney — mentioned in Despatches	

F.A. Edwards Lt Col
Cmdg 1/4 Leicestershire Regt.

D. D. & L., London E.C
(10342) Wt W5300/P713 750,000 3/18 E 688 Forms/C2118/16.

Instructions regarding War Diaries and Intelligence Summaries are contained in F. S. Regs., Part II. and the Staff Manual respectively. Title pages will be prepared in manuscript.

WAR DIARY
or
~~INTELLIGENCE SUMMARY.~~
(Erase heading not required.)

Army Form C. 2118.

1/4 Leicester R.

Place	Date	Hour	Summary of Events and Information	Remarks and references to Appendices
	1919			
BOUSIES	Jan 1 to Jan 15		Salvaging and Filling in	
	Jan 16 to Jan 31		Garrison Duty.	

F. H. Edwards Lt Col
1/4 Leic. R.

D. D. & L., London E.C.
(10341) W1 W5300/P713 750,000 3/18 E 638 Forms/C2118/16.

Instructions regarding War Diaries and Intelligence Summaries are contained in F. S. Regs., Part II. and the Staff Manual respectively. Title pages will be prepared in manuscript.

WAR DIARY
or
INTELLIGENCE SUMMARY.
(Erase heading not required.)

Vol 48

Army Form C. 2118.

Place	Date	Hour	Summary of Events and Information	Remarks and references to Appendices
BOUSIES.	Feb. 1st to Feb. 24th		GARRISON DUTY AT BOUSIES. (Feb. 24th BATTALION MOVED TO SOLESMES.	
SOLESMES.	Feb. 25th to Feb. 28th		GARRISON DUTY AT SOLESMES.	

J. H. Edwards.
Lt. Col. Cmdg. 1/4 Bn: The Leicestershire Regt.

D. D. & L., London, E.C.
(A10266) Wt W5300/P713 750,000 2/18 Sch. 52 Forms/C2118/16

Instructions regarding War Diaries and Intelligence Summaries are contained in F. S. Regs., Part II. and the Staff Manual respectively. Title pages will be prepared in manuscript.

WAR DIARY

~~or~~

~~INTELLIGENCE SUMMARY.~~

(Erase heading not required.)

Army Form C. 2118.

Place	Date	Hour	Summary of Events and Information	Remarks and references to Appendices
SOLESMES	1st MARCH 1919 to 9th MARCH 1919		GARRISON DUTY AT SOLESMES.	
	10th MARCH 1919		Bn leaves SOLESMES and proceeds to new billets at ST HILAIRE.	
ST. HILAIRE	10th MARCH 1919 to 31st MARCH 1919		GARRISON DUTY AT ST HILAIRE	

Capt and Adj

for C.O. 1/4 Leicestershire Rgt

D. D. & L., London, E.C.
(A10266) Wt W5300/P713 750,000 2/18 Sch. 52 Forms/C2118/16

Army Form C. 2118.

1/4 Leicester Rgt

WAR DIARY
or
~~INTELLIGENCE SUMMARY.~~
(Erase heading not required.)

Instructions regarding War Diaries and Intelligence Summaries are contained in F. S. Regs., Part II. and the Staff Manual respectively. Title pages will be prepared in manuscript.

VR 50

Place	Date	Hour	Summary of Events and Information	Remarks and references to Appendices
	APRIL '19			
ST HILAIRE	1 -	6	Garrison duty at ST HILAIRE	
,,			2 Drafts of 3 Officers + 80 O.R's leave for 53rd + 54th P.O.W Coys on 4th April 1919.	
,,			1 Draft of 3 Officers + 80 O.R's leave for 183rd P.O.W. Coy on 6th April '19	
INCHY.	7		Bn move to billets at INCHY.	
,,	8	-30	Bn at CADRE strength. Garrison duty at INCHY.	
,,			17 O.R's proceed to 178 P.O.W Coy on 14th April 1919.	
,,			Lt Col F.H. Edwards MC left the Bn to take over command of 51st BEDFORDSHIRE REGT on 24th April 1919.	
			MAJOR L.F.H.W. de SZARAMOWICZ commands the CADRE.	

W.L. Brass
Capt + Adj
for O.C 1/4 Bn Leicestershire Regt.

D. D. & L., London, E.C.
(A10266) Wt W5300/P713 750,000 2/18 Sch. 52 Forms/C2118/16

Instructions regarding War Diaries and Intelligence Summaries are contained in F. S. Regs., Part II. and the Staff Manual respectively. Title pages will be prepared in manuscript.

WAR DIARY

or

~~INTELLIGENCE SUMMARY.~~

(Erase heading not required.)

Army Form C. 2118.

1/4 Leicester R.

VII 51

Place	Date 1919	Hour	Summary of Events and Information	Remarks and references to Appendices
INCHY. -BEAUMONT.	1st -31st	MAY MAY	Cadre in charge of stores at INCHY - BEAUMONT.	
			31 May 1919 W.L. Bass Captain for O.C. 1/4 Leicestershire Rgt.	

4TH BATTALION, THE LEICESTERSHIRE REGIMENT.
No.........
Date.........

D. D. & L., London, E.C.
(A10266) Wt W5300/P713 750,000 2/15 Sch. 52 Forms/C2118/11

Army Form C. 2118.

Instructions regarding War Diaries and Intelligence Summaries are contained in F. S. Regs., Part II. and the Staff Manual respectively. Title pages will be prepared in manuscript.

WAR DIARY
or
INTELLIGENCE SUMMARY.
(Erase heading not required.)

1/4 Bn. Leicestershire Regt.

Place	Date	Hour	Summary of Events and Information	Remarks and references to Appendices
INCHY	June 1st to 23rd		Cadre awaiting orders to proceed to England.	
	June 24th		Capt & Adjt. W. L. Bass M.C. and Lt. A.F. Castle and 23 ORs proceeded to ENGLAND with the Colours, leaving behind the Equipment Guard consisting of Major F.F.H.W. de Szaramowicz, Capt & Q.M. M.F. Shepherd D.C.M. and 12 ORs.	
	June 25th		Equipment Guard moved to CAUDRY.	
CAUDRY	June 25th to 30th		Equipment Guard awaiting orders to proceed to ENGLAND.	

F.H. Szaramowicz
Major
O/c Equip Gd. 1/4 Leics Regt
2/7/19.

D. D. & L., London, E.C.
(10344) W1 W5300/P713 550,000 3/18 E 2688 Forms/C2118/18.

www.ingramcontent.com/pod-product-compliance
Lightning Source LLC
Chambersburg PA
CBHW082356010526
44111CB00041B/2548

* 9 7 8 1 4 7 4 5 2 1 4 8 2 *